Dive Into Python 3

Mark Pilgrim

apress®

Dive Into Python 3

ISBN-13 (pbk): 978-1-4302-2415-0

ISBN-13 (electronic): 978-1-4302-2416-7

Lead Editor: Duncan Parkes
Technical Reviewer: Simon Willison
Editorial Board: Clay Andres, Steve Anglin, Mark Beckner, Ewan Buckingham, Tony Campbell, Gary Cornell, Jonathan Gennick, Michelle Lowman, Matthew Moodie, Jeffrey Pepper, Frank Pohlmann, Ben Renow-Clarke, Dominic Shakeshaft, Matt Wade, Tom Welsh
Project Managers: Richard Dal Porto and Debra Kelly
Copy Editors: Nancy Sixsmith, Heather Lang, Patrick Meader, and Sharon Terdeman
Compositor: folio 2
Indexer: Julie Grady

Distributed to the book trade worldwide by Springer-Verlag New York, Inc., 233 Spring Street, 6th Floor, New York, NY 10013. Phone 1-800-SPRINGER, fax 201-348-4505, e-mail orders-ny@springer-sbm.com, or visit http://www.springeronline.com.

For information on translations, please e-mail info@apress.com, or visit http://www.apress.com.

Apress and friends of ED books may be purchased in bulk for academic, corporate, or promotional use. eBook versions and licenses are also available for most titles. For more information, reference our Special Bulk Sales–eBook Licensing web page at http://www.apress.com/info/bulksales.

For Michael

Contents at a Glance

Contents

Foreword

Seven years ago, I'd have looked at you incredulously and probably laughed if you had told me I would be sitting here today writing the foreword to a book, much less the foreword to a programming book. Yet here I am.

Seven years ago, I was just a test engineer with some scripting skills and a systems administration background. I had little programming experience and even less passion for it.

One day, a soon-to-be-coworker of mine mentioned this "new" scripting language called Python. He said it was easy to learn and might add to my skill set. I was wary because programmers seemed to be so separated from my "real world" of tests and systems and users. But his description also made me curious, so I visited the nearest bookstore and bought the first book on the subject I found.

The book I bought was the original *Dive Into Python*, by Mark Pilgrim. I have to believe that I am not the only person who can say, without exaggeration, that Mark's book changed my life and career forever.

The combination of Mark's book, his passion for Python, his presentation of the material, and even the Python (the language itself) fundamentally altered the way I thought. The combination drove me not just to read "yet another book about tech stuff"; it drove me to code, to represent my ideas in a completely new and exciting way. Mark's passion for the language inspired me with a newfound passion.

Now, seven years later, I'm a contributor to the Python standard library—an active community member—and I teach the language to as many people as I can. I use it in my free time, I use it at my job, and I contribute to it in between my daughter's naps. *Dive Into Python*—and Python itself—changed me.

Python is neither the prettiest nor most flexible language out there. But it is clean, simple, and powerful. Its elegance lies in its simplicity and its practicality. Its flexibility enables you (or anyone) to get something—anything—done simply by "keeping out of your way."

I've said for some time the beauty of Python is that it scales "up." It is useful for someone who wants only to do some math or write a simple script. And it is equally useful for programmers who want to create large-scale systems, web frameworks, and multimillion dollar video-sharing sites.

Python has not been without its warts, though. Building a language is, at least in my mind, much like learning to program. It's an evolutionary process where you constantly have to question the decisions you've made and be willing to correct those decisions.

Python 3 admits to some of those mistakes with its new fixes, removing some of the old warts, while also possibly introducing some new ones. Python 3 shows a self-awareness and willingness to evolve in much-needed ways you don't see in a lot of things.

Python 3 does not redefine, fundamentally alter, or suddenly invalidate all the Python you knew before. Rather, it takes something that is time-proven and battle-worn and improves on it in rational, practical ways.

Python 3 doesn't represent the end of the evolution of the language. New features, syntax, and libraries continue to be added; and it will probably be added, tweaked, and removed for as long as Python carries on.

Python 3 is simply a cleaner, more evolved platform for you, the reader, to get things done with.

Like Python 3, *Dive Into Python 3* represents the evolution of something that was already very good becoming something even better. Mark's passion, wit, and engaging style are still there; and the material has been expanded, improved, and updated. But like Python 3 itself, version 3 of this series fundamentally remains the thing that originally gave me such a passion for programming.

Python's simplicity is infectious. The passion of its community, not to mention the passion with which the language is created and maintained, remains astounding.

I hope Mark's passion, and Python itself, inspires you as it did me seven years ago. I hope you find Python, and Python 3, to be as practical and powerful as the hundreds of thousands of programmers and companies that use it across the world.

Jesse Noller
Python Developer

About the Author

■By day, Mark Pilgrim is a developer advocate for open source and open standards. By night, he is a husband and father who lives in North Carolina with his wife, his two sons, and his big, slobbery dog. He spends his copious free time sunbathing, skydiving, and making up autobiographical information.

About the Technical Reviewer

 Simon Willison is a speaker, writer, developer and all-around web technology enthusiast. Simon works for Guardian News and Media as a technical architect for both guardian.co.uk and the recently launched Guardian Developer Network.

Before joining the Guardian Simon worked as a consultant for clients that included the BBC, Automattic, and GCap Media. He is a past member of Yahoo!'s Technology Development team (his projects included the initial prototype of FireEagle, Yahoo!'s location broker API). Prior to Yahoo!, he worked at the *Lawrence Journal-World*, an award winning local newspaper in Kansas.

Simon is a co-creator of the Django web framework, and a passionate advocate for Open Source and standards-based development. He maintains a popular web development weblog at `http://simonwillison.net`.

Acknowledgments

The author would like to thank his wife for her never-ending support and encouragement, without which this book would still be an item on an ever-growing wish list.

Thank you to Raymond Hettinger for relicensing his alphametics solver so I could use it as the basis for Chapter 8.

Thank you to Jesse Noller for patiently explaining so many things to me at PyCon 2009, so that I could explain them to everyone else.

Finally, thank you to the many people who gave me feedback during the public writing process, especially Giulio Piancastelli, Florian Wollenschein, and all the good people of python.reddit.com.

Installing Python

Welcome to Python 3. Let's dive in. In this chapter, you'll install the version of Python 3 that's right for you.

Which Python Is Right for You?

The first thing you need to do with Python is install it. Or do you?

If you're using an account on a hosted server, your Internet service provider (ISP) might have already installed Python 3. If you're running Linux at home, you might already have Python 3, too. Most popular GNU/Linux distributions come with Python 2 in the default installation; a small but growing number of distributions also include Python 3. (As you'll see in this chapter, you can have more than one version of Python installed on your computer.) Mac OS X includes a command-line version of Python 2, but (as of this writing) it does not include Python 3. Microsoft Windows does not come with any version of Python. But don't despair! You can point and click your way through installing Python, regardless of which operating system you have.

The easiest way to check for Python 3 on your Linux or Mac OS X system is to get to a command line. On Linux, look in your Applications menu for a program called Terminal. (It might be in a submenu such as Accessories or System.) On Mac OS X, there is an application called **Terminal.app** in your **/Application/Utilities/** folder.

Once you're at a command-line prompt, just type **python3** (all lowercase, no spaces) and see what happens. On my home Linux system, Python 3 is already installed, and this command gets me into the Python interactive shell, as shown in Listing 0-1.

Listing 0-1. Python Interactive Shell

```
mark@atlantis:~$ python3
Python 3.0.1+ (r301:69556, Apr 15 2009, 17:25:52)
[GCC 4.3.3] on linux2
Type "help", "copyright", "credits" or "license" for more information.
>>>
```

Type **exit()** and press Enter to exit the Python interactive shell.

My web hosting provider also runs Linux and provides command-line access, but as Listing 0-2 shows, my server does not have Python 3 installed. (Boo!)

Listing 0-2. Python Interactive Shell

```
mark@manganese:~$ python3
bash: python3: command not found
```

So back to the question that started this section: "Which Python is right for you?" The answer is simple: whichever one runs on the computer you already have.

Installing on Microsoft Windows

Windows comes in two architectures these days: 32-bit and 64-bit. Of course, there are lots of different *versions* of Windows—XP, Vista, and Windows 7—but Python runs on all of them. The more important distinction is 32-bit versus 64-bit. If you have no idea what architecture you're running, it's probably 32-bit.

Visit `http://python.org/download/` and download the appropriate Python 3 Windows installer for your architecture. Your choices will look something like these:

- Python 3.1 Windows installer (Windows binary—does not include source)

- Python 3.1 Windows AMD64 installer (Windows AMD64 binary—does not include source)

I don't want to include direct download links here because minor updates of Python happen all the time and I don't want to be responsible for you missing important updates. You should always install the most recent version of Python 3.x unless you have some esoteric reason not to.

Once your download is complete, double-click the `.msi` file. Windows will display a security alert because you're about to be running executable code. The official Python installer is digitally signed by the Python Software Foundation, the nonprofit corporation that oversees Python development. Don't accept imitations!

Click the Run button to launch the Python 3 installer.

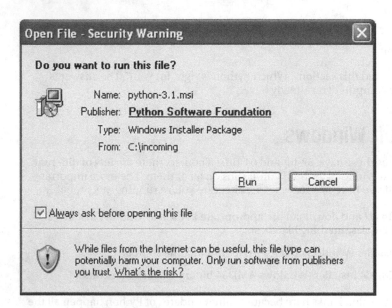

The first question the installer will ask you is whether you want to install Python 3 for all users or just for you. The default choice is "Install for all users," which is the best choice unless you have a good reason to choose otherwise. (One reason why you might want to choose "Install just for me" is that you are installing Python on your company's computer and you don't have administrative rights on your Windows account. But then why are you installing Python without permission from your company's Windows administrator? Don't get me in trouble here!)

Click the Next button to accept your choice of installation type.

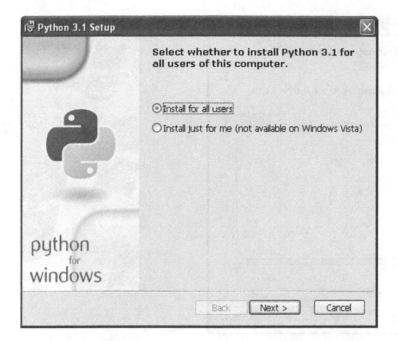

Next, the installer will prompt you to choose a destination directory. The default for all versions of Python 3.1.x is C:\Python31\, which should work well for most users unless you have a specific reason to change it. If you maintain a separate drive letter for installing applications, you can browse to it using the embedded controls or simply type the pathname in the box below. You are not limited to installing Python on the C: drive; you can install it on any drive, in any folder.

Click the Next button to accept your choice of destination directory.

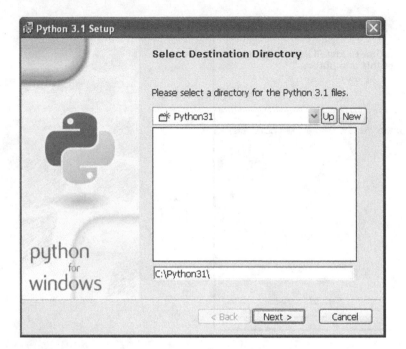

Although the next page looks complicated, it's not really difficult. Like many installers, you have the option not to install every single component of Python 3. If disk space is especially tight, you can exclude certain components.

- Register Extensions allows you to double-click Python scripts (.py files) and run them (recommended but not required). This option doesn't require any disk space, so there is little point in excluding it.

- Tcl/Tk is the graphics library used by the Python shell, which you will use throughout this book. I strongly recommend keeping this option.

- Documentation installs a help file that contains much of the information on http://docs.python.org. This option is recommended if you are on dialup or have limited Internet access.

- Utility Scripts includes the 2to3.py script, which you'll learn about later in this book. It is required if you want to learn about migrating existing Python 2 code to Python 3. If you have no existing Python 2 code, you can skip this option.

- Test suite is a collection of scripts used to test the Python interpreter. You will not use it in this book, nor have I ever used it in the course of programming in Python. Completely optional.

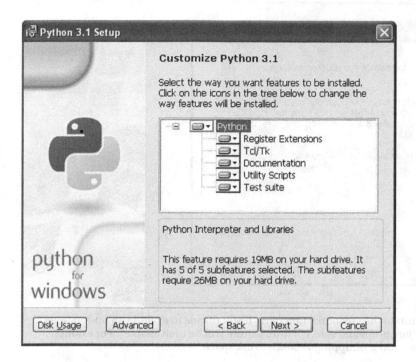

If you don't know how much disk space you have, click the Disk Usage button. The installer will list your drive letters, compute how much space is available on each drive, and calculate how much would be left after installation.

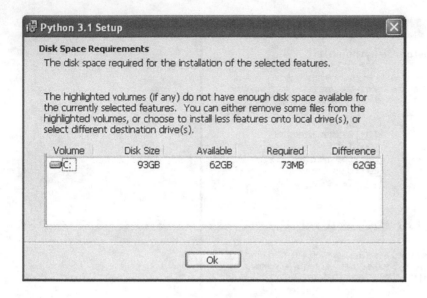

Click the OK button to return to the customization page. If you decide to exclude an option, select the drop-down button before the option and select "Entire feature will be unavailable". For example, excluding the Test suite will save you a whopping 7908KB of disk space.

Click the Next button to accept your choice of options.

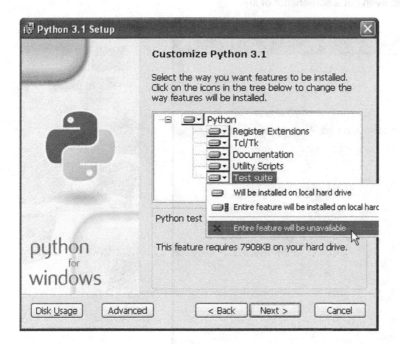

The installer will copy all the necessary files to your chosen destination directory. (This happens so quickly, I had to try it three times to even get a screenshot of it!)

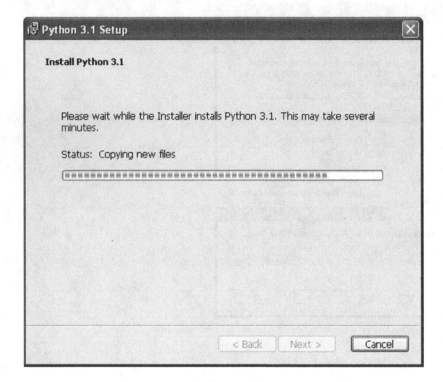

Click the Finish button to exit the installer.

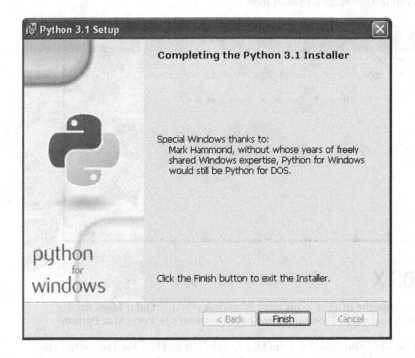

In your Start menu, there should be a new item called Python 3.1, in which you find a program called IDLE. Select this item to run the interactive Python shell.

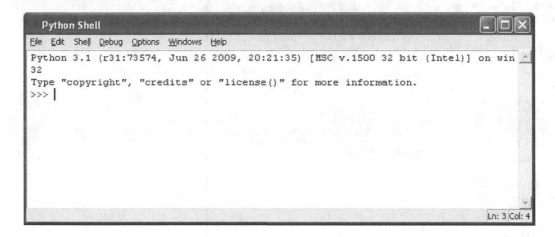

Installing on Mac OS X

All modern Macintosh computers use the Intel chip (as most Windows PCs do). Older Macs used PowerPC chips. You don't need to understand the difference because there's just one Mac Python installer for all Macs.

Visit http://python.org/download/ and download the Mac installer. It will be called something like Python 3.1 Mac Installer Disk Image, although the version number might vary. Be sure to download version 3.x, not 2.x.

Your browser should automatically mount the disk image and open a Finder window to show you the contents. (If this doesn't happen, you'll need to find the disk image in your Downloads folder and double-click to mount it. It will be named something like python-3.1.dmg.) The disk image contains a number of text files (Build.txt, License.txt, ReadMe.txt) and the actual installer package, Python.mpkg.

Double-click the `Python.mpkg` installer package to launch the Mac Python installer.

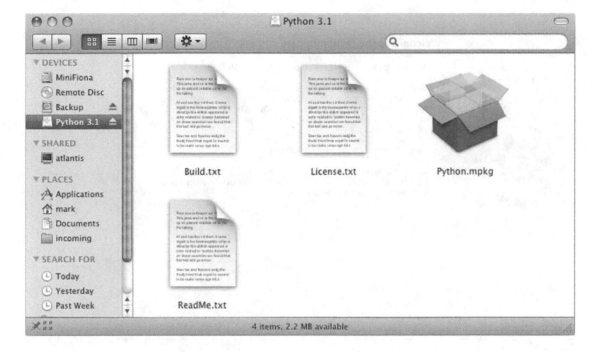

The first page of the installer gives a brief description of Python itself. It then refers you to the `ReadMe.txt` file (which you didn't read, did you?) for more details.

Click the Continue button to move along.

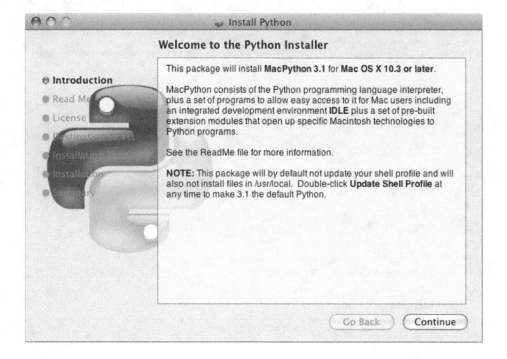

The next page actually contains some important information: Python requires Mac OS X 10.3 or later. If you are still running Mac OS X 10.2, you should upgrade. Apple no longer provides security updates for your operating system, and your computer is probably at risk if you ever go online. Also, you can't run Python 3.

Click the Continue button to advance.

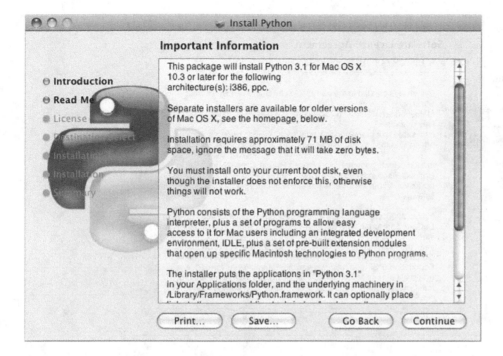

Like all good installers, the Python installer displays the software license agreement. Python is open source and its license is approved by the Open Source Initiative. Python has had a number of owners and sponsors throughout its history, each of which has left its mark on the software license. But the end result is this: Python is open source, and you are allowed use it on any platform, for any purpose, without fee or obligation of reciprocity.

Click the Continue button once again.

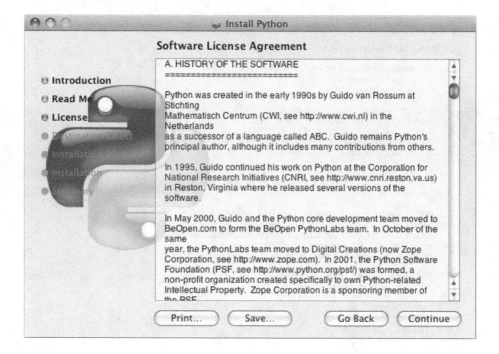

Because of quirks in the standard Apple installer framework, you must "agree" to the software license to complete the installation. Because Python is open source, you are really "agreeing" that the license is granting you additional rights instead of taking them away.

Click the Agree button to continue.

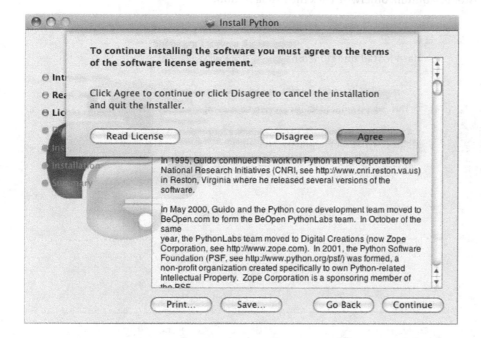

The next screen allows you to change your install location. You must install Python on your boot drive, but because of limitations of the installer, it does not enforce it. In truth, I have never had the need to change the install location.

From this screen, you can also customize the installation to exclude certain features. If you want to do this, click the Customize button; otherwise click the Install button.

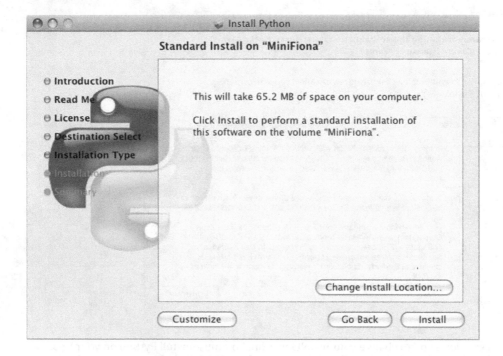

If you choose Custom Install, the installer will present you with the following list of features:

- Python Framework is the guts of Python, and it is both selected and disabled because it must be installed.

- GUI Applications includes IDLE, the graphical Python shell that you will use throughout this book. I strongly recommend keeping this option selected.

- "UNIX command-line tools" includes the command-line python3 application. I strongly recommend keeping this option, too.

- Python Documentation contains much of the information on http://docs.python.org. This option is recommended if you are on dialup or have limited Internet access.

- "Shell profile updater" controls whether to update your shell profile (used in Terminal.app) to ensure that this version of Python is on the search path of your shell. You probably don't need to change it.

- "Fix system Python" should not be changed. It tells your Mac to use Python 3 as the default Python for all scripts, including built-in system scripts from Apple. This would be very bad because most of those scripts are written for Python 2, and they would fail to run properly under Python 3.

Click the Install button to continue.

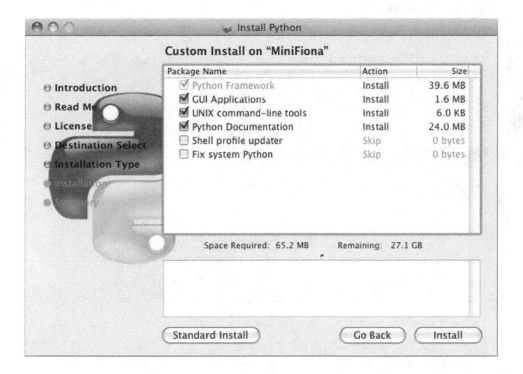

Because it installs system-wide frameworks and binaries in **/usr/local/bin/**, the installer will ask you for an administrative password. There is no way to install Mac Python without administrator privileges.

After supplying the password, click the OK button to begin the installation.

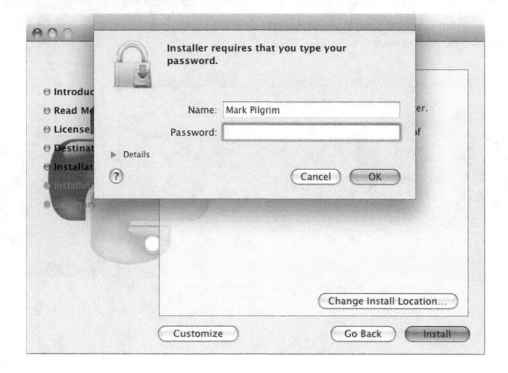

The installer will display a progress meter while it installs the features you've selected.

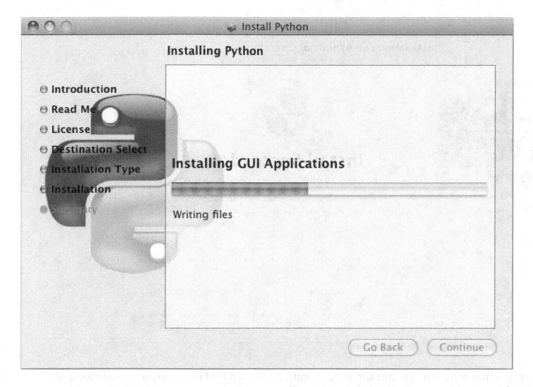

Assuming that all went well, the installer will show you a big green check mark to tell you that the installation completed successfully.

Click the Close button to exit the installer.

Assuming that you didn't change the install location, you can find the newly installed files in the Python 3.1 folder within your /Applications folder. The most important piece is IDLE, the graphical Python shell.

Double-click IDLE to launch the graphical Python shell.

The Python shell is where you will spend most of your time exploring Python. Examples throughout this book will assume that you can find your way into the Python shell.

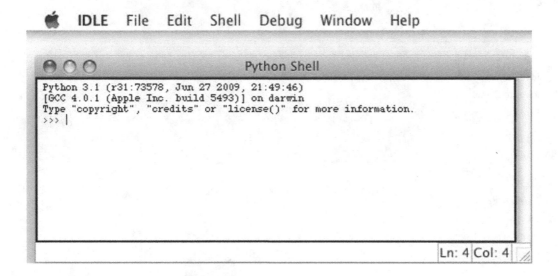

Installing on Ubuntu Linux

Modern Linux distributions are backed by vast repositories of precompiled applications, ready to install. The exact details vary by distribution. In Ubuntu Linux, the easiest way to install Python 3 is through the **Add/Remove** application in your Applications menu.

When you first launch the **Add/Remove** application, it will show you a list of preselected applications in different categories. Some are already installed; most are not. Because the repository contains more than 10,000 applications, there are different filters you can apply to see small parts of the repository. The default filter ("Canonical-maintained applications") is a small subset of the total number of applications that are officially supported by Canonical, the company that creates and maintains Ubuntu Linux.

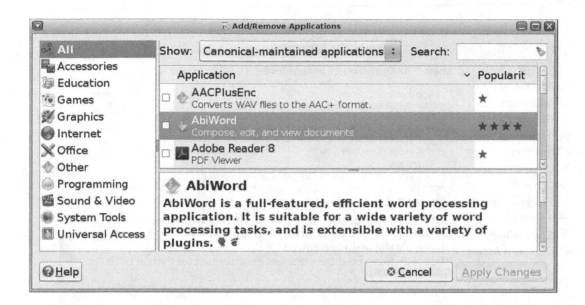

Python 3 is not maintained by Canonical, so the first step is to drop down this filter menu and select "All Open Source applications".

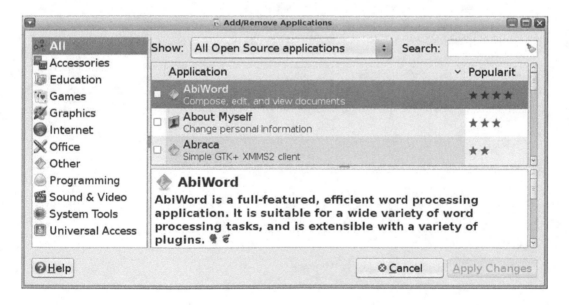

Once you've widened the filter to include all open source applications, use the Search box immediately after the filter menu to search for Python 3.

Now the list of applications narrows to just those matching Python 3. You'll check two packages. The first is `Python (v3.0)`, which contains the Python interpreter.

The second package you want is immediately above: `IDLE (using Python-3.0)`. This is a graphical Python shell that you will use throughout this book.

After you've checked those two packages, click the Apply Changes button to continue.

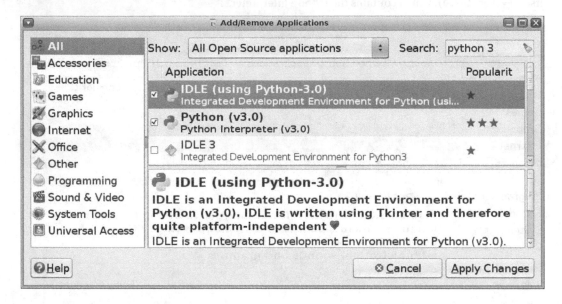

The package manager will ask you to confirm that you want to add both IDLE (using Python-3.0) and Python (v3.0).

Click the Apply button to continue.

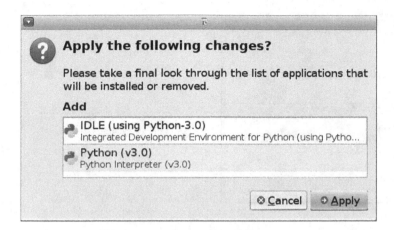

The package manager will show you a progress meter while it downloads the necessary packages from Canonical's Internet repository.

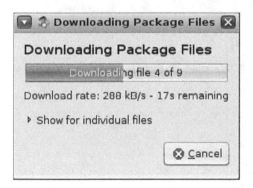

Once the packages are downloaded, the package manager will automatically begin installing them.

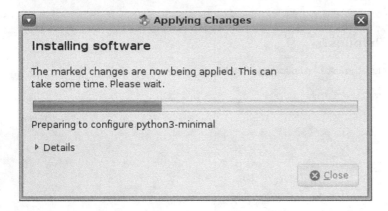

If all went well, the package manager will confirm that both packages were successfully installed. From here, you can double-click IDLE to launch the Python shell or click the Close button to exit the package manager.

You can always relaunch the Python shell by going to your Applications menu, choosing the Programming submenu, and selecting IDLE.

The Python shell is where you will spend most of your time exploring Python. Examples throughout this book will assume that you can find your way into the Python shell.

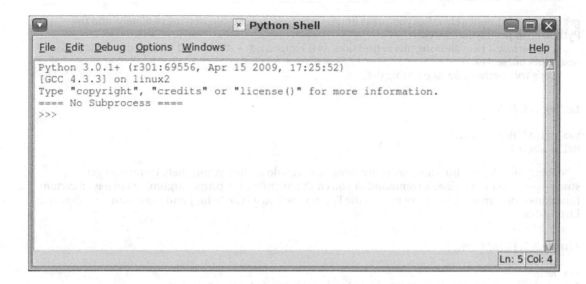

Installing on Other Platforms

Python 3 is available on a number of different platforms. In particular, it is available in virtually every Linux-, BSD-, and Solaris-based distribution. For example, RedHat Linux uses the yum package manager; FreeBSD has its ports and packages collection; Solaris has pkgadd and friends. A quick web search for "Python 3" + "your operating system" will tell you whether a Python 3 package is available and how to install it.

Using the Python Shell

The Python shell is where you can explore Python syntax, get interactive help for commands, and debug short programs. The graphical Python shell (named IDLE) also contains a decent text editor that supports Python syntax coloring and integrates with the Python shell. If you don't already have a favorite text editor, you should give IDLE a try.

First things first. The Python shell itself is an amazing interactive playground. Throughout this book, you'll see examples like the one shown in Listing 0-3.

Listing 0-3. Evaluating Expressions in the Python Interactive Shell

```
>>> 1 + 1
2
```

The three angle brackets, >>>, denote the Python shell prompt. Don't type that part. That's just to let you know that this example is meant to be followed in the Python shell.

1 + 1 is the part you type. You can type any valid Python expression or command in the Python shell. Don't be shy; it won't bite! The worst that will happen is you'll get an error message. Commands

get executed immediately (after you press Enter), expressions get evaluated immediately, and the Python shell prints out the result.

2 is the result of evaluating this expression. As it happens, 1 + 1 is a valid Python expression. The result, of course, is 2.

Let's try another one (see Listing 0-4).

Listing 0-4. Hello World!

```
>>> print('Hello world!')
Hello world!
```

Pretty simple, no? But there are more things you can do in the Python shell. If you ever get stuck—you can't remember a command or you can't remember the proper arguments to pass a certain function—you can get interactive help in the Python shell. Just type help() and press Enter, as shown in Listing 0-5.

Listing 0-5. Help?

```
>>> help
Type help() for interactive help, or help(object) for help about object.
```

There are two modes of help. You can get help about a single object, which just prints out the documentation and returns you to the Python shell prompt. You can also enter help mode, where instead of evaluating Python expressions, you just type keywords or command names and it will print out whatever it knows about that command.

To enter the interactive help mode, type help() and press Enter, as shown in Listing 0-6.

Listing 0-6. Interactive Help Mode

```
>>> help()
Welcome to Python 3.1! This is the online help utility.

If this is your first time using Python, you should definitely check out
the tutorial on the Internet at http://docs.python.org/tutorial/.

Enter the name of any module, keyword, or topic to get help on writing
Python programs and using Python modules. To quit this help utility and
return to the interpreter, just type "quit".

To get a list of available modules, keywords, or topics, type "modules",
"keywords", or "topics". Each module also comes with a one-line summary
of what it does; to list the modules whose summaries contain a given word
such as "spam", type "modules spam".

help>
```

Note that the prompt changes from >>> to help>. This reminds you that you're in the interactive help mode. Now you can enter any keyword, command, module name, function name—pretty much anything Python understands—and read documentation on it (see Listing 0-7).

Listing 0-7. Interactive Help Mode

```
help> print                                                          (1)
Help on built-in function print in module builtins:

print(...)
    print(value, ..., sep=' ', end='\n', file=sys.stdout)

    Prints the values to a stream, or to sys.stdout by default.
    Optional keyword arguments:
    file: a file-like object (stream); defaults to the current sys.stdout.
    sep:  string inserted between values, default a space.
    end:  string appended after the last value, default a newline.

help> PapayaWhip                                                      (2)
no Python documentation found for 'PapayaWhip'

help> quit                                                           (3)

You are now leaving help and returning to the Python interpreter.
If you want to ask for help on a particular object directly from the
interpreter, you can type "help(object)". Executing "help('string')"
has the same effect as typing a particular string at the help> prompt.
>>>                                                                  (4)
```

The following notes refer to the numbered lines in Listing 0-7:

1. To get documentation on the **print()** function, just type **print** and press Enter. The interactive help mode will display something akin to a man page: the function name, a brief synopsis, the function's arguments and their default values, and so on. If the documentation seems opaque to you, don't panic. You'll learn more about all these concepts in the next few chapters.

2. Of course, the interactive help mode doesn't know everything. If you type something that isn't a Python command, module, function, or other built-in keyword, the interactive help mode will just shrug its virtual shoulders.

3. To quit the interactive help mode, type **quit** and then press Enter.

4. The prompt changes back to >>> to signal that you've left the interactive help mode and returned to the Python shell.

IDLE, the graphical Python shell, also includes a Python–aware text editor. You'll see how to use it in the next chapter.

Python Editors and IDEs

IDLE is not the only game in town when it comes to writing programs in Python. While IDLE is useful to get started with learning the language itself, many developers prefer other text editors or integrated development environments (IDEs). I won't cover them here, but the Python community maintains a list of Python-aware editors at http://wiki.python.org/moin/PythonEditors that covers a wide range of supported platforms and software licenses.

You might also want to check out the list of Python-aware IDEs at
`http://wiki.python.org/moin/IntegratedDevelopmentEnvironments`, although few of them support
Python 3 yet. One that does is PyDev (`http://pydev.sourceforge.net/`), a plugin for Eclipse
(`http://eclipse.org/`) that turns Eclipse into a full-fledged Python IDE. Both Eclipse and PyDev are
cross-platform and open source.

On the commercial front, there is ActiveState's Komodo IDE at
`http://www.activestate.com/komodo/`. It has per-user licensing, but students can get a discount, and a
free time-limited trial version is available.

I've been programming in Python for nine years, and I edit my Python programs in GNU Emacs and
debug them in the command-line Python shell. There's no right or wrong way to develop in Python. Find
a way that works for you!

CHAPTER 1

■■■

Your First Python Program

Books about programming usually start with a bunch of boring chapters about fundamentals and eventually work up to building something useful. Let's skip all that. Listing 1-1 is a complete working Python program that probably makes absolutely no sense to you. Don't worry about that because you'll dissect it line by line. But read through it first and see what, if anything, you can make of it.

Listing 1-1. humansize.py

```python
SUFFIXES = {1000: ['KB', 'MB', 'GB', 'TB', 'PB', 'EB', 'ZB', 'YB'],
            1024: ['KiB', 'MiB', 'GiB', 'TiB', 'PiB', 'EiB', 'ZiB', 'YiB']}

def approximate_size(size, a_kilobyte_is_1024_bytes=True):
    '''Convert a file size to human-readable form.

    Keyword arguments:
    size -- file size in bytes
    a_kilobyte_is_1024_bytes -- if True (default), use multiples of 1024
                                if False, use multiples of 1000

    Returns: string

    '''
    if size < 0:
        raise ValueError('number must be non-negative')

    multiple = 1024 if a_kilobyte_is_1024_bytes else 1000
    for suffix in SUFFIXES[multiple]:
        size /= multiple
        if size < multiple:
            return '{0:.1f} {1}'.format(size, suffix)

    raise ValueError('number too large')

if __name__ == '__main__':
    print(approximate_size(1000000000000, False))
```

```
print(approximate_size(1000000000000))
```

Now let's run this program on the command line. On Windows, it will look something like Listing 1-2.

Listing 1-2. Running humansize.py on Windows

```
c:\home\diveintopython3\examples> c:\python31\python.exe humansize.py
1.0 TB
931.3 GiB
```

On Mac OS X or Linux, it would look something like Listing 1-3.

Listing 1-3. Running humansize.py on Mac OS X

```
you@localhost:~/diveintopython3/examples$ python3 humansize.py
1.0 TB
931.3 GiB
```

What just happened? You executed your first Python program. You called the Python interpreter on the command line, and you passed the name of the script you wanted Python to execute. The script defines a single function, the `approximate_size()` function, which takes an exact file size in bytes and calculates a pretty (but approximate) size. You've probably seen this in Windows Explorer; or the Mac OS X Finder; or Nautilus, Dolphin, or Thunar on Linux. If you display a folder of documents as a multicolumn list, it will display a table with the document icon, document name, size, type, last-modified date, and so on. If the folder contains a 1093-byte file named `TODO`, your file manager won't display `TODO 1093 bytes`; it'll say something like `TODO 1 KB` instead. That's what the `approximate_size()` function does.

Look at the bottom of the script; you'll see two calls to `print(approximate_size(`*arguments*`))`. These are function calls that call the `approximate_size()` function and pass a number of arguments; then take the return value and pass it straight on to the `print()` function. The `print()` function is built in; you'll never see an explicit declaration of it. You can just use it anytime, anywhere. (There are lots of built-in functions and even more functions that are separated into modules. Patience, Grasshopper.)

So why does running the script on the command line give you the same output every time? You'll get to that soon. First, let's look at that `approximate_size()` function.

Declaring Functions

Although Python has functions like most other languages, it doesn't have separate header files like C++ or `interface`/`implementation` sections like Pascal. When you need a function, just declare it, as shown in Listing 1-4.

Listing 1-4. Declaring the approximate_size() Function

```
def approximate_size(size, a_kilobyte_is_1024_bytes=True):
```

The keyword `def` starts the function declaration, followed by the function name, and then followed by the arguments in parentheses. Multiple arguments are separated with commas.

Note that the function doesn't define a return datatype. Python functions do not specify the datatype of their return value; they don't even specify whether they return a value. (In fact, every Python function returns a value; if the function ever executes a `return` statement, it will return that value; otherwise, it will return `None`, the Python null value.)

■ In some languages, functions (that return a value) start with `function`, and subroutines (that do not return a value) start with `sub`. There are no subroutines in Python. Everything is a function, all functions return a value (even if it's `None`), and all functions start with `def`.

The `approximate_size()` function takes the two arguments `size` and `a_kilobyte_is_1024_bytes`, but neither argument specifies a datatype. In Python, variables are never explicitly typed. Python figures out what type a variable is and keeps track of it internally.

■ In Java and other statically typed languages, you must specify the datatype of the function return value and each function argument. In Python, you never explicitly specify the datatype of anything. Based on what value you assign, Python keeps track of the datatype internally.

Optional and Named Arguments

Python allows function arguments to have default values; if the function is called without the argument, the argument gets its default value. Furthermore, arguments can be specified in any order by using named arguments.

Let's take another look at that `approximate_size()` function declaration (see Listing 1-5).

Listing 1-5. Declaring the Approximate_size() Function

```
def approximate_size(size, a_kilobyte_is_1024_bytes=True):
```

The second argument, `a_kilobyte_is_1024_bytes`, specifies a default value of `True`. This means the argument is optional; you can call the function without it, and Python will act as if you had called it with `True` as a second parameter.

Now look at the bottom of the script (see Listing 1-6).

Listing 1-6. The if __name__=='__main__' Block

```
if __name__ == '__main__':
    print(approximate_size(1000000000000, False))   (1)
    print(approximate_size(1000000000000))          (2)
```

The following notes refer to the numbered lines in Listing 1-6:

1. This calls the `approximate_size()` function with two arguments. Within the `approximate_size()` function, `a_kilobyte_is_1024_bytes` will be `False` because you explicitly passed `False` as the second argument.

2. This calls the `approximate_size()` function with only one argument. But that's okay because the second argument is optional! Because the caller doesn't specify, the second argument defaults to `True`, as defined by the function declaration.

You can also pass values into a function by name (see Listing 1-7).

Listing 1-7. Function Parameters by Name

```
>>> from humansize import approximate_size
>>> approximate_size(4000, a_kilobyte_is_1024_bytes=False)        (1)
'4.0 KB'
>>> approximate_size(size=4000, a_kilobyte_is_1024_bytes=False)   (2)
'4.0 KB'
>>> approximate_size(a_kilobyte_is_1024_bytes=False, size=4000)   (3)
'4.0 KB'
>>> approximate_size(a_kilobyte_is_1024_bytes=False, 4000)        (4)
  File "<stdin>", line 1
SyntaxError: non-keyword arg after keyword arg
>>> approximate_size(size=4000, False)                            (5)
  File "<stdin>", line 1
SyntaxError: non-keyword arg after keyword arg
```

1. This calls the `approximate_size()` function with **4000** for the first argument (**size**) and `False` for the argument named **a_kilobyte_is_1024_bytes**. (That happens to be the second argument, but it doesn't matter, as you'll see in a minute.)

2. This calls the `approximate_size()` function with **4000** for the argument named **size** and `False` for the argument named **a_kilobyte_is_1024_bytes**. (These named arguments happen to be in the same order as the arguments are listed in the function declaration, but that doesn't matter, either.)

3. This calls the `approximate_size()` function with `False` for the argument named **a_kilobyte_is_1024_bytes** and **4000** for the argument named **size**. (See? I told you the order didn't matter.)

4. This call fails because you have a named argument followed by an unnamed (positional) argument, and that never works. Reading the argument list from left to right, once you have a single named argument, the rest of the arguments must also be named.

5. This call fails, too, for the same reason as the previous call. Is that surprising? After all, you passed **4000** for the argument named **size**, so that `False` value was meant for **a_kilobyte_is_1024_bytes argument**. But Python doesn't work that way. As soon as you have a named argument, all arguments to the right of it need to be named arguments, too.

Writing Readable Code

I won't bore you with a long finger-wagging speech about the importance of documenting your code. Just know that code is written once but read many times, and the most important audience for your code is the future you (six months after you write it and after you've forgotten everything, but need to fix something).

Python makes it easy to write readable code, so take advantage of it. You'll thank me in six months.

Documentation Strings

You can document a Python function by giving it a *document string* (*docstring*). In this program, the approximate_size() function has a docstring (see Listing 1-8).

Listing 1-8. The Approximate_size() Function's Docstring

```
def approximate_size(size, a_kilobyte_is_1024_bytes=True):
    '''Convert a file size to human-readable form.

    Keyword arguments:
    size -- file size in bytes
    a_kilobyte_is_1024_bytes -- if True (default), use multiples of 1024
                                if False, use multiples of 1000

    Returns: string

    '''
```

Triple quotes signify a multiline string. Everything between the start and end quotes is part of a single string, including carriage returns, leading whitespace, and other quote characters. You can use them anywhere, but you'll see them most often used when defining a docstring.

■ Triple quotes are also an easy way to define a string with both single and double quotes, like qq/.../ in Perl 5.

Everything between the triple quotes is the function's docstring, which documents what the function does. A docstring must be the first thing defined in a function (on the next line after the function declaration). You don't technically need to give your function a docstring, but you always should. I know you've heard this in every programming class you've ever taken, but Python gives you an added incentive: the docstring is available at runtime as an attribute of the function.

■ Many Python integrated development environments (IDEs) use docstrings to provide context-sensitive documentation, so that when you type a function name, its docstring appears as a tooltip. This can be incredibly helpful, but it's only as good as the docstrings you write.

The import Search Path

Before continuing, I want to briefly mention the library search path. Python looks in several places when you try to import a module. Specifically, it looks in all the directories defined in `sys.path` (see Listing 1-9). This is just a list, and you can easily view it or modify it with standard list methods. (You'll learn more about lists in Chapter 2.)

Listing 1-9. Introducing sys.path

```
>>> import sys                                                    (1)
>>> sys.path                                                      (2)
['',
 '/usr/lib/python31.zip',
 '/usr/lib/python3.1',
 '/usr/lib/python3.1/plat-linux2@EXTRAMACHDEPPATH@',
 '/usr/lib/python3.1/lib-dynload',
 '/usr/lib/python3.1/dist-packages',
 '/usr/local/lib/python3.1/dist-packages']
>>> sys                                                           (3)
<module 'sys' (built-in)>
>>> sys.path.insert(0, '/home/mark/diveintopython3/examples')    (4)
>>> sys.path                                                      (5)
['/home/mark/diveintopython3/examples',
 '',
 '/usr/lib/python31.zip',
 '/usr/lib/python3.1',
 '/usr/lib/python3.1/plat-linux2@EXTRAMACHDEPPATH@',
 '/usr/lib/python3.1/lib-dynload',
 '/usr/lib/python3.1/dist-packages',
 '/usr/local/lib/python3.1/dist-packages']
```

1. Importing the **sys** module makes all its functions and attributes available.

2. **sys.path** is a list of directory names that constitute the current search path. (Yours will look different, depending on your operating system, what version of Python you're running, and where it was originally installed.) Python will look through these directories (in this order) for a **.py** file whose name matches what you're trying to import.

3. Actually, I lied; the truth is more complicated than that because not all modules are stored as .py files. Some, like the **sys** module, are *built-in modules*; they are actually baked right into Python itself. Built-in modules behave just like regular modules, but their Python source code is not available because they're not written in Python! (The **sys** module is written in C.)

4. You can add a new directory to Python's search path at runtime by adding the directory name to **sys.path**; Python will then look in that directory as well, whenever you try to import a module. The effect lasts as long as Python is running.

5. By using **sys.path.insert(0, new_path)**, you inserted a new directory as the first item of the **sys.path** list (and therefore at the beginning of Python's search path). This is almost always what you want. In case of naming conflicts (for example, if Python ships with version 2 of a particular library, but you want to use version 3), it ensures that your modules will be found and used instead of the modules that came with Python.

Everything Is an Object

In case you missed it, I just said that Python functions have attributes and that those attributes are available at runtime. Like everything else in Python, a function is an object.

Run the interactive Python shell (see Listing 1-10) and follow along.

Listing 1-10. Exploring the humansize Module

```
>>> import humansize                                    (1)
>>> print(humansize.approximate_size(4096, True))       (2)
4.0 KiB
>>> print(humansize.approximate_size.__doc__)           (3)
Convert a file size to human-readable form.

    Keyword arguments:
    size -- file size in bytes
    a_kilobyte_is_1024_bytes -- if True (default), use multiples of 1024
                                if False, use multiples of 1000

    Returns: string
```

1. The first line imports the **humansize** program as a module   a chunk of code that you can use interactively or from a larger Python program. After you import a module, you can reference any of its public functions, classes, or attributes. Modules can do this to access functionality in other modules, and you can do it in the Python interactive shell, too. This is an important concept, and you'll see a lot more of it throughout this book.

2. When you want to use functions defined in imported modules, you need to include the module name. So you can't just say **approximate_size**; it must be **humansize.approximate_size**. If you've used classes in Java, this should feel vaguely familiar.

3.   Instead of calling the function as you would expect to, you asked for one of the function's attributes: __doc__.

■ import in Python is like require in Perl. After you import a Python module, you access its functions with *module.function*; after you require a Perl module, you access its functions with *module::function*.

What's an Object?

Everything in Python is an object, and everything can have attributes and methods. All functions have a built-in attribute, __doc__, which returns the docstring defined in the function's source code. The sys module is an object that has (among other things) an attribute called path. And so forth.

Still, this doesn't answer the more fundamental question. What is an object, anyway? Different programming languages define *object* in different ways. In some, it means that all objects must have attributes and methods; in others, it means that all objects are subclassable. In Python, the definition is looser. Some objects have neither attributes nor methods, but they could. Not all objects are subclassable. But everything is an object in the sense that it can be assigned to a variable or passed as an argument to a function.

You may have heard the term *first-class object* in other programming contexts. In Python, functions are first-class objects. You can pass a function as an argument to another function. Modules are first-class objects. You can pass an entire module as an argument to a function. Classes are first-class objects, and individual instances of a class are also first-class objects.

This is important, so I'm going to repeat it in case you missed it the first few times: *everything in Python is an object*. Strings are objects. Lists are objects. Functions are objects. Classes are objects. Class instances are objects. Even modules are objects.

Indenting Code

Python functions have no explicit begin or end, and no curly braces to mark where the function code starts and stops. As you can see in Listing 1-11, the only delimiter is a colon (:) and the indentation of the code itself.

Listing 1-11. Indentation in the approximate_size() Function

```
def approximate_size(size, a_kilobyte_is_1024_bytes=True):   (1)
    if size < 0:                                             (2)
        raise ValueError('number must be non-negative')      (3)
                                                             (4)
    multiple = 1024 if a_kilobyte_is_1024_bytes else 1000
    for suffix in SUFFIXES[multiple]:                        (5)
        size /= multiple
        if size < multiple:
            return '{0:.1f} {1}'.format(size, suffix)

    raise ValueError('number too large')
```

1. Code blocks are defined by their indentation. By *code block*, I mean functions, if statements, for loops, while loops, and so forth. Indenting starts a block, and unindenting ends it. There are no explicit braces, brackets, or keywords. This means that whitespace is significant and must be consistent. In this example, the function code is indented four spaces. It doesn't need to be four spaces; it just needs to be consistent. The first line that is not indented marks the end of the function.

2. In Python, an if statement is followed by a code block. If the if expression evaluates to true, the indented block is executed; otherwise, it falls to the else block (if any). Note the lack of parentheses around the expression.

3. This line is inside the if code block. The raise statement will raise an exception (of type ValueError), but only if size < 0.

4. This is *not* the end of the function. Completely blank lines don't count. They can make the code more readable, but they don't count as code block delimiters. The function continues on the next line.

5. The for loop also marks the start of a code block. Code blocks can contain multiple lines as long as they are all indented the same amount. This for loop has three lines of code in it. There is no other special syntax for multiline code blocks; just indent and get on with your life.

After some initial protests and several snide analogies to Fortran, you will make peace with Python's use of whitespace and start seeing its benefits. One major benefit is that all Python programs look similar because indentation is a language requirement and not a matter of style. This makes it easier to read and understand other people's Python code.

■ Python uses carriage returns to separate statements; it uses a colon and indentation to separate code blocks.

C++ and Java use semicolons to separate statements and curly braces to separate code blocks.

Exceptions

Exceptions are everywhere in Python. Virtually every module in the standard Python library uses them, and Python will raise them in a lot of different circumstances. You'll see them repeatedly throughout this book.

What is an exception? Usually it's an error, an indication that something went wrong. (Not all exceptions are errors, but never mind that for now.) Some programming languages encourage the use of error return codes, which you *check*. Python encourages the use of exceptions, which you *handle*.

When an error occurs in the Python shell, it prints out some details about the exception and how it happened, and that's that. This is called an *unhandled exception*. When the exception was raised, there was no code to explicitly notice it and deal with it, so it bubbled its way back up to the top level of the Python shell, which spits out some debugging information and calls it a day. In the shell, that's no big deal, but if that happened while your actual Python program was running, the entire program would come to a screeching halt if nothing handles the exception. Maybe that's what you want; maybe it isn't.

■ Unlike Java, Python functions don't declare which exceptions they might raise. It's up to you to determine what possible exceptions you need to catch.

An exception doesn't need results in a complete program crash, though. Exceptions can be *handled*. Sometimes an exception happens because you have a bug in your code (such as accessing a variable that doesn't exist), but sometimes an exception is something you can anticipate. If you're opening a file, it might not exist. If you're importing a module, it might not be installed. If you're connecting to a database, it might be unavailable or you might not have the correct security credentials to access it. If you know that a line of code might raise an exception, you should handle the exception using a `try...except` block.

■ Python uses `try...except` blocks to handle exceptions and the `raise` statement to generate them. Java and C++ use `try...catch` blocks to handle exceptions and the `throw` statement to generate them.

The `approximate_size()` function raises exceptions in two different cases: if the given `size` is larger than the function is designed to handle or if it's less than zero. Listing 1-12 shows the second case.

Listing 1-12. Raising an Exception in the approximate_size() Function

```
if size < 0:
    raise ValueError('number must be non-negative')
```

The syntax for raising an exception is simple enough. Use the `raise` statement, followed by the exception name, and an optional human-readable string for debugging purposes. The syntax is reminiscent of calling a function. (In reality, exceptions are implemented as classes, and this `raise` statement is actually creating an instance of the `ValueError` class and passing the string `'number must be non-negative'` to its initialization method. But we're getting ahead of ourselves!)

■ You don't have to handle an exception in the function that raises it. If one function doesn't handle it, the exception is passed to the calling function, then to that function's calling function, and so on "up the stack." If the exception is never handled, your program will crash. When your program crashes, Python will print a block of debugging information called a *traceback*, and that's the end of that. Again, maybe that's what you want; it depends on what your program does.

Catching Import Errors

One of Python's built-in exceptions is `ImportError`, which is raised when you try to import a module and fail. This can happen for a variety of reasons, but the simplest case is when the module doesn't exist in your import search path. You can use this to include optional features in your program. For example, the `chardet` library in Chapter 16 provides character encoding auto-detection. Perhaps your program wants to use this library if it exists, but continue gracefully if the user hasn't installed it. You can do this with a `try..except` block, as shown in Listing 1-13.

Listing 1-13. Catching an Import Error

```
try:
  import chardet
except ImportError:
  chardet = None
```

Later, you can check for the presence of the `chardet` module with a simple `if` statement (see Listing 1-14).

Listing 1-14. Using a Module if it Is Available

```
if chardet:
  # do something
else:
  # continue anyway
```

Another common use of the `ImportError` exception is when two modules implement a common application programming interface (API), but one is more desirable than the other. (Maybe it's faster or uses less memory.) You can try to import one module but fall back to a different module if the first import fails. For example, Chapter 12 talks about two modules that implement a common API called the `ElementTree` API. The first, `lxml`, is a third-party module that you need to download and install yourself. The second, `xml.etree.ElementTree`, is slower but is part of the Python 3 standard library. Listing 1-15 shows how to try to import one module but settle for another.

Listing 1-15. Catching an Import Error to Load a Fallback Module Instead

```
try:
    from lxml import etree
except ImportError:
    import xml.etree.ElementTree as etree
```

By the end of this `try..except` block, you have imported a module and named it `etree`. Because both modules implement a common API, the rest of your code doesn't need to keep checking which module got imported. And because the module that did get imported is always called `etree`, the rest of your code doesn't need to be littered with `if` statements to call differently named modules.

Unbound Variables

Take another look at the Listing 1-16 line of code from the `approximate_size()` function.

Listing 1-16. Assigning a Value to a Variable

```
multiple = 1024 if a_kilobyte_is_1024_bytes else 1000
```

You never declare the variable `multiple`; you just assign a value to it (see Listing 1-17). That's okay because Python lets you do that. Python doesn't let you reference a variable that has never been assigned a value; trying to do so will raise a `NameError` exception.

Listing 1-17. Accessing a Variable Never Assigned a Value

```
>>> x
Traceback (most recent call last):
  File "<stdin>", line 1, in <module>
NameError: name 'x' is not defined
>>> x = 1
>>> x
1
```

You will thank Python for this one day.

Running Scripts

Python modules are objects and have several useful attributes. One of these attributes makes it easy to test your modules as you write them by including a special block of code that executes when you run the Python file on the command line. Take the last few lines of `humansize.py` (see Listing 1-18).

Listing 1-18. If if __name__ == '__main__' Block

```
if __name__ == '__main__':
    print(approximate_size(1000000000000, False))
    print(approximate_size(1000000000000))
```

■ Like C, Python uses == for comparison and = for assignment. Unlike C, Python does not support inline assignment, so there's no chance of accidentally assigning the value you thought you were comparing.

So what makes this `if` statement special? Well, modules are objects, and all modules have a built-in attribute `__name__`. A module's `__name__` depends on how you're using the module. If you `import` the module, `__name__` is the module's file name without a directory path or file extension, as shown in Listing 1-19.

Listing 1-19. Modules Have Properties

```
>>> import humansize
>>> humansize.__name__
'humansize'
```

But you can also run the module directly as a standalone program, in which case __name__ will be a special default value: __main__. Python will evaluate this if statement, find a true expression, and execute the if code block. As shown in Listing 1-20, the __main__ block prints two values.

Listing 1-20. Running a Script from the Command Line

```
c:\home\diveintopython3> c:\python31\python.exe humansize.py
1.0 TB
931.3 GiB
```

And that's your first Python program!

Further Reading Online

- *PEP 257*: Docstring Conventions explains what distinguishes a good docstring from a great docstring. http://www.python.org/dev/peps/pep-0257

- *Python Tutorial*: Documentation Strings also touches on the subject. http://docs.python.org/3.1/tutorial/controlflow.html#documentation-strings

- *PEP 8*: Style guide for Python Code discusses good indentation style. http://www.python.org/dev/peps/pep-0008

- *Python Reference Manual*: Explains what it means to say that everything in Python is an object (because some people are pedants and like to discuss that sort of thing at great length). http://docs.python.org/3.1/reference/datamodel.html#objects-values-and-types

CHAPTER 2

■ ■ ■

Native Datatypes

Let's cast aside your first Python program for just a minute and talk about datatypes. In Python, every value has a datatype, but you don't need to declare the datatype of variables. How does that work? Based on each variable's original assignment, Python figures out what type it is and keeps tracks of that internally.

Python has many native datatypes. Here are the important ones:

- **Booleans** are either `True` or `False`.

- **Numbers** can be integers (`1` and `2`), floats (`1.1` and `1.2`), fractions (`1/2` and `2/3`), or even complex numbers (`i`, the square root of `-1`).

- **Strings** are sequences of Unicode characters, *e.g.*, an HTML document.

- **Bytes** and **byte arrays**, *e.g.*, a JPEG image file.

- **Lists** are ordered sequences of values.

- **Tuples** are ordered, immutable sequences of values.

- **Sets** are unordered bags of values.

- **Dictionaries** are unordered bags of key-value pairs.

Of course, there are a lot more types than these. Everything is an object in Python, so there are types like *module, function, class, method, file,* and even *compiled code*. You've already seen some of these: modules have names, functions have docstrings, and so on. You'll learn about classes in Chapter 7 and files in Chapter 11.

Strings and bytes are important enough—and complicated enough—that they get their own chapter (see Chapter 4). Let's look at the others first.

Booleans

Booleans are either true or false. Python has two constants, cleverly named `True` and `False`, which can be used to assign boolean values directly. Expressions can also evaluate to a boolean value. In certain places (like `if` statements), Python expects an expression to evaluate to a boolean value. These places are called *boolean contexts*. You can use virtually any expression in a boolean context, and Python will try to determine its truth value. Different datatypes have different rules about which values are true or false in a boolean context. (This will make more sense once you see some concrete examples later in this chapter.)

For example, take this snippet from `humansize.py`, shown in Listing 2-1.

Listing 2-1. *An if Statement*

```
if size < 0:
    raise ValueError('number must be non-negative')
```

`size` is an integer, `0` is an integer, and `<` is a numerical operator. The result of the expression `size < 0` is always a boolean. You can test this yourself in the Python interactive shell, as shown in Listing 2-2.

Listing 2-2. *Testing Comparisons*

```
>>> size = 1
>>> size < 0
False
>>> size = 0
>>> size < 0
False
>>> size = -1
>>> size < 0
True
```

Due to some legacy issues left over from Python 2, booleans can be treated as numbers: `True` is `1`; `False` is `0` (see Listing 2-3).

Listing 2-3. *Booleans as Numbers*

```
>>> True + True
2
>>> True - False
1
>>> True * False
0
>>> True / False
Traceback (most recent call last):
  File "<stdin>", line 1, in <module>
ZeroDivisionError: int division or modulo by zero
```

Ew, ew, ew! Don't do that. Forget I even mentioned it.

Numbers

Numbers are awesome, not least because there are so many to choose from. Python supports both integers and floating point numbers. There's no type declaration to distinguish them; Python tells them apart by the presence or absence of a decimal point.

Listing 2-4. Integers and Floating Point Numbers

```
>>> type(1)              (1)
<class 'int'>
>>> isinstance(1, int)   (2)
True
>>> 1 + 1                (3)
2
>>> 1 + 1.0              (4)
2.0
>>> type(2.0)
<class 'float'>
```

The following notes refer to the numbered lines in Listing 2-4:

1. You can use the `type()` function to check the type of any value or variable. As you might expect, 1 is an `int`.

2. You can use the `isinstance()` function to check whether a value or variable is of a given type.

3. Adding an `int` to an `int` yields an `int`.

4. Adding an `int` to a `float` yields a `float`. Python coerces the `int` into a `float` to perform the addition, then returns a `float` as the result.

Coercing Integers to Floats and Vice Versa

As you saw in Listing 2-4, some operators (like addition) coerce integers to floating point numbers, as needed. You can also coerce them yourself, as shown in Listing 2-5.

Listing 2-5. Converting Integers to Floating Point Numbers

```
>>> float(2)                    (1)
2.0
>>> int(2.0)                    (2)
2
>>> int(2.5)                    (3)
2
>>> int(-2.5)                   (4)
-2
>>> 1.12345678901234567890      (5)
1.1234567890123457
>>> type(1000000000000000)      (6)
<class 'int'>
```

1. You can explicitly coerce an `int` to a `float` by calling the `float()` function.

2. Unsurprisingly, you can also coerce a `float` to an `int` by calling `int()`.

3. The `int()` function will truncate, not round.

4. The int() function truncates negative numbers towards 0. It's a true truncate function, not a floor function.

5. Floating point numbers are accurate to 15 decimal places.

6. Integers can be arbitrarily large.

■ Python 2 had separate types for int and long. The int datatype was limited by sys.maxint, which varied by platform but was usually (2**32)-1. Python 3 has just one integer type, which behaves mostly like the old long type from Python 2. See PEP 237 for details at http://www.python.org/dev/peps/pep-0237.

Common Numerical Operations

You can do all kinds of magical things with numbers, as shown in Listing 2-6.

Listing 2-6. Numerical Operations

```
>>> 11 / 2        (1)
5.5
>>> 11 // 2       (2)
5
>>> -11 // 2      (3)
-6
>>> 11.0 // 2     (4)
5.0
>>> 11 ** 2       (5)
121
>>> 11 % 2        (6)
1
```

1. The / operator performs floating point division. It returns a **float** even if both the numerator and denominator are **ints**.

2. The // operator performs a quirky kind of integer division. When the result is positive, you can think of it as truncating (not rounding) to 0 decimal places, but be careful with that.

3. When integer-dividing negative numbers, the // operator rounds "up" to the nearest integer. Mathematically speaking, it's rounding "down" because -6 is less than -5, but it could trip you up if you're expecting it to truncate to -5.

4. The // operator doesn't always return an integer. If either the numerator or denominator is a **float**, it will still round to the nearest integer, but the actual return value will be a **float**.

5. The ** operator means "raised to the power of." 11**2 is 121.

6. The % operator gives the remainder after performing integer division. 11 divided by 2 is 5 with a remainder of 1, so the result here is 1.

■ In Python 2, the / operator usually meant integer division, but you could make it behave like floating point division by including a special directive in your code. In Python 3, the / operator always means floating point division. See PEP 238 for details at http://www.python.org/dev/peps/pep-0238/.

Fractions

Python isn't limited to integers and floating point numbers. It can also do all the fancy math you learned in high school and promptly forgot about, as shown in Listing 2-7.

Listing 2-7. Using Fractions

```
>>> import fractions              (1)
>>> x = fractions.Fraction(1, 3)  (2)
>>> x
Fraction(1, 3)
>>> x * 2                         (3)
Fraction(2, 3)
>>> fractions.Fraction(6, 4)      (4)
Fraction(3, 2)
>>> fractions.Fraction(0, 0)      (5)
Traceback (most recent call last):
  File "<stdin>", line 1, in <module>
  File "fractions.py", line 96, in __new__
    raise ZeroDivisionError('Fraction(%s, 0)' % numerator)
ZeroDivisionError: Fraction(0, 0)
```

1. To start using fractions, import the **fractions** module.

2. To define a fraction, create a **Fraction** object and pass in the numerator and denominator.

3. You can perform all the usual mathematical operations with fractions. Operations return a new **Fraction** object: 2 * (1/3) = (2/3)

4. The **Fraction** object reduces fractions automatically: (6/4) = (3/2)

5. Python has the good sense not to create a fraction with a zero denominator.

Trigonometry

You can also do basic trigonometry in Python, as shown in Listing 2-8.

Listing 2-8. *Sines and Cosines*

```
>>> import math
>>> math.pi                    (1)
3.1415926535897931
>>> math.sin(math.pi / 2)   (2)
1.0
>>> math.tan(math.pi / 4)   (3)
0.99999999999999989
```

1. The `math` module has a constant for π, the ratio of a circle's circumference to its diameter.

2. The `math` module has all the basic trigonometric functions, including `sin()`, `cos()`, `tan()`, and variants like `asin()`.

3. Note that Python does *not* have infinite precision. For example, `tan(π / 4)` should return `1.0`, not `0.99999999999999989`.

Numbers in a Boolean Context

You can use numbers in a boolean context, such as an `if` statement. Zero values are false, and non-zero values are true, as shown in Listing 2-9.

Listing 2-9. *Numbers in a Boolean Context*

```
>>> def is_it_true(anything):        (1)
...     if anything:
...       print("yes, it's true")
...     else:
...       print("no, it's false")
...
>>> is_it_true(1)                    (2)
yes, it's true
>>> is_it_true(-1)
yes, it's true
>>> is_it_true(0)
no, it's false
>>> is_it_true(0.1)                  (3)
yes, it's true
>>> is_it_true(0.0)
no, it's false
>>> import fractions
```

```
>>> is_it_true(fractions.Fraction(1, 2))   (4)
yes, it's true
>>> is_it_true(fractions.Fraction(0, 1))
no, it's false
```

1. Did you know you can define your own functions in the Python interactive shell? Just press ENTER at the end of each line, and ENTER on a blank line to finish.

2. In a boolean context, non-zero integers are true; 0 is false.

3. Non-zero floating point numbers are true; 0.0 is false. Be careful with this one! If there's the slightest rounding error (not impossible, as you saw in the previous section), then Python will be testing 0.0000000000001 instead of 0 and will return True.

4. Fractions can also be used in a boolean context. Fraction(0, n) is false for all values of n. All other fractions are true.

Lists

Lists are Python's workhorse datatype. When I say "list," you might be thinking "array whose size I have to declare in advance, that can contain only items of the same type, and so on." Don't think like that. Lists are much cooler than arrays.

■ A list in Python is like an array in Perl 5. In Perl 5, variables that store arrays always start with the @ character; in Python, variables can be named anything, and Python keeps track of the datatype internally.

Creating a List

Creating a list is easy: use square brackets to wrap a comma-separated list of values, as shown in Listing 2-10.

Listing 2-10. Creating Lists

```
>>> a_list = ['a', 'b', 'mpilgrim', 'z', 'example']  (1)
>>> a_list
['a', 'b', 'mpilgrim', 'z', 'example']
>>> a_list[0]                                         (2)
'a'
>>> a_list[4]                                         (3)
'example'
>>> a_list[-1]                                        (4)
'example'
>>> a_list[-3]                                        (5)
'mpilgrim'
```

1. First, you define a list of five items. Note that these items retain their original order. This is not an accident: a list is an ordered set of items.

2. A list can be used like a zero-based array. The first item of any non-empty list is always a_list[0].

3. The last item of this five-item list is a_list[4] because lists are always zero-based.

4. A negative index accesses items from the end of the list, counting backwards. The last item of any non-empty list is always a_list[-1].

5. If the negative index is confusing to you, think of it this way: a_list[-n] == a_list[len(a_list) - n]. So in this list, a_list[-3] == a_list[5 - 3] == a_list[2].

Slicing a List

Once you define a list, you can get any part of it as a new list. This is called *slicing* the list (see Listing 2-11).

Listing 2-11. Slicing Lists

```
>>> a_list
['a', 'b', 'mpilgrim', 'z', 'example']
>>> a_list[1:3]              (1)
['b', 'mpilgrim']
>>> a_list[1:-1]            (2)
['b', 'mpilgrim', 'z']
>>> a_list[0:3]            (3)
['a', 'b', 'mpilgrim']
>>> a_list[:3]             (4)
['a', 'b', 'mpilgrim']
>>> a_list[3:]             (5)
['z', 'example']
>>> a_list[:]              (6)
['a', 'b', 'mpilgrim', 'z', 'example']
```

1. You can get a part of a list, called a "slice", by specifying two indexes. The return value is a new list containing all the items of the list, in order, starting with the first slice index (in this case a_list[1]), up to, but not including, the second slice index (in this case a_list[3]).

2. Slicing works if one or both of the slice indexes is negative. If it helps, you can think of it this way: reading the list from left to right, the first slice index specifies the first item you want, and the second slice index specifies the first item you don't want. The return value is everything in between.

3. Lists are zero-based, so a_list[0:3] returns the first three items of the list, starting at a_list[0], up to, but not including, a_list[3].

4. If the left slice index is 0, you can leave it out, and 0 is implied. So a_list[:3] is the same as a_list[0:3] because the starting 0 is implied.

5. Similarly, if the right slice index is the length of the list, you can leave it out. So
   a_list[3:] is the same as a_list[3:5] because this list has five items. There is
   a pleasing symmetry here; in this five-item list, a_list[:3] returns the first
   three items, and a_list[3:] returns the last two items. In fact, a_list[:n]
   always returns the first n items, and a_list[n:] returns the rest, regardless of
   the length of the list.

6. If both slice indexes are left out, all items of the list are included. But this is
   not the same as the original a_list variable. It is a new list that happens to
   have all the same items. a_list[:] is shorthand for making a complete copy of
   a list. Once you make a copy of a list, you can modify each copy independently
   without affecting the other.

Adding Items to a List

A list in Python is much more than an array in Java (although it can be used as one if that's really all you
want out of life). A better analogy would be to Java's **ArrayList** class, which can hold arbitrary objects
and can expand dynamically as new items are added.

There are four ways to add items to a list Listing 2-12 shows all of them.

Listing 2-12. Adding Items to a List

```
>>> a_list = ['a']
>>> a_list = a_list + [2.0, 3]        (1)
>>> a_list                            (2)
['a', 2.0, 3]
>>> a_list.append(True)               (3)
>>> a_list
['a', 2.0, 3, True]
>>> a_list.extend(['four', 'Ω'])      (4)
>>> a_list
['a', 2.0, 3, True, 'four', 'Ω']
>>> a_list.insert(0, 'Ω')             (5)
>>> a_list
['Ω', 'a', 2.0, 3, True, 'four', 'Ω']
```

1. The + operator concatenates lists to create a new list. A list can contain any
   number of items, and there is no size limit (other than available memory).
   However, if memory is a concern, you should be aware that list concatenation
   creates a second list in memory. In this case, that new list is assigned
   immediately to the existing a_list variable. So this line of code is really a
   two-step process—concatenation then assignment—that can (temporarily)
   consume a lot of memory when you're dealing with large lists.

2. A list can contain items of any datatype, and the items in a single list don't all
   need to be the same type. Here we have a list containing a string, a floating
   point number, and an integer.

3. The append() method adds a single item to the end of the list; note that there
   are now *four* different datatypes in the list!

4. Lists are implemented as classes. "Creating" a list is really instantiating a class. As such, a list has methods that operate on it. The extend() method takes one argument—a list—and appends each of the argument's items to the original list.

5. The insert() method inserts a single item into a list. The first argument is the index of the first item in the list that will get bumped out of position. List items do not need to be unique; for example, there are now two separate items with the value 'Ω': the first item, a_list[0], and the last item, a_list[6].

■ a_list.insert(0, value) is like the unshift() function in Perl. It adds an item to the beginning of the list, and all the other items have their positional index bumped up to make room.

Listing 2-13 takes a closer look at the difference between append() and extend().

Listing 2-13. append() and extend()

```
>>> a_list = ['a', 'b', 'c']
>>> a_list.extend(['d', 'e', 'f'])  (1)
>>> a_list
['a', 'b', 'c', 'd', 'e', 'f']
>>> len(a_list)                     (2)
6
>>> a_list[-1]
'f'
>>> a_list.append(['g', 'h', 'i'])  (3)
>>> a_list
['a', 'b', 'c', 'd', 'e', 'f', ['g', 'h', 'i']]
>>> len(a_list)                     (4)
7
>>> a_list[-1]
['g', 'h', 'i']
```

1. The extend() method takes a single argument, which is always a list, and adds each of the items of that list to a_list.

2. If you start with a list of three items and extend it with a list of three more items, you end up with a list of six items.

3. On the other hand, the append() method takes a single argument, which can be any datatype. Here, you're calling the append() method with a list of three items.

4. If you start with a list of six items and append a list onto it, you end up with... a list of seven items. Why seven? Because the last item (which you just appended) *is itself a list*. Lists can contain any type of data, including other lists. That might be what you want, or it might not. But it's what you asked for, and it's what you got.

Searching For Values in a List

Python has several methods for searching a list, as shown in Listing 2-14.

Listing 2-14. Searching a List

```
>>> a_list = ['a', 'b', 'new', 'mpilgrim', 'new']
>>> a_list.count('new')         (1)
2
>>> 'new' in a_list             (2)
True
>>> 'c' in a_list
False
>>> a_list.index('mpilgrim')  (3)
3
>>> a_list.index('new')         (4)
2
>>> a_list.index('c')           (5)
Traceback (innermost last):
  File "<interactive input>", line 1, in ?
ValueError: list.index(x): x not in list
```

1. As you might expect, the count() method returns the number of occurrences of a specific value in a list.

2. If all you want to know is whether a value is in the list or not, the in operator is slightly faster than using the count() method. The in operator always returns True or False; it does not tell you where in the list the value is.

3. If you need to know exactly where in the list a value is, call the index() method. By default, it searches the entire list, although you can specify a second argument of the (0-based) index to start from. You can even specify a third argument of the (0-based) index to stop the search.

4. The index() method finds the *first* occurrence of a value in the list. In this case, 'new' occurs twice in the list, in a_list[2] and a_list[4]; however, the index() method returns only the index of the first occurrence.

5. As you might *not* expect, if the value is not found in the list, the index() method raises an exception.

Wait, what? That's right: the index() method raises an exception if it doesn't find the value in the list. This is notably different from most languages, which return some invalid index (like -1). While this might seem annoying at first, I think you will come to appreciate it. It means your program will crash at the source of the problem instead of failing strangely and silently later. Remember: -1 is a valid list index. If the index() method returned -1, that could lead to some not-so-fun debugging sessions!

Removing Items from a List

Lists can expand and contract automatically. You've seen the expansion part, but there are also several different ways to remove items from a list, as shown in Listing 2-15.

Listing 2-15. Removing Items from a List

```
>>> a_list = ['a', 'b', 'new', 'mpilgrim', 'new']
>>> a_list[1]
'b'
>>> del a_list[1]          (1)
>>> a_list
['a', 'new', 'mpilgrim', 'new']
>>> a_list[1]              (2)
'new'
```

1. You can use the `del` statement to delete a specific item from a list.

2. Accessing index 1 after deleting index 1 does *not* result in an error. All items after the deleted item shift their positional index to "fill the gap" created by deleting the item.

What if you don't know the positional index? That's not a problem: you can remove items by value instead, as shown in Listing 2-16.

Listing 2-16. Removing Items by Value

```
>>> a_list.remove('new')  (1)
>>> a_list
['a', 'mpilgrim', 'new']
>>> a_list.remove('new')  (2)
>>> a_list
['a', 'mpilgrim']
>>> a_list.remove('new')
Traceback (most recent call last):
  File "<stdin>", line 1, in <module>
ValueError: list.remove(x): x not in list
```

1. You can also remove an item from a list with the `remove()` method. The `remove()` method takes a *value* and removes the first occurrence of that value from the list. Again, all items after the deleted item will have their positional indexes bumped down to "fill the gap." Lists never have gaps.

2. You can call the `remove()` method as often as you like, but it raises an exception if you try to remove an item that isn't in the list.

Removing Items from a List: Bonus Round

Another interesting list method is `pop()`. The `pop()` method is yet another way to remove items from a list, but with a twist (see Listing 2-17).

Listing 2-17. pop()

```
>>> a_list = ['a', 'b', 'new', 'mpilgrim']
>>> a_list.pop()    (1)
'mpilgrim'
>>> a_list
['a', 'b', 'new']
>>> a_list.pop(1)   (2)
'b'
>>> a_list
['a', 'new']
>>> a_list.pop()
'new'
>>> a_list.pop()
'a'
>>> a_list.pop()    (3)
Traceback (most recent call last):
  File "<stdin>", line 1, in <module>
IndexError: pop from empty list
```

1. When called without arguments, the pop() list method removes the last item in the list *and* returns the value it removed.

2. You can pop arbitrary items from a list. Just pass a positional index to the pop() method, and it will remove that item, shift all the items after it to "fill the gap," and return the value it removed.

3. Calling pop() on an empty list raises an exception.

■ Calling the pop() list method without an argument is like calling the pop() function in Perl. It removes the last item from the list and returns the value of the removed item. Perl has another function, shift(), that removes the first item and returns its value; in Python, this is equivalent to a_list.pop(0).

Lists in a Boolean Context

You can also use a list in a boolean context, such as an if statement (see Listing 2-18).

Listing 2-18. A List in a Boolean Context

```
>>> def is_it_true(anything):
...     if anything:
...         print("yes, it's true")
...     else:
...         print("no, it's false")
...
>>> is_it_true([])              (1)
```

```
no, it's false
>>> is_it_true(['a'])            (2)
yes, it's true
>>> is_it_true([False])          (3)
yes, it's true
```

1. In a boolean context, an empty list is false.

2. Any list with at least one item is true.

3. Any list with at least one item is true. The value of the items is irrelevant.

Tuples

A tuple is an immutable list. As long as you don't try to change it, a tuple acts just like a list (see Listing 2-19).

Listing 2-19. Tuples Behave a Lot Like Lists

```
>>> a_tuple = ("a", "b", "mpilgrim", "z", "example")   (1)
>>> a_tuple
('a', 'b', 'mpilgrim', 'z', 'example')
>>> a_tuple[0]                                          (2)
'a'
>>> a_tuple[-1]                                         (3)
'example'
>>> a_tuple[1:3]                                        (4)
('b', 'mpilgrim')
```

1. A tuple is defined in the same way as a list, except that the whole set of elements is enclosed in parentheses instead of square brackets.

2. The elements of a tuple have a defined order, just like a list. Tuple indexes are zero-based, just like a list, so the first element of a non-empty tuple is always a_tuple[0].

3. Negative indexes count from the end of the tuple, just like a list.

4. Slicing works too, just like a list. When you slice a list, you get a new list; when you slice a tuple, you get a new tuple.

The major difference between tuples and lists is that tuples cannot be changed. In technical terms, tuples are immutable. In practical terms, they have no methods that would allow you to change them. Lists have methods like append(), extend(), insert(), remove(), and pop(). Tuples have none of these methods. You can slice a tuple (because that creates a new tuple), and you can check whether a tuple contains a particular value (because that doesn't change the tuple), and... that's about it, as shown in Listing 2-20.

Listing 2-20. Tuples have few methods

```
# continued from the previous example
>>> a_tuple
('a', 'b', 'mpilgrim', 'z', 'example')
>>> a_tuple.append("new")              (1)
Traceback (innermost last):
  File "<interactive input>", line 1, in ?
AttributeError: 'tuple' object has no attribute 'append'
>>> a_tuple.remove("z")                (2)
Traceback (innermost last):
  File "<interactive input>", line 1, in ?
AttributeError: 'tuple' object has no attribute 'remove'
>>> a_tuple.index("example")           (3)
4
>>> "z" in a_tuple                     (4)
True
```

1. You can't add elements to a tuple. Tuples have no append() or extend() method.

2. You can't remove elements from a tuple. Tuples have no remove() or pop() method.

3. You *can* find elements in a tuple because this doesn't change the tuple.

4. You can also use the in operator to check whether an element exists in the tuple.

So what are tuples good for?

- Tuples are faster than lists. You should use a tuple instead of a list if you're defining a constant set of values and all you're ever going to do with the tuple is iterate through it.

- Tuples make your code safer if you "write-protect" data that doesn't need to be changed. Using a tuple instead of a list is like having an implied assert statement that shows this data is constant, and that special thought (and a specific function) is required to override that.

- Some tuples can be used as dictionary keys, as you'll see later in this chapter. (Lists can never be used as dictionary keys.)

■ Tuples can be converted into lists, and vice-versa. The built-in tuple() function takes a list and returns a tuple with the same elements, and the list() function takes a tuple and returns a list. In effect, tuple() freezes a list, and list() thaws a tuple.

Tuples in a Boolean Context

You can use tuples in a boolean context, such as an `if` statement, as shown in Listing 2-21.

Listing 2-21. Tuples in a Boolean Context

```
>>> def is_it_true(anything):
...    if anything:
...      print("yes, it's true")
...    else:
...      print("no, it's false")
...
>>> is_it_true(())              (1)
no, it's false
>>> is_it_true(('a', 'b'))      (2)
yes, it's true
>>> is_it_true((False,))        (3)
yes, it's true
>>> type((False))               (4)
<class 'bool'>
>>> type((False,))
<class 'tuple'>
```

1. In a boolean context, an empty tuple is false.

2. Any tuple with at least one item is true.

3. Any tuple with at least one item is true. The value of the items is irrelevant—but what's that comma doing there?

4. To create a tuple of one item, you need a comma after the value. Without the comma, Python just assumes you have an extra pair of parentheses, which is harmless, but it doesn't create a tuple.

Assigning Multiple Values at Once

Here's a cool programming shortcut: in Python, you can use a tuple to assign multiple values at once, as shown in Listing 2-22.

Listing 2-22. Assigning Multiple Values at Once

```
>>> v = ('a', 2, True)
>>> (x, y, z) = v          (1)
>>> x
'a'
>>> y
2
>>> z
True
```

1. v is a tuple of three elements, and (x, y, z) is a tuple of three variables. Assigning one to the other assigns each of the values of v to each of the variables, in order.

This has all kinds of uses. I often want to assign names to a range of values. Suppose you want to assign names to a range of values. You can use the built-in range() function with multi-variable assignment to quickly assign consecutive values, as shown in Listing 2-23.

Listing 2-23. Assigning Consecutive Values

```
>>> (MONDAY, TUESDAY, WEDNESDAY, THURSDAY, FRIDAY, SATURDAY, SUNDAY) = range(7)   (1)
>>> MONDAY                                                                        (2)
0
>>> TUESDAY
1
>>> SUNDAY
6
```

1. The built-in range() function constructs a sequence of integers. (Technically, the range() function returns an iterator, not a list or a tuple, but you'll learn the significance of that distinction in Chapter 7.) MONDAY, TUESDAY, WEDNESDAY, THURSDAY, FRIDAY, SATURDAY, and SUNDAY are the variables you're defining. (This example comes from the calendar module, a fun little module that prints calendars, like the UNIX program cal. The calendar module defines integer constants for days of the week.)

2. Now each variable has a value: MONDAY is 0, TUESDAY is 1, and so forth.

You can also use multi-variable assignment to build functions that return multiple values, simply by returning a tuple of all the values. The caller can treat it as a single tuple, or it can assign the values to individual variables. Many standard Python libraries do this, including the os module, which you'll learn about in Chapter 3.

Sets

A set is an unordered "bag" of unique values. A single set can contain values of any datatype. Once you have two sets, you can do standard set operations like union, intersection, and set difference.

Creating a set is as easy as creating a list (see Listing 2-24).

Listing 2-24. Creating a Set from Scratch

```
>>> a_set = {1}        (1)
>>> a_set
{1}
>>> type(a_set)        (2)
<class 'set'>
>>> a_set = {1, 2}     (3)
>>> a_set
{1, 2}
```

1. To create a set with one value, put the value in curly brackets ({}).

2. Sets are actually implemented as classes, but don't worry about that until Chapter 7.

3. To create a set with multiple values, separate the values with commas and wrap everything up with curly brackets.

You can also create a set out of a list, as shown in Listing 2-25.

Listing 2-25. *Creating a Set from a List*

```
>>> a_list = ['a', 'b', 'mpilgrim', True, False, 42]
>>> a_set = set(a_list)                    (1)
>>> a_set                                  (2)
{'a', False, 'b', True, 'mpilgrim', 42}
>>> a_list                                 (3)
['a', 'b', 'mpilgrim', True, False, 42]
```

1. To create a set from a list, use the **set()** function. (Pedants who know how sets are implemented will point out that this is not really calling a function, but instantiating a class. I *promise* you will learn the difference later in this book (in Chapter 7). For now, just know that **set()** acts like a function, and it returns a set.)

2. As I mentioned earlier, a single set can contain values of any datatype. And, as I also mentioned earlier, sets are *unordered*. This set does not remember the original order of the list that was used to create it. If you were to add items to this set, it would not remember the order in which you added them.

3. The original list is unchanged.

So you don't have any values yet? No problem: You can create an empty set, as shown in Listing 2-26.

Listing 2-26. *Empty Sets*

```
>>> a_set = set()      (1)
>>> a_set              (2)
set()
>>> type(a_set)        (3)
<class 'set'>
>>> len(a_set)         (4)
0
>>> not_sure = {}      (5)
>>> type(not_sure)
<class 'dict'>
```

1. To create an empty set, call **set()** with no arguments.

2. The printed representation of an empty set looks a bit strange. Were you expecting {}, perhaps? That would denote an empty dictionary, not an empty set. You'll learn about dictionaries later in this chapter.

3. Despite the strange printed representation, this *is* a set...

4. ... and this set has no members.

5. Due to historical quirks carried over from Python 2, you cannot create an empty set with two curly brackets. This code creates an empty dictionary, not an empty set.

Modifying a Set

There are two different ways to add values to an existing set: the `add()` method and the `update()` method, as shown in Listings 2-27 and 2-28.

Listing 2-27. Adding Members to a Set

```
>>> a_set = {1, 2}
>>> a_set.add(4)    (1)
>>> a_set
{1, 2, 4}
>>> len(a_set)      (2)
3
>>> a_set.add(1)    (3)
>>> a_set
{1, 2, 4}
>>> len(a_set)      (4)
3
```

1. The `add()` method takes a single argument, which can be any datatype, and adds the given value to the set.

2. This set now has three members.

3. Sets are bags of *unique* values. If you try to add a value that already exists in the set, nothing happens. You won't even get an error.

4. This set *still* has three members.

Listing 2-28. Adding Multiple Members to a Set

```
>>> a_set = {1, 2, 3}
>>> a_set
{1, 2, 3}
>>> a_set.update({2, 4, 6})                    (1)
>>> a_set                                      (2)
{1, 2, 3, 4, 6}
>>> a_set.update({3, 6, 9}, {1, 2, 3, 5, 8, 13})   (3)
>>> a_set
{1, 2, 3, 4, 5, 6, 8, 9, 13}
>>> a_set.update([10, 20, 30])                 (4)
>>> a_set
{1, 2, 3, 4, 5, 6, 8, 9, 10, 13, 20, 30}
```

1. The update() method takes one argument—a set—and adds all its members to the original set. It's as if you called the add() method with each member of the set.

2. Duplicate values are ignored because sets cannot contain duplicates.

3. You can actually call the update() method with any number of arguments. When called with two sets, the update() method adds all the members of each set to the original set, dropping duplicates.

4. The update() method can take objects of a number of different datatypes, including lists. When called with a list, the update() method adds all the items of the list to the original set.

Removing Items from a Set

There are three ways to remove individual values from a set. The first two, discard() and remove(), have one subtle difference: remove() can throw an exception, but discard() never will (see Listing 2-29).

Listing 2-29. discard() vs. remove()

```
>>> a_set = {1, 3, 6, 10, 15, 21, 28, 36, 45}
>>> a_set
{1, 3, 36, 6, 10, 45, 15, 21, 28}
>>> a_set.discard(10)                      (1)
>>> a_set
{1, 3, 36, 6, 45, 15, 21, 28}
>>> a_set.discard(10)                      (2)
>>> a_set
{1, 3, 36, 6, 45, 15, 21, 28}
>>> a_set.remove(21)                       (3)
>>> a_set
{1, 3, 36, 6, 45, 15, 28}
>>> a_set.remove(21)                       (4)
Traceback (most recent call last):
  File "<stdin>", line 1, in <module>
KeyError: 21
```

1. The discard() method takes a single value as an argument and removes that value from the set.

2. If you call the discard() method with a value that doesn't exist in the set, it does nothing. It doesn't raise an error; it just does nothing.

3. The remove() method also takes a single value as an argument, and it also removes that value from the set.

4. Here's the difference: if the value doesn't exist in the set, the remove() method raises a KeyError exception.

Like lists, sets have a pop() method, as shown in Listing 2-30.

Listing 2-30. Popping from a Set

```
>>> a_set = {1, 3, 6, 10, 15, 21, 28, 36, 45}
>>> a_set.pop()                                      (1)
1
>>> a_set.pop()
3
>>> a_set.pop()
36
>>> a_set
{6, 10, 45, 15, 21, 28}
>>> a_set.clear()                                    (2)
>>> a_set
set()
>>> a_set.pop()                                      (3)
Traceback (most recent call last):
  File "<stdin>", line 1, in <module>
KeyError: 'pop from an empty set'
```

1. The pop() method removes a single value from a set and returns the value. However, sets are unordered, so there is no "last" value in a set, which means there is no way to control which value gets removed. It is essentially random.

2. The clear() method removes *all* values from a set, leaving you with an empty set. This is equivalent to a_set = set(), which would create a new empty set and overwrite the previous value of the a_set variable.

3. Attempting to pop a value from an empty set will raise a KeyError exception.

Common Set Operations

Python's set type supports several common set operations, as shown in Listing 2-31.

Listing 2-31. Set Operations

```
>>> a_set = {2, 4, 5, 9, 12, 21, 30, 51, 76, 127, 195}
>>> 30 in a_set                                              (1)
True
>>> 31 in a_set
False
>>> b_set = {1, 2, 3, 5, 6, 8, 9, 12, 15, 17, 18, 21}
>>> a_set.union(b_set)                                       (2)
{1, 2, 195, 4, 5, 6, 8, 12, 76, 15, 17, 18, 3, 21, 30, 51, 9, 127}
>>> a_set.intersection(b_set)                                (3)
{9, 2, 12, 5, 21}
>>> a_set.difference(b_set)                                  (4)
{195, 4, 76, 51, 30, 127}
>>> a_set.symmetric_difference(b_set)                        (5)
{1, 3, 4, 6, 8, 76, 15, 17, 18, 195, 127, 30, 51}
```

1. To test whether a value is a member of a set, use the `in` operator. This works with sets just as it does with lists.

2. The `union()` method returns a new set containing all the elements that are in *either* set.

3. The `intersection()` method returns a new set containing all the elements that are in *both* sets.

4. The `difference()` method returns a new set containing all the elements that are in `a_set` but not `b_set`.

5. The `symmetric_difference()` method returns a new set containing all the elements that are in *exactly* one of the sets.

Three of these methods are symmetric, as shown in Listing 2-32.

Listing 2-32. Symmetric Set Methods

```
# continued from the previous example
>>> b_set.symmetric_difference(a_set)                               (1)
{3, 1, 195, 4, 6, 8, 76, 15, 17, 18, 51, 30, 127}
>>> b_set.symmetric_difference(a_set) == a_set.symmetric_difference(b_set)  (2)
True
>>> b_set.union(a_set) == a_set.union(b_set)                        (3)
True
>>> b_set.intersection(a_set) == a_set.intersection(b_set)          (4)
True
>>> b_set.difference(a_set) == a_set.difference(b_set)              (5)
False
```

1. The symmetric difference of `a_set` from `b_set` *looks* different than the symmetric difference of `b_set` from `a_set`, but you need to bear in mind that sets are unordered. Any two sets that contain all the same values (with none left over) are considered equal.

2. And that's exactly what happens here. Don't be fooled by the Python Shell's printed representation of these sets. They contain the same values, so they are equal.

3. The union of two sets is also symmetric.

4. The intersection of two sets is also symmetric.

5. The difference of two sets is not symmetric. That makes sense; it's analogous to subtracting one number from another. The order of the operands matters.

Finally, there are a few questions you can ask of sets, as shown in Listing 2-33.

Listing 2-33. More Symmetric Set Methods

```
>>> a_set = {1, 2, 3}
>>> b_set = {1, 2, 3, 4}
>>> a_set.issubset(b_set)      (1)
True
>>> b_set.issuperset(a_set)   (2)
True
>>> a_set.add(5)              (3)
>>> a_set.issubset(b_set)
False
>>> b_set.issuperset(a_set)
False
```

1. a_set is a subset of b_set—all the members of a_set are also members of b_set.

2. Asking the same question in reverse, b_set is a superset of a_set, because all the members of a_set are also members of b_set.

3. As soon as you add a value to a_set that is not in b_set, both tests return **False**.

Sets in a Boolean Context

You can use sets in a boolean context, such as an **if** statement (see Listing 2-34).

Listing 2-34. Sets in a Boolean Context

```
>>> def is_it_true(anything):
...    if anything:
...       print("yes, it's true")
...    else:
...       print("no, it's false")
...
>>> is_it_true(set())          (1)
no, it's false
>>> is_it_true({'a'})          (2)
yes, it's true
>>> is_it_true({False})        (3)
yes, it's true
```

1. In a boolean context, an empty set is false.

2. Any set with at least one item is true.

3. Any set with at least one item is true. The value of the items is irrelevant.

Dictionaries

A dictionary is an unordered set of key-value pairs. When you add a key to a dictionary, you must also add a value for that key. (You can always change the value later.) Python dictionaries are optimized for retrieving the value when you know the key, but not the other way around.

■ A dictionary in Python is like a hash in Perl 5. In Perl 5, variables that store hashes always start with a % character. In Python, variables can be named anything, and Python keeps track of the datatype internally.

Creating a Dictionary

Creating a dictionary is easy. The syntax is similar to sets, but instead of values, you have key-value pairs. Once you have a dictionary, you can look up a value by its key, as shown in Listing 2-35.

Listing 2-35. Creating Dictionaries

```
>>> a_dict = {'server': 'db.diveintopython3.org', 'database': 'mysql'}  (1)
>>> a_dict
{'server': 'db.diveintopython3.org', 'database': 'mysql'}
>>> a_dict['server']                                                     (2)
'db.diveintopython3.org'
>>> a_dict['database']                                                   (3)
'mysql'
>>> a_dict['db.diveintopython3.org']                                     (4)
Traceback (most recent call last):
  File "<stdin>", line 1, in <module>
KeyError: 'db.diveintopython3.org'
```

1. First, you create a new dictionary with two items and assign it to the variable a_dict. Each item is a key-value pair, and the whole set of items is enclosed in curly braces.

2. 'server' is a key, and its associated value, referenced by a_dict['server'], is 'db.diveintopython3.org'.

3. 'database' is a key, and its associated value, referenced by a_dict['database'], is 'mysql'.

4. You can get values by key, but you can't get keys by value. So a_dict['server'] is 'db.diveintopython3.org', but a_dict['db.diveintopython3.org'] raises an exception because 'db.diveintopython3.org' is not a key.

Modifying a Dictionary

Dictionaries do not have any predefined size limit. You can add new key-value pairs to a dictionary at any time, or you can modify the value of an existing key. Listing 2-36 continues the Python Shell session from Listing 2-35.

Listing 2-36. Modifying Dictionary Values

```
>>> a_dict
{'server': 'db.diveintopython3.org', 'database': 'mysql'}
>>> a_dict['database'] = 'blog'    (1)
>>> a_dict
{'server': 'db.diveintopython3.org', 'database': 'blog'}
>>> a_dict['user'] = 'mark'        (2)
>>> a_dict                         (3)
{'server': 'db.diveintopython3.org', 'user': 'mark', 'database': 'blog'}
>>> a_dict['user'] = 'dora'        (4)
>>> a_dict
{'server': 'db.diveintopython3.org', 'user': 'dora', 'database': 'blog'}
>>> a_dict['User'] = 'mark'        (5)
>>> a_dict
{'User': 'mark', 'server': 'db.diveintopython3.org', 'user': 'dora', 'database': 'blog'}
```

1. You cannot have duplicate keys in a dictionary. Assigning a value to an existing key wipes out the old value.

2. You can add new key-value pairs at any time. This syntax is identical to the syntax for modifying existing values.

3. The new dictionary item (key 'user', value 'mark') appears to be in the middle. In fact, it was just a coincidence that the items appeared to be in order in the first example; it is equally a coincidence that they appear to be out of order now.

4. Assigning a value to an existing dictionary key simply replaces the old value with the new one.

5. Will this change the value of the 'user' key back to 'mark'? No! Look at the key closely—that's a capital U in "User". Dictionary keys are case-sensitive, so this statement is creating a new key-value pair, not overwriting an existing one. It might look similar to you, but it's completely different as far as Python is concerned.

Mixed-Value Dictionaries

Dictionaries aren't just for strings. Dictionary values can be any datatype, including integers, booleans, arbitrary objects, or even other dictionaries. And within a single dictionary, the values don't all need to be the same type; you can mix and match as needed. Dictionary keys are more restricted, but they can also be strings, integers, and a few other types. You can also mix and match key datatypes within a dictionary.

In fact, you've already seen a dictionary with non-string keys and values in the `humansize.py` script in Chapter 1 (see Listing 2-37).

Listing 2-37. A Dictionary of Lists

```
SUFFIXES = {1000: ['KB', 'MB', 'GB', 'TB', 'PB', 'EB', 'ZB', 'YB'],
            1024: ['KiB', 'MiB', 'GiB', 'TiB', 'PiB', 'EiB', 'ZiB', 'YiB']}
```

Let's tear this example apart in the interactive shell (see Listing 2-38).

Listing 2-38. Nested Dictionary Access

```
>>> SUFFIXES = {1000: ['KB', 'MB', 'GB', 'TB', 'PB', 'EB', 'ZB', 'YB'],
...              1024: ['KiB', 'MiB', 'GiB', 'TiB', 'PiB', 'EiB', 'ZiB', 'YiB']}
>>> len(SUFFIXES)       (1)
2
>>> 1000 in SUFFIXES    (2)
True
>>> SUFFIXES[1000]      (3)
['KB', 'MB', 'GB', 'TB', 'PB', 'EB', 'ZB', 'YB']
>>> SUFFIXES[1024]      (4)
['KiB', 'MiB', 'GiB', 'TiB', 'PiB', 'EiB', 'ZiB', 'YiB']
>>> SUFFIXES[1000][3]   (5)
'TB'
```

1. As it does with lists and sets, the `len()` function gives you the number of keys in a dictionary.

2. And, as with lists and sets, you can use the `in` operator to test whether a specific key is defined in a dictionary.

3. `1000` *is* a key in the `SUFFIXES` dictionary; its value is a list of eight items (eight strings, to be precise).

4. Similarly, `1024` is a key in the `SUFFIXES` dictionary; its value is also a list of eight items.

5. `SUFFIXES[1000]` is a list, so you can address individual items in the list by their zero-based index.

Dictionaries in a Boolean Context

You can also use a dictionary in a boolean context, such as an `if` statement (see Listing 2-39).

Listing 2-39. Dictionaries in a Boolean Context

```
>>> def is_it_true(anything):
...     if anything:
...       print("yes, it's true")
...     else:
...       print("no, it's false")
...
>>> is_it_true({})           (1)
no, it's false
>>> is_it_true({'a': 1})     (2)
yes, it's true
```

1. In a boolean context, an empty dictionary is false.

2. Any dictionary with at least one key-value pair is true.

None

None is a special constant in Python. It is a null value. None is not the same as False. None is not 0, nor is it an empty string. Comparing None to anything other than None always returns False.

None is the only null value. It has its own datatype (NoneType), and you can assign None to any variable; however, you cannot create other NoneType objects. All variables with a value of None are equal to each other. Listing 2-40 shows some of the properties of None.

Listing 2-40. Properties of None

```
>>> type(None)
<class 'NoneType'>
>>> None == False
False
>>> None == 0
False
>>> None == ''
False
>>> None == None
True
>>> x = None
>>> x == None
True
>>> y = None
>>> x == y
True
```

None in a Boolean Context

In a boolean context, None is false and not None is true (see Listing 2-41).

Listing 2-41. None in a Boolean Context

```
>>> def is_it_true(anything):
...    if anything:
...      print("yes, it's true")
...    else:
...      print("no, it's false")
...
>>> is_it_true(None)
no, it's false
>>> is_it_true(not None)
yes, it's true
```

Further Reading Online

The following list of resources can help you drill down on several of the subjects discussed in this chapter in greater detail:

- *Boolean operations*: `http://docs.python.org/3.1/library/stdtypes.html#boolean-operations-and-or-not`

- *Numeric types*: `http://docs.python.org/3.1/library/stdtypes.html#numeric-types-int-float-long-complex`

- *Sequence types*: `http://docs.python.org/3.1/library/stdtypes.html#sequence-types-str-unicode-list-tuple-buffer-xrange`

- *Set types*: `http://docs.python.org/3.1/library/stdtypes.html#set-types-set-frozenset`

- *Mapping types*: `http://docs.python.org/3.1/library/stdtypes.html#mapping-types-dict`

- `fractions` *module*: `http://docs.python.org/3.1/library/fractions.html`

- `math` *module*: `http://docs.python.org/3.1/library/math.html`

- *PEP 237: Unifying Long Integers and Integers*: `http://www.python.org/dev/peps/pep-0237/`

- PEP 238: Changing the Division Operator: `http://www.python.org/dev/peps/pep-0238/`

CHAPTER 3

■ ■ ■

Comprehensions

This chapter will teach you about list comprehensions, dictionary comprehensions, and set comprehensions—three related concepts centered around one very powerful technique. But first, I want to take a little detour into two modules that will help you navigate your local file system.

Working With Files and Directories

Python 3 comes with a module called **os**, which stands for *operating system*. The **os** module contains a host of functions to get information on—and, in some cases, to manipulate—local directories, files, processes, and environment variables. Python does its best to offer a unified API across all supported operating systems so your programs can run on any computer with as little platform-specific code as possible.

The Current Working Directory

When you're just getting started with Python, you're going to spend a lot of time in the Python shell. Throughout this book, you will see examples that go like this:

1. Import one of the modules in the examples folder

2. Call a function in that module

3. Explain the result

If you don't know about the current working directory, step 1 will probably fail with an `ImportError`. Why? Because Python will look for the examples module in the import search path, but it won't find it because the **examples** folder isn't one of the directories in the search path. To get past this, you can do one of two things:

- Add the **examples** folder to the import search path, or

- Change the current working directory to the **examples** folder

The current working directory is an invisible property that Python holds in memory at all times. There is always a current working directory, whether you're in the Python shell, running your own Python script from the command line, or running a Python CGI script on a web server somewhere.

The **os** module contains two functions to deal with the current working directory, as shown in Listing 3-1.

Listing 3-1. The Current Working Directory

```
>>> import os                                          (1)
>>> print(os.getcwd())                                 (2)
C:\Python31
>>> os.chdir('/Users/pilgrim/diveintopython3/examples')  (3)
>>> print(os.getcwd())                                 (4)
C:\Users\pilgrim\diveintopython3\examples
```

1. The **os** module comes with Python; you can import it anytime, anywhere.

2. Use the **os.getcwd()** function to get the current working directory. When you run the graphical Python shell, the current working directory starts as the directory where the Python shell executable is. On Windows, this depends on where you installed Python; the default directory is **c:\Python31**. If you run the Python shell from the command line, the current working directory starts as the directory you were in when you ran **python3**.

3. Use the **os.chdir()** function to change the current working directory.

4. When I called the **os.chdir()** function, I used a Linux-style pathname (forward slashes, no drive letter) even though I'm on Windows. This is one of the places where Python tries to paper over the differences between operating systems.

Working with Filenames and Directory Names

While we're on the subject of directories, I want to point out the **os.path** module. **os.path** contains functions for manipulating filenames and directory names, as shown in Listing 3-2.

Listing 3-2. Working with Filenames

```
>>> import os
>>> print(os.path.join('/Users/pilgrim/diveintopython3/examples/', 'humansize.py'))   (1)
/Users/pilgrim/diveintopython3/examples/humansize.py
>>> print(os.path.join('/Users/pilgrim/diveintopython3/examples', 'humansize.py'))    (2)
/Users/pilgrim/diveintopython3/examples\humansize.py
>>> print(os.path.expanduser('~'))                                                    (3)
c:\Users\pilgrim
>>> print(os.path.join(os.path.expanduser('~'), 'diveintopython3', 'examples', ↵
'humansize.py'))                                                                      (4)
c:\Users\pilgrim\diveintopython3\examples\humansize.py
```

1. The `os.path.join()` function constructs a pathname out of one or more partial pathnames. In this case, it simply concatenates strings.

2. In this slightly less trivial case, `join` will add an extra slash to the pathname before joining it to the filename. It's a backslash instead of a forward slash, because I constructed this example on Windows. If you replicate this example on Linux or Mac OS X, you'll see a forward slash instead. Python can access the file no matter what kind of slashes you use in the pathname.

3. The `os.path.expanduser()` function will expand a pathname that uses ~ to represent the current user's home directory. This works on any platform where users have a home directory, including Linux, Mac OS X, and Windows. The returned path does not have a trailing slash, but the `os.path.join()` function doesn't mind.

4. Combining these techniques, you can easily construct pathnames for directories and files in the user's home directory. The `os.path.join()` function can take any number of arguments. I was overjoyed when I discovered this, since `addSlashIfNecessary()` is one of the stupid little functions I always need to write when building up my toolbox in a new language. Do not write this stupid little function in Python; smart people have already taken care of it for you.

`os.path` also contains functions to split full pathnames, directory names, and filenames into their constituent parts, as shown in Listing 3-3.

Listing 3-3. Splitting Pathnames

```
>>> pathname = '/Users/pilgrim/diveintopython3/examples/humansize.py'
>>> os.path.split(pathname)                              (1)
('/Users/pilgrim/diveintopython3/examples', 'humansize.py')
>>> (dirname, filename) = os.path.split(pathname)        (2)
>>> dirname                                              (3)
'/Users/pilgrim/diveintopython3/examples'
>>> filename                                             (4)
'humansize.py'
>>> (shortname, extension) = os.path.splitext(filename)  (5)
>>> shortname
'humansize'
>>> extension
'.py'
```

1. The `split` function splits a full pathname and returns a tuple containing the path and filename.

2. Remember way back in Chapter 2 when I said you could use multi-variable assignment to return multiple values from a function? The `os.path.split()` function does exactly that. You assign the return value of the `split` function into a tuple of two variables. Each variable receives the value of the corresponding element of the returned tuple.

3. The first variable, `dirname`, receives the value of the first element of the tuple returned from the `os.path.split()` function, the file path.

4. The second variable, `filename`, receives the value of the second element of the tuple returned from the `os.path.split()` function, the filename.

5. `os.path` also contains the `os.path.splitext()` function, which splits a filename and returns a tuple containing the filename and the file extension. You use the same technique to assign each of them to separate variables.

Listing Directories

The `glob` module is another tool in the Python standard library. It's an easy way to get the contents of a directory programmatically. As shown in Listing 3-4, it uses the sort of wildcards you may already be familiar with from working on the command line.

Listing 3-4. Listing with Wildcards

```
>>> os.chdir('/Users/pilgrim/diveintopython3/')
>>> import glob
>>> glob.glob('examples/*.xml')                   (1)
['examples\\feed-broken.xml',
 'examples\\feed-ns0.xml',
 'examples\\feed.xml']
>>> os.chdir('examples/')                          (2)
>>> glob.glob('*test*.py')                         (3)
['alphameticstest.py',
 'pluraltest1.py',
 'pluraltest2.py',
 'pluraltest3.py',
 'pluraltest4.py',
 'pluraltest5.py',
 'pluraltest6.py',
 'romantest1.py',
 'romantest10.py',
 'romantest2.py',
 'romantest3.py',
 'romantest4.py',
 'romantest5.py',
 'romantest6.py',
 'romantest7.py',
 'romantest8.py',
 'romantest9.py']
```

1. The `glob` module takes a wildcard and returns the path of all files and directories matching the wildcard. In this example, the wildcard is a directory path plus `*.xml`, which will match all `.xml` files in the `examples` subdirectory.

2. Now change the current working directory to the `examples` subdirectory. The `os.chdir()` function can take relative pathnames.

3. You can include multiple wildcards in your glob pattern. This example finds all the files in the current working directory that end in a `.py` extension and contain the word `test` anywhere in their filename.

Getting File Metadata

Every modern file system stores metadata about each file: creation date, last-modified date, file size, and so on. Python provides a single API to access this metadata, as shown in Listing 3-5. You don't need to open the file; all you need is the filename.

Listing 3-5. Getting File Metadata

```
>>> import os
>>> print(os.getcwd())                     (1)
c:\Users\pilgrim\diveintopython3\examples
>>> metadata = os.stat('feed.xml')         (2)
>>> metadata.st_mtime                       (3)
1247520344.9537716
>>> import time                             (4)
>>> time.localtime(metadata.st_mtime)       (5)
time.struct_time(tm_year=2009, tm_mon=7, tm_mday=13, tm_hour=17,
  tm_min=25, tm_sec=44, tm_wday=0, tm_yday=194, tm_isdst=1)
>>> metadata.st_size                              (6)
3070
>>> import humansize
>>> humansize.approximate_size(metadata.st_size)  (7)
'3.0 KiB'
```

1. The current working directory is the examples folder.

2. feed.xml is a file in the examples folder. Calling the os.stat() function returns an object that contains several different types of metadata about the file.

3. st_mtime is the modification time, but it's in a format that isn't terribly useful. (Technically, it's the number of seconds since the Epoch, which is defined as the first second of January 1, 1970. Seriously.)

4. The time module is part of the Python standard library. It contains functions to convert between different time representations, format time values into strings, and fiddle with time zones.

5. The time.localtime() function converts a time value from seconds-since-the-Epoch (from the st_mtime property returned from the os.stat() function) into a more useful structure of year, month, day, hour, minute, second, and so on. This file was last modified on July 13, 2009, at around 5:25 PM.

6. The os.stat() function also returns the size of a file, in the st_size property. The file feed.xml is 3070 bytes.

7. You can pass the st_size property to the approximate_size() function.

Constructing Absolute Pathnames

In the previous section, the glob.glob() function returned a list of relative pathnames. The first example had pathnames like 'examples\feed.xml', and the second example had even shorter relative pathnames like 'romantest1.py'. As long as you stay in the same current working directory, these relative pathnames will work for opening files or getting file metadata. But if you want to construct an absolute

pathname—that is, one that includes all the directory names back to the root directory or drive letter—
then you'll need the **os.path.realpath()** function, as shown in Listing 3-6.

Listing 3-6. Constructing an Absolute Pathname

```
>>> import os
>>> print(os.getcwd())
c:\Users\pilgrim\diveintopython3\examples
>>> print(os.path.realpath('feed.xml'))
c:\Users\pilgrim\diveintopython3\examples\feed.xml
```

List Comprehensions

A list comprehension provides a compact way of mapping a list to another list by applying a function to
each of the elements of the list (see Listing 3-7).

Listing 3-7. Constructing a List with a List Comprehension

```
>>> a_list = [1, 9, 8, 4]
>>> [elem * 2 for elem in a_list]        (1)
[2, 18, 16, 8]
>>> a_list                               (2)
[1, 9, 8, 4]
>>> a_list = [elem * 2 for elem in a_list]  (3)
>>> a_list
[2, 18, 16, 8]
```

1. To make sense of this, look at it from right to left. **a_list** is the list you're
   mapping. The Python interpreter loops through **a_list** one element at a time,
   temporarily assigning the value of each element to the variable **elem**. Python
   then applies the function **elem * 2** and appends that result to the returned list.

2. A list comprehension creates a new list; it does not change the original list.

3. It is safe to assign the result of a list comprehension to the variable you're
   mapping. Python constructs the new list in memory, and when the list
   comprehension is complete, it assigns the result to the original variable.

You can use any Python expression in a list comprehension, including the functions in the **os**
module for manipulating files and directories, as shown in Listing 3-8.

Listing 3-8. Constructing a List of Files with a List Comprehension and Wildcards

```
>>> import os, glob
>>> glob.glob('*.xml')                                      (1)
['feed-broken.xml', 'feed-ns0.xml', 'feed.xml']
>>> [os.path.realpath(f) for f in glob.glob('*.xml')]   (2)
['c:\\Users\\pilgrim\\diveintopython3\\examples\\feed-broken.xml',
 'c:\\Users\\pilgrim\\diveintopython3\\examples\\feed-ns0.xml',
 'c:\\Users\\pilgrim\\diveintopython3\\examples\\feed.xml']
```

1. This returns a list of all the `.xml` files in the current working directory.

2. This list comprehension takes that list of `.xml` files and transforms it into a list of full pathnames.

List comprehensions can also filter items, as in Listing 3-9, producing a result that can be smaller than the original list.

Listing 3-9. Filtering a List of Files

```
>>> import os, glob
>>> [f for f in glob.glob('*.py') if os.stat(f).st_size > 6000]   (1)
['pluraltest6.py',
 'romantest10.py',
 'romantest6.py',
 'romantest7.py',
 'romantest8.py',
 'romantest9.py']
```

1. To filter a list, you can include an `if` clause at the end of the list comprehension. The expression after the `if` keyword will be evaluated for each item in the list. If the expression evaluates to `True`, the item will be included in the output. This list comprehension looks at the list of all `.py` files in the current directory, and the `if` expression filters that list by testing whether the size of each file is greater than 6000 bytes. There are six such files, so the list comprehension returns a list of six filenames.

All the examples of list comprehensions so far have featured simple expressions—multiply a number by a constant, call a single function, or simply return the original list item (after filtering). But there's no limit to how complex a list comprehension can be, as shown in Listing 3-10.

Listing 3-10. A complex List Comprehension

```
>>> import os, glob
>>> [(os.stat(f).st_size, os.path.realpath(f)) for f in glob.glob('*.xml')]          (1)
[(3074, 'c:\\Users\\pilgrim\\diveintopython3\\examples\\feed-broken.xml'),
 (3386, 'c:\\Users\\pilgrim\\diveintopython3\\examples\\feed-ns0.xml'),
 (3070, 'c:\\Users\\pilgrim\\diveintopython3\\examples\\feed.xml')]
>>> import humansize
>>> [(humansize.approximate_size(os.stat(f).st_size), f) for f in glob.glob('*.xml')]  (2)
[('3.0 KiB', 'feed-broken.xml'),
 ('3.3 KiB', 'feed-ns0.xml'),
 ('3.0 KiB', 'feed.xml')]
```

1. This list comprehension finds all the `.xml` files in the current working directory, gets the size of each file (by calling the `os.stat()` function), and constructs a tuple of the file size and the absolute path of each file (by calling the `os.path.realpath()` function).

2. This comprehension builds on the previous one to call the `approximate_size()` function with the file size of each `.xml` file.

Dictionary Comprehensions

A dictionary comprehension is like a list comprehension, but it constructs a dictionary instead of a list (see Listing 3-11).

Listing 3-11. Constructing a Dictionary with a Dictionary Comprehension

```
>>> import os, glob
>>> metadata = [(f, os.stat(f)) for f in glob.glob('*test*.py')]     (1)
>>> metadata[0]                                                       (2)
('alphameticstest.py', nt.stat_result(st_mode=33206, st_ino=0, st_dev=0,
 st_nlink=0, st_uid=0, st_gid=0, st_size=2509, st_atime=1247520344,
 st_mtime=1247520344, st_ctime=1247520344))
>>> metadata_dict = {f:os.stat(f) for f in glob.glob('*test*.py')}   (3)
>>> type(metadata_dict)                                              (4)
<class 'dict'>
>>> list(metadata_dict.keys())                                       (5)
['romantest8.py', 'pluraltest1.py', 'pluraltest2.py', 'pluraltest5.py',
 'pluraltest6.py', 'romantest7.py', 'romantest10.py', 'romantest4.py',
 'romantest9.py', 'pluraltest3.py', 'romantest1.py', 'romantest2.py',
 'romantest3.py', 'romantest5.py', 'romantest6.py', 'alphameticstest.py',
 'pluraltest4.py']
>>> metadata_dict['alphameticstest.py'].st_size                     (6)
2509
```

1. This is not a dictionary comprehension; it's a list comprehension. It finds all .py files with test in their names, then constructs a tuple of the filename and the file metadata (from calling the os.stat() function).

2. Each item of the resulting list is a tuple.

3. This is a dictionary comprehension. The syntax is similar to a list comprehension, with two differences. First, it is enclosed in curly braces instead of square brackets. Second, instead of a single expression for each item, it contains two expressions separated by a colon. The expression before the colon (f in this example) is the dictionary key; the expression after the colon (os.stat(f) in this example) is the value.

4. A dictionary comprehension returns a dictionary.

5. The keys of this particular dictionary are simply the filenames returned from the call to glob.glob('*test*.py').

6. The value associated with each key is the return value from the os.stat() function. That means we can "look up" a file by name in this dictionary to get its file metadata. One of the pieces of metadata is st_size, the file size. The file alphameticstest.py is 2509 bytes long.

Like list comprehensions, you can include an `if` clause in a dictionary comprehension to filter the input sequence based on an expression that is evaluated with each item, as shown in Listing 3-12.

Listing 3-12. Filtering a Dictionary

```
>>> import os, glob, humansize
>>> humansize_dict = {os.path.splitext(f)[0]:humansize.approximate_size↩
(os.stat(f).st_size) \
...                      for f in glob.glob('*') if os.stat(f).st_size > 6000}    (1)
>>> list(humansize_dict.keys())                                                   (2)
['romantest9', 'romantest8', 'romantest7', 'romantest6', 'romantest10', 'pluraltest6']
>>> humansize_dict['romantest9']                                                  (3)
'6.5 KiB'
```

1. This dictionary comprehension constructs a list of all the files in the current working directory (`glob.glob('*')`), filters that list to include only those files larger than `6000` bytes (`if os.stat(f).st_size > 6000`), and uses that filtered list to construct a dictionary whose keys are the filename minus the extension (`os.path.splitext(f)[0]`) and whose values are the approximate size of each file (`humansize.approximate_size(os.stat(f).st_size)`).

2. As you saw in a previous example, there are six such files, thus there are six items in this dictionary.

3. The value of each key is the string returned from the `approximate_size()` function.

Fun with Dictionary Comprehensions

Listing 3-13 shows a trick with dictionary comprehensions that might be useful someday: swapping the keys and values of a dictionary.

Listing 3-13. Swapping Dictionary Keys and Values

```
>>> a_dict = {'a': 1, 'b': 2, 'c': 3}
>>> {value:key for key, value in a_dict.items()}
{1: 'a', 2: 'b', 3: 'c'}
```

Set Comprehensions

Not to be left out, sets have their own comprehension syntax as well. It is remarkably similar to the syntax for dictionary comprehensions, as shown in Listing 3-14. The only difference is that sets just have values instead of key-value pairs.

Listing 3-14. Constructing a Set

```
>>> a_set = set(range(10))
>>> a_set
{0, 1, 2, 3, 4, 5, 6, 7, 8, 9}
>>> {x ** 2 for x in a_set}              (1)
{0, 1, 4, 81, 64, 9, 16, 49, 25, 36}
>>> {x for x in a_set if x % 2 == 0}  (2)
{0, 8, 2, 4, 6}
>>> {2**x for x in range(10)}            (3)
{32, 1, 2, 4, 8, 64, 128, 256, 16, 512}
```

1. Set comprehensions can take a set as input. This set comprehension calculates the squares of the set of numbers from 0 to 9.

2. Like list comprehensions and dictionary comprehensions, set comprehensions can contain an **if** clause to filter each item before returning it in the result set.

3. Set comprehensions do not need to take a set as input; they can take any sequence.

Further Reading Online

- os module: http://docs.python.org/3.1/library/os.html

- "os—Portable access to operating system specific features" by Doug Hellmann: http://www.doughellmann.com/PyMOTW/os/

- os.path module: http://docs.python.org/3.1/library/os.path.html

- "os.path—Platform-independent manipulation of file names" by Doug Hellmann: http://www.doughellmann.com/PyMOTW/ospath/

- glob module: http://docs.python.org/3.1/library/glob.html

- "glob—Filename pattern matching" by Doug Hellmann: http://www.doughellmann.com/PyMOTW/glob/

- time module: http://docs.python.org/3.1/library/time.html

- "time—Functions for manipulating clock time" by Doug Hellmann: http://www.doughellmann.com/PyMOTW/time/

- List comprehensions: http://docs.python.org/3.1/tutorial/datastructures.html#list-comprehensions

- Nested list comprehensions: http://docs.python.org/3.1/tutorial/datastructures.html#nested-list-comprehensions w

- Looping techniques: http://docs.python.org/3.1/tutorial/datastructures.html#looping-techniques

CHAPTER 4

■ ■ ■

Strings

Did you know that the people of Bougainville have the smallest alphabet in the world? Their Rotokas alphabet is composed of only 12 letters: A, E, G, I, K, O, P, R, S, T, U, and V. On the other end of the spectrum, languages such as Chinese, Japanese, and Korean have thousands of characters. English, of course, has 26 letters—52 if you count uppercase and lowercase letters separately—plus a handful of !@#$%& punctuation marks.

When people talk about *text*, they're thinking of *characters and symbols on the computer screen*. But computers don't deal in characters and symbols; they deal in bits and bytes. Every piece of text you've ever seen on a computer screen is actually stored in a particular *character encoding*. Very roughly speaking, character encoding provides a mapping between the stuff you see on your screen and the stuff your computer actually stores in memory and on disk. There are many different character encodings; some are optimized for particular languages such as Russian or Chinese or English; others can be used for multiple languages.

In reality, it's even more complicated than that. Many characters are common to multiple encodings, but each encoding might use a different sequence of bytes to actually store those characters in memory or on disk. So you can think of character encoding as a kind of decryption key. Whenever someone gives you a sequence of bytes—a file, a web page, whatever—and claims that it is *text*, you need to know what character encoding was used so you can decode the bytes into characters. If you get the wrong key or no key at all, you're left with the unenviable task of cracking the code yourself. Chances are you'll get it wrong, and the result will be gibberish.

Surely you've seen web pages with strange question-mark-like characters where apostrophes should be. The author didn't declare the character encoding correctly, your browser was left guessing, and the result was a mix of expected and unexpected characters. In English, it's merely annoying; in other languages, the result can be completely unreadable.

There are character encodings for each major language in the world. Because each language is different, and memory and disk space have historically been expensive, each character encoding is optimized for a particular language (by that, I mean each encoding uses the same numbers [0–255] to represent that language's characters). For instance, you're probably familiar with ASCII encoding, which stores English characters as numbers ranging from 0 to 127 (65 is capital *A*, 97 is lowercase *a*, and so on). English has a very simple alphabet, so it can be completely expressed in fewer than 128 numbers. For those of you who can count in base 2, that's 7 out of the 8 bits in a byte.

Western European languages such as French, Spanish, and German have more letters than English. Or, more precisely, they have letters combined with various diacritical marks (such as the ñ character in Spanish). The most common encoding for these languages is CP-1252, also called *Windows-1252* because it is widely used on Microsoft Windows. The CP-1252 encoding shares characters with ASCII in the 0–127 range, but then extends into the 128–255 range for characters such as n-with-a-tilde-over-it (241), u-with-two-dots-over-it (252), and so on. It's still a single-byte encoding, though; the highest possible number, 255, fits in one byte.

Then there are languages such as Chinese, Japanese, and Korean, which have so many characters that they require multiple-byte character sets. That is, each "character" is represented by a two-byte number from 0–65535. But different multibyte encodings still share the same problem as different single-byte encodings: they each use the same numbers to mean different things. The range of numbers is broader because there are many more characters to represent.

That was mostly okay in a non-networked world, in which text was something you typed and occasionally printed. There wasn't much *plain text.* Source code was ASCII, and everyone else used word processors, which defined their own (non-text) formats that tracked character encoding information along with rich styling, and so on. People read these documents with the same word processing program as the original author, so everything worked, more or less.

Now think about the rise of global networks such as e-mail and the Web. Lots of plain text flying around the globe, being authored on one computer, transmitted through a second computer, and received and displayed by a third computer. Computers can see only numbers, but the numbers could mean different things. Oh no! What to do? Systems had to be designed to carry encoding information along with every piece of plain text. Remember, it's the decryption key that maps computer-readable numbers to human-readable characters. A missing decryption key means garbled text, gibberish, or worse.

Now think about trying to store multiple pieces of text in the same place, for example in the same database table that holds all the e-mail you've ever received. You still need to store the character encoding alongside each piece of text so you can display it properly. Think that's hard? Try searching your e-mail database, which means converting between multiple encodings on the fly. Doesn't that sound fun?

Now think about the possibility of multilingual documents, where characters from several languages are next to each other in the same document. (Hint: programs that tried to do this typically used escape codes to switch "modes." Poof, you're in Russian koi8-r mode, so 241 means   ; poof, now you're in Mac Greek mode, so 241 means   .) And you'll want to search *those* documents, too.

Now cry a lot because everything you thought you knew about strings is wrong, and there ain't no such thing as plain text.

Unicode

Enter Unicode.

Unicode is a system designed to represent *every* character from *every* language. Unicode represents each letter, character, or ideograph as a 4-byte number. Each number represents a unique character used in at least one of the world's languages. (Not all the numbers are used, but more than 65535 of them are, so 2 bytes wouldn't be sufficient.) Characters that are used in multiple languages generally have the same number unless there is a good etymological reason not to. Regardless, there is exactly one number per character, and exactly one character per number. Every number always means just one thing; there are no modes to keep track of. U+0041 is always 'A', even if your language doesn't have an 'A' in it.

On the face of it, this seems like a great idea. One encoding to rule them all. Multiple languages per document. No more to switching modes midstream between encodings. But right away, the obvious question should leap out at you. Four bytes? For every single character? That seems awfully wasteful, especially for languages such as English and Spanish, which need less than 1 byte (256 numbers) to express every possible character. In fact, it's wasteful even for ideograph-based languages (such as Chinese), which never need more than two bytes per character.

There is a Unicode encoding that uses 4 bytes per character. It's called UTF-32 because 32 bits = 4 bytes. UTF-32 is a straightforward encoding; it takes each Unicode character (a 4-byte number) and represents the character with that same number. This has some advantages, the most important being that you can find the Nth character of a string in constant time because the Nth character starts at the 4×Nth byte. It also has several disadvantages, the most obvious being that it takes 4 freaking bytes to store every freaking character.

Even though there are a lot of Unicode characters, it turns out that most people will never use anything beyond the first 65535. Thus, there is another Unicode encoding, called UTF-16 (because 16 bits = 2 bytes). UTF-16 encodes every character from 0–65535 as 2 bytes; it then uses some dirty hacks if you actually need to represent the rarely used *astral plane* Unicode characters beyond 65535. The most obvious advantage: UTF-16 is twice as space-efficient as UTF-32 because every character requires only 2 bytes to store instead of 4 bytes (except for the ones that don't). And you can still easily find the Nth character of a string in constant time if you assume that the string doesn't include any astral plane characters, which is a good assumption right up until the moment that it's not.

But there are also not-obvious disadvantages to both UTF-32 and UTF-16. Different computer systems store individual bytes in different ways. That means that the character U+4E2D could be stored in UTF-16 as either 4E 2D or 2D 4E, depending on whether the system is big-endian or little-endian. (For UTF-32, there are even more possible byte orderings.) As long as your documents never leave your computer, you're safe—different applications on the same computer use the same byte order. But the minute you want to transfer documents between systems, perhaps on a worldwide web of some sort, you'll need a way to indicate which order your bytes are stored. Otherwise, the receiving system has no way of knowing whether the 2-byte sequence 4E 2D means U+4E2D or U+2D4E.

To solve this problem, the multi-byte Unicode encodings define a *Byte Order Mark*, which is a special nonprintable character that you can include at the beginning of your document to indicate what order your bytes are in. For UTF-16, the Byte Order Mark is U+FEFF. If you receive a UTF-16 document that starts with the bytes FF FE, you know the byte ordering is one way; if it starts with FE FF, you know the byte ordering is reversed.

Still, UTF-16 isn't exactly ideal, especially if you're dealing with a lot of ASCII characters. If you think about it, even a Chinese web page contains a lot of ASCII characters—all the elements and attributes surrounding the printable Chinese characters. Being able to find the Nth character in constant time is nice, but there's still the nagging problem of those astral plane characters. You can't *guarantee* that every character is exactly 2 bytes, so you can't *really* find the Nth character in constant time unless you maintain a separate index. And boy, there sure is a lot of ASCII text in the world.

Other people pondered these questions, and they came up with a solution: UTF-8.

UTF-8 is a *variable-length encoding system* for Unicode. That is, different characters take up a different number of bytes. For ASCII characters (A-Z, and so on), UTF-8 uses just 1 byte per character. In fact, it uses the exact same bytes; the first 128 characters (0–127) in UTF-8 are indistinguishable from ASCII. *Extended Latin* characters such as ñ and ö end up taking 2 bytes. (The bytes are not simply the Unicode code point AS they would be in UTF-16; there is some serious bit-twiddling involved.) Chinese characters such as 中 end up taking 3 bytes. The rarely used astral plane characters take 4 bytes.

Disadvantages: because each character can take a different number of bytes, finding the Nth character is an O(n) operation (the longer the string, the longer it takes to find a specific character). Also, there is bit-twiddling involved to encode characters into bytes and decode bytes into characters.

Advantages: super-efficient encoding of common ASCII characters. No worse than UTF-16 for extended Latin characters. Better than UTF-32 for Chinese characters. Also (and you'll have to trust me on this because I'm not going to show you the math) there are no byte-ordering issues because of the exact nature of the bit twiddling. A document encoded in UTF-8 uses the exact same stream of bytes on any computer.

Diving In

In Python 3, all strings are sequences of Unicode characters. There is no such thing as a Python string encoded in UTF-8, or a Python string encoded as CP-1252. "Is this string UTF-8?" is an invalid question. UTF-8 is a way of encoding characters as a sequence of bytes. If you want to take a string and turn it into a sequence of bytes in a particular character encoding, Python 3 can help you with that. If you want to take a sequence of bytes and turn it into a string, Python 3 can help you with that, too (see Listing 4-1). Bytes are not characters; bytes are bytes. Characters are an abstraction. A string is a sequence of those abstractions.

Listing 4-1. Introducing Strings

```
>>> s = '深入 Python'      (1)
>>> len(s)               (2)
9
>>> s[0]                 (3)
'深'
>>> s + ' 3'             (4)
'深入 Python 3'
```

The following notes refer to the numbered lines in Listing 4-1:

1. To create a string, enclose it in quotes. Python strings can be defined with either single quotes (') or double quotes (").

2. The built-in `len()` function returns the length of the string, (that is, the number of characters). This is the same function you use to find the length of a list. A string is like a list of characters.

3. Just as you can get individual items out of a list, you can get individual characters out of a string using index notation.

4. Just like lists, you can concatenate strings using the + operator.

Formatting Strings

Let's take another look at `humansize.py` (see Listing 4-2).

Listing 4-2. Strings in the approximate_size() Function

```
SUFFIXES = {1000: ['KB', 'MB', 'GB', 'TB', 'PB', 'EB', 'ZB', 'YB'],        (1)
            1024: ['KiB', 'MiB', 'GiB', 'TiB', 'PiB', 'EiB', 'ZiB', 'YiB']}

def approximate_size(size, a_kilobyte_is_1024_bytes=True):
    '''Convert a file size to human-readable form.                         (2)

    Keyword arguments:
    size – file size in bytes
    a_kilobyte_is_1024_bytes – if True (default), use multiples of 1024
                               if False, use multiples of 1000
```

```
Returns: string

'''                                                              (3)
if size < 0:
    raise ValueError('number must be non-negative')             (4)

multiple = 1024 if a_kilobyte_is_1024_bytes else 1000
for suffix in SUFFIXES[multiple]:
    size /= multiple
    if size < multiple:
        return '{0:.1f} {1}'.format(size, suffix)               (5)

raise ValueError('number too large')
```

1. `'KB'`, `'MB'`, and `'GB'`, and so on are strings.

2. Function docstrings are strings. This docstring spans multiple lines, so it uses three-in-a-row quotes to start and end the string.

3. These three-in-a-row quotes end the docstring.

4. There's another string being passed to the exception as a human-readable error message.

5. There's a... whoa, what the heck is that?

Python 3 supports formatting values into strings. Although this can include very complicated expressions, the most basic usage is to insert a value into a string with single placeholder (see Listing 4-3).

Listing 4-3. Basic String Formatting

```
>>> username = 'mark'
>>> password = 'PapayaWhip'                                     (1)
>>> "{0}'s password is {1}".format(username, password)          (2)
"mark's password is PapayaWhip"
```

1. No, my password is not really `PapayaWhip`.

2. There's a lot going on here. First, that's a method call on a string literal. Strings are objects, and objects have methods. Second, the whole expression evaluates to a string. Third, {0} and {1} are *replacement fields*, which are replaced by the arguments passed to the `format()` method.

Compound Field Names

The previous example shows the simplest case, in which the replacement fields are simply integers. Integer replacement fields are treated as positional indices into the argument list of the `format()` method. That means that {0} is replaced by the first argument (`username`, in this case), {1} is replaced by the second argument (`password`), and so on. You can have as many positional indices as you have arguments, and you can have as many arguments as you want. But replacement fields are much more powerful than that, as shown in Listing 4-4.

Listing 4-4. *String Formatting with Compound Field Names*

```
>>> import humansize
>>> si_suffixes = humansize.SUFFIXES[1000]         (1)
>>> si_suffixes
['KB', 'MB', 'GB', 'TB', 'PB', 'EB', 'ZB', 'YB']
>>> '1000{0[0]} = 1{0[1]}'.format(si_suffixes)  (2)
'1000KB = 1MB'
```

1. Instead of calling any function in the `humansize` module, you're just grabbing one of the data structures it defines: the list of *SI* (powers-of-1000) suffixes.

2. This looks complicated, but it's not. `{0}` would refer to the first argument passed to the `format()` method: `si_suffixes`. But `si_suffixes` is a list. So `{0[0]}` refers to the first item of the list, which is the first argument passed to the `format()` method: `'KB'`. Meanwhile, `{0[1]}` refers to the second item of the same list: `'MB'`. Everything outside the curly braces—including `1000`, the equals sign, and the spaces—is untouched. The final result is the string `'1000KB = 1MB'`.

What this example shows is that *format specifers* can access items and properties of data structures using (almost) Python syntax. This is called *compound field names*. The following compound field names work:

- Passing a list and accessing an item of the list by index (as in the previous example)

- Passing a dictionary and accessing a value of the dictionary by key

- Passing a module and accessing its variables and functions by name

- Passing a class instance and accessing its properties and methods by name

- *Any combination of the previous names*

Just to blow your mind, Listing 4-5 shows an example that combines all of them.

Listing 4-5. *Complex String Formatting*

```
>>> import humansize
>>> import sys
>>> '1MB = 1000{0.modules[humansize].SUFFIXES[1000][0]}'.format(sys)
'1MB = 1000KB'
```

Here's how it works:

- The `sys` module holds information about the currently running Python instance. Because you just imported it, you can pass the `sys` module as an argument to the `format()` method. So the replacement field `{0}` refers to the `sys` module.

- `sys.modules` is a dictionary of all the modules that have been imported in this Python instance. The keys are the module names as strings; the values are the module objects. So the replacement field `{0.modules}` refers to the dictionary of imported modules.

- `sys.modules['humansize']` is the `humansize` module that you just imported. The replacement field `{0.modules[humansize]}` refers to the `humansize` module. Note the slight difference in syntax here. In real Python code, the keys of the `sys.modules` dictionary are strings; to refer to them, you need to put quotes around the module name (for example, `'humansize'`). But within a replacement field, you skip the quotes around the dictionary key name (for example, `humansize`). Complex string formatting is defined in PEP 3101, which states, "The rules for parsing an item key are very simple. If it starts with a digit, then it is treated as a number; otherwise it is used as a string."

- `sys.modules['humansize'].SUFFIXES` is the dictionary defined at the top of the `humansize` module. The replacement field `{0.modules[humansize].SUFFIXES}` refers to that dictionary.

- `sys.modules['humansize'].SUFFIXES[1000]` is a list of SI suffixes: `['KB', 'MB', 'GB', 'TB', 'PB', 'EB', 'ZB', 'YB']`. So the replacement field `{0.modules[humansize].SUFFIXES[1000]}` refers to that list.

- `sys.modules['humansize'].SUFFIXES[1000][0]` is the first item of the list of SI suffixes: `'KB'`. Therefore, the complete replacement field `{0.modules[humansize].SUFFIXES[1000][0]}` is replaced by the two-character string `KB`.

Format Specifiers

But wait! There's more! Let's take another look at that strange line of code from `humansize.py` (see Listing 4-6).

Listing 4-6. String Formatting in the approximate_size() Function

```
if size < multiple:
    return '{0:.1f} {1}'.format(size, suffix)
```

`{1}` is replaced with the second argument passed to the `format()` method, which is `suffix`. But what is `{0:.1f}`? It consists of two things: `{0}`, which you recognize, and `:.1f`, which you don't. The second half (including after the colon) defines the *format specifier*, which further refines how the replaced variable should be formatted.

■ Format specifiers allow you to munge the replacement text in a variety of useful ways, similar to the `printf()` function in C. You can add zero- or space-padding, align strings, control decimal precision, and even convert numbers to hexadecimal.

Within a replacement field, a colon (:) marks the start of the format specifier. The format specifier .1 means "round to the nearest tenth" (that is, display only one digit after the decimal point). The format specifier f means *fixed-point number* (as opposed to exponential notation or some other decimal representation). Thus, given a size of 698.24 and suffix of 'GB', the formatted string would be '698.2 GB' because 698.24 gets rounded to one decimal place; then the suffix is appended after the number (see Listing 4-7).

Listing 4-7. Formatting Floating-Point Numbers

```
>>> '{0:.1f} {1}'.format(698.24, 'GB')
'698.2 GB'
```

For all the gory details on format specifiers, consult the Format Specification Mini-Language in the official Python documentation: http://docs.python.org/3.0/library/string.html#format-specification-mini-language.

Other Common String Methods

Besides formatting, strings can do a number of other useful tricks (see Listing 4-8).

Listing 4-8. String Methods

```
>>> s = '''Finished files are the re-    (1)
... sult of years of scientif-
... ic study combined with the
... experience of years.'''
>>> s.splitlines()                       (2)
['Finished files are the re-',
 'sult of years of scientif-',
 'ic study combined with the',
 'experience of years.']
>>> print(s.lower())                     (3)
finished files are the re-
sult of years of scientif-
ic study combined with the
experience of years.
>>> s.lower().count('f')                 (4)
6
```

1. You can input multiline strings in the Python interactive shell. Once you start a multiline string with triple quotation marks, just press Enter and the interactive shell will prompt you to continue the string. Typing the closing triple quotation marks ends the string, and the next Enter will execute the command (in this case, assigning the string to s).

2. The splitlines() method takes one multiline string and returns a list of strings, one for each line of the original. Note that the carriage returns at the end of each line are not included.

3. The `lower()` method converts the entire string to lowercase. (Similarly, the `upper()` method converts a string to uppercase.)

4. The `count()` method counts the number of occurrences of a substring. Yes, there really are six *f*s in that sentence!

Listing 4-9 shows another common case. Let's say you have a list of key-value pairs in the form `key1=value1&key2=value2` and you want to split them up and make a dictionary of the form {`key1: value1, key2: value2`}.

Listing 4-9. Splitting Strings

```
>>> query = 'user=pilgrim&database=master&password=PapayaWhip'
>>> a_list = query.split('&')                              (1)
>>> a_list
['user=pilgrim', 'database=master', 'password=PapayaWhip']
>>> a_list_of_lists = [v.split('=', 1) for v in a_list]    (2)
>>> a_list_of_lists
[['user', 'pilgrim'], ['database', 'master'], ['password', 'PapayaWhip']]
>>> a_dict = dict(a_list_of_lists)                         (3)
>>> a_dict
{'password': 'PapayaWhip', 'user': 'pilgrim', 'database': 'master'}
```

1. The `split()` string method takes one argument, a delimiter, and splits a string into a list of strings based on the delimiter. Here, the delimiter is an ampersand character, but it could be anything.

2. Now you have a list of strings, each with a key, followed by an equals sign, followed by a value. You can use a list comprehension to iterate over the entire list and split each string into two strings based on the first equals sign. (In theory, a value could contain an equals sign, too. If we just used `'key=value=foo'.split('=')`, we would end up with a three-item list `['key', 'value', 'foo']`.)

3. Finally, Python can turn that list of lists into a dictionary simply by passing it to the `dict()` function.

■ The previous example looks a lot like parsing query parameters in a URL, but real-life URL parsing is actually more complicated than this. If you're dealing with URL query parameters, you're better off using the `urllib.parse.parse_qs()` function, which handles some not-so-obvious edge cases.

Slicing a String

Once you've defined a string, you can get any part of it as a new string. This is called *slicing* the string. Slicing strings works exactly the same as slicing lists, which makes sense because strings are just sequences of characters. Listing 4-10 shows how string slicing works.

Listing 4-10. String Slicing

```
>>> a_string = 'My alphabet starts where your alphabet ends.'
>>> a_string[3:11]          (1)
'alphabet'
>>> a_string[3:-3]          (2)
'alphabet starts where your alphabet en'
>>> a_string[0:2]           (3)
'My'
>>> a_string[:18]           (4)
'My alphabet starts'
>>> a_string[18:]           (5)
' where your alphabet ends.'
```

1. You can get a part of a string, called a *slice*, by specifying two indices. The return value is a new string containing all the characters of the string, in order, starting with the first slice index (in this case, a_string[0]), up to but not including the second slice index (in this case, a_string[2]).

2. Like slicing lists, you can use negative indices to slice strings.

3. Strings are zero-based, so a_string[0:3] returns the first three items of the string, starting at a_string[0], up to but not including a_string[3].

4. If the left slice index is 0, you can leave it out, and 0 is implied. So a_string[:18] is the same as a_string[0:18] because the starting 0 is implied.

5. Similarly, if the right slice index is the length of the string, you can leave it out. So a_string[18:] is the same as a_string[18:44] because this string has 44 characters. There is a pleasing symmetry here. In this 44-character string, a_string[:18] returns the first 18 characters, and a_string[18:] returns everything but the first 18 characters. In fact, a_string[:n] will always return the first n characters, and a_string[n:] will return the rest, regardless of the length of the string.

Strings versus Bytes

Bytes are bytes; characters are an abstraction. An immutable sequence of Unicode characters is called a string. An immutable sequence of numbers between 0 and 255 is called a **bytes** object (see Listing 4-11).

Listing 4-11. bytes Objects

```
>>> by = b'abcd\x65'  (1)
>>> by
b'abcde'
>>> type(by)          (2)
<class 'bytes'>
```

```
>>> len(by)            (3)
5
>>> by += b'\xff'      (4)
>>> by
b'abcde\xff'
>>> len(by)            (5)
6
>>> by[0]              (6)
97
>>> by[0] = 102        (7)
Traceback (most recent call last):
  File "<stdin>", line 1, in <module>
TypeError: 'bytes' object does not support item assignment
```

1. To define a **bytes** object, use the b'' *byte literal* syntax. Each byte within the byte literal can be an ASCII character or an encoded hexadecimal number from \x00 to \xff (0–255).

2. The type of a **bytes** object is **bytes**.

3. Just like lists and strings, you can get the length of a **bytes** object with the built-in len() function.

4. Just like lists and strings, you can use the + operator to concatenate **bytes** objects. The result is a new **bytes** object.

5. Concatenating a 5-byte **bytes** object and a 1-byte **bytes** object gives you a 6-byte **bytes** object.

6. Just like lists and strings, you can use index notation to get individual bytes in a **bytes** object. The items of a string are strings; the items of a **bytes** object are integers (specifically, integers between 0–255).

7. A **bytes** object is immutable; you can't assign individual bytes. If you need to change individual bytes, you can use string slicing and concatenation operators (which work the same as strings), or you can convert the **bytes** object into a **bytearray** object.

If you need to modify a sequence of bytes, you need to explicitly convert it into a byte array, as shown in Listing 4-12.

Listing 4-12. Converting Bytes to Byte Arrays

```
>>> by = b'abcd\x65'
>>> barr = bytearray(by)   (1)
>>> barr
bytearray(b'abcde')
>>> len(barr)              (2)
5
>>> barr[0] = 102          (3)
>>> barr
bytearray(b'fbcde')
```

1. To convert an **bytes** object into a mutable **bytearray** object, use the built-in **bytearray()** function.

2. All the methods and operations you can do on a **bytes** object, you can do on a **bytearray** object, too.

3. The one difference is that with the **bytearray** object, you can assign individual bytes using index notation. The assigned value must be an integer between 0–255.

The one thing you can *never* do is mix bytes and strings (see Listing 4-13).

Listing 4-13. Trying to Mix Bytes and Strings

```
>>> by = b'd'
>>> s = 'abcde'
>>> by + s                           (1)
Traceback (most recent call last):
  File "<stdin>", line 1, in <module>
TypeError: can't concat bytes to str
>>> s.count(by)                      (2)
Traceback (most recent call last):
  File "<stdin>", line 1, in <module>
TypeError: Can't convert 'bytes' object to str implicitly
>>> s.count(by.decode('ascii'))  (3)
1
```

1. You can't concatenate bytes and strings. They are two different datatypes.

2. You can't count the occurrences of bytes in a string because there are no bytes in a string. A string is a sequence of characters. Did you mean "count the occurrences of the string that you would get after decoding this sequence of bytes in a particular character encoding?" If so, you'll need to say that explicitly. Python 3 won't implicitly convert bytes to strings or strings to bytes.

3. By an amazing coincidence, this line of code says "count the occurrences of the string that you would get after decoding this sequence of bytes in this particular character encoding."

And here is the link between strings and bytes: **bytes** objects have a **decode()** method that takes a character encoding and returns a string, and strings have an **encode()** method that takes a character encoding and returns a **bytes** object. In Listing 4-13, the decoding was relatively straightforward—converting a sequence of bytes n the ASCII encoding into a string of characters. But as you can see in Listing 4-14, the same process works with any encoding that supports the characters of the string—even legacy (non-Unicode) encodings.

Listing 4-14. Explicitly Converting Between Bytes and Strings

```
>>> a_string = '深入 Python'         (1)
>>> len(a_string)
9
>>> by = a_string.encode('utf-8')    (2)
>>> by
```

```
b'\xe6\xb7\xb1\xe5\x85\xa5 Python'
>>> len(by)
13
>>> by = a_string.encode('gb18030')    (3)
>>> by
b'\xc9\xee\xc8\xeb Python'
>>> len(by)
11
>>> by = a_string.encode('big5')       (4)
>>> by
b'\xb2`\xa4J Python'
>>> len(by)
11
>>> roundtrip = by.decode('big5')      (5)
>>> roundtrip
'深入 Python'
>>> a_string == roundtrip
True
```

1. This is a string. It has 9 characters.

2. This is a **bytes** object. It has 13 bytes. It is the sequence of bytes you get when you take **a_string** and encode it in UTF-8.

3. This is a **bytes** object. It has 11 bytes. It is the sequence of bytes you get when you take **a_string** and encode it in GB18030.

4. This is a **bytes** object. It has 11 bytes. It is an entirely different sequence of bytes that you get when you take **a_string** and encode it in Big5.

5. This is a string. It has 9 characters. It is the sequence of characters you get when you take **by** and decode it using the Big5 encoding algorithm. It is identical to the original string.

Character Encoding of Python Source Code

Python 3 assumes that your source code (that is, each .py file) is encoded in UTF-8.

■ In Python 2, the default encoding for .py files was ASCII. In Python 3, the default encoding is UTF-8.

If you want to use a different encoding within your Python code, you can put an encoding declaration on the first line of each file. The declaration shown in Listing 4-15 defines a .py file to be Windows-1252.

Listing 4-15. Declaring a Character Encoding in the .py File

```
# -*- coding: windows-1252 -*-
```

Technically, the character encoding override can also be on the second line if the first line is a UNIX-like `hash-bang` command (see Listing 4-16).

Listing 4-16. Declaring a Character Encoding After the hash-bang

```
#!/usr/bin/python3
# -*- coding: windows-1252 -*-
```

For more information, consult *PEP 263: Defining Python Source Code Encodings* at `http://www.python.org/dev/peps/pep-0263/`

Further Reading Online

For more information on Unicode in Python, see the following:

- *Python Unicode HOWTO*: `http://docs.python.org/3.0/howto/unicode.html`

- *What's New In Python 3: Text vs. Data Instead of Unicode vs. 8-bit*: `http://docs.python.org/3.0/whatsnew/3.0.html#text-vs-data-instead-of-unicode-vs-8-bit`

For more information on Unicode in general, see the following:

- *The Absolute Minimum Every Software Developer Absolutely, Positively Must Know About Unicode and Character Sets (No Excuses!)*: `http://www.joelonsoftware.com/articles/Unicode.html`

- *On the goodness of Unicode*: `http://www.tbray.org/ongoing/When/200x/2003/04/06/Unicode`

- *On character strings*: `http://www.tbray.org/ongoing/When/200x/2003/04/13/Strings`

- *Characters vs. bytes*: `http://www.tbray.org/ongoing/When/200x/2003/04/26/UTF`

For more information on character encoding in other formats, see the following:

- *Character encoding in XML*: `http://feedparser.org/docs/character-encoding.html`

- *Character encoding in HTML*: `http://blog.whatwg.org/the-road-to-html-5-character-encoding`

For more information on strings and string formatting, see the following:

- *string module*: `http://docs.python.org/3.1/library/string.html`

- *Format string syntax*: `http://docs.python.org/3.1/library/string.html#formatstrings`

- *Format specification mini-language*: `http://docs.python.org/3.1/library/string.html#format-specification-mini-language`

- *PEP 3101: Advanced String Formatting*: `http://www.python.org/dev/peps/pep-3101`

CHAPTER 5

■ ■ ■

Regular Expressions

Every modern programming language has built-in functions for working with strings. In Python, strings have methods for searching and replacing: index(), find(), split(), count(), replace(), and so on. But these methods are limited to the simplest of cases. For example, the index() method looks for a single, hard-coded substring, and the search is always case-sensitive. To do case-insensitive searches of a string s, you must call s.lower() or s.upper() and make sure that your search strings are the appropriate case to match. The replace() and split() methods have the same limitations.

If your goal can be accomplished with string methods, you should use them. They're fast, simple, and easy to read; and there's a lot to be said for fast, simple, and readable code. But if you use a lot of different string functions with if statements to handle special cases, or if you're chaining calls to split() and join() to slice and dice your strings, you might need to move up to regular expressions.

Regular expressions are a powerful and (mostly) standardized way of searching, replacing, and parsing text with complex patterns of characters. Although the regular expression syntax is tight and unlike normal code, the result can end up being *more* readable than a hand-rolled solution that uses a long chain of string functions. There are even ways of embedding comments within regular expressions, so you can include fine-grained documentation within them.

■ If you used regular expressions in other languages (such as Perl, JavaScript, or PHP), Python's syntax will be very familiar. Read the summary of the re module to get an overview of the available functions and their arguments.

Case Study: Street Addresses

This series of examples was inspired by a real-life problem I had in my day job several years ago, when I needed to scrub and standardize street addresses exported from a legacy system before importing them into a newer system. (See, I don't just make this stuff up; it's actually useful.) Listing 5-1 shows how I approached the problem.

Listing 5-1. String Substitution

```
>>> s = '100 NORTH MAIN ROAD'
>>> s.replace('ROAD', 'RD.')                (1)
'100 NORTH MAIN RD.'
>>> s = '100 NORTH BROAD ROAD'
>>> s.replace('ROAD', 'RD.')                (2)
'100 NORTH BRD. RD.'
>>> s[:-4] + s[-4:].replace('ROAD', 'RD.')  (3)
'100 NORTH BROAD RD.'
>>> import re                               (4)
>>> re.sub('ROAD$', 'RD.', s)               (5)
'100 NORTH BROAD RD.'
```

The following notes refer to the numbered lines in Listing 5-1:

1. My goal is to standardize a street address so that `'ROAD'` is always abbreviated as `'RD.'`. At first glance, I thought this was simple enough that I could just use the string method `replace()`. After all, all the data was already uppercase, so case mismatches would not be a problem. And the search string `'ROAD'` was a constant. And in this deceptively simple example, `s.replace()` does indeed work.

2. Life, unfortunately, is full of counterexamples, and I quickly discovered this one. The problem here is that `'ROAD'` appears twice in the address: once as part of the street name `'BROAD'` and once as its own word. The `replace()` method sees these two occurrences and blindly replaces both of them; meanwhile, I see my addresses getting destroyed.

3. To solve the problem of addresses with more than one `'ROAD'` substring, you could resort to something like this: search and replace `'ROAD'` only in the last four characters of the address (`s[-4:]`) and leave the string alone (`s[:-4]`). But you can see that this is already getting unwieldy. For example, the pattern is dependent on the length of the string you're replacing. (If you were replacing `'STREET'` with `'ST.'`, you would need to use `s[:-6]` and `s[-6:].replace(...)`.) Would you like to come back in six months and debug this? I know I wouldn't.

4. It's time to move up to regular expressions. In Python, all functionality related to regular expressions is contained in the `re` module.

5. Take a look at the first parameter: `'ROAD$'`. This is a simple regular expression that matches `'ROAD'` only when it occurs at the end of a string. The $ means "end of the string." (There is a corresponding character, the caret, ^, which means "beginning of the string.") Using the `re.sub()` function, search the string s for the regular expression `'ROAD$'` and replace it with `'RD.'`. This matches the ROAD at the end of the string s, but does *not* match the ROAD that's part of the word BROAD because that's in the middle of s.

Continuing with my story of scrubbing addresses, I soon discovered that the previous example, matching `'ROAD'` at the end of the address, was not good enough because not all addresses included a street designation at all. Some addresses simply ended with the street name. I got away with it most of the time, but if the street name was `'BROAD'`, the regular expression would match `'ROAD'` at the end of the string as part of the word `'BROAD'`, which is not what I wanted. Listing 5-2 shows my predicament.

Listing 5-2. String Substitution with Regular Expressions

```
>>> s = '100 BROAD'
>>> re.sub('ROAD$', 'RD.', s)
'100 BRD.'
>>> re.sub('\\bROAD$', 'RD.', s)     (1)
'100 BROAD'
>>> re.sub(r'\bROAD$', 'RD.', s)     (2)
'100 BROAD'
>>> s = '100 BROAD ROAD APT. 3'
>>> re.sub(r'\bROAD$', 'RD.', s)     (3)
'100 BROAD ROAD APT. 3'
>>> re.sub(r'\bROAD\b', 'RD.', s)    (4)
'100 BROAD RD. APT 3'
```

1. What I *really* wanted was to match `'ROAD'` when it was at the end of the string *and* it was its own word (and not a part of some larger word). To express this in a regular expression, you use \b, which means "a word boundary must occur right here." In Python, this is complicated by the fact that the \ character in a string must itself be escaped. This is sometimes referred to as the *backslash plague*, and it is one reason why regular expressions are easier in Perl than in Python. On the down side, Perl mixes regular expressions with other syntax, so if you have a bug, it might be hard to tell whether it's a bug in syntax or a bug in your regular expression.

2. To work around the backslash plague, you can use what is called a *raw* string, by prefixing the string with the letter r. This tells Python that nothing in this string should be escaped; `'\t'` is a tab character, but r`'\t'` is really the backslash character \ followed by the letter t. I recommend always using raw strings when dealing with regular expressions; otherwise, things get too confusing too quickly (and regular expressions are confusing enough already).

3. Unfortunately (*sigh*), I soon found more cases that contradicted my logic. In this case, the street address contained the word `'ROAD'` as a whole word by itself, but it wasn't at the end because the address had an apartment number after the street designation. Because `'ROAD'` isn't at the very end of the string, it doesn't match, so the entire call to `re.sub()` ends up replacing nothing at all, and you get the original string back, which is not what you want.

4. To solve this problem, I removed the $ character and added another \b. Now the regular expression reads "match `'ROAD'` when it's a whole word by itself anywhere in the string," whether at the end, the beginning, or somewhere in the middle.

Case Study: Roman Numerals

You've most likely seen Roman numerals, even if you didn't recognize them. You might have seen them in copyrights of old movies and television shows ("Copyright MCMXLVI" instead of "Copyright

1946"), or on the dedication walls of libraries or universities ("established MDCCCLXXXVIII" instead of "established 1888"). You might also have seen them in outlines and bibliographical references. It's a system of representing numbers that really does date back to the ancient Roman empire (hence the name).

In Roman numerals, there are seven characters that are repeated and combined in various ways to represent numbers:

I = 1

V = 5

X = 10

L = 50

C = 100

D = 500

M = 1000

The following are some general rules for constructing Roman numerals:

- Characters are additive. I is 1, II is 2, and III is 3. VI is 6 (literally, "5 and 1"), VII is 7, and VIII is 8.

- The tens characters (I, X, C, and M) can be repeated up to three times. At 4, you need to subtract from the next highest fives character. You can't represent 4 as IIII; instead, it is represented as IV ("1 less than 5"). The number 40 is written as XL (10 less than 50), 41 as XLI, 42 as XLII, 43 as XLIII, and then 44 as XLIV (10 less than 50, then 1 less than 5).

- Similarly, at 9, you need to subtract from the next highest tens character: 8 is VIII, but 9 is IX (1 less than 10), not VIIII (because the I character can't be repeated four times). The number 90 is XC, 900 is CM.

- The fives characters can't be repeated. The number 10 is always represented as X, never as VV. The number 100 is always C, never LL.

- Roman numerals are always written highest to lowest, and read left to right, so the order of characters matters very much. DC is 600; CD is a completely different number (400, 100 less than 500). CI is 101; IC is not even a valid Roman numeral (because you can't subtract 1 directly from 100; you would need to write it as XCIX, for 10 less than 100, then 1 less than 10).

Checking for Thousands

What would it take to validate that an arbitrary string is a valid Roman numeral? Let's take it one digit at a time. Because Roman numerals are always written highest to lowest, let's start with the highest: the thousands place. For numbers 1000 and higher, the thousands are represented by a series of M characters (see Listing 5-3).

Listing 5-3. Validating the Thousands Place of a Roman Numeral

```
>>> import re
>>> pattern = '^M?M?M?$'          (1)
>>> re.search(pattern, 'M')       (2)
<SRE_Match object at 0106FB58>
>>> re.search(pattern, 'MM')      (3)
<SRE_Match object at 0106C290>
>>> re.search(pattern, 'MMM')     (4)
<SRE_Match object at 0106AA38>
>>> re.search(pattern, 'MMMM')    (5)
>>> re.search(pattern, '')        (6)
<SRE_Match object at 0106F4A8>
```

1. This pattern has three parts. ^ matches what follows only at the beginning of the string. If this were not specified, the pattern would match no matter where the M characters were, which is not what you want. You want to make sure that the M characters, if they're there, are at the beginning of the string. M? optionally matches a single M character. Because this is repeated three times, you're matching anywhere from zero to three M characters in a row. And $ matches the end of the string. When combined with the ^ character at the beginning, the pattern must match the entire string, with no other characters before or after the M characters.

2. The essence of the re module is the search() function, which takes a regular expression (pattern) and a string ('M') to try to match against the regular expression. If a match is found, search() returns an object that has various methods to describe the match; if no match is found, search() returns None, the Python null value. All you care about at the moment is whether the pattern matches, which you can tell by just looking at the return value of search(). 'M' matches this regular expression because the first optional M matches and the second and third optional M characters are ignored.

3. 'MM' matches because the first and second optional M characters match, and the third M is ignored.

4. 'MMM' matches because all three M characters match.

5. 'MMMM' does not match. All three M characters match, but then the regular expression insists on the string ending (because of the $ character), and the string doesn't end yet (because of the fourth M). So search() returns None.

6. Interestingly, an empty string also matches this regular expression because all the M characters are optional.

Checking for Hundreds

The hundreds place is more difficult than the thousands because there are several mutually exclusive ways it could be expressed, depending on its value:

100 = C

200 = CC

300 = CCC

400 = CD

500 = D

600 = DC

700 = DCC

800 = DCCC

900 = CM

There are four possible patterns:

- CM

- CD

- Zero to three C characters (zero if the hundreds place is 0)

- D, followed by zero to three C characters

The last two patterns can be combined:

- an optional D, followed by zero to three C characters

Listing 5-4 shows how to validate the hundreds place of a Roman numeral.

Listing 5-4. Validating the Hundreds Place of a Roman Numeral

```
>>> import re
>>> pattern = '^M?M?M?(CM|CD|D?C?C?C?)$'    (1)
>>> re.search(pattern, 'MCM')                (2)
<SRE_Match object at 01070390>
>>> re.search(pattern, 'MD')                 (3)
<SRE_Match object at 01073A50>
>>> re.search(pattern, 'MMMCCC')             (4)
<SRE_Match object at 010748A8>
>>> re.search(pattern, 'MCMC')               (5)
>>> re.search(pattern, '')                   (6)
<SRE_Match object at 01071D98>
```

1.   This pattern starts out the same as the previous one, checking for the beginning of the string (^) and then the thousands place (M?M?M?). Then it has the new part, in parentheses, which defines a set of three mutually exclusive patterns, separated by vertical bars: CM, CD, and D?C?C?C? (which is an optional D, followed by zero to three optional C characters). The regular expression parser checks for each of these patterns in order (from left to right), takes the first one that matches, and ignores the rest.

2.   'MCM' matches because the first M matches, the second and third M characters are ignored, and the CM matches (so the CD and D?C?C?C? patterns are never even considered). MCM is the Roman numeral representation of 1900.

3. `'MD'` matches because the first M matches, the second and third M characters are ignored, and the D?C?C?C? pattern matches D (each of the three C characters is optional and ignored). MD is the Roman numeral representation of 1500.

4. `'MMMCCC'` matches because all three M characters match, and the D?C?C?C? pattern matches CCC (the D is optional and is ignored). MMMCCC is the Roman numeral representation of 3300.

5. `'MCMC'` does not match. The first M matches, the second and third M characters are ignored, and the CM matches, but then the $ does not match because you're not at the end of the string yet (you still have an unmatched C character). The C does *not* match as part of the D?C?C?C? pattern because the mutually exclusive CM pattern has already matched.

6. Interestingly, an empty string still matches this pattern because all the M characters are optional and ignored, and the empty string matches the D?C?C?C? pattern where all the characters are optional and ignored.

Whew! See how quickly regular expressions can get nasty? And I've covered only the thousands and hundreds places of Roman numerals. But if you followed all that, the tens and ones places are easy because they're exactly the same pattern. But let's look at another way to express the pattern.

Using the {n,m} Syntax

In the previous section, you were dealing with a pattern in which the same character could be repeated up to three times. There is another way to express this in regular expressions, which some people find more readable. First look at the method we already used in the previous example, shown again in Listing 5-5.

Listing 5-5. Validating the Hundreds Place with the ? Wildcard

```
>>> import re
>>> pattern = '^M?M?M?$'
>>> re.search(pattern, 'M')        (1)
<_sre.SRE_Match object at 0x008EE090>
>>> pattern = '^M?M?M?$'
>>> re.search(pattern, 'MM')       (2)
<_sre.SRE_Match object at 0x008EEB48>
>>> pattern = '^M?M?M?$'
>>> re.search(pattern, 'MMM')      (3)
<_sre.SRE_Match object at 0x008EE090>
>>> re.search(pattern, 'MMMM')     (4)
>>>
```

1. This matches the start of the string, and then the first optional M character, but not the second and third M (but that's okay because they're optional), and then the end of the string.

2. This matches the start of the string, and then the first and second optional M character, but not the third M (but that's okay because it's optional), and then the end of the string.

3.   This matches the start of the string, and then all three optional M, and then the end of the string.

4.   This matches the start of the string, and then all three optional M, but then does not match the the end of the string (because there is still one unmatched M), so the pattern does not match and returns None.

Now let's see how to accomplish the same thing with a {n,m} wildcard (see Listing 5-6).

Listing 5-6. Validating the Hundreds Place with the {n,m} Wildcard

```
>>> pattern = '^M{0,3}$'          (1)
>>> re.search(pattern, 'M')       (2)
<_sre.SRE_Match object at 0x008EEB48>
>>> re.search(pattern, 'MM')      (3)
<_sre.SRE_Match object at 0x008EE090>
>>> re.search(pattern, 'MMM')     (4)
<_sre.SRE_Match object at 0x008EEDA8>
>>> re.search(pattern, 'MMMM')    (5)
>>>
```

1.   This pattern says, "Match the start of the string, then anywhere from zero to three M characters, and then the end of the string." The 0 and 3 can be any numbers; if you want to match at least one but no more than three M characters, you could say M{1,3}.

2.   This matches the start of the string, then one M out of a possible three, and then the end of the string.

3.   This matches the start of the string, then two M out of a possible three, and then the end of the string.

4.   This matches the start of the string, then three M out of a possible three, and then the end of the string.

5.   This matches the start of the string and then three M out of a possible three, but then *does* not match the end of the string. The regular expression allows for up to only three M characters before the end of the string, but you have four, so the pattern does not match and returns None.

Checking for Tens and Ones

Now let's expand the Roman numeral regular expression to cover the tens and ones place. Listing 5-7 shows the check for tens.

Listing 5-7. Validating the Tens and Ones Place of a Roman Numeral

```
>>> pattern = '^M?M?M?(CM|CD|D?C?C?C?)(XC|XL|L?X?X?X?)$'
>>> re.search(pattern, 'MCMXL')        (1)
<_sre.SRE_Match object at 0x008EEB48>
>>> re.search(pattern, 'MCML')         (2)
<_sre.SRE_Match object at 0x008EEB48>
```

```
>>> re.search(pattern, 'MCMLX')     (3)
<_sre.SRE_Match object at 0x008EEB48>
>>> re.search(pattern, 'MCMLXXX')    (4)
<_sre.SRE_Match object at 0x008EEB48>
>>> re.search(pattern, 'MCMLXXXX')   (5)
>>>
```

1. This matches the start of the string, then the first optional M, then CM, then XL, and then the end of the string. Remember, the (A|B|C) syntax means "match exactly one of A, B, or C." You match XL, so you ignore the XC and L?X?X?X? choices and then move on to the end of the string. MCMXL is the Roman numeral representation of **1940**.

2. This matches the start of the string, then the first optional M, then CM, and then L?X?X?X?. Of the L?X?X?X?, it matches the L and skips all three optional X characters. Then you move to the end of the string. MCML is the Roman numeral representation of **1950**.

3. This matches the start of the string, then the first optional M, then CM, then the optional L and the first optional X, skips the second and third optional X, and then the end of the string. MCMLX is the Roman numeral representation of **1960**.

4. This matches the start of the string, then the first optional M, then CM, then the optional L and all three optional X characters, and then the end of the string. MCMLXXX is the Roman numeral representation of **1980**.

5. This matches the start of the string, then the first optional M, then CM, then the optional L and all three optional X characters, but it fails to match the end of the string because there is still one more X unaccounted for. So the entire pattern fails to match and returns **None**. MCMLXXXX is not a valid Roman numeral.

The expression for the ones place follows the same pattern. I'll spare you the details and show you the end result (see Listing 5-8).

Listing 5-8. The End Result

```
>>> pattern = '^M?M?M?(CM|CD|D?C?C?C?)(XC|XL|L?X?X?X?)(IX|IV|V?I?I?I?)$'
```

So what does that look like using this alternate {n,m} syntax? Listing 5-9 shows the new syntax.

Listing 5-9. Validating the Tens and Ones Place with {n,m} Syntax

```
>>> pattern = '^M{0,3}(CM|CD|D?C{0,3})(XC|XL|L?X{0,3})(IX|IV|V?I{0,3})$'
>>> re.search(pattern, 'MDLV')              (1)
<_sre.SRE_Match object at 0x008EEB48>
>>> re.search(pattern, 'MMDCLXVI')          (2)
<_sre.SRE_Match object at 0x008EEB48>
>>> re.search(pattern, 'MMMDCCCLXXXVIII')   (3)
<_sre.SRE_Match object at 0x008EEB48>
>>> re.search(pattern, 'I')                 (4)
<_sre.SRE_Match object at 0x008EEB48>
```

1. This matches the start of the string, then one of a possible three M characters, and then D?C{0,3}. Of that, it matches the optional D character and zero of three possible C characters. Moving on, it matches L?X{0,3} by matching the optional L character and zero of three possible X characters. Then it matches V?I{0,3} by matching the optional V and zero of three possible I characters, and finally the end of the string. MDLV is the Roman numeral representation of 1555.

2. This matches the start of the string, then two of a possible three M characters, then the D?C{0,3} with a D and one of three possible C characters, then L?X{0,3} with an L and one of three possible X characters, then V?I{0,3} with a V and one of three possible I characters, and then the end of the string. MMDCLXVI is the Roman numeral representation of 2666.

3. This matches the start of the string, then three out of three M characters, then D?C{0,3} with a D and three out of three C characters, then L?X{0,3} with an L and three out of three X characters, then V?I{0,3} with a V and three out of three I characters, and then the end of the string. MMMDCCCLXXXVIII is the Roman numeral representation of 3888, and it's the longest Roman numeral you can write without extended syntax.

4. Watch closely. (I feel like a magician. Watch closely kids; I'm going to pull a rabbit out of my hat.) This matches the start of the string, then zero out of three M, then matches D?C{0,3} by skipping the optional D and matching zero out of three C, then matches L?X{0,3} by skipping the optional L and matching zero out of three X, and then matches V?I{0,3} by skipping the optional V and matching one out of three I. Then the end of the string. Whoa.

If you followed all that and understood it on the first try, you're doing better than I did. Now imagine trying to understand someone else's regular expressions in the middle of a critical function of a large program. Or even imagine coming back to your own regular expressions a few months later. I've done it, and it's not a pretty sight.

Now let's explore an alternate syntax that can help keep your expressions maintainable.

Verbose Regular Expressions

So far, you've just been dealing with what I'll call "compact" regular expressions. As you've seen, they are difficult to read, and even if you figure out what one does, that's no guarantee that you'll be able to understand it six months later. What you really need is inline documentation.

Python allows you to do this with something called *verbose regular expressions*. A verbose regular expression is different from a compact regular expression in two ways:

*   Whitespace is ignored. Spaces, tabs, and carriage returns are not matched as spaces, tabs, and carriage returns. They're not matched at all. (If you want to match a space in a verbose regular expression, you'll need to escape it by putting a backslash in front of it.)

*   Comments are ignored. A comment in a verbose regular expression is just like a comment in Python code: it starts with a # character and goes until the end of the line. In this case, it's a comment within a multiline string instead of within your source code, but it works the same way.

This will be more clear with an example. Let's revisit the compact regular expression you've been working with, and make it a verbose regular expression. Listing 5-10 shows how.

Listing 5-10. A Verbose Regular Expression

```
>>> pattern = '''
    ^                       # beginning of string
    M{0,3}                  # thousands - 0 to 3 Ms
    (CM|CD|D?C{0,3})        # hundreds - 900 (CM), 400 (CD), 0-300 (0 to 3 Cs),
    #                                   or 500-800 (D, followed by 0 to 3 Cs)
    (XC|XL|L?X{0,3})        # tens - 90 (XC), 40 (XL), 0-30 (0 to 3 Xs),
    #                                 or 50-80 (L, followed by 0 to 3 Xs)
    (IX|IV|V?I{0,3})        # ones - 9 (IX), 4 (IV), 0-3 (0 to 3 Is),
    #                               or 5-8 (V, followed by 0 to 3 Is)
    $                       # end of string
    '''
>>> re.search(pattern, 'M', re.VERBOSE)                    (1)
<_sre.SRE_Match object at 0x008EEB48>
>>> re.search(pattern, 'MCMLXXXIX', re.VERBOSE)            (2)
<_sre.SRE_Match object at 0x008EEB48>
>>> re.search(pattern, 'MMMDCCCLXXXVIII', re.VERBOSE)      (3)
<_sre.SRE_Match object at 0x008EEB48>
>>> re.search(pattern, 'M')                                (4)
```

1. The most important thing to remember when using verbose regular expressions is that you need to pass an extra argument when working with them: re.VERBOSE is a constant defined in the re module, signaling that the pattern should be treated as a verbose regular expression. As you can see, this pattern has quite a bit of whitespace (all of which is ignored) and several comments (all of which are ignored). Once you ignore the whitespace and the comments, this is exactly the same regular expression as in the previous section, but it's a lot more readable.

2. This matches the start of the string, then one of a possible three M characters, then CM, then L and three of a possible three X characters, then IX, and then the end of the string.

3. This matches the start of the string, then three of a possible three M characters, then D and three of a possible three C characters, then L and three of a possible three X characters, then V and three of a possible three I characters, and then the end of the string.

4. This does not match. Why? Because it doesn't have the re.VERBOSE flag, so the re.search function is treating the pattern as a compact regular expression, with significant whitespace and literal hash marks. Python can't auto-detect whether a regular expression is verbose. Python assumes that every regular expression is compact unless you explicitly state that it is verbose.

Case Study: Parsing Phone Numbers

So far, you've concentrated on matching whole patterns. Either the pattern matches or it doesn't. But regular expressions are much more powerful than that. When a regular expression *does* match, you can pick out specific pieces of it. You can find out what matched where.

This example came from another real-world problem I encountered, again from a previous day job. The problem: parsing an American phone number. The client wanted to be able to enter the number free form (in a single field); but then wanted to store the area code, trunk, number, and optionally an extension separately in the company's database. I scoured the Web and found many examples of regular expressions that purported to do this, but none of them was permissive enough.

Here are the phone numbers that had to be accepted:

800-555-1212

800 555 1212

800.555.1212

(800) 555-1212

1-800-555-1212

800-555-1212-1234

800-555-1212x1234

800-555-1212 ext. 1234

work 1-(800) 555.1212 #1234

Quite a variety! In each of these cases, I need to know that the area code was 800, the trunk was 555, and the rest of the phone number was 1212. For those with an extension, I need to know that the extension was 1234.

Let's work through developing a solution for phone number parsing. Listing 5-11 shows the first step.

Listing 5-11. Parsing Phone Numbers: Attempt 1

```
>>> phonePattern = re.compile(r'^(\d{3})-(\d{3})-(\d{4})$')   (1)
>>> phonePattern.search('800-555-1212').groups()              (2)
('800', '555', '1212')
>>> phonePattern.search('800-555-1212-1234')                  (3)
>>> phonePattern.search('800-555-1212-1234').groups()         (4)
Traceback (most recent call last):
  File "<stdin>", line 1, in <module>
AttributeError: 'NoneType' object has no attribute 'groups'
```

1. Always read regular expressions from left to right. This one matches the beginning of the string and then (\d{3}). What's \d{3}? Well, \d means "any numeric digit" (0-9). The {3} means "match exactly three numeric digits"; it's a variation on the {n,m} syntax you saw earlier. Putting it all in parentheses means "match exactly three numeric digits *and then remember them as a group* that I can ask for later." Then match a literal hyphen. Then match another group of exactly three digits. Then another literal hyphen. Then another group of exactly four digits. Then match the end of the string.

2. To get access to the groups that the regular expression parser remembered along the way, use the groups() method on the object that the search() method returns. It will return a tuple of however many groups were defined in the regular expression. In this case, you defined three groups: one with three digits, another with three digits, and one with four digits.

3. This regular expression is not the final answer because it doesn't handle a phone number with an extension on the end. For that, you'll need to expand the regular expression.

4. And this is why you should never "chain" the search() and groups() methods in production code. If the search() method returns no matches, it returns None, not a regular expression match object. Calling None.groups() raises a perfectly obvious exception: None doesn't have a groups() method. (Of course, it's slightly less obvious when you get this exception from deep within your code. Yes, I speak from experience here.)

Let's try to handle some of those edge cases (see Listing 5-12).

Listing 5-12. Parsing Phone Numbers: Attempt 2

```
>>> phonePattern = re.compile(r'^(\d{3})-(\d{3})-(\d{4})-(\d+)$')    (1)
>>> phonePattern.search('800-555-1212-1234').groups()               (2)
('800', '555', '1212', '1234')
>>> phonePattern.search('800 555 1212 1234')                        (3)
>>>
>>> phonePattern.search('800-555-1212')                             (4)
>>>
```

1. This regular expression is almost identical to the previous one. Just as before, you match the beginning of the string, then a remembered group of three digits, then a hyphen, then a remembered group of three digits, then a hyphen, and then a remembered group of four digits. What's new is that you then match another hyphen and a remembered group of one or more digits; then the end of the string.

2. The groups() method now returns a tuple of four elements because the regular expression now defines four groups to remember.

3. Unfortunately, this regular expression is not the final answer, either because it assumes that the different parts of the phone number are separated by hyphens. What if they're separated by spaces, or commas, or dots? You need a more general solution to match several different types of separators.

4. Oops! Not only does this regular expression not do everything you want, but it's actually a step backward because now you can't parse phone numbers *without* an extension. That's not what you wanted at all; if the extension is there, you want to know what it is; if it's not there, you still want to know what the different parts of the main number are.

Listing 5-13 shows the regular expression to handle separators between the different parts of the phone number.

Listing 5-13. Parsing Phone Numbers: Attempt 3

```
>>> phonePattern = re.compile(r'^(\d{3})\D+(\d{3})\D+(\d{4})\D+(\d+)$')   (1)
>>> phonePattern.search('800 555 1212 1234').groups()  (2)
('800', '555', '1212', '1234')
>>> phonePattern.search('800-555-1212-1234').groups()  (3)
('800', '555', '1212', '1234')
>>> phonePattern.search('80055512121234')              (4)
>>>
>>> phonePattern.search('800-555-1212')                (5)
>>>
```

1. Hang on to your hat. You're matching the beginning of the string, then a group of three digits, and then \D+. What the heck is that? Well, \D matches any character *except* a numeric digit, and + means "1 or more." So \D+ matches one or more characters that are not digits. This is what you're using instead of a literal hyphen to try to match different separators.

2. Using \D+ instead of - means you can now match phone numbers where the parts are separated by spaces instead of hyphens.

3. Of course, phone numbers separated by hyphens still work, too.

4. Unfortunately, this is still not the final answer because it assumes that there is a separator. What if the phone number is entered without any spaces or hyphens at all?

5. Oops! This still hasn't fixed the problem of requiring extensions. Now you have two problems, but you can solve both of them with the same technique.

Listing 5-14 shows the regular expression for handling phone numbers *without* separators.

Listing 5-14. Parsing Phone Numbers: Attempt 4

```
>>> phonePattern = re.compile(r'^(\d{3})\D*(\d{3})\D*(\d{4})\D*(\d*)$')   (1)
>>> phonePattern.search('80055512121234').groups()       (2)
('800', '555', '1212', '1234')
>>> phonePattern.search('800.555.1212 x1234').groups()  (3)
('800', '555', '1212', '1234')
```

```
>>> phonePattern.search('800-555-1212').groups()            (4)
('800', '555', '1212', '')
>>> phonePattern.search('(800)5551212 x1234')               (5)
>>>
```

1. The only change you made since that last step is changing + to *. Instead of \D+
   between the parts of the phone number, you now match on \D*. Remember
   that + means 1 or more? Well, * means zero or more. So now you should be
   able to parse phone numbers even when there are no separator characters
   at all.

2. Lo and behold, it actually works. Why? You matched the beginning of the
   string, then a remembered group of three digits (**800**), then zero non-numeric
   characters, then a remembered group of three digits (**555**), then zero non-
   numeric characters, then a remembered group of four digits (**1212**), then zero
   non-numeric characters, then a remembered group of an arbitrary number of
   digits (**1234**), and then the end of the string.

3. Other variations also work now: dots instead of hyphens, and both a space and
   an x before the extension.

4. Finally, you solved the other problem: extensions are optional again. If no
   extension is found, the **groups()** method still returns a tuple of four elements,
   but the fourth element is just an empty string.

5. I hate to be the bearer of bad news, but you're not finished yet. What's the
   problem here? There's an extra character before the area code, but the regular
   expression assumes that the area code is the first thing at the beginning of the
   string. No problem; you can use the same technique of "zero or more non-
   numeric characters" to skip over the leading characters before the area code.
   Listing 5-15 shows how to handle leading characters in phone numbers.

Listing 5-15. Parsing Phone Numbers: Attempt 5

```
>>> phonePattern = re.compile(r'^\D*(\d{3})\D*(\d{3})\D*(\d{4})\D*(\d*)$')  (1)
>>> phonePattern.search('(800)5551212 ext. 1234').groups()                 (2)
('800', '555', '1212', '1234')
>>> phonePattern.search('800-555-1212').groups()                           (3)
('800', '555', '1212', '')
>>> phonePattern.search('work 1-(800) 555.1212 #1234')                     (4)
>>>
```

1. This is the same as in the previous example, except now you're matching \D*,
   zero or more non-numeric characters, before the first remembered group (the
   area code). Notice that you're not remembering these non-numeric characters
   (they're not in parentheses). If you find them, you'll just skip over them and
   then start remembering the area code whenever you get to it.

2. You can successfully parse the phone number, even with the leading left
   parenthesis before the area code. (The right parenthesis after the area code is
   already handled; it's treated as a non-numeric separator and matched by the
   \D* after the first remembered group.)

3. Just a sanity check to make sure you haven't broken anything that used to work. Because the leading characters are entirely optional, this matches the beginning of the string, then zero non-numeric characters, then a remembered group of three digits (**800**), then one non-numeric character (the hyphen), then a remembered group of three digits (**555**), then one non-numeric character (the hyphen), then a remembered group of four digits (**1212**), then zero non-numeric characters, then a remembered group of zero digits, and then the end of the string.

4. This is where regular expressions make me want to gouge my eyes out with a blunt object. Why doesn't this phone number match? Because there's a **1** before the area code, but you assumed that all the leading characters before the area code were non-numeric characters (\D*). Aargh.

Let's back up for a second. So far, the regular expressions have all matched from the beginning of the string. But now you see that there may be an indeterminate amount of stuff at the beginning of the string that you want to ignore. Instead of trying to match it all just to skip over it, let's take a different approach: don't explicitly match the beginning of the string at all. This approach is shown in Listing 5-16.

Listing 5-16. Parsing Phone Numbers: Attempt 6

```
>>> phonePattern = re.compile(r'(\d{3})\D*(\d{3})\D*(\d{4})\D*(\d*)$')   (1)
>>> phonePattern.search('work 1-(800) 555.1212 #1234').groups()          (2)
('800', '555', '1212', '1234')
>>> phonePattern.search('800-555-1212')                                  (3)
('800', '555', '1212', '')
>>> phonePattern.search('80055512121234')                                (4)
('800', '555', '1212', '1234')
```

1. Note the lack of ^ in this regular expression. You are not matching the beginning of the string any more. There's nothing that says you need to match the entire input with your regular expression. The regular expression engine will do the hard work of figuring out where the input string starts to match and go from there.

2. Now you can successfully parse a phone number that includes leading characters and a leading digit, plus any number of any kind of separators around each part of the phone number.

3. Sanity check. This still works.

4. This still works, too.

See how quickly a regular expression can get out of control? Take a quick glance at any of the previous iterations. Can you tell the difference between one and the next?

While you still understand the final answer (and it is the final answer; if you've discovered a case it doesn't handle, I don't want to know about it), let's write it out as a verbose regular expression before you forget why you made the choices you made (see Listing 5-17).

Listing 5-17. Parsing Phone Numbers: Verbose Edition

```
>>> phonePattern = re.compile(r'''
                # don't match beginning of string, number can start anywhere
    (\d{3})     # area code is 3 digits (e.g. '800')
    \D*         # optional separator is any number of non-digits
    (\d{3})     # trunk is 3 digits (e.g. '555')
    \D*         # optional separator
    (\d{4})     # rest of number is 4 digits (e.g. '1212')
    \D*         # optional separator
    (\d*)       # extension is optional and can be any number of digits
    $           # end of string
    ''', re.VERBOSE)
>>> phonePattern.search('work 1-(800) 555.1212 #1234').groups()  (1)
('800', '555', '1212', '1234')
>>> phonePattern.search('800-555-1212')                          (2)
('800', '555', '1212', '')
```

1. Other than being spread out over multiple lines, this is exactly the same regular expression as the last step, so it's no surprise that it parses the same inputs.

2. Final sanity check. Yes, this still works. You're done.

Further Reading Online

For more information, see the following resources:

- *re module:* http://docs.python.org/3.1/library/re.html

- *Regular expression HOWTO:* http://www.amk.ca/python/howto/regex/

CHAPTER 6

■ ■ ■

Closures and Generators

For reasons passing all understanding, I have always been fascinated by languages. Not programming languages. Well yes, programming languages, but also natural languages. Take English. English is a schizophrenic language that borrows words from German, French, Spanish, and Latin (to name a few). Actually, *borrows* is the wrong word; *pillages* is more like it. Or perhaps *assimilates*—like the Borg. Yes, I like that.

```
We are the Borg. Your linguistic and etymological distinctiveness will be added to
our own. Resistance is futile.
```

In this chapter, you'll learn about plural nouns. Also about functions that return other functions, advanced regular expressions, and generators. But first, let's talk about how to make plural nouns. (If you haven't read the chapter on regular expressions, now would be a good time. This chapter assumes that you understand the basics of regular expressions, and it quickly descends into more advanced uses.)

If you grew up in an English-speaking country or learned English in a formal school setting, you're probably familiar with the basic rules:

- If a word ends in *S*, *X*, or *Z*, add *ES*. *Bass* becomes *basses*, *fax* becomes *faxes*, and *waltz* becomes *waltzes*.

- If a word ends in a noisy *H*, add *ES*; if it ends in a silent *H*, just add *S*. What's a noisy *H*? One that gets combined with other letters to make a sound that you can hear. So *coach* becomes *coaches*, and *rash* becomes *rashes* because you can hear the *CH* and *SH* sounds when you say them. But *cheetah* becomes *cheetahs* because the H is silent.

- If a word ends in *Y* that sounds like *I*, change the *Y* to *IES*; if the *Y* is combined with a vowel to sound like something else, just add *S*. So *vacancy* becomes *vacancies*, but *day* becomes *days*.

- If all else fails, just add *S* and hope for the best.

I know, there are a lot of exceptions. *Man* becomes *men*, and *woman* becomes *women*, but *human* becomes *humans*. *Mouse* becomes *mice*, and *louse* becomes *lice*, but *house* becomes *houses*. *Knife* becomes *knives*, and *wife* becomes *wives*, but *lowlife* becomes *lowlifes*. And don't even get me started on words that are their own plural, such as *sheep*, *deer*, and *haiku*.)

Other languages, of course, are completely different.

Let's design a Python library that automatically pluralizes English nouns. We'll start with just these four rules, but keep in mind that you'll inevitably need to add more.

I Know, Let's Use Regular Expressions!

So you're looking at words, which means that you're looking at strings of characters (at least in English). You have rules that say you need to find different combinations of characters and then do different things to them. This sounds like a job for regular expressions! (See Listing 6-1.)

Listing 6-1. A plural() Function

```
import re

def plural(noun):
    if re.search('[sxz]$', noun):               (1)
        return re.sub('$', 'es', noun)          (2)
    elif re.search('[^aeioudgkprt]h$', noun):
        return re.sub('$', 'es', noun)
    elif re.search('[^aeiou]y$', noun):
        return re.sub('y$', 'ies', noun)
    else:
        return noun + 's'
```

The following notes refer to the numbered lines in Listing 6-1:

1. This is a regular expression, but it uses a syntax you didn't see in Chapter 5. The square brackets mean "match exactly one of these characters." So [sxz] means s, or x, or z, but only one of them. The $ should be familiar; it matches the end of string. Combined, this regular expression tests whether noun ends with s, x, or z.

2. This re.sub() function performs regular expression-based string substitutions. Let's look at regular expression substitutions in more detail (see Listing 6-2).

Listing 6-2. re.search() and re.sub()

```
>>> import re
>>> re.search('[abc]', 'Mark')      (1)
<_sre.SRE_Match object at 0x001C1FA8>
>>> re.sub('[abc]', 'o', 'Mark')    (2)
'Mork'
>>> re.sub('[abc]', 'o', 'rock')    (3)
'rook'
>>> re.sub('[abc]', 'o', 'caps')    (4)
'oops'
```

1. Does the string Mark contain a, b, or c? Yes, it contains a.

2. Okay, now find a, b, or c; and replace it with o. Mark becomes Mork.

3. The same function turns rock into rook.

4. You might think this would turn caps into oaps, but it doesn't. The re.sub() function replaces *all* the matches, not just the first one. So this regular expression turns caps into oops because both the c and the a get turned into o.

And now, back to the plural() function (see Listing 6-3).

Listing 6-3. A plural() Function

```
def plural(noun):
    if re.search('[sxz]$', noun):
        return re.sub('$', 'es', noun)           (1)
    elif re.search('[^aeioudgkprt]h$', noun):    (2)
        return re.sub('$', 'es', noun)           (3)
    elif re.search('[^aeiou]y$', noun):
        return re.sub('y$', 'ies', noun)
    else:
        return noun + 's'
```

1. Here, you're replacing the end of the string (matched by $) with the string es. In other words, adding es to the string. You could accomplish the same thing with string concatenation, for example noun + 'es', but I chose to use regular expressions for each rule for reasons that will become clear later in the chapter.

2. Look closely; this is another new variation. The ^ as the first character inside the square brackets means something special: negation. [^abc] means any single character *except* a, b, or c. So [^aeioudgkprt] means any character except a, e, i, o, u, d, g, k, p, r, or t. Then that character needs to be followed by h, followed by end of string. You're looking for words that end in *H* where the *H* can be heard.

3. Same pattern here: match words that end in *Y* where the character before the Y is *not* a, e, i, o, or u. You're looking for words that end in *Y* that sounds like *I*.

Let's look at negation regular expressions in more detail (see Listing 6-4).

Listing 6-4. Negation Regular Expressions

```
>>> import re
>>> re.search('[^aeiou]y$', 'vacancy')   (1)
<_sre.SRE_Match object at 0x001C1FA8>
>>> re.search('[^aeiou]y$', 'boy')       (2)
>>>
>>> re.search('[^aeiou]y$', 'day')
>>>
>>> re.search('[^aeiou]y$', 'pita')      (3)
>>>
```

1. vacancy matches this regular expression because it ends in cy; and c is not a, e, i, o, or u.

2. boy does not match because it ends in oy, and you specifically said that the character before the y could not be o. day does not match because it ends in ay.

3. pita does not match because it does not end in y.

When a noun ends in a consonant followed by the letter y, the y turns into ies, as shown in Listing 6-5.

Listing 6-5. *Y Turns to IES*

```
>>> re.sub('y$', 'ies', 'vacancy')            (1)
'vacancies'
>>> re.sub('y$', 'ies', 'agency')
'agencies'
>>> re.sub('([^aeiou])y$', r'\1ies', 'vacancy')  (2)
'vacancies'
```

1. This regular expression turns vacancy into vacancies and agency into agencies, which is what you wanted. Note that it would also turn boy into boies, but that will never happen in the function because you called the re.search() function first to find out whether you should do this call to the re.sub() function.

2. It is possible to combine these two regular expressions (one to find out if the rule applies and another to actually apply it) into a single regular expression. Here's what that would look like. Most of it should look familiar: you're using a remembered group, which you learned about in Chapter 5. The group is used to remember the character before the letter y. Then in the substitution string, you use a new syntax, \1, which means "Hey, that first group you remembered? Put it right here." In this case, you remember the c before the y; when you do the substitution, the c remains a c, and y is replaced by ies. (If you have more than one remembered group, you can use \2, \3, and so on.)

Regular expression substitutions are extremely powerful, and the \1 syntax makes them even more powerful. But combining the entire operation into one regular expression is also much harder to read, and it doesn't directly map to the way you first described the pluralizing rules. You originally laid out rules such as "If the word ends in *S*, *X*, or *Z*, add *ES*." If you look at this function, you have two lines of code that say "If the word ends in *S*, *X*, or *Z*, add *ES*." It doesn't get much more direct than that.

A List of Functions

Now you're going to add a level of abstraction. You started by defining a list of rules: if this, do that; otherwise, go to the next rule. Let's temporarily complicate part of the program so you can simplify another part (see Listing 6-6).

Listing 6-6. A Plural Framework

```
import re

def match_sxz(noun):
    return re.search('[sxz]$', noun)

def apply_sxz(noun):
    return re.sub('$', 'es', noun)

def match_h(noun):
    return re.search('[^aeioudgkprt]h$', noun)

def apply_h(noun):
    return re.sub('$', 'es', noun)

def match_y(noun):                              (1)
    return re.search('[^aeiou]y$', noun)

def apply_y(noun):                              (2)
    return re.sub('y$', 'ies', noun)

def match_default(noun):
    return True

def apply_default(noun):
    return noun + 's'

rules = ((match_sxz, apply_sxz),                (3)
         (match_h, apply_h),
         (match_y, apply_y),
         (match_default, apply_default)
         )

def plural(noun):
    for matches_rule, apply_rule in rules:      (4)
        if matches_rule(noun):
            return apply_rule(noun)
```

1. Now, each match rule is its own function that returns the results of calling the
    re.search() function.

2. Each apply rule is also its own function, which calls the re.sub() function to
    apply the appropriate pluralization rule.

3. Instead of having one function, plural(), with multiple rules, you have the
    rules data structure, which is a sequence of pairs of functions.

4. Because the rules have been broken out into a separate data structure, the new plural() function can be reduced to a few lines of code. Using a for loop, you can pull out the match and apply rules two at a time (one match, one apply) from the rules structure. On the first iteration of the for loop, matches_rule will get match_sxz, and apply_rule will get apply_sxz. On the second iteration (assuming that you get that far), matches_rule will be assigned match_h, and apply_rule will be assigned apply_h. The function is guaranteed to return something eventually because the final match rule (match_default) simply returns True, meaning that the corresponding apply rule (apply_default) will always be applied.

The reason this technique works is that everything in Python is an object, including functions. The rules data structure contains functions—not names of functions, but actual function objects. When they get assigned in the for loop, matches_rule and apply_rule are actual functions that you can call. On the first iteration of the for loop, this is equivalent to calling matches_sxz(noun) and (if it returns a match) calling apply_sxz(noun).

If this additional level of abstraction is confusing, try unrolling the function to see the equivalence. The entire for loop is equivalent to Listing 6-7.

Listing 6-7. An Equivalent Plural Framework

```
def plural(noun):
    if match_sxz(noun):
        return apply_sxz(noun)
    if match_h(noun):
        return apply_h(noun)
    if match_y(noun):
        return apply_y(noun)
    if match_default(noun):
        return apply_default(noun)
```

The benefit here is that the plural() function is now simplified. It takes a sequence of rules, defined elsewhere, and iterates through them in a generic fashion:

1. Get a match rule.

2. Does it match? Yes? Call the apply rule and return the result.

3. No match? Go to step 1.

The rules could be defined anywhere, in any way. The plural() function doesn't care.

Was adding this level of abstraction worth it? Well, not yet. Let's consider what it would take to add a new rule to the function. In the first example, it would require adding an if statement to the plural() function. In this second example, it would require adding two functions, match_foo() and apply_foo(), and then updating the rules sequence to specify where in the order the new match and apply functions should be called relative to the other rules.

But this is really just a stepping stone to the next section. Let's move on.

A List of Patterns

Defining separate named functions for each match and apply rule isn't really necessary. You never call them directly; you add them to the rules sequence and call them through there. Furthermore, each function follows one of two patterns. All the match functions call re.search(), and all the apply functions call re.sub(). Let's factor out the patterns so that defining new rules can be easier (see Listing 6-8).

Listing 6-8. build_match_and_apply_functions()

```
import re

def build_match_and_apply_functions(pattern, search, replace):
    def matches_rule(word):                          (1)
        return re.search(pattern, word)
    def apply_rule(word):                            (2)
        return re.sub(search, replace, word)
    return (matches_rule, apply_rule)                (3)
```

1. build_match_and_apply_functions() is a function that builds other functions dynamically. It takes pattern, search, and replace; then defines a matches_rule() function that calls re.search() with the pattern that was passed to the build_match_and_apply_functions() function and the word that was passed to the matches_rule() function you're building. Whoa.

2. Building the apply function works the same way. The apply function is a function that takes one parameter, and calls re.sub() with the search and replace parameters that were passed to the build_match_and_apply_functions() function, and the word that was passed to the apply_rule() function you're building. This technique of using the values of outside parameters within a dynamic function is called a *closure*. You're essentially defining constants within the apply function you're building: it takes one parameter (word), but it then acts on that plus two other values (search and replace) that were set when you defined the apply function.

3. Finally, the build_match_and_apply_functions() function returns a tuple of two values: the two functions you just created. The constants you defined within those functions (pattern within the match_rule() function, and search and replace within the apply_rule() function) stay with those functions, even after you return from build_match_and_apply_functions(). That's insanely cool.

If this is incredibly confusing (and it should be; this is weird stuff), it might become clearer when you see how to use it (see Listing 6-9).

Listing 6-9. A Tuple of Tuples

```
patterns = \                                          (1)
  (
    ('[sxz]$',            '$',   'es'),
    ('[^aeioudgkprt]h$',  '$',   'es'),
    ('(qu|[^aeiou])y$',   'y$',  'ies'),
    ('$',                 '$',   's')                 (2)
  )
rules = [build_match_and_apply_functions(pattern, search, replace)  (3)
         for (pattern, search, replace) in patterns]
```

1. Our pluralization "rules" are now defined as a tuple of tuples of *strings* (not functions). The first string in each group is the regular expression pattern that you would use in re.search() to see whether this rule matches. The second and third strings in each group are the search and replace expressions you would use in re.sub() to actually apply the rule to turn a noun into its plural.

2. There's a slight change here in the fallback rule. In the previous example, the match_default() function simply returned True, meaning that if none of the more specific rules matched, the code would simply add an s to the end of the given word. This example does something functionally equivalent. The final regular expression asks whether the word has an end ($ matches the end of a string). Of course, every string has an end, even an empty string, so this expression always matches. Thus, it serves the same purpose as the match_default() function that always returned True: it ensures that if no more specific rule matches, the code adds an s to the end of the given word.

3. This line is magic. It takes the sequence of strings in patterns and turns them into a sequence of functions. How? By *mapping* the strings to the build_match_and_apply_functions() function. That is, it takes each triplet of strings and calls the build_match_and_apply_functions() function with those three strings as arguments. The build_match_and_apply_functions() function returns a tuple of two functions. This means that rules ends up being functionally equivalent to the previous example: a list of tuples, in which each inner tuple is a pair of functions. The first function is the match function that calls re.search(), and the second function is the apply function that calls re.sub().

Rounding out this version of the script is the main entry point, the plural() function (see Listing 6-10).

Listing 6-10. A Generic plural() Function

```
def plural(noun):
    for matches_rule, apply_rule in rules:    (1)
        if matches_rule(noun):
            return apply_rule(noun)
```

1. Because the rules list is the same as the previous example (really, it is), it should come as no surprise that the plural() function hasn't changed at all. It's completely generic; it takes a list of rule functions and calls them in order. It doesn't care how the rules are defined. In the previous example, they were defined as separate named functions. Now they are built dynamically by mapping the output of the build_match_and_apply_functions() function onto a list of raw strings. It doesn't matter; the plural() function still works the same way.

A File of Patterns

You've factored out all the duplicate code and added enough abstractions so that the pluralization rules are defined in a list of strings. The next logical step is to take these strings and put them in a separate file, in which they can be maintained separately from the code that uses them.

First, let's create a text file that contains the rules you want (see Listing 6-11). No fancy data structures, just whitespace-delimited strings in three columns. Let's call it plural4-rules.txt.

Listing 6-11. Rules in a File

```
[sxz]$                  $       es
[^aeioudgkprt]h$        $       es
[^aeiou]y$              y$      ies
$                       $       s
```

Now let's see how you can use this rules file (see Listing 6-12).

Listing 6-12. Reading the Rules

```
import re

def build_match_and_apply_functions(pattern, search, replace):  (1)
    def matches_rule(word):
        return re.search(pattern, word)
    def apply_rule(word):
        return re.sub(search, replace, word)
    return [matches_rule, apply_rule]

rules = []
with open('plural4-rules.txt', encoding='utf-8') as pattern_file:  (2)
    for line in pattern_file:                                      (3)
        pattern, search, replace = line.split(None, 3)            (4)
        rules.append(build_match_and_apply_functions(            (5)
                pattern, search, replace))
```

1. The build_match_and_apply_functions() function has not changed. You're still using closures to build two functions dynamically that use variables defined in the outer function.

2. The global open() function opens a file and returns a file object. In this case, the file we're opening contains the pattern strings for pluralizing nouns. The with statement creates what's called a *context*: when the with block ends, Python will automatically close the file, even if an exception is raised inside the with block. You'll learn more about with blocks and file objects in Chapter 11.

3. The for line in <fileobject> idiom reads data from the open file, one line at a time, and assigns the text to the line variable. You'll learn more about reading from files in Chapter 11.

4. Each line in the file really has three values, but they're separated by whitespace (tabs or spaces, it makes no difference). To split it out, use the split() string method. The first argument to the split() method is None, which means "split on any whitespace (tabs or spaces, it makes no difference)." The second argument is 3, which means split on whitespace three times and then leave the rest of the line alone. A line like [sxz]$ $ es will be broken up into the list ['[sxz]$', '$', 'es'], which means that pattern will get '[sxz]$', search will get '$', and replace will get 'es'. That's a lot of power in one little line of code.

5. Finally, you pass pattern, search, and replace to the build_match_and_apply_functions() function, which returns a tuple of functions. You append this tuple to the rules list, and rules ends up storing the list of match and apply functions that the plural() function expects.

The improvement here is that you've completely separated the pluralization rules into an external file, so it can be maintained separately from the code that uses it. Code is code, data is data, and life is good.

Generators

Wouldn't it be grand to have a generic plural() function that parses the rules file? Get rules, check for a match, apply appropriate transformation, go to next rule. That's all the plural() function has to do, and that's all the plural() function should do.

Listing 6-13. A Generator Function

```
def rules():
    with open('plural5-rules.txt', encoding='utf-8') as pattern_file:
        for line in pattern_file:
            pattern, search, replace = line.split(None, 3)
            yield build_match_and_apply_functions(pattern, search, replace)

def plural(noun, rules_filename='plural5-rules.txt'):
    for matches_rule, apply_rule in rules():
        if matches_rule(noun):
            return apply_rule(noun)
    raise ValueError('no matching rule for {0}'.format(noun))
```

How the heck does *that* work? Let's look at an interactive example first (see Listing 6-14).

Listing 6-14. How the Heck Generators Work

```
>>> def make_counter(x):
...     print('entering make_counter')
```

```
...        while True:
...            yield x                     (1)
...            print('incrementing x')
...            x = x + 1
...
>>> counter = make_counter(2)             (2)
>>> counter                               (3)
<generator object at 0x001C9C10>
>>> next(counter)                         (4)
entering make_counter
2
>>> next(counter)                         (5)
incrementing x
3
>>> next(counter)                         (6)
incrementing x
4
```

1. The presence of the yield keyword in make_counter means that this is not a normal function. It is a special kind of function that generates values one at a time. You can think of it as a resumable function. Calling it will return a *generator* that can be used to generate successive values of x.

2. To create an instance of the make_counter generator, just call it like any other function. Note that this does not actually execute the function code. You can tell this because the first line of the make_counter() function calls print(), but nothing has been printed yet.

3. The make_counter() function returns a generator object.

4. The next() function takes a generator object and returns its next value. The first time you call next() with the counter generator, it executes the code in make_counter() up to the first yield statement; then returns the value that was yielded. In this case, it will be 2 because you originally created the generator by calling make_counter(2).

5. Repeatedly calling next() with the same generator object resumes exactly where it left off and continues until it hits the next yield statement. All variables (local, state, and so on) are saved on yield and restored on next(). The next line of code waiting to be executed calls print(), which prints incrementing x. After that, the statement x = x + 1. Then it loops through the while loop again, and the first thing it hits is the statement yield x, which saves the state of everything and returns the current value of x (now 3).

6. The second time you call next(counter), you do all the same things again, but this time x is now 4.

Because make_counter sets up an infinite loop, you could theoretically do this forever, and it would just keep incrementing x and spitting out values.

A Fibonacci Generator

Let's look at a more productive use of generators (see Listing 6-15).

Listing 6-15. *A Fibonacci Generator*

```
def fib(max):
    a, b = 0, 1          (1)
    while a < max:
        yield a          (2)
        a, b = b, a + b  (3)
```

1. The Fibonacci sequence is a sequence of numbers in which each number is the sum of the two numbers before it. It starts with 0 and 1, goes up slowly at first; then more and more rapidly. To start the sequence, you need two variables: a starts at 0, and b starts at 1.

2. a is the current number in the sequence, so yield it.

3. b is the next number in the sequence, so assign that to a, but also calculate the next value (a + b) and assign that to b for later use. Note that this happens in parallel: if a is 3 and b is 5, then a, b = b, a + b will set a to 5 (the previous value of b) and b to 8 (the sum of the previous values of a and b).

So you have a function that spits out successive Fibonacci numbers. Sure, you could do that with recursion, but this way is easier to read (see Listing 6-16). Also, it works well with for loops.

Listing 6-16. *Calling the Fibonacci Generator*

```
>>> from fibonacci import fib
>>> for n in fib(1000):        (1)
...     print(n, end=' ')      (2)
0 1 1 2 3 5 8 13 21 34 55 89 144 233 377 610 987
>>> list(fib(1000))            (3)
[0, 1, 1, 2, 3, 5, 8, 13, 21, 34, 55, 89, 144, 233, 377, 610, 987]
```

1. You can use a generator such as fib() in a for loop directly. The for loop will automatically call the next() function to get values from the fib() generator and assign them to the for loop index variable (n).

2. Each time through the for loop, n gets a new value from the yield statement in fib(), and all you have to do is print it out. Once fib() runs out of numbers (a becomes bigger than max, which in this case is 1000), the for loop exits gracefully.

3. This is a useful idiom: pass a generator to the list() function, and it will iterate through the entire generator (just like the for loop in the previous example) and return a list of all the values.

A Plural Rule Generator

Let's go back to plural5.py and see how this version of the plural() function works (see Listing 6-17).

Listing 6-17. Plural Rules as a Generator Function

```
def rules(rules_filename):
    with open(rules_filename, encoding='utf-8') as pattern_file:
        for line in pattern_file:
            pattern, search, replace = line.split(None, 3)          (1)
            yield build_match_and_apply_functions(pattern, search, replace)  (2)

def plural(noun, rules_filename='plural5-rules.txt'):
    for matches_rule, apply_rule in rules(rules_filename):          (3)
        if matches_rule(noun):
            return apply_rule(noun)
    raise ValueError('no matching rule for {0}'.format(noun))
```

1. No magic here. Remember that the lines of the rules file have three values separated by whitespace, so you use line.split(None, 3) to get the three "columns" and assign them to three local variables.

2. *And then you yield.* What do you yield? Two functions, built dynamically with your old friend, build_match_and_apply_functions(), which is identical to the previous examples. In other words, rules() is a generator that spits out match and apply functions *on demand.*

3. Because rules() is a generator, you can use it directly in a for loop. The first time through the for loop, you will call the rules() function, which will open the pattern file, read the first line, dynamically build a match function and an apply function from the patterns on that line, and yield the dynamically built functions. The second time through the for loop, you will pick up exactly where you left off in rules() (which was in the middle of the for line in pattern_file loop). The first thing it will do is read the next line of the file (which is still open), dynamically build another match and apply function based on the patterns on that line in the file, and yield the two functions.

What have you gained over stage 4? Startup time. In stage 4, when you imported the plural4 module, it read the entire patterns file and built a list of all the possible rules before you could even think about calling the plural() function. With generators, you can do everything lazily: you read the first rule and create functions and try them, and if that works you don't ever read the rest of the file or create any other functions.

What have you lost? Performance! Every time you call the plural() function, the rules() generator starts over from the beginning—which means reopening the patterns file and reading from the beginning, one line at a time.

What if you could have the best of both worlds: minimal startup cost (don't execute any code on import) *and* maximum performance (don't build the same functions over and over again). Oh, and you still want to keep the rules in a separate file (because code is code and data is data), just as long as you never have to read the same line twice.

To do that, you'll need to build your own iterator. But before you do *that*, you need to learn about Python classes.

Further Reading Online

For more information, see the following resources:

- *PEP 255: Simple Generators*: http://www.python.org/dev/peps/pep-0255/

- *Understanding Python's* with *statement*: http://effbot.org/zone/python-with-statement.htm

- *Closures in Python*: http://ynniv.com/blog/2007/08/closures-in-python.html

- *Fibonacci numbers*: http://en.wikipedia.org/wiki/Fibonacci_number

- *English irregular plural nouns*: http://www2.gsu.edu/~wwwesl/egw/crump.htm

CHAPTER 7

■ ■ ■

Classes and Iterators

Generators are really just a special case of *iterators*. A function that yields values is a nice, compact way of building an iterator without building an iterator. Let me show you what I mean by that.

Remember the Fibonacci generator from Chapter 6? Listing 7-1 shows it as a built-from-scratch iterator:

Listing 7-1. A Fibonacci Iterator

```
class Fib:
    '''iterator that yields numbers in the Fibonacci sequence'''

    def __init__(self, max):
        self.max = max

    def __iter__(self):
        self.a = 0
        self.b = 1
        return self

    def __next__(self):
        fib = self.a
        if fib > self.max:
            raise StopIteration
        self.a, self.b = self.b, self.a + self.b
        return fib
```

Let's take that one line at a time (see Listing 7-2).

Listing 7-2. Class?

```
class Fib:
```

class? What's a class?

Defining Classes

Python is fully object-oriented: you can define your own classes, inherit from your own or built-in classes, and instantiate the classes you define.

Defining a class in Python is simple. As with functions, there is no separate interface definition. Just define the class and then start coding. A Python class starts with the reserved word class, followed by the class name. Technically, that's all that is required because a class doesn't need to inherit from any other class, as shown in Listing 7-3.

Listing 7-3. The Simplest Class

```
class PapayaWhip:   (1)
    pass            (2)
```

The following notes refer to the numbered lines in Listing 7-3:

1. The name of this class is PapayaWhip, and it doesn't inherit from any other class. Class names are usually capitalized, *EachWordLikeThis*, but this is only a convention, not a requirement.

2. You probably guessed this, but everything in a class is indented, just like the code within a function, if statement, for loop, or any other block of code. The first line not indented is outside the class.

This PapayaWhip class doesn't define any methods or attributes, but syntactically there needs to be something in the definition thus the pass statement. This is a Python reserved word that just means "move along; nothing to see here". It's a statement that does nothing, and it's a good placeholder when you're stubbing out functions or classes.

■ The pass statement in Python is like an empty set of curly braces ({}) in Java or C.

Many classes are inherited from other classes, but this one is not. Many classes define methods, but this one does not. There is nothing that a Python class absolutely must have, other than a name. In particular, C++ programmers might find it odd that Python classes don't have explicit constructors and destructors. Although it's not required, Python classes *can* have something similar to a constructor: the __init__() method.

The __init__() Method

This example shows the initialization of the Fib class using the __init__ method (see Listing 7-4).

Listing 7-4. The __init__ Method

```
class Fib:
    '''iterator that yields numbers in the Fibonacci sequence'''  (1)

    def __init__(self, max):                                       (2)
```

1. Classes can (and should) have docstrings, too, just like modules and functions.

2. The __init__() method is called immediately after an instance of the class is created. It would be tempting but technically incorrect to call this the constructor of the class. It's tempting because it looks like a C++ constructor (by convention, the __init__() method is the first method defined for the class), acts like one (it's the first piece of code executed in a newly created instance of the class), and even sounds like one. Incorrect! The object has already been constructed by the time the __init__() method is called, and you already have a valid reference to the new instance of the class.

The first argument of every class method, including the __init__() method, is always a reference to the current instance of the class. By convention, this argument is named self. This argument fills the role of the reserved word this in C++ or Java, but self is not a reserved word in Python; it's merely a naming convention. Nonetheless, please don't call it anything but self; this is a very strong convention.

In the __init__() method, self refers to the newly created object; in other class methods, it refers to the instance whose method was called. Although you need to specify self explicitly when defining the method, you do *not* specify it when calling the method; Python will add it for you automatically.

Instantiating Classes

Instantiating classes in Python is a straightforward process. To instantiate a class, simply call the class as if it were a function, passing the arguments that the __init__() method requires. The return value will be the newly created object (see Listing 7-5).

Listing 7-5. Class Attributes

```
>>> import fibonacci2
>>> fib = fibonacci2.Fib(100)  (1)
>>> fib                        (2)
<fibonacci2.Fib object at 0x00DB8810>
>>> fib.__class__              (3)
<class 'fibonacci2.Fib'>
>>> fib.__doc__               (4)
'iterator that yields numbers in the Fibonacci sequence'
```

1. You are creating an instance of the Fib class (defined in the fibonacci2 module) and assigning the newly created instance to the variable fib. You are passing one parameter, 100, which will end up as the max argument in the Fib __init__() method.

2. fib is now an instance of the Fib class.

3. Every class instance has a built-in attribute, __class__, which is the object's class. Java programmers might be familiar with the Class class, which contains methods such as getName() and getSuperclass() to get metadata information about an object. In Python, this kind of metadata is available through attributes, but the idea is the same.

4. You can access the instance's docstring (just as with a function or a module). All instances of a class share the same docstring.

■ In Python, simply call a class as if it were a function to create a new instance of the class. There is no explicit new operator as in C++ or Java.

Instance Variables

Now on to the next line (see Listing 7-6).

Listing 7-6. Instance Variables

```
class Fib:
    def __init__(self, max):
        self.max = max          (1)
```

1. What is self.max? It's an instance variable. It is completely separate from max, which was passed into the __init__() method as an argument. self.max is "global" to the instance. That means that you can access it from other methods.

Listing 7-7 further illustrates how instance variables work.

Listing 7-7. Instance Variables Across Methods

```
class Fib:
    def __init__(self, max):
        self.max = max          (1)
    .
    .
    .
    def __next__(self):
        fib = self.a
        if fib > self.max:      (2)
```

1. self.max is defined in the __init__() method.

2. And it's referenced in the __next__() method.

Instance variables are specific to one instance of a class. For example, if you create two Fib instances with different maximum values, they will each remember its own values, as shown in Listing 7-8.

Listing 7-8. Each Instance Maintains its Own State

```
>>> import fibonacci2
>>> fib1 = fibonacci2.Fib(100)
>>> fib2 = fibonacci2.Fib(200)
>>> fib1.max
100
>>> fib2.max
200
```

A Fibonacci Iterator

Now you're ready to learn how to build an iterator (see Listing 7-9). An iterator is just a class that defines an __iter__() method.

Listing 7-9. Building an Iterator from Scratch

```
class Fib:                                    (1)
    def __init__(self, max):                  (2)
        self.max = max

    def __iter__(self):                       (3)
        self.a = 0
        self.b = 1
        return self

    def __next__(self):                       (4)
        fib = self.a
        if fib > self.max:
            raise StopIteration               (5)
        self.a, self.b = self.b, self.a + self.b
        return fib                            (6)
```

1. To build an iterator from scratch, fib needs to be a class, not a function.

2. "Calling" Fib(max) is really creating an instance of this class and calling its __init__() method with max. The __init__() method saves the maximum value as an instance variable so other methods can refer to it later.

3. The __iter__() method is called whenever someone calls iter(fib). (As you'll see in a minute, a for loop will call this automatically, but you can also call it yourself manually.) After performing beginning-of-iteration initialization (in this case, resetting self.a and self.b, the two counters), the __iter__() method can return any object that implements a __next__() method. In this case (and in most cases), __iter__() simply returns self because this class implements its own __next__() method.

4. The __next__() method is called whenever someone calls next() on an iterator of an instance of a class. That will make more sense in a minute.

5.   When the __next__() method raises a StopIteration exception, this signals to the caller that the iteration is exhausted. Unlike most exceptions, this is not an error; it's a normal condition that just means the iterator has no more values to generate. If the caller is a for loop, it will notice this StopIteration exception and gracefully exit the loop. (In other words, it will swallow the exception.) This little bit of magic is actually the key to using iterators in for loops.

6.   To spit out the next value, an iterator's __next__() method simply returns the value. Do not use yield here; that's a bit of syntactic sugar that applies only when you're using generators. Here you're creating your own iterator from scratch; use return instead.

All three of these class methods (__init__, __iter__, and __next__) begin and end with a pair of underscore (_) characters. Why is that? There's nothing magical about it, but it usually indicates that they are "special methods."

■ The only thing special about special methods is that they aren't called directly; Python calls them when you use some other syntax on the class or an instance of the class.

Thoroughly confused yet? Excellent. Let's see how to call this iterator (see Listing 7-10).

Listing 7-10. Running the Built-from-Scratch Iterator

```
>>> from fibonacci2 import Fib
>>> for n in Fib(1000):
...     print(n, end=' ')
0 1 1 2 3 5 8 13 21 34 55 89 144 233 377 610 987
```

Why, it's exactly the same! It's byte for byte identical to how you called Fibonacci-as-a-generator in Chapter 6 (modulo one capital letter). But how?

There's a bit of magic involved in for loops. Here's what happens:

•   The for loop calls Fib(1000), as shown. This returns an instance of the Fib class. Call it fib_inst.

•   Secretly, and quite cleverly, the for loop calls iter(fib_inst), which returns an iterator object. Call it fib_iter. In this case, fib_iter == fib_inst because the __iter__() method returns self, but the for loop doesn't know (or care) about that.

•   To "loop through" the iterator, the for loop calls next(fib_iter), which calls the __next__() method on the fib_iter object (it does the next-Fibonacci-number calculations and returns a value). The for loop takes this value and assigns it to n; then executes the body of the for loop for that value of n.

- How does the for loop know when to stop? I'm glad you asked! When next(fib_iter) raises a StopIteration exception, the for loop will swallow the exception and gracefully exit. (Any other exception will pass through and be raised as usual.) And where have you seen a StopIteration exception? In the __next__() method, of course!

A Plural Rule Iterator

Now it's time for the finale. Let's rewrite the plural rules generator that you saw in Chapter 6 as an iterator (see Listing 7-11).

Listing 7-11. A LazyRules Class

```
class LazyRules:
    rules_filename = 'plural6-rules.txt'

    def __init__(self):
        self.pattern_file = open(self.rules_filename, encoding='utf-8')
        self.cache = []

    def __iter__(self):
        self.cache_index = 0
        return self

    def __next__(self):
        self.cache_index += 1
        if len(self.cache) >= self.cache_index:
            return self.cache[self.cache_index - 1]

        if self.pattern_file.closed:
            raise StopIteration

        line = self.pattern_file.readline()
        if not line:
            self.pattern_file.close()
            raise StopIteration

        pattern, search, replace = line.split(None, 3)
        funcs = build_match_and_apply_functions(
            pattern, search, replace)
        self.cache.append(funcs)
        return funcs

rules = LazyRules()
```

So this is a class that implements __iter__() and __next__() so it can be used as an iterator. Then you instantiate the class and assign it to rules. This happens just once   on import.

Let's take the class one bite at a time (see Listing 7-12).

Listing 7-12. Initializing the Iterator

```
class LazyRules:
    rules_filename = 'plural6-rules.txt'

    def __init__(self):
        self.pattern_file = open(self.rules_filename, encoding='utf-8')   (1)
        self.cache = []                                                   (2)
```

1. When you instantiate the LazyRules class, open the pattern file but don't read anything from it. (That comes later.)

2. After opening the patterns file, initialize the cache. You'll use these later (in the __next__() method) as you read the patterns from the pattern file.

Before you continue, take a closer look at rules_filename. It's not defined within the __iter__() method. In fact, it's not defined within *any* method. It's defined at the class level. It's a *class variable*, and although you can access it just like an instance variable (self.rules_filename), it is shared across all instances of the LazyRules class. See Listing 7-13.

Listing 7-13. Class Attributes and Instance Attributes

```
>>> import plural6
>>> r1 = plural6.LazyRules()
>>> r2 = plural6.LazyRules()
>>> r1.rules_filename                              (1)
'plural6-rules.txt'
>>> r2.rules_filename
'plural6-rules.txt'
>>> r2.rules_filename = 'r2-override.txt'          (2)
>>> r2.rules_filename
'r2-override.txt'
>>> r1.rules_filename
'plural6-rules.txt'
>>> r2.__class__.rules_filename                    (3)
'plural6-rules.txt'
>>> r2.__class__.rules_filename = 'papayawhip.txt' (4)
>>> r1.rules_filename
'papayawhip.txt'
>>> r2.rules_filename                              (5)
'r2-overridetxt'
```

1. Each instance of the class inherits the rules_filename attribute with the value defined by the class.

2. Changing the attribute's value in one instance does not affect other instances.

3. Nor does it change the class attribute. You can access the class attribute (as opposed to an individual instance's attribute) by using the special __class__ attribute to access the class itself.

4.   If you change the class attribute, all instances that are still inheriting that value (such as r1) will be affected.

5.   Instances that have overridden that attribute (such as r2) will not be affected.

And now back to the show (see Listings 7-14 and 7-15).

Listing 7-14. The __iter__ Method

```
def __iter__(self):        (1)
    self.cache_index = 0   (2)
    return self            (3)
```

1.   The __iter__() method will be called every time someone (a for loop, for example) calls iter(rules).

2.   This is the place to reset the counter that you'll use to retrieve items from the cache (that we haven't built yet patience, Grasshopper).

3.   Finally, the __iter__() method returns self, which signals that this class will take care of returning its own values throughout an iteration.

Listing 7-15. The End of the __next__ Method

```
def __next__(self):                               (1)
    .
    .
    .
    pattern, search, replace = line.split(None, 3)
    funcs = build_match_and_apply_functions(      (2)
        pattern, search, replace)
    self.cache.append(funcs)                      (3)
    return funcs
```

1.   The __next__() method gets called whenever someone (a for loop, for example) calls next(rules). This method will make sense only if we start at the end and work backward. So let's do that.

2.   The last part of this function should look familiar, at least. The build_match_and_apply_functions() function hasn't changed; it's the same as it ever was.

3.   The only difference is that, before returning the match and apply functions (which are stored in the tuple funcs), you'll save them in self.cache.

Now moving backward (see Listing 7-16).

Listing 7-16. The Middle of the __next__ Method

```
def __next__(self):
    .
    .
    .
    line = self.pattern_file.readline()   (1)
    if not line:                          (2)
        self.pattern_file.close()
        raise StopIteration               (3)
    .
    .
    .
```

1. A bit of advanced file trickery here. The readline() method (singular, not plural) reads exactly one line from an open file   specifically, the next line. (File objects are iterators, too! Iterators all the way down.)

2. If there was a line for readline() to read, line would not be an empty string. Even if the file contained a blank line, line would end up as the one-character string '\n' (a carriage return). If line is really an empty string, there are no more lines to read from the file.

3. When you reach the end of the file, close the file and raise the magic StopIteration exception. Remember, you got to this point because you needed a match and apply function for the next rule. The next rule comes from the next line of the file, but there is no next line! Therefore, you have no value to return. The iteration is over. (♫ The party's over... ♫)

Now you're moving backward all the way to the start of the __next__() method (see Listing 7-17).

Listing 7-17. The Beginning of the __next__ Method

```
def __next__(self):
    self.cache_index += 1
    if len(self.cache) >= self.cache_index:
        return self.cache[self.cache_index - 1]    (1)

    if self.pattern_file.closed:
        raise StopIteration                        (2)
    .
    .
    .
```

1. `self.cache` will be a list of the functions you need to match and apply individual rules. (At least *that* should sound familiar!) `self.cache_index` keeps track of which cached item you should return next. If you haven't exhausted the cache yet (that is, if the length of `self.cache` is greater than `self.cache_index`), you have a cache hit! Hooray! You can return the match and apply functions from the cache instead of building them from scratch.

2. On the other hand, if you don't get a hit from the cache, *and* the file object has been closed (which could happen farther down the method, as you saw in the previous code snippet), there's nothing more you can do. If the file is closed, it means you've exhausted it   you've already read through every line from the pattern file, and you've already built and cached the match and apply functions for each pattern. The file is exhausted; the cache is exhausted; everybody's exhausted. Wait, what? Hang in there, you're almost done.

Putting it all together, here's what happens:

- When the module is imported, it creates a single instance of the `LazyRules` class, called `rules`, which opens the pattern file but does not read from it.

- When asked for the first match and apply function, it checks its cache but finds the cache is empty. So it reads a single line from the pattern file, builds the match and apply functions from those patterns, and then caches them.

- For the sake of argument, suppose that the very first rule matched. If so, no further match and apply functions are built, and no further lines are read from the pattern file.

- Furthermore, for the sake of argument, suppose that the caller calls the `plural()` function *again* to pluralize a different word. The `for` loop in the `plural()` function will call `iter(rules)`, which will reset the cache index but will not reset the open file object.

- The first time through, the `for` loop will ask for a value from `rules`, which will invoke its `__next__()` method. This time, however, the cache is primed with a single pair of match and apply functions, corresponding to the patterns in the first line of the pattern file. Because they were built and cached in the course of pluralizing the previous word, they're retrieved from the cache. The cache index increments, and the open file is never touched.

- Suppose that the first rule does *not* match this time around. So the `for` loop comes around again and asks for another value from `rules`. This invokes the `__next__()` method a second time. This time, the cache is exhausted   it contained only one item, and you're asking for a second   so the `__next__()` method continues. It reads another line from the open file, builds match and apply functions out of the patterns, and caches them.

- This read-build-and-cache process will continue as long as the rules being read from the pattern file don't match the word you're trying to pluralize. If you do find a matching rule before the end of the file, you simply use it and stop with the file still open. The file pointer will stay wherever you stopped reading, waiting for the next `readline()` command. In the meantime, the cache now has more items in it, and if you start all over again trying to pluralize a new word, each of those items in the cache will be tried before reading the next line from the pattern file.

You have achieved pluralization nirvana, combining all three goals:

- *Minimal startup cost*: the only thing that happens on import is instantiating a single class and opening a file (but not reading from it).

- *Maximum performance*: the previous example would read through the file and build functions dynamically every time you wanted to pluralize a word. This version will cache functions as soon as they're built, and in the worst case, it will only read through the pattern file once, no matter how many words you pluralize.

- *Separation of code and data*: all the patterns are stored in a separate file. Code is code, and data is data, and never the twain shall meet.

Further Reading Online

For more information, refer to the following online sources:

- *Iterator types*:
  http://docs.python.org/3.1/library/stdtypes.html#iterator-types

- *PEP 234: Iterators*: http://www.python.org/dev/peps/pep-0234

- *PEP 255: Simple Generators*: http://www.python.org/dev/peps/pep-0255/

- *Generator Tricks for systems programmers*: http://www.dabeaz.com/generators/

CHAPTER 8

■ ■ ■

Advanced Iterators

HAWAII + IDAHO + IOWA + OHIO == STATES. Or, to put it another way, 510199 + 98153 + 9301 + 3593 == 621246. Am I speaking in tongues? No, it's just a puzzle.

Let me spell it out for you in Listing Listing 8-1.

Listing 8-1. An Alphametics Puzzle

```
HAWAII + IDAHO + IOWA + OHIO == STATES
510199 + 98153 + 9301 + 3593 == 621246

H = 5
A = 1
W = 0
I = 9
D = 8
O = 3
S = 6
T = 2
E = 4
```

Puzzles like this are called *cryptarithms* or *alphametics*. The letters spell out actual words, but if you replace each letter with a digit from 0–9, it also "spells" an arithmetic equation. The trick is to figure out which letter maps to each digit. All the occurrences of each letter must map to the same digit, no digit can be repeated, and no "word" can start with the digit 0.

The most well-known alphametic puzzle is SEND + MORE = MONEY.

In this chapter, we'll dive into an incredible Python program originally written by Raymond Hettinger. This program (shown in Listing 8-2) solves alphametic puzzles *in just 14 lines of code*.

Listing 8-2. An Alphametics Solver

```python
import re
import itertools

def solve(puzzle):
    words = re.findall('[A-Z]+', puzzle.upper())
    unique_characters = set(''.join(words))
    assert len(unique_characters) <= 10, 'Too many letters'
    first_letters = {word[0] for word in words}
    n = len(first_letters)
    sorted_characters = ''.join(first_letters) + \
        ''.join(unique_characters - first_letters)
    characters = tuple(ord(c) for c in sorted_characters)
    digits = tuple(ord(c) for c in '0123456789')
    zero = digits[0]
    for guess in itertools.permutations(digits, len(characters)):
        if zero not in guess[:n]:
            equation = puzzle.translate(dict(zip(characters, guess)))
            if eval(equation):
                return equation

if __name__ == '__main__':
    import sys
    for puzzle in sys.argv[1:]:
        print(puzzle)
        solution = solve(puzzle)
        if solution:
            print(solution)
```

You can run the program from the command line. On Linux, it would look like Listing 8-3. (These may take a while, depending on the speed of your computer, and there is no progress bar. Just be patient!)

Listing 8-3. Running the Alphametics Solver

```
you@localhost:~/diveintopython3/examples$ python3 alphametics.py \
    "HAWAII + IDAHO + IOWA + OHIO == STATES"
HAWAII + IDAHO + IOWA + OHIO = STATES
510199 + 98153 + 9301 + 3593 == 621246
you@localhost:~/diveintopython3/examples$ python3 alphametics.py \
    "I + LOVE + YOU == DORA"
I + LOVE + YOU == DORA
1 + 2784 + 975 == 3760
you@localhost:~/diveintopython3/examples$ python3 alphametics.py \
    "SEND + MORE == MONEY"
SEND + MORE == MONEY
9567 + 1085 == 10652
```

Finding All Occurrences of a Pattern

The first thing this alphametics solver does is find all the letters (A–Z) in the puzzle, as shown in Listing 8-4.

Listing 8-4. The re.findall() Function

```
>>> import re
>>> re.findall('[0-9]+', '16 2-by-4s in rows of 8')   (1)
['16', '2', '4', '8']
>>> re.findall('[A-Z]+', 'SEND + MORE == MONEY')       (2)
['SEND', 'MORE', 'MONEY']
```

1. The re module is Python's implementation of regular expressions. re has a nifty function called findall() that takes a regular expression pattern and a string and finds all occurrences of the pattern within the string. In this case, the pattern matches sequences of numbers. The findall() function returns a list of all the substrings that matched the pattern.

2. Here the regular expression pattern matches sequences of letters. Again, the return value is a list and each item in the list is a string that matched the regular expression pattern.

Listing 8-5 shows another example that will stretch your brain a little.

Listing 8-5. The Sixth Sick Sheikh

```
>>> re.findall(' s.*? s', "The sixth sick sheikh's sixth sheep's sick.")
[' sixth s', " sheikh's s", " sheep's s"]
```

Surprised? The regular expression looks for a space, an s, and then the shortest possible series of any character (.*?), then a space, then another s. Well, looking at that input string, I see five matches:

The **sixth s**ick sheikh's sixth sheep's sick.

The sixth **sick s**heikh's sixth sheep's sick.

The sixth sick **sheikh's s**ixth sheep's sick.

The sixth sick sheikh's **sixth s**heep's sick.

The sixth sick sheikh's sixth **sheep's s**ick.

But the re.findall() function only returned three matches. Specifically, it returned the first, the third, and the fifth. Why is that? Because it doesn't return overlapping matches. The first match overlaps with the second, so the first is returned and the second is skipped. Then the third overlaps with the fourth, so the third is returned and the fourth is skipped. Finally, the fifth is returned. Three matches, not five.

This has nothing to do with the alphametics solver; I just thought it was interesting.

Finding the Unique Items in a Sequence

Sets make it trivial to find the unique items in a sequence (see Listing 8-6).

Listing 8-6. Unique Items in a List

```
>>> a_list = ['The', 'sixth', 'sick', "sheik's", 'sixth', "sheep's", 'sick']
>>> set(a_list)                      (1)
{'sixth', 'The', "sheep's", 'sick', "sheik's"}
>>> a_string = 'EAST IS EAST'
>>> set(a_string)                    (2)
{'A', ' ', 'E', 'I', 'S', 'T'}
>>> words = ['SEND', 'MORE', 'MONEY']
>>> ''.join(words)                   (3)
'SENDMOREMONEY'
>>> set(''.join(words))              (4)
{'E', 'D', 'M', 'O', 'N', 'S', 'R', 'Y'}
```

1. Given a list of several strings, the `set()` function will return a set of unique strings from the list. This makes sense if you think of it like a **for** loop. Take the first item from the list, put it in the set. Second. Third. Fourth. Fifth—wait, that one's in the set already. It only gets listed once, because Python sets don't allow duplicates. Fifth. Sixth. Seventh—again, a duplicate, so it only gets listed once. The end result? All the unique items in the original list, without any duplicates. The original list doesn't even need to be sorted first.

2. The same technique works with strings, since a string is just a sequence of characters.

3. Given a list of strings, `''.join(a_list)` concatenates all the strings together into one.

4. So, given a list of strings, this line of code returns all the unique characters across all the strings, with no duplicates.

The alphametics solver uses this technique to get a list of all the unique characters in the puzzle (see Listing 8-7).

Listing 8-7. Finding Unique Letters in the Alphametic Solver

```
unique_characters = set(''.join(words))
```

This list is later used to assign digits to characters as the solver iterates through the possible solutions.

Making Assertions

Like many programming languages, Python has an **assert** statement. Listing 8-8 shows how it works.

Listing 8-8. The assert Statement

```
>>> assert 1 + 1 == 2                                          (1)
>>> assert 1 + 1 == 3                                          (2)
Traceback (most recent call last):
  File "<stdin>", line 1, in <module>
AssertionError
>>> assert 2 + 2 == 5, "Only for very large values of 2"  (3)
Traceback (most recent call last):
  File "<stdin>", line 1, in <module>
AssertionError: Only for very large values of 2
```

1. The **assert** statement is followed by any valid Python expression. In this case, the expression 1 + 1 == 2 evaluates to True, so the **assert** statement does nothing.

2. However, if the Python expression evaluates to False, the **assert** statement will raise an **AssertionError**.

3. You can also include a human-readable message that is printed if the **AssertionError** is raised.

Therefore, this line of code:

```
assert len(unique_characters) <= 10, 'Too many letters'
```

…is equivalent to this:

```
if len(unique_characters) > 10:
  raise AssertionError('Too many letters')
```

The alphametics solver uses this exact **assert** statement to bail out early if the puzzle contains more than ten unique letters. Since each letter is assigned a unique digit, and there are only ten digits, a puzzle with more than ten unique letters can not possibly have a solution.

Generator Expressions

As Listing 8-9 shows, a generator expression is like a generator function without the function.

117

Listing 8-9. Generator Expressions

```
>>> unique_characters = {'E', 'D', 'M', 'O', 'N', 'S', 'R', 'Y'}
>>> gen = (ord(c) for c in unique_characters)   (1)
>>> gen                                          (2)
<generator object <genexpr> at 0x00BADC10>
>>> next(gen)                                    (3)
69
>>> next(gen)
68
>>> tuple(ord(c) for c in unique_characters)     (4)
(69, 68, 77, 79, 78, 83, 82, 89)
```

1. A generator expression is like an anonymous function that yields values. The expression itself looks like a list comprehension, but it's wrapped in parentheses instead of square brackets.

2. The generator expression returns an iterator.

3. Calling next(gen) returns the next value from the iterator.

4. If you like, you can iterate through all the possible values and return a tuple, list, or set, by passing the generator expression to tuple(), list(), or set(). In these cases, you don't need an extra set of parentheses—just pass the "bare" expression ord(c) for c in unique_characters to the tuple() function, and Python figures out that it's a generator expression.

■ Using a generator expression instead of a list comprehension can save both CPU and RAM. If you're building a list just to throw it away (for example, passing it to tuple() or set()), use a generator expression instead!

Listing 8-10 shows another way to accomplish the same thing, using a generator function:

Listing 8-10. A Generator Function

```
def ord_map(a_string):
    for c in a_string:
        yield ord(c)

gen = ord_map(unique_characters)
```

The generator expression is more compact but functionally equivalent.

Calculating Permutations ... the Lazy Way

First of all, what the heck are permutations? As used here, it's a mathematical concept. (There are actually several definitions, depending on the kind of math you're doing. Here I'm talking about combinatorics, but if that doesn't mean anything to you, don't worry about it.)

The idea is that you take a list of things (could be numbers, could be letters, could be dancing bears) and find all the possible ways to split them up into smaller lists. All the smaller lists have the same size, which can be as small as 1 and as large as the total number of items. Oh, and nothing can be repeated. Mathematicians say things like "let's find the permutations of 3 different items taken 2 at a time," which means you have a sequence of 3 items and you want to find all the possible ordered pairs. Listing 8-11 shows a function that generates permutations.

Listing 8-11. Generating Permutations

```
>>> import itertools                             (1)
>>> perms = itertools.permutations([1, 2, 3], 2) (2)
>>> next(perms)                                  (3)
(1, 2)
>>> next(perms)
(1, 3)
>>> next(perms)
(2, 1)                                           (4)
>>> next(perms)
(2, 3)
>>> next(perms)
(3, 1)
>>> next(perms)
(3, 2)
>>> next(perms)                                  (5)
Traceback (most recent call last):
  File "<stdin>", line 1, in <module>
StopIteration
```

1. The `itertools` module has all kinds of fun stuff in it, including a `permutations()` function that does all the hard work of finding permutations.

2. The `permutations()` function takes a sequence (here a list of three integers) and a number, which is the number of items you want in each smaller group. The function returns an iterator, which you can use in a `for` loop or any old place that iterates. Here I'll step through the iterator manually to show all the values.

3. The first permutation of `[1, 2, 3]` taken 2 at a time is `(1, 2)`.

4. Note that permutations are ordered: `(2, 1)` is different than `(1, 2)`.

5. That's it! Those are all the permutations of `[1, 2, 3]` taken 2 at a time. Pairs like `(1, 1)` and `(2, 2)` never show up, because they contain repeats so they aren't valid permutations. When there are no more permutations, the iterator raises a `StopIteration` exception.

The `permutations()` function doesn't have to take a list. It can take any sequence—even a string, as Listing 8-12 shows.

Listing 8-12. Permutations of a String

```
>>> import itertools
>>> perms = itertools.permutations('ABC', 3)   (1)
>>> next(perms)
('A', 'B', 'C')                                        (2)
>>> next(perms)
('A', 'C', 'B')
>>> next(perms)
('B', 'A', 'C')
>>> next(perms)
('B', 'C', 'A')
>>> next(perms)
('C', 'A', 'B')
>>> next(perms)
('C', 'B', 'A')
>>> next(perms)
Traceback (most recent call last):
  File "<stdin>", line 1, in <module>
StopIteration
>>> list(itertools.permutations('ABC', 3))      (3)
[('A', 'B', 'C'), ('A', 'C', 'B'),
 ('B', 'A', 'C'), ('B', 'C', 'A'),
 ('C', 'A', 'B'), ('C', 'B', 'A')]
```

1. A string is just a sequence of characters. For the purposes of finding permutations, the string `'ABC'` is equivalent to the list `['A', 'B', 'C']`.

2. The first permutation of the 3 items `['A', 'B', 'C']`, taken 3 at a time, is `('A', 'B', 'C')`. There are five other permutations—the same three characters in every conceivable order.

3. Since the `permutations()` function always returns an iterator, an easy way to debug permutations is to pass that iterator to the built-in `list()` function to see all the permutations immediately.

Other Fun Stuff in the itertools Module

But wait, there's more. See Listings 8-13 and 8-14.

Listing 8-13. Combinations

```
>>> import itertools
>>> list(itertools.product('ABC', '123'))   (1)
[('A', '1'), ('A', '2'), ('A', '3'),
 ('B', '1'), ('B', '2'), ('B', '3'),
 ('C', '1'), ('C', '2'), ('C', '3')]
```

```
>>> list(itertools.combinations('ABC', 2))   (2)
[('A', 'B'), ('A', 'C'), ('B', 'C')]
```

1.   The `itertools.product()` function returns an iterator containing the Cartesian product of two sequences.

2.   The `itertools.combinations()` function returns an iterator containing all the possible combinations of the given sequence of the given length. This is like the `itertools.permutations()` function, except combinations don't include items that are duplicates of other items in a different order. So `itertools.permutations('ABC', 2)` will return both `('A', 'B')` and `('B', 'A')` (among others), but `itertools.combinations('ABC', 2)` will not return `('B', 'A')` because it is a duplicate of `('A', 'B')` in a different order.

Listing 8-14. A File as a List

```
>>> names = list(open('examples/favorite-people.txt', encoding='utf-8'))   (1)
>>> names
['Dora\n', 'Ethan\n', 'Wesley\n', 'John\n', 'Anne\n',
'Mike\n', 'Chris\n', 'Sarah\n', 'Alex\n', 'Lizzie\n']
>>> names = [name.rstrip() for name in names]                              (2)
>>> names
['Dora', 'Ethan', 'Wesley', 'John', 'Anne',
'Mike', 'Chris', 'Sarah', 'Alex', 'Lizzie']
>>> names = sorted(names)                                                  (3)
>>> names
['Alex', 'Anne', 'Chris', 'Dora', 'Ethan',
'John', 'Lizzie', 'Mike', 'Sarah', 'Wesley']
>>> names = sorted(names, key=len)                                         (4)
>>> names
['Alex', 'Anne', 'Dora', 'John', 'Mike',
'Chris', 'Ethan', 'Sarah', 'Lizzie', 'Wesley']
```

1.   This idiom **returns** a list of the lines in a text file.

2.   Unfortunately (for this example), the `list(open(`*filename*`))` idiom also includes the carriage returns at the end of each line. This list comprehension uses the `rstrip()` string method to strip trailing whitespace from each line. (Strings also have an `lstrip()` method to strip leading whitespace, and a `strip()` method which strips both.)

3.   The `sorted()` function takes a list and returns it sorted. By default, it sorts alphabetically.

4.   But the `sorted()` function can also take a function as the `key` parameter, and it sorts by that key. In this case, the sort function is `len()`, so it sorts by len(*each item*). Shorter names come first, then longer, then longest.

What does this have to do with the `itertools` module? I'm glad you asked. Take a look at Listing 8-15.

Listing 8-15. The groupby()Function

```
…continuing from the previous interactive shell…
>>> import itertools
>>> groups = itertools.groupby(names, len)   (1)
>>> groups
<itertools.groupby object at 0x00BB20C0>
>>> list(groups)
[(4, <itertools._grouper object at 0x00BA8BF0>),
 (5, <itertools._grouper object at 0x00BB4050>),
 (6, <itertools._grouper object at 0x00BB4030>)]
>>> groups = itertools.groupby(names, len)    (2)
>>> for name_length, name_iter in groups:     (3)
...     print('Names with {0:d} letters:'.format(name_length))
...     for name in name_iter:
...         print(name)
...
Names with 4 letters:
Alex
Anne
Dora
John
Mike
Names with 5 letters:
Chris
Ethan
Sarah
Names with 6 letters:
Lizzie
Wesley
```

1. The `itertools.groupby()` function takes a sequence and a key function, and returns an iterator that generates pairs. Each pair contains the result of `key_function(each item)` and another iterator containing all the items that shared that key result.

2. Calling the `list()` function "exhausted" the iterator, meaning you've already generated every item in the iterator to make the list. There's no "reset" button on an iterator; you can't just start over once you've exhausted it. If you want to loop through it again (say, in the upcoming **for** loop), you need to call `itertools.groupby()` again to create a new iterator.

3. In this example, given a list of names already sorted by length, `itertools.groupby(names, len)` will put all the 4-letter names in one iterator, all the 5-letter names in another iterator, and so on. The `groupby()` function is completely generic; it could group strings by first letter, numbers by their number of factors, or any other key function you can think of.

■ The `itertools.groupby()` function only works if the input sequence is already sorted by the grouping function. In the preceding example, you grouped a list of names by the `len()` function. That only worked because the input list was already sorted by length.

Are you watching closely? Look at Listing 8-16.

Listing 8-16. zip and zip_longest

```
>>> list(range(0, 3))
[0, 1, 2]
>>> list(range(10, 13))
[10, 11, 12]
>>> list(itertools.chain(range(0, 3), range(10, 13)))        (1)
[0, 1, 2, 10, 11, 12]
>>> list(zip(range(0, 3), range(10, 13)))                    (2)
[(0, 10), (1, 11), (2, 12)]
>>> list(zip(range(0, 3), range(10, 14)))                    (3)
[(0, 10), (1, 11), (2, 12)]
>>> list(itertools.zip_longest(range(0, 3), range(10, 14)))  (4)
[(0, 10), (1, 11), (2, 12), (None, 13)]
```

1. The `itertools.chain()` function takes two iterators and returns an iterator that contains all the items from the first iterator, followed by all the items from the second iterator. (Actually, it can take any number of iterators, and it chains them all in the order they were passed to the function.)

2. The `zip()` function does something prosaic that turns out to be extremely useful: it takes any number of sequences and returns an iterator which returns tuples of the first items of each sequence, then the second items of each, then the third, and so on.

3. The `zip()` function stops at the end of the shortest sequence. `range(10, 14)` has 4 items (10, 11, 12, and 13), but `range(0, 3)` only has 3, so the `zip()` function returns an iterator of 3 items.

4. On the other hand, the `itertools.zip_longest()` function stops at the end of the *longest* sequence, inserting **None** values for items past the end of the shorter sequences.

OK, that was all very interesting, but how does it relate to the alphametics solver? Listing 8-17 shows how.

Listing 8-17. Using the zip() Function to Pair Numbers and Letters

```
>>> characters = ('S', 'M', 'E', 'D', 'O', 'N', 'R', 'Y')
>>> guess = ('1', '2', '0', '3', '4', '5', '6', '7')
>>> tuple(zip(characters, guess))  (1)
(('S', '1'), ('M', '2'), ('E', '0'), ('D', '3'),
 ('O', '4'), ('N', '5'), ('R', '6'), ('Y', '7'))
>>> dict(zip(characters, guess))    (2)
{'E': '0', 'D': '3', 'M': '2', 'O': '4',
 'N': '5', 'S': '1', 'R': '6', 'Y': '7'}
```

1. Given a list of letters and a list of digits (each represented here as 1-character strings), the `zip` function will create a pairing of letters and digits, in order.

2. Why is that cool? Because that data structure happens to be exactly the right structure to pass to the `dict()` function to create a dictionary that uses letters as keys and their associated digits as values. (This isn't the only way to do it, of course. You could use a dictionary comprehension to create the dictionary directly.) Although the printed representation of the dictionary lists the pairs in a different order (dictionaries have no "order" per se), you can see that each letter is associated with the digit, based on the ordering of the original `characters` and `guess` sequences.

The alphametics solver uses this technique to create a dictionary that maps letters in the puzzle to digits in the solution, for each possible solution (see Listing 8-18).

Listing 8-18. The zip() Function in the Alphametics Solver

```
characters = tuple(ord(c) for c in sorted_characters)
digits = tuple(ord(c) for c in '0123456789')
...
for guess in itertools.permutations(digits, len(characters)):
    ...
    equation = puzzle.translate(dict(zip(characters, guess)))
```

But what is this `translate()` method? Ah, now you're getting to the *really* fun part.

A New Kind of String Manipulation

Python strings have many methods. You learned about some of those methods in the Strings chapter: `lower()`, `count()`, and `format()`. Now I want to introduce you to a powerful but little-known string manipulation technique—the `translate()` method, shown in Listing 8-19.

Listing 8-19. The translate() String Method

```
>>> translation_table = {ord('A'): ord('O')}   (1)
>>> translation_table                           (2)
{65: 79}
>>> 'MARK'.translate(translation_table)         (3)
'MORK'
```

1. String translation starts with a translation table, which is just a dictionary that maps one character to another. Actually, "character" is incorrect—the translation table really maps one *byte* to another.

2. Remember, bytes in Python 3 are integers. The ord() function returns the ASCII value of a character, which, in the case of A–Z, is always a byte from 65 to 90.

3. The translate() method on a string takes a translation table and runs the string through it. That is, it replaces all occurrences of the keys of the translation table with the corresponding values, in this case, "translating" MARK to MORK.

What does this have to do with solving alphametic puzzles? As it turns out, everything (see Listing 8-20).

Listing 8-20. The translate() Method is the Key

```
>>> characters = tuple(ord(c) for c in 'SMEDONRY')   (1)
>>> characters
(83, 77, 69, 68, 79, 78, 82, 89)
>>> guess = tuple(ord(c) for c in '91570682')        (2)
>>> guess
(57, 49, 53, 55, 48, 54, 56, 50)
>>> translation_table = dict(zip(characters, guess)) (3)
>>> translation_table
{68: 55, 69: 53, 77: 49, 78: 54, 79: 48, 82: 56, 83: 57, 89: 50}
>>> 'SEND + MORE == MONEY'.translate(translation_table)  (4)
'9567 + 1085 == 10652'
```

1. Using a generator expression, we quickly compute the byte values for each character in a string. characters is an example of the value of sorted_characters in the alphametics.solve() function.

2. Using another generator expression, we quickly compute the byte values for each digit in this string. The result, guess, is of the form returned by the itertools.permutations() function in the alphametics.solve() function.

3. This translation table is generated by zipping **characters** and **guess** together and building a dictionary from the resulting sequence of pairs. This is exactly what the **alphametics.solve()** function does inside the **for** loop.

4. Finally, we pass this translation table to the **translate()** method of the original puzzle string. This converts each letter in the string to the corresponding digit (based on the letters in **characters** and the digits in **guess**). The result is a valid Python expression, as a string.

That's pretty impressive. But what can you do with a string that happens to be a valid Python expression?

Evaluating Arbitrary Strings as Python Expressions

This is the final piece of the puzzle (or rather, the final piece of the puzzle solver). After all that fancy string manipulation, we're left with a string like **'9567 + 1085 == 10652'**. But that's a string, and what good is a string? Enter **eval()**, the universal Python evaluation tool (see Listing 8-21).

Listing 8-21. The eval() Function

```
>>> eval('1 + 1 == 2')
True
>>> eval('1 + 1 == 3')
False
>>> eval('9567 + 1085 == 10652')
True
```

But wait, there's more! The **eval()** function isn't limited to Boolean expressions. It can handle *any* Python expression and returns *any* datatype (see Listing 8-22).

Listing 8-22. Evaluating Python Expressions

```
>>> eval('"A" + "B"')
'AB'
>>> eval('"MARK".translate({65: 79})')
'MORK'
>>> eval('"AAAAA".count("A")')
5
>>> eval('["*"] * 5')
['*', '*', '*', '*', '*']
```

And that's not all—look at Listing 8-23!

Listing 8-23. Referencing Global Variables in an eval() Expression

```
>>> x = 5
>>> eval("x * 5")           (1)
25
>>> eval("pow(x, 2)")       (2)
25
>>> import math
>>> eval("math.sqrt(x)")    (3)
2.2360679774997898
```

1.   The expression that **eval()** takes can reference global variables defined outside
     the **eval()**. If called within a function, it can reference local variables too.

2.   And functions.

3.   And modules.

Hey, wait a minute…take a look at Listing 8-24.

Listing 8-24. Dangerous eval() Expressions

```
>>> import subprocess
>>> eval("subprocess.getoutput('ls ~')")                    (1)
'Desktop         Library         Pictures  \
 Documents       Movies          Public    \
 Music           Sites'
>>> eval("subprocess.getoutput('rm /some/random/file')")    (2)
```

1.   The **subprocess** module allows you to run arbitrary shell commands and get
     the result as a Python string.

2.   Arbitrary shell commands can have permanent consequences.

It's even worse than that, because there's a global **__import__()** function that takes a module name
as a string, imports the module, and returns a reference to it. Combined with the power of **eval()**, you
can construct a single expression that will wipe out all your files, as Listing 8-25 shows.

Listing 8-25. Very Dangerous eval() Expressions

```
>>> eval("__import__('subprocess').getoutput('rm /some/random/file')")  (1)
```

1.   Now imagine the output of **'rm -rf ~'**. Actually there wouldn't be any output,
     but you wouldn't have any files left either.

Say it with me: "**eval()** is evil!"

Well, the evil part is evaluating arbitrary expressions from untrusted sources. You should only use eval() on trusted input. Of course, the trick is figuring out what's trusted. But here's something I know for certain: you should **not** take this alphametics solver and put it on the Internet as a fun little web service. Don't make the mistake of thinking, "Gosh, the function does a lot of string manipulation before getting a string to evaluate; *I can't imagine how someone could exploit that.*" Someone *will* figure out how to sneak nasty executable code past all that string manipulation (stranger things have happened), and then you can kiss your server goodbye.

But surely there's *some* way to evaluate expressions safely? To put eval() in a sandbox where it can't access or harm the outside world? Well, yes and no, see Listing 8-26.

Listing 8-26. Hacking eval()

```
>>> x = 5
>>> eval("x * 5", {}, {})               (1)
Traceback (most recent call last):
  File "<stdin>", line 1, in <module>
  File "<string>", line 1, in <module>
NameError: name 'x' is not defined
>>> eval("x * 5", {"x": x}, {})         (2)
>>> import math
>>> eval("math.sqrt(x)", {"x": x}, {})  (2)
Traceback (most recent call last):
  File "<stdin>", line 1, in <module>
  File "<string>", line 1, in <module>
NameError: name 'math' is not defined
```

1. The second and third parameters passed to the eval() function act as the global and local namespaces for evaluating the expression. In this case, they are both empty, which means that when the string "x * 5" is evaluated, there is no reference to x in either the global or local namespace, so eval() throws an exception.

2. You can selectively include specific values in the global namespace by listing them individually. Then those—and only those—variables will be available during evaluation.

3. Even though you just imported the math module, you didn't include it in the namespace passed to the eval() function, so the evaluation failed.

Gee, that was easy. Let's go make an alphametics web service now!

Not so fast…. Now look at Listing 8-27.

Listing 8-27. Hacking the Hack

```
>>> eval("pow(5, 2)", {}, {})                      (1)
25
>>> eval("__import__('math').sqrt(5)", {}, {})     (2)
2.2360679774997898
```

1. Even though you've passed empty dictionaries for the global and local namespaces, all of Python's built-in functions are still available during evaluation. So pow(5, 2) works, because 5 and 2 are literals, and pow() is a built-in function.

2. Unfortunately (and if you don't see why it's unfortunate, read on), the __import__() function is also a built-in function, so it works too.

That means you can still do nasty things, even if you explicitly set the global and local namespaces to empty dictionaries when calling eval(), as in Listing 8-28.

Listing 8-28. Still Dangerous

```
>>> eval("__import__('subprocess').getoutput('rm /some/random/file')", {}, {})
```

Oops. I'm glad I didn't make that alphametics web service. Is there *any* way to use eval() safely? Again, yes and no. See Listing 8-29.

Listing 8-29. Finally Safe?

```
>>> eval("__import__('math').sqrt(5)",
...     {"__builtins__":None}, {})            (1)
Traceback (most recent call last):
  File "<stdin>", line 1, in <module>
  File "<string>", line 1, in <module>
NameError: name '__import__' is not defined
>>> eval("__import__('subprocess').getoutput('rm -rf /')",
...     {"__builtins__":None}, {})            (2)
Traceback (most recent call last):
  File "<stdin>", line 1, in <module>
  File "<string>", line 1, in <module>
NameError: name '__import__' is not defined
```

1. To evaluate untrusted expressions safely, you need to define a global namespace dictionary that maps "__builtins__" to None, the Python null value. Internally, the "built-in" functions are contained within a pseudo-module called "__builtins__". This pseudo-module (that is, the set of built-in functions) is made available to evaluated expressions unless you explicitly override it.

2. Be sure you've overridden __builtins__. Not __builtin__, __built-ins__, or some other variation that will work just fine but expose you to catastrophic risks.

So eval() is safe now? Well, yes and no (see Listing 8-30).

Listing 8-30. The Expression That Never Ends

```
>>> eval("2 ** 2147483647",
...     {"__builtins__":None}, {})            (1)
```

1. Even without access to `__builtins__`, you can still launch a denial-of-service attack. For example, trying to raise `2` to the `2147483647th` power will spike your server's CPU utilization to 100% for quite some time. (If you're trying this in the interactive shell, press Ctrl-C a few times to break out of it.) Technically this expression will return a value eventually, but in the meantime your server will be doing a whole lot of nothing.

In the end, it *is* possible to safely evaluate untrusted Python expressions, for some definition of "safe" that turns out not to be terribly useful in real life. It's fine if you're just playing around, and it's fine if you only ever pass it trusted input. But anything else is just asking for trouble.

Putting It All Together

To recap: this program solves alphametic puzzles by brute force, that is, through an exhaustive search of all possible solutions. To do so, it…

1. Finds all the letters in the puzzle with the `re.findall()` function

2. Finds all the *unique* letters in the puzzle with sets and the `set()` function

3. Checks if there are more than 10 unique letters (meaning the puzzle is definitely unsolvable) with an `assert` statement

4. Converts the letters to their ASCII equivalents with a generator object

5. Calculates all the possible solutions with the `itertools.permutations()` function

6. Converts each possible solution to a Python expression with the `translate()` string method

7. Tests each possible solution by evaluating the Python expression with the `eval()` function

8. Returns the first solution that evaluates to `True`

…all in just 14 lines of code.

Further Reading Online

- Raymond Hettinger's "Easy AI with Python" talk at PyCon 2009: `http://blip.tv/file/1947373/`

- Recipe 576615: Raymond Hettinger's original alphametics solver for Python 2: `http://code.activestate.com/recipes/576615/`

- More of Raymond Hettinger's recipes in the ActiveState Code repository: `http://code.activestate.com/recipes/users/178123/`

- Alphametics on Wikipedia: `http://en.wikipedia.org/wiki/Verbal_arithmetic`

- Alphametics Index: `http://www.tkcs-collins.com/truman/alphamet/index.shtml`

Many thanks to Raymond Hettinger for agreeing to relicense his code so I could port it to Python 3 and use it as the basis for this chapter.

CHAPTER 9

■ ■ ■

Unit Testing

In this chapter, you're going to write and debug a set of utility functions to convert to and from Roman numerals. You saw the mechanics of constructing and validating Roman numerals in Chapter 5. Now step back and consider what it would take to expand that into a two-way utility.

The rules for Roman numerals lead to a number of interesting observations:

- There is only one correct way to represent a particular number as a Roman numeral.

- The converse is also true: if a string of characters is a valid Roman numeral, it represents only one number (that is, it can only be interpreted one way).

- There is a limited range of numbers that can be expressed as Roman numerals, specifically 1 through 3999. The Romans did have several ways of expressing larger numbers, for instance by having a bar over a numeral to represent that its normal value should be multiplied by 1000. For the purposes of this chapter, let's stipulate that Roman numerals go from 1 to 3999.

- There is no way to represent 0 in Roman numerals.

- There is no way to represent negative numbers in Roman numerals.

- There is no way to represent fractions or non-integer numbers in Roman numerals.

Let's start mapping out what a `roman.py` module should do. It will have two main functions, `to_roman()` and `from_roman()`. The `to_roman()` function should take an integer from 1 to 3999 and return the Roman numeral representation as a string…

Stop right there. Now let's do something a little unexpected: write a test case that checks whether the `to_roman()` function does what you want it to. You read that right: you're going to write code that tests code that you haven't written yet.

This is called *unit testing*. The set of two conversion functions—`to_roman()`, and later `from_roman()`—can be written and tested as a unit, separate from any larger program that imports them. Python has a framework for unit testing, the appropriately-named `unittest` module.

Unit testing is an important part of an overall testing-centric development strategy. If you write unit tests, it is important to write them early (preferably before writing the code they test), and to keep them updated as code and requirements change. Unit testing is not a replacement for higher-level functional or system testing, but it is important in all phases of development:

- Before writing code, it forces you to detail your requirements in a useful fashion.

- While writing code, it keeps you from over-coding. When all the test cases pass, the function is complete.

- When refactoring code, it assures you that the new version behaves the same way as the old version.

- When maintaining code, it helps you cover your ass when someone comes screaming that your latest change broke their old code. ("But, boss, all the unit tests passed when I checked it in...")

- When writing code in a team, it increases confidence that the code you're about to commit isn't going to break someone else's code, because you can run their unit tests first. (I've seen this sort of process in code sprints. A team breaks up the assignment; everybody takes the specs for their task, writes unit tests, then shares their unit tests with the rest of the team. That way, nobody goes off too far into developing code that doesn't play well with others.)

A Single Question

A test case answers a single question about the code it is testing. A test case should be able to...

- ...run completely by itself, without any human input. Unit testing is about automation.

- ...determine by itself whether the function it is testing has passed or failed, without a human interpreting the results.

- ...run in isolation, separate from any other test cases (even if they test the same functions). Each test case is an island.

Let's build a test case for the first requirement. The to_roman() function should return the Roman numeral representation for all integers 1 to 3999.

It is not immediately obvious how the code in Listing 9-1 does ... well, *anything*. It defines a class that has no __init__() method. The class *does* have another method, but it is never called. The entire script has a __main__ block, but it doesn't reference the class or its method. But it does do something, I promise.

Listing 9-1. Your First Test

```
import roman1
import unittest

class KnownValues(unittest.TestCase):                    (1)
    known_values = ( (1, 'I'),
                     (2, 'II'),
                     (3, 'III'),
```

```
    (4, 'IV'),
    (5, 'V'),
    (6, 'VI'),
    (7, 'VII'),
    (8, 'VIII'),
    (9, 'IX'),
    (10, 'X'),
    (50, 'L'),
    (100, 'C'),
    (500, 'D'),
    (1000, 'M'),
    (31, 'XXXI'),
    (148, 'CXLVIII'),
    (294, 'CCXCIV'),
    (312, 'CCCXII'),
    (421, 'CDXXI'),
    (528, 'DXXVIII'),
    (621, 'DCXXI'),
    (782, 'DCCLXXXII'),
    (870, 'DCCCLXX'),
    (941, 'CMXLI'),
    (1043, 'MXLIII'),
    (1110, 'MCX'),
    (1226, 'MCCXXVI'),
    (1301, 'MCCCI'),
    (1485, 'MCDLXXXV'),
    (1509, 'MDIX'),
    (1607, 'MDCVII'),
    (1754, 'MDCCLIV'),
    (1832, 'MDCCCXXXII'),
    (1993, 'MCMXCIII'),
    (2074, 'MMLXXIV'),
    (2152, 'MMCLII'),
    (2212, 'MMCCXII'),
    (2343, 'MMCCCXLIII'),
    (2499, 'MMCDXCIX'),
    (2574, 'MMDLXXIV'),
    (2646, 'MMDCXLVI'),
    (2723, 'MMDCCXXIII'),
    (2892, 'MMDCCCXCII'),
    (2975, 'MMCMLXXV'),
    (3051, 'MMMLI'),
    (3185, 'MMMCLXXXV'),
    (3250, 'MMMCCL'),
    (3313, 'MMMCCCXIII'),
    (3408, 'MMMCDVIII'),
    (3501, 'MMMDI'),
    (3610, 'MMMDCX'),
    (3743, 'MMMDCCXLIII'),
    (3844, 'MMMDCCCXLIV'),
    (3888, 'MMMDCCCLXXXVIII'),
    (3940, 'MMMCMXL'),
```

```
                   (3999, 'MMMCMXCIX'))              (2)

    def test_to_roman_known_values(self):           (3)
        '''to_roman should give known result with known input'''
        for integer, numeral in self.known_values:
            result = roman1.to_roman(integer)        (4)
            self.assertEqual(numeral, result)        (5)

if __name__ == '__main__':
    unittest.main()
```

1. To write a test case, first subclass the `TestCase` class of the `unittest` module. This class provides many useful methods you can use in your test case to test specific conditions.

2. This is a list of integer/numeral pairs that I verified manually. It includes the lowest ten numbers, the highest number, every number that translates to a single-character Roman numeral, and a random sampling of other valid numbers. You don't need to test every possible input, but you should try to test all the obvious edge cases.

3. Every individual test is its own method, which must take no parameters and return no value. If the method exits normally without raising an exception, the test is considered passed; if the method raises an exception, the test is considered failed.

4. Here you call the actual `to_roman()` function. (Well, the function hasn't been written yet, but once it is, this is the line that will call it.) Notice that you have now defined the API for the `to_roman()` function: it must take an integer (the number to convert) and return a string (the Roman numeral representation). If the API is different from that, this test is considered failed. Also notice that you are not trapping any exceptions when you call `to_roman()`. This is intentional. `to_roman()` shouldn't raise an exception when you call it with valid input, and these input values are all valid. If `to_roman()` raises an exception, this test is considered failed.

5. Assuming the `to_roman()` function was defined correctly, called correctly, completed successfully, and returned a value, the last step is to check whether it returned the *right* value. This is a common question, and the `TestCase` class provides a method, `assertEqual`, to check whether two values are equal. If the result returned from `to_roman()` (`result`) does not match the known value you were expecting (`numeral`), `assertEqual` will raise an exception and the test will fail. If the two values are equal, `assertEqual` will do nothing. If every value returned from `to_roman()` matches the known value you expect, `assertEqual` never raises an exception, so `test_to_roman_known_values` eventually exits normally, which means `to_roman()` has passed this test.

Once you have a test case, you can start coding the `to_roman()` function. First, you should stub it out as an empty function and make sure the tests fail (see Listing 9-2). If the tests succeed before you've written any code, your tests aren't testing your code at all! Unit testing is a dance: tests lead, code follows. Write a test that fails, then code until it passes.

Listing 9-2. A Stub Function

```
def to_roman(n):
    '''convert integer to Roman numeral'''
    pass                                    (1)
```

1. At this stage, you want to define the API of the to_roman() function, but you
   don't want to code it yet. (Your test needs to fail first.) To stub it out, use the
   Python reserved word **pass**, which does precisely nothing.

Execute romantest1.py on the command line to run the test. If you call it with the -v command-line
option, it will give more verbose output so you can see exactly what's going on as each test case runs.
With any luck, your output should look like Listing 9-3.

Listing 9-3. Hooray, Your Test Fails

```
you@localhost:~/diveintopython3/examples$ python3 romantest1.py -v
test_to_roman_known_values (__main__.KnownValues)                (1)
to_roman should give known result with known input ... FAIL      (2)

======================================================================
FAIL: to_roman should give known result with known input
----------------------------------------------------------------------
Traceback (most recent call last):
  File "romantest1.py", line 73, in test_to_roman_known_values
    self.assertEqual(numeral, result)
AssertionError: 'I' != None                                      (3)

----------------------------------------------------------------------
Ran 1 test in 0.016s                                             (4)

FAILED (failures=1)                                              (5)
```

1. Running the script runs unittest.main(), which runs each test case. Each
   test case is a method within a class in romantest.py. There is no required
   organization of these test classes; they can each contain a single test method,
   or you can have one class that contains multiple test methods. The only
   requirement is that each test class must inherit from unittest.TestCase.

2. For each test case, the **unittest** module will print out the **docstring** of the
   method and whether that test passed or failed. As expected, this test case fails.

3. For each failed test case, **unittest** displays the trace information showing
   exactly what happened. In this case, the call to assertEqual() raised an
   AssertionError because it was expecting to_roman(1) to return 'I', but it
   didn't. (Since there was no explicit return statement, the function returned
   None, the Python null value.)

4. After the detail of each test, **unittest** displays a summary of how many tests were performed and how long it took.

5. Overall, the test run failed because at least one test case did not pass. When a test case doesn't pass, **unittest** distinguishes between failures and errors. A failure is a call to an **assertXYZ** method, like **assertEqual** or **assertRaises**, that fails because the asserted condition is not true or the expected exception was not raised. An error is any other sort of exception raised in the code you're testing or the unit test case itself.

Now, finally, you can write the **to_roman()** function, as shown in Listing 9-4.

Listing 9-4. A Real to_roman() Function

```
roman_numeral_map = (('M',  1000),
                     ('CM', 900),
                     ('D',  500),
                     ('CD', 400),
                     ('C',  100),
                     ('XC', 90),
                     ('L',  50),
                     ('XL', 40),
                     ('X',  10),
                     ('IX', 9),
                     ('V',  5),
                     ('IV', 4),
                     ('I',  1))                    (1)

def to_roman(n):
    '''convert integer to Roman numeral'''
    result = ''
    for numeral, integer in roman_numeral_map:
        while n >= integer:                        (2)
            result += numeral
            n -= integer
    return result
```

1. **roman_numeral_map** is a tuple of tuples that defines three things: the character representations of the most basic Roman numerals; the order of the Roman numerals (in descending value order, from M all the way down to I); the value of each Roman numeral. Each inner tuple is a pair of (**numeral**, **value**) and includes not just single-character Roman numerals; it also defines two-character pairs like **CM** (one hundred less than one thousand). This makes the **to_roman()** function code simpler.

2. Here's where the rich data structure of **roman_numeral_map** pays off, because you don't need any special logic to handle the subtraction rule. To convert to Roman numerals, simply iterate through **roman_numeral_map** looking for the largest integer value less than or equal to the input. Once found, add the Roman numeral representation to the end of the output, subtract the corresponding integer value from the input, lather, rinse, repeat.

If you're still not clear how the `to_roman()` function works, add a `print()` call to the end of the `while` loop, as shown in Listing 9-5.

Listing 9-5. A Debugging Version of the to_roman() Function

```
while n >= integer:
    result += numeral
    n -= integer
    print('subtracting {0} from input, adding {1} to output'.format(integer, numeral))
```

With the debug `print()` statements, the output looks like Listing 9-6.

Listing 9-6. Debugging the to_roman() Function

```
>>> import roman1
>>> roman1.to_roman(1424)
subtracting 1000 from input, adding M to output
subtracting 400 from input, adding CD to output
subtracting 10 from input, adding X to output
subtracting 10 from input, adding X to output
subtracting 4 from input, adding IV to output
'MCDXXIV'
```

So the `to_roman()` function appears to work, at least in this manual spot check. But will it pass the test case you wrote? See Listing 9-7.

Listing 9-7. Hooray, Your Test Passes

```
you@localhost:~/diveintopython3/examples$ python3 romantest1.py -v
test_to_roman_known_values (__main__.KnownValues)
to_roman should give known result with known input ... ok

----------------------------------------------------------------------
Ran 1 test in 0.016s

OK
```

1. The `to_roman()` function passes the "known values" test case. It's not comprehensive, but it does put the function through its paces with a variety of inputs, including inputs that produce every single-character Roman numeral, the largest possible input (**3999**), and the input that produces the longest possible Roman numeral (**3888**). At this point, you can be reasonably confident that the function works for any good input value you could throw at it.

"Good" input? Hmm. What about bad input?

Halt and Catch Fire

It is not enough to test that functions succeed when given good input; you must also test that they fail when given bad input (see Listing 9-8). And not just any sort of failure; they must fail in the way you expect.

Listing 9-8. A Bug from Bad Input

```
>>> import roman1
>>> roman1.to_roman(4000)
'MMMM'
>>> roman1.to_roman(5000)
'MMMMM'
>>> roman1.to_roman(9000)   (1)
'MMMMMMMMM'
```

1. That's definitely not what you wanted—that's not even a valid Roman numeral! In fact, each of these numbers is outside the range of acceptable input, but the function returns a bogus value anyway. Silently returning bad values is *baaaaaaad*; if a program is going to fail, it is far better that it fail quickly and noisily. "Halt and catch fire," as the saying goes. The Pythonic way to halt and catch fire is to raise an exception.

The question to ask yourself is, "How can I express this as a testable requirement?" The `to_roman()` function should raise an `OutOfRangeError` when given an integer greater than `3999`.

What would that test look like? It would look at lot like Listing 9-9.

Listing 9-9. A Test for Too-large Numbers

```
class ToRomanBadInput(unittest.TestCase):                              (1)
    def test_too_large(self):                                          (2)
        '''to_roman should fail with large input'''
        self.assertRaises(roman2.OutOfRangeError, roman2.to_roman, 4000)  (3)
```

1. Like the previous test case, you create a class that inherits from `unittest.TestCase`. You can have more than one test per class (as you'll see later in this chapter), but I chose to create a new class here because this test is something different than the last one. We'll keep all the good input tests together in one class and all the bad input tests together in another.

2. Like the previous test case, the test itself is a method of the class, with a name starting with `test`.

3. The `unittest.TestCase` class provides the `assertRaises` method, which takes the following arguments: the exception you're expecting, the function you're testing, and the arguments you're passing to that function. (If the function you're testing takes more than one argument, pass them all to `assertRaises`, in order, and it will pass them right along to the function you're testing.)

Pay close attention to this last line of code. Instead of calling `to_roman()` directly and manually checking that it raises a particular exception (by wrapping it in a `try...except` block), the `assertRaises` method has encapsulated all of that for us. All you do is tell it what exception you're expecting (`roman2.OutOfRangeError`), the function (`to_roman()`), and the function's arguments (`4000`). The `assertRaises` method takes care of calling `to_roman()` and checking that it raises `roman2.OutOfRangeError`.

Also note that you're passing the `to_roman()` function itself as an argument; you're not calling it, and you're not passing the name of it as a string. Have I mentioned recently how handy it is that everything in Python is an object?

So what happens when you run the test suite with this new test? See Listing 9-10.

Listing 9-10. Your Second Test Produces ... an Error

```
you@localhost:~/diveintopython3/examples$ python3 romantest2.py -v
test_to_roman_known_values (__main__.KnownValues)
to_roman should give known result with known input ... ok
test_too_large (__main__.ToRomanBadInput)
to_roman should fail with large input ... ERROR                          (1)


======================================================================
ERROR: to_roman should fail with large input
----------------------------------------------------------------------
Traceback (most recent call last):
  File "romantest2.py", line 78, in test_too_large
    self.assertRaises(roman2.OutOfRangeError, roman2.to_roman, 4000)
AttributeError: 'module' object has no attribute 'OutOfRangeError'      (2)


----------------------------------------------------------------------
Ran 2 tests in 0.000s

FAILED (errors=1)
```

1. You should have expected this to fail (since you haven't written any code to pass it yet), but... it didn't actually fail, it had an error instead. This is a subtle but important distinction. A unit test actually has *three* return values: pass, fail, and error. *Pass*, of course, means that the test passed—the code did what you expected. *Fail* is what the previous test case did (until you wrote code to make it pass)—it executed the code but the result was not what you expected. *Error* means that the code didn't even execute properly.

2. Why didn't the code execute properly? The traceback tells all. The module you're testing doesn't have an exception called `OutOfRangeError`. Remember, you passed this exception to the `assertRaises()` method, because it's the exception you want the function to raise given an out-of-range input. But the exception doesn't exist, so the call to the `assertRaises()` method failed. It never got a chance to test the `to_roman()` function; it didn't get that far.

To solve this problem, you need to define the `OutOfRangeError` exception in `roman2.py`, as shown in Listing 9-11.

Listing 9-11. Defining a Custom Exception

```
class OutOfRangeError(ValueError):  (1)
    pass                            (2)
```

1. Exceptions are classes. An "out of range" error is a kind of value error—the argument value is out of its acceptable range. So this exception inherits from the built-in **ValueError** exception. This is not strictly necessary (it could just inherit from the base **Exception** class), but it feels right.

2. Exceptions don't actually do anything, but you need at least one line of code to make a class. Calling **pass** does precisely nothing, but it's a line of Python code, so that makes it a class.

Now run the test suite again (see Listing 9-12).

Listing 9-12. Hooray, Your Second Test Fails

```
you@localhost:~/diveintopython3/examples$ python3 romantest2.py -v
test_to_roman_known_values (__main__.KnownValues)
to_roman should give known result with known input ... ok
test_too_large (__main__.ToRomanBadInput)
to_roman should fail with large input ... FAIL                        (1)


=======================================================================
FAIL: to_roman should fail with large input
-----------------------------------------------------------------------
Traceback (most recent call last):
  File "romantest2.py", line 78, in test_too_large
    self.assertRaises(roman2.OutOfRangeError, roman2.to_roman, 4000)
AssertionError: OutOfRangeError not raised by to_roman               (2)


-----------------------------------------------------------------------
Ran 2 tests in 0.016s

FAILED (failures=1)
```

1. The new test is still not passing, but it's not returning an error either. Instead, the test is failing. That's progress! It means the call to the **assertRaises()** method succeeded this time, and the unit test framework actually tested the **to_roman()** function.

2. Of course, the **to_roman()** function isn't raising the **OutOfRangeError** exception you just defined, because you haven't told it to do that yet. That's excellent news! It means this is a valid test case—it fails before you write the code to make it pass.

Now you can write the code to make this test pass (see Listing 9-13).

Listing 9-13. A to_roman() Function that Checks for Too-large Input

```
def to_roman(n):
    '''convert integer to Roman numeral'''
    if n > 3999:
        raise OutOfRangeError('number out of range (must be less than 4000)')  (1)

    result = ''
    for numeral, integer in roman_numeral_map:
```

```
        while n >= integer:
            result += numeral
            n -= integer
    return result
```

1. This is straightforward: if the given input (n) is greater than **3999**, raise an
    OutOfRangeError exception. The unit test does not check the human-readable
    string that accompanies the exception, although you could write another test
    that did check it (but watch out for internationalization issues for strings that
    vary by the user's language or environment).

Does this make the test pass? Let's find out. See Listing 9-14.

Listing 9-14. Hooray, Your Second Test Passes

```
you@localhost:~/diveintopython3/examples$ python3 romantest2.py -v
test_to_roman_known_values (__main__.KnownValues)
to_roman should give known result with known input ... ok
test_too_large (__main__.ToRomanBadInput)
to_roman should fail with large input ... ok                          (1)

----------------------------------------------------------------

Ran 2 tests in 0.000s

OK
```

1. Hooray! Both tests pass. Because you worked iteratively, bouncing back and
    forth between testing and coding, you can be sure that the two lines of code
    you just wrote were the cause of that one test going from "fail" to "pass." That
    kind of confidence doesn't come cheap, but it will pay for itself over the
    lifetime of your code.

More Halting, More Fire

Along with testing numbers that are too large, you need to test numbers that are too small. As we
noted at the beginning of this chapter, Roman numerals cannot express 0 or negative numbers. But
Listing 9-15 shows that we have some more tests to write.

Listing 9-15. Another Bug from Negative Input

```
>>> import roman2
>>> roman2.to_roman(0)
''
>>> roman2.to_roman(-1)
''
```

Well *that's* not good. Let's add tests for each of these conditions (see Listing 9-16).

Listing 9-16. Tests for Zero and Negative Numbers

```
class ToRomanBadInput(unittest.TestCase):
    def test_too_large(self):
        '''to_roman should fail with large input'''
        self.assertRaises(roman3.OutOfRangeError, roman3.to_roman, 4000)  (1)

    def test_zero(self):
        '''to_roman should fail with 0 input'''
        self.assertRaises(roman3.OutOfRangeError, roman3.to_roman, 0)     (2)

    def test_negative(self):
        '''to_roman should fail with negative input'''
        self.assertRaises(roman3.OutOfRangeError, roman3.to_roman, -1)    (3)
```

1. The test_too_large() method has not changed since the previous step. I'm including it here to show where the new code fits.

2. Here's a new test: the test_zero() method. Like the test_too_large() method, it tells the assertRaises() method defined in unittest.TestCase to call our to_roman() function with a parameter of 0, and check that it raises the appropriate exception, OutOfRangeError.

3. The test_negative() method is almost identical, except it passes -1 to the to_roman() function. If either of these new tests does *not* raise an OutOfRangeError (either because the function returns an actual value, or because it raises some other exception), the test is considered failed.

Now check that the tests fail (see Listing 9-17):

Listing 9-17. Hooray, Your New Tests Fail

```
you@localhost:~/diveintopython3/examples$ python3 romantest3.py -v
test_to_roman_known_values (__main__.KnownValues)
to_roman should give known result with known input ... ok
test_negative (__main__.ToRomanBadInput)
to_roman should fail with negative input ... FAIL
test_too_large (__main__.ToRomanBadInput)
to_roman should fail with large input ... ok
test_zero (__main__.ToRomanBadInput)
to_roman should fail with 0 input ... FAIL

======================================================================
FAIL: to_roman should fail with negative input
----------------------------------------------------------------------
Traceback (most recent call last):
  File "romantest3.py", line 86, in test_negative
    self.assertRaises(roman3.OutOfRangeError, roman3.to_roman, -1)
AssertionError: OutOfRangeError not raised by to_roman


======================================================================
```

```
FAIL: to_roman should fail with 0 input
----------------------------------------------------------------------
Traceback (most recent call last):
  File "romantest3.py", line 82, in test_zero
    self.assertRaises(roman3.OutOfRangeError, roman3.to_roman, 0)
AssertionError: OutOfRangeError not raised by to_roman


----------------------------------------------------------------------
Ran 4 tests in 0.000s

FAILED (failures=2)
```

Excellent. Both tests failed, as expected. Now let's switch over to the code and see what we can do to make them pass (see Listing 9-18).

Listing 9-18. Catching Out-of-Range Input

```
def to_roman(n):
    '''convert integer to Roman numeral'''
    if not (0 < n < 4000):                                         (1)
        raise OutOfRangeError('number out of range (must be 1..3999)')  (2)

    result = ''
    for numeral, integer in roman_numeral_map:
        while n >= integer:
            result += numeral
            n -= integer
    return result
```

1. This is a nice Pythonic shortcut: multiple comparisons at once. This is equivalent to if not ((0 < n) and (n < 4000)), but it's much easier to read. This one line of code should catch inputs that are too large, negative, or zero.

2. If you change your conditions, make sure to update your human-readable error strings to match. The unittest framework won't care, but it'll make it difficult to do manual debugging if your code is throwing incorrectly-described exceptions.

I could present a whole series of unrelated examples to show that the multiple-comparisons-at-once shortcut works, but instead I'll just run the unit tests and prove it (see Listing 9-19).

Listing 9-19. Hooray, All Tests Pass

```
you@localhost:~/diveintopython3/examples$ python3 romantest3.py -v
test_to_roman_known_values (__main__.KnownValues)
to_roman should give known result with known input ... ok
test_negative (__main__.ToRomanBadInput)
to_roman should fail with negative input ... ok
test_too_large (__main__.ToRomanBadInput)
to_roman should fail with large input ... ok
test_zero (__main__.ToRomanBadInput)
to_roman should fail with 0 input ... ok
```

```
-------------------------------------------------------------------
Ran 4 tests in 0.016s

OK
```

And One More Thing …

There was one more functional requirement for converting numbers to Roman numerals: dealing with non-integers. Listing 9-20 shows the bug.

Listing 9-20. A Bug with Non-Integer Inputs

```
>>> import roman3
>>> roman3.to_roman(1.0)   (1)
'I'
>>> roman3.to_roman(0.5)   (2)
''
```

    1.   Oh, that's bad.

    2.   Oh, that's even worse. Both of these cases should raise an exception. Instead, they give bogus results.

Testing for non-integers is not difficult. First, define a `NonIntegerError` exception, as shown in Listing 9-21.

Listing 9-21. Defining Another Exception

```
class OutOfRangeError(ValueError): pass
class NotIntegerError(ValueError): pass
```

Next, write a test case that checks for the `NonIntegerError` exception, as shown in Listing 9-22.

Listing 9-22. Testing for Non-Integers

```
class ToRomanBadInput(unittest.TestCase):
    .
    .
    .
    def test_non_integer(self):
        '''to_roman should fail with non-integer input'''
        self.assertRaises(roman4.NotIntegerError, roman4.to_roman, 0.5)
```

Now check that the test fails properly, as shown in Listing 9-23.

Listing 9-23. Hooray, the Latest Test Fails

```
you@localhost:~/diveintopython3/examples$ python3 romantest4.py -v
test_to_roman_known_values (__main__.KnownValues)
to_roman should give known result with known input ... ok
test_negative (__main__.ToRomanBadInput)
to_roman should fail with negative input ... ok
test_non_integer (__main__.ToRomanBadInput)
to_roman should fail with non-integer input ... FAIL
test_too_large (__main__.ToRomanBadInput)
to_roman should fail with large input ... ok
test_zero (__main__.ToRomanBadInput)
to_roman should fail with 0 input ... ok


======================================================================
FAIL: to_roman should fail with non-integer input
----------------------------------------------------------------------
Traceback (most recent call last):
  File "romantest4.py", line 90, in test_non_integer
    self.assertRaises(roman4.NotIntegerError, roman4.to_roman, 0.5)
AssertionError: NotIntegerError not raised by to_roman


----------------------------------------------------------------------
Ran 5 tests in 0.000s

FAILED (failures=1)
```

Write the code that makes the test pass (see Listing 9-24).

Listing 9-24. Code to Reject Non-Integers

```
def to_roman(n):
    '''convert integer to Roman numeral'''
    if not (0 < n < 4000):
        raise OutOfRangeError('number out of range (must be 1..3999)')
    if not isinstance(n, int):                                            (1)
        raise NotIntegerError('non-integers can not be converted')        (2)

    result = ''
    for numeral, integer in roman_numeral_map:
        while n >= integer:
            result += numeral
            n -= integer
    return result
```

1. The built-in `isinstance()` function tests whether a variable is a particular type (or, technically, any descendant type).

2. If the argument n is not an `int`, raise our newly minted `NotIntegerError` exception.

Finally, check that the code does indeed make the test pass (see Listing 9-25).

Listing 9-25. Hooray, All Tests Pass

```
you@localhost:~/diveintopython3/examples$ python3 romantest4.py -v
test_to_roman_known_values (__main__.KnownValues)
to_roman should give known result with known input ... ok
test_negative (__main__.ToRomanBadInput)
to_roman should fail with negative input ... ok
test_non_integer (__main__.ToRomanBadInput)
to_roman should fail with non-integer input ... ok
test_too_large (__main__.ToRomanBadInput)
to_roman should fail with large input ... ok
test_zero (__main__.ToRomanBadInput)
to_roman should fail with 0 input ... ok

----------------------------------------------------------------------
Ran 5 tests in 0.000s

OK
```

The `to_roman()` function passes all of its tests, and I can't think of any more tests, so it's time to move on to `from_roman()`.

A Pleasing Symmetry

Converting a string from a Roman numeral to an integer sounds more difficult than converting an integer to a Roman numeral. Certainly there is the issue of validation. It's easy to check if an integer is greater than 0, but a bit harder to check whether a string is a valid Roman numeral. But we already constructed a regular expression to check for Roman numerals, so that part is done. That leaves the problem of converting the string itself. As we'll see in a minute, thanks to the rich data structure we defined to map individual Roman numerals to integer values, the nitty-gritty of the `from_roman()` function is as straightforward as the `to_roman()` function.

But first, the tests. We'll need a "known values" test to spot-check for accuracy. Our test suite already contains a mapping of known values; let's reuse that (see Listing 9-26).

Listing 9-26. Testing for Known Values Again

```
    def test_from_roman_known_values(self):
        '''from_roman should give known result with known input'''
        for integer, numeral in self.known_values:
            result = roman5.from_roman(numeral)
            self.assertEqual(integer, result)
```

There's a pleasing symmetry here. The `to_roman()` and `from_roman()` functions are inverses of each other. The first converts integers to specially formatted strings, the second converts specially formatted strings to integers. In theory, we should be able to "round-trip" a number by passing to the `to_roman()` function to get a string, then passing that string to the `from_roman()` function to get an integer, and end up with the same number.

In vaguely mathematical terms, n = from_roman(to_roman(n)) for all values of n. In this case, *all values* means any number between 1..3999, since that is the valid range of inputs to the to_roman() function. We can express this symmetry in a test case (see Listing 9-27) that runs through all the values 1..3999, calls to_roman(), calls from_roman(), and checks that the output is the same as the original input.

Listing 9-27. A Round-Trip Test

```
class RoundtripCheck(unittest.TestCase):
    def test_roundtrip(self):
        '''from_roman(to_roman(n))==n for all n'''
        for integer in range(1, 4000):
            numeral = roman5.to_roman(integer)
            result = roman5.from_roman(numeral)
            self.assertEqual(integer, result)
```

These new tests won't even fail yet. We haven't defined a from_roman() function at all, so they'll just raise errors, as shown in Listing 9-28.

Listing 9-28. Round-Trip Test Produces an Error

```
you@localhost:~/diveintopython3/examples$ python3 romantest5.py
E.E....
======================================================================
ERROR: test_from_roman_known_values (__main__.KnownValues)
from_roman should give known result with known input
----------------------------------------------------------------------
Traceback (most recent call last):
  File "romantest5.py", line 78, in test_from_roman_known_values
    result = roman5.from_roman(numeral)
AttributeError: 'module' object has no attribute 'from_roman'

======================================================================
ERROR: test_roundtrip (__main__.RoundtripCheck)
from_roman(to_roman(n))==n for all n
----------------------------------------------------------------------
Traceback (most recent call last):
  File "romantest5.py", line 103, in test_roundtrip
    result = roman5.from_roman(numeral)
AttributeError: 'module' object has no attribute 'from_roman'

----------------------------------------------------------------------
Ran 7 tests in 0.019s

FAILED (errors=2)
```

A quick stub function will solve that problem (see Listing 9-29).

Listing 9-29. A from_roman() Stub Function

```
def from_roman(s):
    '''convert Roman numeral to integer'''
```

(Hey, did you notice that? I defined a function with nothing but a docstring. That's legal Python. In fact, some programmers swear by it. "Don't stub; document!")

Now the test cases will actually fail, as shown in Listing 9-30.

Listing 9-30. Round-Trip Tests Fail (as Expected)

```
you@localhost:~/diveintopython3/examples$ python3 romantest5.py
F.F....
======================================================================
FAIL: test_from_roman_known_values (__main__.KnownValues)
from_roman should give known result with known input
----------------------------------------------------------------------
Traceback (most recent call last):
  File "romantest5.py", line 79, in test_from_roman_known_values
    self.assertEqual(integer, result)
AssertionError: 1 != None


======================================================================
FAIL: test_roundtrip (__main__.RoundtripCheck)
from_roman(to_roman(n))==n for all n
----------------------------------------------------------------------
Traceback (most recent call last):
  File "romantest5.py", line 104, in test_roundtrip
    self.assertEqual(integer, result)
AssertionError: 1 != None


----------------------------------------------------------------------
Ran 7 tests in 0.002s

FAILED (failures=2)
```

Now it's time to write the **from_roman()** function (see Listing 9-31).

Listing 9-31. The from_roman() Function

```
def from_roman(s):
    """convert Roman numeral to integer"""
    result = 0
    index = 0
    for numeral, integer in roman_numeral_map:
        while s[index:index+len(numeral)] == numeral:   (1)
            result += integer
            index += len(numeral)
    return result
```

1. The pattern here is the same as the to_roman() function. You iterate through your Roman numeral data structure (a tuple of tuples), but instead of matching the highest integer values as often as possible, you match the "highest" Roman numeral character strings as often as possible.

If you're not clear how from_roman() works, add a print statement to the end of the while loop, as shown in Listing 9-32.

Listing 9-32. Debugging the from_roman() Function

```
def from_roman(s):
    """convert Roman numeral to integer"""
    result = 0
    index = 0
    for numeral, integer in roman_numeral_map:
        while s[index:index+len(numeral)] == numeral:
            result += integer
            index += len(numeral)
            print('found', numeral, 'of length', len(numeral), ', adding', integer)

>>> import roman5
>>> roman5.from_roman('MCMLXXII')
found M , of length 1, adding 1000
found CM of length 2, adding 900
found L of length 1, adding 50
found X of length 1, adding 10
found X of length 1, adding 10
found I of length 1, adding 1
found I of length 1, adding 1
1972
```

Time to re-run the tests (see Listing 9-33).

Listing 9-33. The from_roman() Tests Pass

```
you@localhost:~/diveintopython3/examples$ python3 romantest5.py
.......
----------------------------------------------------------------------
Ran 7 tests in 0.060s

OK
```

There are two pieces of exciting news here. The first is that the from_roman() function works for good input, at least for all the known values included in the test. The second is that the "round-trip" test also passed. Combined with the known values tests, you can be reasonably sure that both the to_roman() and from_roman() functions work properly for all possible good values. This is not guaranteed; it is theoretically possible that to_roman() has a bug that produces the wrong Roman numeral for some particular set of inputs, *and* that from_roman() has a reciprocal bug that produces the same wrong integer values for exactly that set of Roman numerals that to_roman() generated incorrectly. If that possibility bothers you, write more comprehensive test cases until it doesn't bother you.

More Bad Input

Now that the `from_roman()` function works properly with good input, it's time to fit in the last piece of the puzzle: making it work properly with bad input. That means finding a way to look at a string and determine if it's a valid Roman numeral. This is inherently more difficult than validating numeric input in the `to_roman()` function, but you have a powerful tool at your disposal: regular expressions. (If you're not familiar with regular expressions, now would be a good time to read Chapter 5.)

As you saw in Chapter 5, there are several simple rules for constructing a Roman numeral, using the letters M, D, C, L, X, V, and I. Let's review the rules:

- Sometimes characters are additive. I is 1, II is 2, and III is 3. VI is 6 (literally, "5 and 1"), VII is 7, and VIII is 8.

- The tens characters (I, X, C, and M) can be repeated up to three times. At 4, you need to subtract from the next highest fives character. You can't represent 4 as IIII; instead, it is represented as IV ("1 less than 5"). 40 is written as XL ("10 less than 50"), 41 as XLI, 42 as XLII, 43 as XLIII, and then 44 as XLIV ("10 less than 50, then 1 less than 5").

- Sometimes characters are… the opposite of additive. By putting certain characters before others, you subtract from the final value. For example, at 9, you need to subtract from the next highest tens character: 8 is VIII, but 9 is IX ("1 less than 10"), not VIIII (since the I character can not be repeated four times). 90 is XC, 900 is CM.

- The fives characters can not be repeated. 10 is always represented as X, never as VV. 100 is always C, never LL.

- Roman numerals are read left to right, so the order of characters matters very much. DC is 600; CD is a completely different number (400, "100 less than 500"). CI is 101; IC is not even a valid Roman numeral (because you can't subtract 1 directly from 100; you would need to write it as XCIX, "10 less than 100, then 1 less than 10").

Thus, one useful test would be to ensure that the `from_roman()` function fails when you pass it a string with too many repeated numerals (see Listing 9-34). How many is "too many" depends on the numeral.

Listing 9-34. Testing for Too Many Repeated Numerals

```
class FromRomanBadInput(unittest.TestCase):
    def test_too_many_repeated_numerals(self):
        '''from_roman should fail with too many repeated numerals'''
        for s in ('MMMM', 'DD', 'CCCC', 'LL', 'XXXX', 'VV', 'IIII'):
            self.assertRaises(roman6.InvalidRomanNumeralError, roman6.from_roman, s)
```

Another useful test would be to check that certain patterns aren't repeated, as shown in Listing 9-35. For example, IX is 9, but IXIX is never valid.

Listing 9-35. Testing for Too Many Repeated Pairs of Numerals

```
def test_repeated_pairs(self):
    '''from_roman should fail with repeated pairs of numerals'''
    for s in ('CMCM', 'CDCD', 'XCXC', 'XLXL', 'IXIX', 'IVIV'):
        self.assertRaises(roman6.InvalidRomanNumeralError, roman6.from_roman, s)
```

A third test could check that numerals appear in the correct order, from highest to lowest value. For example, CL is 150, but LC is never valid, because the numeral for 50 can never come before the numeral for 100. This test (shown in Listing 9-36) includes a randomly chosen set of invalid antecedents: I before M, V before X, and so on.

Listing 9-36. Testing for Malformed Antecedents

```
def test_malformed_antecedents(self):
    '''from_roman should fail with malformed antecedents'''
    for s in ('IIMXCC', 'VX', 'DCM', 'CMM', 'IXIV',
              'MCMC', 'XCX', 'IVI', 'LM', 'LD', 'LC'):
        self.assertRaises(roman6.InvalidRomanNumeralError, roman6.from_roman, s)
```

Each of these tests relies the from_roman() function raising a new exception, InvalidRomanNumeralError, which we haven't defined yet. Let's define it (see Listing 9-37).

Listing 9-37. Defining an Exception for Invalid Roman Numerals

```
class InvalidRomanNumeralError(ValueError): pass
```

All three of these tests should fail, since the from_roman() function doesn't currently have any validity checking (see Listing 9-38). (If they don't fail now, then what the heck are they testing?)

Listing 9-38. Hooray, the from_roman() Tests Fail

```
you@localhost:~/diveintopython3/examples$ python3 romantest6.py
FFF.......
======================================================================
FAIL: test_malformed_antecedents (__main__.FromRomanBadInput)
from_roman should fail with malformed antecedents
----------------------------------------------------------------------
Traceback (most recent call last):
  File "romantest6.py", line 113, in test_malformed_antecedents
    self.assertRaises(roman6.InvalidRomanNumeralError, roman6.from_roman, s)
AssertionError: InvalidRomanNumeralError not raised by from_roman

======================================================================
FAIL: test_repeated_pairs (__main__.FromRomanBadInput)
from_roman should fail with repeated pairs of numerals
----------------------------------------------------------------------
```

```
Traceback (most recent call last):
  File "romantest6.py", line 107, in test_repeated_pairs
    self.assertRaises(roman6.InvalidRomanNumeralError, roman6.from_roman, s)
AssertionError: InvalidRomanNumeralError not raised by from_roman

======================================================================
FAIL: test_too_many_repeated_numerals (__main__.FromRomanBadInput)
from_roman should fail with too many repeated numerals
----------------------------------------------------------------------
Traceback (most recent call last):
  File "romantest6.py", line 102, in test_too_many_repeated_numerals
    self.assertRaises(roman6.InvalidRomanNumeralError, roman6.from_roman, s)
AssertionError: InvalidRomanNumeralError not raised by from_roman

----------------------------------------------------------------------
Ran 10 tests in 0.058s

FAILED (failures=3)
```

Now, all we need to do is add the regular expression to test for valid Roman numerals into the from_roman() function, as shown in Listing 9-39. The regular expression is lifted straight from Chapter 5.

Listing 9-39. Validating Roman Numerals

```
roman_numeral_pattern = re.compile('''
    ^                   # beginning of string
    M{0,3}              # thousands - 0 to 3 Ms
    (CM|CD|D?C{0,3})    # hundreds - 900 (CM), 400 (CD), 0-300 (0 to 3 Cs),
                        #            or 500-800 (D, followed by 0 to 3 Cs)
    (XC|XL|L?X{0,3})    # tens - 90 (XC), 40 (XL), 0-30 (0 to 3 Xs),
                        #        or 50-80 (L, followed by 0 to 3 Xs)
    (IX|IV|V?I{0,3})    # ones - 9 (IX), 4 (IV), 0-3 (0 to 3 Is),
                        #        or 5-8 (V, followed by 0 to 3 Is)
    $                   # end of string
    ''', re.VERBOSE)

def from_roman(s):
    '''convert Roman numeral to integer'''
    if not roman_numeral_pattern.search(s):
        raise InvalidRomanNumeralError('Invalid Roman numeral: {0}'.format(s))

    result = 0
    index = 0
    for numeral, integer in roman_numeral_map:
        while s[index : index + len(numeral)] == numeral:
            result += integer
            index += len(numeral)
    return result
```

And re-run the tests… (See Listing 9-40.)

Listing 9-40. Hooray, the from_roman() Tests Pass

```
you@localhost:~/diveintopython3/examples$ python3 romantest7.py
..........
----------------------------------------------------------------------
Ran 10 tests in 0.066s

OK
```

And the anticlimax award of the year goes to… the word OK, which is printed by the unittest module when all the tests pass.

CHAPTER 10

■ ■ ■

Refactoring

Despite your best efforts to write comprehensive unit tests, bugs happen. What do I mean by *bug*? A bug is a test case you haven't written yet. There's a bug in the Roman numeral converter, as shown in Listing 10-1.

Listing 10-1. A Bug

```
>>> import roman7
>>> roman7.from_roman('')      (1)
0
```

1. This is a bug. An empty string should raise an InvalidRomanNumeralError exception, just like any other sequence of characters that don't represent a valid Roman numeral.

After reproducing the bug, and before fixing it, you should write a test case that fails, thus illustrating the bug (see Listing 10-2).

Listing 10-2. A Test

```
class FromRomanBadInput(unittest.TestCase):
    .
    .
    .
    def testBlank(self):
        '''from_roman should fail with blank string'''
        self.assertRaises(roman6.InvalidRomanNumeralError, roman6.from_roman, '')      (1)
```

1. Pretty simple stuff here. Call from_roman() with an empty string, and make sure it raises an InvalidRomanNumeralError exception. The hard part was finding the bug; now that you know about it, testing for it is the easy part.

Since your code has a bug, and you now have a test case that tests this bug, the test case will fail, as shown in Listing 10-3.

Listing 10-3. A Test that Fails

```
you@localhost:~/diveintopython3/examples$ python3 romantest8.py -v
from_roman should fail with blank string ... FAIL
from_roman should fail with malformed antecedents ... ok
from_roman should fail with repeated pairs of numerals ... ok
from_roman should fail with too many repeated numerals ... ok
from_roman should give known result with known input ... ok
to_roman should give known result with known input ... ok
from_roman(to_roman(n))==n for all n ... ok
to_roman should fail with negative input ... ok
to_roman should fail with non-integer input ... ok
to_roman should fail with large input ... ok
to_roman should fail with 0 input ... ok


======================================================================
FAIL: from_roman should fail with blank string
----------------------------------------------------------------------
Traceback (most recent call last):
  File "romantest8.py", line 117, in test_blank
    self.assertRaises(roman8.InvalidRomanNumeralError, roman8.from_roman, '')
AssertionError: InvalidRomanNumeralError not raised by from_roman


----------------------------------------------------------------------
Ran 11 tests in 0.171s

FAILED (failures=1)
```

Now, you can fix the bug (see Listing 10-4).

Listing 10-4. A Bug Fix

```
def from_roman(s):
    '''convert Roman numeral to integer'''
    if not s:                                                    (1)
        raise InvalidRomanNumeralError, ('Input can not be blank')
    if not re.search(romanNumeralPattern, s):
        raise InvalidRomanNumeralError, ('Invalid Roman numeral: {}'.format(s))  (2)

    result = 0
    index = 0
    for numeral, integer in romanNumeralMap:
        while s[index:index+len(numeral)] == numeral:
            result += integer
            index += len(numeral)
    return result
```

1. Only two lines of code are required: an explicit check for an empty string and a raise statement.

2. I don't think I've mentioned this yet anywhere in this book, so let this serve as your final lesson in string formatting. Starting in Python 3.1, you can skip the numbers when using positional indexes in a format specifier. That is, instead of using the format specifier {0} to refer to the first parameter to the `format()` method, you can simply use {}, and Python will fill in the proper positional index for you. This works for any number of arguments; the first {} is {0}; the second {} is {1}, and so forth.

Listing 10-5. A Test that Passes

```
you@localhost:~/diveintopython3/examples$ python3 romantest8.py -v
from_roman should fail with blank string ... ok  (1)
from_roman should fail with malformed antecedents ... ok
from_roman should fail with repeated pairs of numerals ... ok
from_roman should fail with too many repeated numerals ... ok
from_roman should give known result with known input ... ok
to_roman should give known result with known input ... ok
from_roman(to_roman(n))==n for all n ... ok
to_roman should fail with negative input ... ok
to_roman should fail with non-integer input ... ok
to_roman should fail with large input ... ok
to_roman should fail with 0 input ... ok


----------------------------------------------------------------------
Ran 11 tests in 0.156s

OK  (2)
```

1. The blank string test case now passes, so the bug is fixed.

2. All the other test cases still pass, which means that this bug fix didn't break anything else. Stop coding.

Coding this way does not make fixing bugs any easier. Simple bugs (like the one shown in Listing 10-5) require simple test cases; complex bugs will require complex test cases. In a testing-centric environment, fixing a bug may *seem* like it takes longer than it otherwise might, since you need to articulate in code exactly what the bug is (to write the test case) and then fix the bug itself. Then, if the test case doesn't pass right away, you need to figure out whether the fix was wrong or whether the test case itself has a bug in it. However, in the long run, this back-and-forth between test code and tested code pays for itself, because bugs are more likely to be fixed correctly the first time. Also, since you can easily rerun *all* the test cases along with any new ones, you are much less likely to break old code when fixing new code. Today's unit test is tomorrow's regression test.

Handling Changing Requirements

Despite your best efforts to pin your customers to the ground and extract exact requirements from them on pain of death via horrible nasty things involving scissors and hot wax, requirements will change. Most customers don't know what they want until they see it, and even if they do, they aren't that good at articulating what they want precisely enough to be useful. Even if they do manage to articulate their needs, they'll want more in the next release anyway. Be prepared to update your test cases as requirements change.

Suppose, for instance, that you wanted to expand the range of the Roman numeral conversion functions. Normally, no character in a Roman numeral can be repeated more than three times in a row. But the Romans were willing to make an exception to that rule by having four *M* characters in a row to represent 4,000. If you make this change, you'll be able to expand the range of convertible numbers from 1 . . .3 999 to 1 . . . 4999. But first, you need to make some changes to your test cases, as shown in Listing 10-6.

Listing 10-6. Changes to Accommodate Larger Roman Numerals

```
class KnownValues(unittest.TestCase):
    known_values = ( (1, 'I'),
                    .
                    .
                    .
                    (3999, 'MMMCMXCIX'),
                    (4000, 'MMMM'),                                         (1)
                    (4500, 'MMMMD'),
                    (4888, 'MMMMDCCCLXXXVIII'),
                    (4999, 'MMMMCMXCIX') )

class ToRomanBadInput(unittest.TestCase):
    def test_too_large(self):
        '''to_roman should fail with large input'''
        self.assertRaises(roman8.OutOfRangeError, roman8.to_roman, 5000)  (2)
    .
    .
    .

class FromRomanBadInput(unittest.TestCase):
    def test_too_many_repeated_numerals(self):
        '''from_roman should fail with too many repeated numerals'''
        for s in ('MMMMM', 'DD', 'CCCC', 'LL', 'XXXX', 'VV', 'IIII'):      (3)
            self.assertRaises(roman8.InvalidRomanNumeralError, roman8.from_roman, s)
    .
    .
    .
```

```
class RoundtripCheck(unittest.TestCase):
    def test_roundtrip(self):
        '''from_roman(to_roman(n))==n for all n'''
        for integer in range(1, 5000):                          (4)
            numeral = roman8.to_roman(integer)
            result = roman8.from_roman(numeral)
            self.assertEqual(integer, result)
```

1. The existing known values don't change (they're all still reasonable values to test), but you need to add a few more in the 4,000 range. Here, I've included **4000** (the shortest), **4500** (the second shortest), **4888** (the longest), and **4999** (the largest).

2. The definition of *large input* has changed. This test used to call **to_roman()** with **4000** and expect an error; now that 4,000 to 4,999 are good values, you need to bump this up to **5000**.

3. The definition of *too many repeated numerals* has also changed. This test used to call **from_roman()** with **'MMMM'** and expect an error; now that MMMM is considered a valid Roman numeral, you need to bump this up to **'MMMMM'**.

4. The sanity check loops through every number in the range, from **1** to **3999**. Since the range has now expanded, this **for** loop needs to be updated as well, to go up to **4999**.

Now, your test cases are up to date with the new requirements, but your code is not, so you expect several of the test cases to fail, as shown in Listing 10-7.

Listing 10-7. Several Test Failures

```
you@localhost:~/diveintopython3/examples$ python3 romantest9.py -v
from_roman should fail with blank string ... ok
from_roman should fail with malformed antecedents ... ok
from_roman should fail with non-string input ... ok
from_roman should fail with repeated pairs of numerals ... ok
from_roman should fail with too many repeated numerals ... ok
from_roman should give known result with known input ... ERROR      (1)
to_roman should give known result with known input ... ERROR         (2)
from_roman(to_roman(n))==n for all n ... ERROR                       (3)
to_roman should fail with negative input ... ok
to_roman should fail with non-integer input ... ok
to_roman should fail with large input ... ok
to_roman should fail with 0 input ... ok


======================================================================
ERROR: from_roman should give known result with known input
----------------------------------------------------------------------
Traceback (most recent call last):
  File "romantest9.py", line 82, in test_from_roman_known_values
    result = roman9.from_roman(numeral)
  File "C:\home\diveintopython3\examples\roman9.py", line 60, in from_roman
    raise InvalidRomanNumeralError('Invalid Roman numeral: {0}'.format(s))
roman9.InvalidRomanNumeralError: Invalid Roman numeral: MMMM
```

```
=======================================================================
ERROR: to_roman should give known result with known input
-----------------------------------------------------------------------
Traceback (most recent call last):
  File "romantest9.py", line 76, in test_to_roman_known_values
    result = roman9.to_roman(integer)
  File "C:\home\diveintopython3\examples\roman9.py", line 42, in to_roman
    raise OutOfRangeError('number out of range (must be 0..3999)')
roman9.OutOfRangeError: number out of range (must be 0..3999)

=======================================================================
ERROR: from_roman(to_roman(n))==n for all n
-----------------------------------------------------------------------
Traceback (most recent call last):
  File "romantest9.py", line 131, in testSanity
    numeral = roman9.to_roman(integer)
  File "C:\home\diveintopython3\examples\roman9.py", line 42, in to_roman
    raise OutOfRangeError('number out of range (must be 0..3999)')
roman9.OutOfRangeError: number out of range (must be 0..3999)


-----------------------------------------------------------------------
Ran 12 tests in 0.171s

FAILED (errors=3)
```

1. The from_roman() known values test will fail as soon as it hits 'MMMM', because
    from_roman() still thinks MMMM is an invalid Roman numeral.

2. The to_roman() known values test will fail as soon as it hits 4000, because
    to_roman() still thinks this value is out of range.

3. The round-trip check will also fail as soon as it hits 4000, because to_roman()
    still thinks this value is out of range.

Now that you have test cases that fail because of the new requirements, you can think about fixing the code to bring it in line with the test cases. One thing that takes some getting used to when you first start coding unit tests is that the code being tested is never ahead of the test cases. While it's behind, you still have some work to do, and as soon as it catches up to the test cases, you stop coding (see Listing 10-8).

Listing 10-8. Code for the New Tests

```
roman_numeral_pattern = re.compile('''
    ^                       # beginning of string
    M{0,4}                  # thousands - 0 to 4 Ms  (1)
    (CM|CD|D?C{0,3})        # hundreds - 900 (CM), 400 (CD), 0-300 (0 to 3 Cs),
                            #            or 500-800 (D, followed by 0 to 3 Cs)
    (XC|XL|L?X{0,3})        # tens - 90 (XC), 40 (XL), 0-30 (0 to 3 Xs),
                            #        or 50-80 (L, followed by 0 to 3 Xs)
    (IX|IV|V?I{0,3})        # ones - 9 (IX), 4 (IV), 0-3 (0 to 3 Is),
                            #        or 5-8 (V, followed by 0 to 3 Is)
    $                       # end of string
```

```
        ''', re.VERBOSE)

def to_roman(n):
    '''convert integer to Roman numeral'''
    if not (0 < n < 5000):                        (2)
        raise OutOfRangeError('number out of range (must be 0..4999)')
    if not isinstance(n, int):
        raise NotIntegerError('non-integers can not be converted')

    result = ''
    for numeral, integer in roman_numeral_map:
        while n >= integer:
            result += numeral
            n -= integer
    return result

def from_roman(s):
    .
    .
    .
```

1. You don't need to make any changes to the from_roman() function at all. The only change is to roman_numeral_pattern. If you look closely, you'll notice that I changed the maximum number of optional M characters from 3 to 4 in the first section of the regular expression. This will allow the Roman numeral equivalents of 4,999 instead of 3,999. The actual from_roman() function is completely generic; it just looks for repeated Roman numeral characters and adds them up, without caring how many times they repeat. The only reason it didn't handle 'MMMM' before is that we explicitly stopped it with the regular expression pattern matching.

2. The to_roman() function needs only one small change, in the range check. Where you used to check 0 < n < 4000, you now check 0 < n < 5000. And you change the error message that you raise to reflect the new acceptable range (1 . . . 4999 instead of 1 . . . 3999). You don't need to make any changes to the rest of the function; it handles the new cases already. It merrily adds 'M' for each thousand that it finds; given 4000, it will spit out 'MMMM'. It didn't do this before only because we explicitly stopped it with the range check.

You may be skeptical that these two small changes are all that you need. Hey, don't take my word for it; see for yourself in Listing 10-9.

Listing 10-9. The Code that Makes the Tests Pass

```
you@localhost:~/diveintopython3/examples$ python3 romantest9.py -v
from_roman should fail with blank string ... ok
from_roman should fail with malformed antecedents ... ok
from_roman should fail with non-string input ... ok
from_roman should fail with repeated pairs of numerals ... ok
from_roman should fail with too many repeated numerals ... ok
from_roman should give known result with known input ... ok
to_roman should give known result with known input ... ok
```

```
from_roman(to_roman(n))==n for all n ... ok
to_roman should fail with negative input ... ok
to_roman should fail with non-integer input ... ok
to_roman should fail with large input ... ok
to_roman should fail with 0 input ... ok


----------------------------------------------------------------------
Ran 12 tests in 0.203s

OK  (1)
```

1.   All the test cases pass. Stop coding.
Comprehensive unit testing means never having to rely on a programmer who says, "Trust me."

Refactoring

The best thing about comprehensive unit testing is not the feeling you get when all your test cases finally pass or even the feeling you get when someone else blames you for breaking their code and you can actually *prove* that you didn't. The best thing about unit testing is that it gives you the freedom to refactor mercilessly.

Refactoring is the process of taking working code and making it work better. Usually, *better* means *faster*, although it can also mean that the code uses less memory or disk space, or simply that it performs more elegantly. Whatever *better* means to you, to your project, in your environment, refactoring is important to the long-term health of any program.

In this chapter, *better* means both *faster* and *easier to maintain*. Specifically, the `from_roman()` function is slower and more complex than I'd like, because of that big nasty regular expression that validates Roman numerals. Now, you might think, "Sure, the regular expression is big and hairy, but how else am I supposed to validate that an arbitrary string is a valid a Roman numeral?"

Here's your answer: There are only 5,000 of them; why don't you just build a lookup table? This idea gets even better when you realize that *you don't need to use regular expressions at all*. As you build the lookup table for converting integers to Roman numerals, you can build the reverse lookup table to convert Roman numerals to integers. By the time you need to check whether an arbitrary string is a valid Roman numeral, you will have collected all the valid Roman numerals. The validation process is reduced to a single dictionary lookup.

Best of all, you already have a complete set of unit tests. You can change over half the code in the module, but the unit tests will stay the same. That means you can prove — to yourself and others — that the new code works just as well as the original(see Listing 10-10).

Listing 10-10. A Completely Different Roman Numeral Converter

```
class OutOfRangeError(ValueError): pass
class NotIntegerError(ValueError): pass
class InvalidRomanNumeralError(ValueError): pass

roman_numeral_map = (('M',  1000),
                     ('CM', 900),
                     ('D',  500),
                     ('CD', 400),
                     ('C',  100),
                     ('XC', 90),
```

```
                        ('L',  50),
                        ('XL', 40),
                        ('X',  10),
                        ('IX', 9),
                        ('V',  5),
                        ('IV', 4),
                        ('I',  1))

to_roman_table = [ None ]
from_roman_table = {}

def to_roman(n):
    '''convert integer to Roman numeral'''
    if not (0 < n < 5000):
        raise OutOfRangeError('number out of range (must be 1..4999)')
    if int(n) != n:
        raise NotIntegerError('non-integers can not be converted')
    return to_roman_table[n]

def from_roman(s):
    '''convert Roman numeral to integer'''
    if not isinstance(s, str):
        raise InvalidRomanNumeralError('Input must be a string')
    if not s:
        raise InvalidRomanNumeralError('Input can not be blank')
    if s not in from_roman_table:
        raise InvalidRomanNumeralError('Invalid Roman numeral: {0}'.format(s))
    return from_roman_table[s]

def build_lookup_tables():
    def to_roman(n):
        result = ''
        for numeral, integer in roman_numeral_map:
            if n >= integer:
                result = numeral
                n -= integer
                break
        if n > 0:
            result += to_roman_table[n]
        return result

    for integer in range(1, 5000):
        roman_numeral = to_roman(integer)
        to_roman_table.append(roman_numeral)
        from_roman_table[roman_numeral] = integer

build_lookup_tables()
```

Let's break down Listing 10-10 into digestible pieces. Arguably, the most important line is the last one, as shown in Listing 10-11.

Listing 10-11. The Most Important Line

```
build_lookup_tables()
```

You will note that is a function call, but there's no `if` statement around it. This is not an `if __name__ == '__main__'` block; it gets called *when the module is imported*. It is important to understand that modules are only imported once and then cached. Importing an already-imported module does nothing, so this code will get called only the first time you import this module.

What does the `build_lookup_tables()` function do? Listing 10-12 illustrates.

Listing 10-12. Building a Lookup Table

```
to_roman_table = [ None ]
from_roman_table = {}
  .
  .
  .
def build_lookup_tables():
    def to_roman(n):                              (1)
        result = ''
        for numeral, integer in roman_numeral_map:
            if n >= integer:
                result = numeral
                n -= integer
                break
        if n > 0:
            result += to_roman_table[n]
        return result

    for integer in range(1, 5000):
        roman_numeral = to_roman(integer)         (2)
        to_roman_table.append(roman_numeral)      (3)
        from_roman_table[roman_numeral] = integer
```

1. This is a clever bit of programming, perhaps too clever. The `to_roman()` function is defined in Listing 10-10; it looks up values in the lookup table and returns them. But the `build_lookup_tables()` function redefines the `to_roman()` function to actually do work (like the previous examples did, before you added a lookup table). Within the `build_lookup_tables()` function, calling `to_roman()` will call this redefined version. Once the `build_lookup_tables()` function exits, the redefined version disappears — it is only defined in the local scope of the `build_lookup_tables()` function.

2. This line of code will call the redefined `to_roman()` function, which actually calculates the Roman numeral.

3. Once you have the result (from the redefined `to_roman()` function), you add the integer and its Roman numeral equivalent to both lookup tables.

Once the lookup tables are built, the rest of the code runs quickly (see Listing 10-13).

Listing 10-13. New to_roman() and from_roman() Functions

```
def to_roman(n):
    '''convert integer to Roman numeral'''
    if not (0 < n < 5000):
        raise OutOfRangeError('number out of range (must be 1..4999)')
    if int(n) != n:
        raise NotIntegerError('non-integers can not be converted')
    return to_roman_table[n]                                    (1)

def from_roman(s):
    '''convert Roman numeral to integer'''
    if not isinstance(s, str):
        raise InvalidRomanNumeralError('Input must be a string')
    if not s:
        raise InvalidRomanNumeralError('Input can not be blank')
    if s not in from_roman_table:
        raise InvalidRomanNumeralError('Invalid Roman numeral: {0}'.format(s))
    return from_roman_table[s]                                  (2)
```

1. After doing the same bounds checking as before, the to_roman() function simply finds the appropriate value in the lookup table and returns it.

2. Similarly, the from_roman() function is reduced to some bounds checking and one line of code: no more regular expressions and no more looping. This code converts to and from Roman numerals in constant time.

But does it work? Why yes, yes it does. And Listing 10-14 proves it.

Listing 10-14. The New Roman Numeral Converter Works

```
you@localhost:~/diveintopython3/examples$ python3 romantest10.py -v
from_roman should fail with blank string ... ok
from_roman should fail with malformed antecedents ... ok
from_roman should fail with non-string input ... ok
from_roman should fail with repeated pairs of numerals ... ok
from_roman should fail with too many repeated numerals ... ok
from_roman should give known result with known input ... ok
to_roman should give known result with known input ... ok
from_roman(to_roman(n))==n for all n ... ok
to_roman should fail with negative input ... ok
to_roman should fail with non-integer input ... ok
to_roman should fail with large input ... ok
to_roman should fail with 0 input ... ok

----------------------------------------------------------------------
Ran 12 tests in 0.031s                                         (1)

OK
```

1. Not that you asked, but it's fast, too — almost ten times as fast! Of course, the comparison isn't not entirely fair, because this version takes longer to import (when it builds the lookup tables). But since the import is only done once, the startup cost is amortized over all the calls to the `to_roman()` and `from_roman()` functions. Since the tests make several thousand function calls (the roundtrip test alone makes 10,000), this savings adds up in a hurry!

The moral of the story?

- Simplicity is a virtue — especially when regular expressions are involved.

- Unit tests can give you the confidence to do large-scale refactoring.

Unit testing is a powerful concept that, if properly implemented, can both reduce maintenance costs and increase flexibility in any long-term project. It is also important to understand that unit testing is not a panacea, a magic problem solver, or a silver bullet. Writing good test cases is hard, and keeping them up to date takes discipline (especially when customers are screaming for critical bug fixes).

Unit testing is not a replacement for other forms of testing, including functional testing, integration testing, and user acceptance testing. But it is feasible, and it does work, and once you've seen it work, you'll wonder how you ever got along without it.

Further Reading Online

For further information on unit testing, visit these sites:

- `unittest` *module*: http://docs.python.org/3.1/library/unittest.html

- *"Simple Smalltalk Testing: With Patterns" by Kent Beck*: This is the article that spawned a thousand unit testing frameworks, including Python's `unittest` module, and it's available at http://www.xprogramming.com/testfram.htm.

CHAPTER 11

∎∎∎

Files

My Windows laptop had 38,493 files before I installed a single application. Installing Python 3 added almost 3,000 files to that total. Files are the primary storage paradigm of every major operating system; the concept is so ingrained that most people would have trouble imagining an alternative. Your computer is, metaphorically speaking, drowning in files.

Reading from Text Files

Before you can read from a file, you need to open it. Opening a file in Python couldn't be easier (see Listing 11-1).

Listing 11-1. Opening a Text File

```
a_file = open('examples/chinese.txt', encoding='utf-8')
```

Python has a built-in open() function, which takes a file name as an argument. Here the file name is 'examples/chinese.txt'. There are five interesting things about this file name:

- It's not just the name of a file; it's a combination of a directory path and a file name. A hypothetical file-opening function could have taken two arguments a directory path and a file name but the open() function takes only one. In Python, whenever you need a "file name," you can include some or all of a directory path as well.

- The directory path uses a forward slash, but I didn't say what operating system I was using. Windows uses backward slashes to denote subdirectories, whereas Mac OS X and Linux use forward slashes. But in Python, forward slashes always Just Work, even on Windows.

- The directory path does not begin with a slash or a drive letter, so it is called a *relative path*. Relative to what, you might ask? (Patience, Grasshopper.)

- It's a string. All modern operating systems (even Windows!) use Unicode to store the names of files and directories. Python 3 fully supports non-ASCII pathnames.

- It doesn't need to be on your local disk. You might have a network drive mounted. That "file" might be a figment of an entirely virtual file system. If your computer considers it a file and can access it as a file, Python can open it.

But that call to the open() function didn't stop at the file name. There's another argument, called encoding. Oh dear, that sounds dreadfully familiar (see Chapter 4).

Character Encoding Rears Its Ugly Head

Bytes are bytes; characters are an abstraction. A string is a sequence of Unicode characters. But a file on disk is not a sequence of Unicode characters; a file on disk is a sequence of bytes. So if you read a "text file" from disk, how does Python convert that sequence of bytes into a sequence of characters? It decodes the bytes according to a specific character-encoding algorithm and returns a sequence of Unicode characters (otherwise known as a string). Listing 11-2 shows what can happen if you forget the encoding parameter when opening a text file.

Listing 11-2. Opening a Text File Without an Encoding Parameter

```
# This example was created on Windows. Other platforms may
# behave differently, for reasons outlined below.
>>> file = open('examples/chinese.txt')
>>> a_string = file.read()
Traceback (most recent call last):
  File "<stdin>", line 1, in <module>
  File "C:\Python31\lib\encodings\cp1252.py", line 23, in decode
    return codecs.charmap_decode(input,self.errors,decoding_table)[0]
UnicodeDecodeError: 'charmap' codec can't decode byte 0x8f in position 28: character
 maps to <undefined>
>>>
```

What just happened? You didn't specify a character encoding, so Python is forced to use the default encoding. What's the default encoding? If you look closely at the traceback, you can see that it's dying in cp1252.py, meaning that Python is using CP-1252 as the default encoding here. (CP-1252 is a common encoding on computers running Microsoft Windows.) The CP-1252 character set doesn't support the characters that are in this file, so the read fails with an ugly UnicodeDecodeError.

But wait, it's worse than that! The default encoding is *platform-dependent*, so this code *might* work on your computer (if your default encoding is UTF-8), but then it will fail when you distribute it to someone else (whose default encoding is different, like CP-1252).

■ If you need to get the default character encoding, import the `locale` module and call `locale.getpreferredencoding()`. On my Windows laptop, it returns `'cp1252'`, but on my Linux box upstairs, it returns `'UTF8'`. I can't even maintain consistency in my own house! Your results may be different (even on Windows), depending on which version of your operating system you have installed and how your regional/language settings are configured. This is why it's so important to specify the encoding every time you open a file.

Stream Objects

So far, all we know is that Python has a built-in function called `open()`. The `open()` function returns a *stream object*, which has methods and attributes for getting information about and manipulating a stream of characters (see Listing 11-3).

Listing 11-3. Attributes of a Stream Object

```
>>> a_file = open('examples/chinese.txt', encoding='utf-8')
>>> a_file.name                                             (1)
'examples/chinese.txt'
>>> a_file.encoding                                         (2)
'utf-8'
>>> a_file.mode                                             (3)
'r'
```

The following notes refer to the numbered lines in Listing 11-3:

1. The `name` attribute reflects the name you passed in to the open() function when you opened the file. It is not normalized to an absolute pathname.

2. Likewise, the encoding attribute reflects the encoding you passed in to the open() function. If you didn't specify the encoding when you opened the file (bad developer!), the encoding attribute will reflect `locale.getpreferredencoding()`.

3. The mode attribute tells you in which mode the file was opened. You can pass an optional mode parameter to the open() function. You didn't specify a mode when you opened this file, so Python defaults to `'r'`, which means "open for reading only in text mode." As you'll see later in this chapter, the file mode serves several purposes; different modes let you write to a file, append to a file, or open a file in binary mode (in which you deal with bytes instead of strings).

■ The documentation for the `open()` function lists all the possible file modes: `http://docs.python.org/3.1/library/io.html#module-interface`

Reading Data from a Text File

After you open a file for reading, you'll probably want to read from it at some point. Listing 11-4 shows you how to do that.

Listing 11-4. Reading from a Text File

```
>>> a_file = open('examples/chinese.txt', encoding='utf-8')
>>> a_file.read()                                               (1)
'Dive Into Python 是为有经验的程序员编写的一本 Python 书\n'
>>> a_file.read()                                               (2)
''
```

1. Once you open a file (with the correct encoding), reading from it is just a matter of calling the stream object's **read( )** method. The result is a string.

2. Somewhat surprisingly, reading the file again does not raise an exception. Python does not consider reading past end-of-file to be an error; it simply returns an empty string.

What if you want to re-read a file? See Listing 11-5.

Listing 11-5. Reading from the Same Text File Twice

```
>>> a_file.read()                       (1)
''
>>> a_file.seek(0)                      (2)
0
>>> a_file.read(16)                     (3)
'Dive Into Python'
>>> a_file.read(1)                      (4)
' '
>>> a_file.read(1)
'是'
>>> a_file.tell()                       (5)
20
```

1. Because you're still at the end of the file, further calls to the stream object's **read( )** method simply return an empty string.

2. The **seek( )** method moves to a specific byte position in a file.

3. The read() method can take an optional parameter: the number of characters to read.

4. If you like, you can even read one character at a time.

5. 16 + 1 + 1 = ... 20?

Let's try that again (see Listing 11-6).

Listing 11-6. Reading from a Specific Position

```
>>> a_file.seek(17)              (1)
17
>>> a_file.read(1)               (2)
'是'
>>> a_file.tell()                (3)
20
```

1. Move to the 17th byte.

2. Read one character.

3. Now you're on the 20th byte.

Do you see it yet? The seek() and tell() methods always count *bytes*, but because you opened this file as text, the read() method counts *characters*. Chinese characters require multiple bytes to encode in UTF-8. The English characters in the file require only one byte each, so you might be misled into thinking that the seek() and read() methods are counting the same thing. But that's true for only some characters.

But wait, it gets worse! (See Listing 11-7.)

Listing 11-7. Mismatch Between Bytes and Characters

```
>>> a_file.seek(18)                     (1)
18
>>> a_file.read(1)                      (2)
Traceback (most recent call last):
  File "<pyshell#12>", line 1, in <module>
    a_file.read(1)
  File "C:\Python31\lib\codecs.py", line 300, in decode
    (result, consumed) = self._buffer_decode(data, self.errors, final)
UnicodeDecodeError: 'utf8' codec can't decode byte 0x98 in position 0: unexpected code byte
```

1. Move to the 18th byte and try to read one character.

2. Why does this fail? Because there isn't a character at the 18th byte. The nearest character starts at the 17th byte (and goes for 3 bytes). Trying to read a character from the middle will fail with a UnicodeDecodeError.

Closing Files

Open files consume system resources, and, depending on the file mode, other programs might not be able to access them. It's important to close files as soon as you're finished with them, as shown in Listing 11-8.

Listing 11-8. Closing an Open Stream Object

```
>>> a_file.close()
```

Well *that* was anticlimactic.

The stream object `a_file` still exists. Calling its `close()` method doesn't destroy the object itself, but it's not terribly useful anymore (see Listing 11-9).

Listing 11-9. Accessing a Closed Stream Object

```
>>> a_file.read()                       (1)
Traceback (most recent call last):
  File "<pyshell#24>", line 1, in <module>
    a_file.read()
ValueError: I/O operation on closed file.
>>> a_file.seek(0)                      (2)
Traceback (most recent call last):
  File "<pyshell#25>", line 1, in <module>
    a_file.seek(0)
ValueError: I/O operation on closed file.
>>> a_file.tell()                       (3)
Traceback (most recent call last):
  File "<pyshell#26>", line 1, in <module>
    a_file.tell()
ValueError: I/O operation on closed file.
>>> a_file.close()                      (4)
>>> a_file.closed                       (5)
True
```

1. You can't read from a closed file; it raises an **IOError** exception.

2. You can't seek in a closed file, either.

3. There's no current position in a closed file, so the `tell()` method also fails.

4. Perhaps surprisingly, calling the `close()` method on a stream object whose file has been closed does *not* raise an exception. It's just a no-op.

5. Closed stream objects do have one useful attribute: the `closed` attribute will confirm that the file is closed.

Closing Files Automatically

Stream objects have an explicit `close()` method, but what happens if your code has a bug and crashes before you call `close()`? That file could theoretically stay open for much longer than necessary. While you're debugging on your local computer, that's not a big deal. On a production server, maybe it is.

Python 2 had a solution for this: the `try..finally` block. That still works in Python 3, and you might see it in other people's code or in older code that was ported to Python 3. But Python 2.5 introduced a cleaner solution, which is now the preferred solution in Python 3: the `with` statement (see Listing 11-10).

Listing 11-10. Closing a Stream Object Automatically

```
with open('examples/chinese.txt', encoding='utf-8') as a_file:
    a_file.seek(17)
    a_character = a_file.read(1)
    print(a_character)
```

This code calls `open()`, but it never calls `a_file.close()`. The `with` statement starts a code block like an `if` statement or a `for` loop. Inside this code block, you can use the variable `a_file` as the stream object returned from the call to `open()`. All the regular stream object methods are available: `seek()`, `read()`, or whatever you need. When the `with` block ends, Python calls `a_file.close()` automatically.

Here's the kicker: no matter how or when you exit the `with` block, Python will close that file   even if you "exit" it via an unhandled exception. That's right; even if your code raises an exception and your entire program comes to a screeching halt, that file will get closed. Guaranteed.

In technical terms, the `with` statement creates a *runtime context*. In these examples, the stream object acts as a *context manager*. Python creates the stream object `a_file` and tells it that it is entering a runtime context. When the `with` code block is completed, Python tells the stream object that it is exiting the runtime context, and the stream object calls its own `close()` method. See Appendix B for details.

There's nothing file-specific about the `with` statement; it's just a generic framework for creating runtime contexts and telling objects that they're entering and exiting a runtime context. If the object in question is a stream object, it does useful file-like things (such as closing the file automatically). But that behavior is defined in the stream object, not in the `with` statement. There are lots of other ways to use context managers that have nothing to do with files. You can even create your own, as you'll see later in this chapter.

Reading Data One Line at a Time

A *line* of a text file is just what you think it is—you type a few words, press Enter, and now you're on a new line. A line of text is a sequence of characters delimited by... what exactly? Well, it's complicated because text files can use several different characters to mark the end of a line. Every operating system has its own convention. Some use a carriage return character, others use a line feed character, and some use both characters at the end of every line.

Now breathe a sigh of relief, because *Python handles line endings automatically* by default. If you say, "I want to read this text file one line at a time," Python will figure out which kind of line ending the text file uses and it will all Just Work.

■ If you need fine-grained control over what's considered a line ending, you can pass the optional `newline` parameter to the `open()` function.

So, how do you actually do it? Read a file one line at a time, that is. It's so simple, it's beautiful (see Listing 11-11).

Listing 11-11. So Simple, It's Beautiful

```
line_number = 0
with open('examples/favorite-people.txt', encoding='utf-8') as a_file:   (1)
    for a_line in a_file:                                                 (2)
        line_number += 1
        print('{:>4} {}'.format(line_number, a_line.rstrip()))           (3)
```

1. Using the `with` pattern, you safely open the file and let Python close it for you.

2. To read a file one line at a time, use a `for` loop. That's it. Besides having explicit methods such as `read()`, *the stream object is also an iterator* that spits out a single line every time you ask for a value.

3. Using the `format()` string method, you can print out the line number and the line itself. The format specifier `{:>4}` means "print this argument right-justified within four spaces." The `a_line` variable contains the complete line, carriage returns and all. The `rstrip()` string method removes the trailing whitespace, including the carriage return characters.

Listing 11-12 shows the output.

Listing 11-12. My Favorite People (in No Particular Order)

```
you@localhost:~/diveintopython3$ python3 examples/oneline.py
   1 Dora
   2 Ethan
   3 Wesley
   4 John
   5 Anne
   6 Mike
   7 Chris
   8 Sarah
   9 Alex
  10 Lizzie
```

■ Did you get this error?

```
you@localhost:~/diveintopython3$ python3 examples/oneline.py
Traceback (most recent call last):
  File "examples/oneline.py", line 4, in <module>
    print('{:>4} {}'.format(line_number, a_line.rstrip()))
ValueError: zero length field name in format
```

If so, you're probably using Python 3.0. You should really upgrade to Python 3.1.

Python 3.0 supported string formatting, but only with explicitly numbered format specifiers. Python 3.1 allows you to omit the argument indexes in your format specifiers. Here is the Python 3.0-compatible version for comparison:

```
print('{0:>4} {1}'.format(line_number, a_line.rstrip()))
```

Writing to Text Files

You can write to files in much the same way that you read from them. First, you open a file and get a stream object, then you use methods on the stream object to write data to the file, and then you close the file.

To open a file for writing, use the open() function and specify the write mode. There are two file modes for writing:

- *Write mode* will overwrite the file. Pass mode='w' to the open() function.

- *Append mode* will add data to the end of the file. Pass mode='a' to the open() function.

Either mode will create the file automatically if it doesn't already exist, so there's never a need for any sort of fiddly "if the file doesn't exist yet, create a new empty file just so you can open it for the first time" function. Just open a file and start writing.

You should always close a file as soon as you're done writing to it in order to release the file handle and ensure that the data is actually written to disk. As with reading data from a file, you can call the stream object's close() method, or you can use the with statement and let Python close the file for you. I bet you can guess which technique I recommend (see Listing 11-13).

Listing 11-13. *Writing to Text Files Using the with Statement*

```
>>> with open('test.log', mode='w', encoding='utf-8') as a_file:   (1)
...     a_file.write('test succeeded')                             (2)
>>> with open('test.log', encoding='utf-8') as a_file:
...     print(a_file.read())
test succeeded
>>> with open('test.log', mode='a', encoding='utf-8') as a_file:   (3)
...     a_file.write('and again')
>>> with open('test.log', encoding='utf-8') as a_file:
...     print(a_file.read())
test succeededand again                                            (4)
```

1. You start boldly by creating the new file `test.log` (or overwriting the existing file) and opening the file for writing. The `mode='w'` parameter means open the file for writing. Yes, that's as dangerous as it sounds. I hope you didn't care about the previous contents of that file (if any) because that data is gone now.

2. You can add data to the newly opened file with the `write` method of the stream object returned by the `open()` function. After the `with` block ends, Python automatically closes the file.

3. That was so much fun; let's do it again. But this time, with `mode='a'` to append to the file instead of overwriting it. Appending will *never* harm the existing contents of the file.

4. Both the original line you wrote and the second line you appended are now in the `test.log` file. Also note that carriage returns are not included. Because you didn't write them explicitly to the file either time, the file doesn't include them. You can write a carriage return with the `'\n'` character. Because you didn't do this, everything you wrote to the file ended up on one line.

Character Encoding Again

Did you notice the `encoding` parameter that got passed in to the `open()` function while you were opening a file for writing? It's important; don't ever leave it out! As you saw in the beginning of this chapter, files don't contain *strings*, they contain *bytes*. Reading a string from a text file works only because you told Python what encoding to use to read a stream of bytes and convert it to a string. Writing text to a file presents the same problem in reverse. You can't write characters to a file; characters are an abstraction. In order to write to the file, Python needs to know how to convert your string into a sequence of bytes. The only way to be sure it's performing the correct conversion is to specify the `encoding` parameter when you open the file for writing.

Binary Files

Not all files contain text. Some of them contain pictures of my dog (see Listing 11-14).

Listing 11-14. Reading Binary Files

```
>>> an_image = open('examples/beauregard.jpg', mode='rb')           (1)
>>> an_image.mode                                                   (2)
'rb'
>>> an_image.name                                                  (3)
'examples/beauregard.jpg'
>>> an_image.encoding                                              (4)
Traceback (most recent call last):
  File "<stdin>", line 1, in <module>
AttributeError: '_io.BufferedReader' object has no attribute 'encoding'
```

1. Opening a file in binary mode is simple but subtle. The only difference from opening it in text mode is that the mode parameter contains a 'b' character.

2. The stream object you get from opening a file in binary mode has many of the same attributes, including mode, which reflects the mode parameter you passed into the open() function.

3. Binary stream objects also have a name attribute, just like text stream objects.

4. Here's one difference, though: a binary stream object has no encoding attribute. That makes sense, right? You're reading (or writing) bytes, not strings, so there's no conversion for Python to do. What you get out of a binary file is exactly what you put into it, no conversion necessary.

Did I mention you're reading bytes? Oh yes you are (see Listing 11-15).

Listing 11-15. Binary Files Contain Bytes, Not Characters

```
>>> an_image.tell()
0
>>> data = image.read(3)      (1)
>>> data
b'\xff\xd8\xff'
>>> type(data)                (2)
<class 'bytes'>
>>> an_image.tell()           (3)
3
>>> an_image.seek(0)
0
>>> data = an_image.read()
>>> len(data)
3150
```

1.   Like text files, you can read binary files a little bit at a time. But there's a crucial difference.

2.   Here's the difference: you're reading bytes, not strings. Because you opened the file in binary mode, the **read()** method takes *the number of bytes to read*, not the number of characters.

3.   That means that there's never an unexpected mismatch between the number you passed into the **read()** method and the position index you get out of the **tell()** method. The **read()** method reads bytes, and the **seek()** and **tell()** methods track the number of bytes read. For binary files, they'll always agree.

Streams Objects from Nonfile Sources

Imagine that you're writing a library, and one of your library functions will read some data from a file. The function could simply take a file name as a string, go open the file for reading, read it, and close it before exiting. But you shouldn't do that. Instead, your API should take *an arbitrary stream object*.

In the simplest case, a stream object is anything with a **read()** method that takes an optional **size** parameter and returns a string. When called with no **size** parameter, the **read()** method should read everything there is to read from the input source and return all the data as a single value. When called with a **size** parameter, it reads that much from the input source and returns that much data. When called again, it picks up where it left off and returns the next chunk of data.

That sounds exactly like the stream object you get from opening a real file. The difference is that *you're not limiting yourself to real files*. The input source that's being "read" could be anything: a web page, a string in memory, or even the output of another program. As long as your functions take a stream object and simply call the object's **read()** method, you can handle any input source that acts like a file, without specific code to handle each kind of input. Listing 11-16 shows how it all works.

Listing 11-16. A Fake File

```
>>> a_string = 'PapayaWhip is the new black.'
>>> import io                               (1)
>>> a_file = io.StringIO(a_string)          (2)
>>> a_file.read()                           (3)
'PapayaWhip is the new black.'
>>> a_file.read()                           (4)
''
>>> a_file.seek(0)                          (5)
0
>>> a_file.read(10)                         (6)
'PapayaWhip'
>>> a_file.tell()
10
>>> a_file.seek(18)
18
>>> a_file.read()
'new black.'
```

1. The `io` module defines the `StringIO` class that you can use to treat a string in memory as a file.

2. To create a stream object out of a string, create an instance of the `io.StringIO()` class and pass it the string you want to use as your "file" data. Now you have a stream object and you can do all sorts of stream-like things with it.

3. Calling the `read()` method "reads" the entire "file" that, in the case of a `StringIO` object, simply returns the original string.

4. Just like a real file, calling the `read()` method again returns an empty string.

5. You can explicitly seek to the beginning of the string, just like seeking through a real file, by using the `seek()` method of the `StringIO` object.

6. You can also read the string in chunks by passing a `size` parameter to the `read()` method.

■ `io.StringIO` lets you treat a string as a text file. There's also an `io.BytesIO` class, which lets you treat a byte array as a binary file.

Handling Compressed Files

The Python standard library contains modules that support reading and writing compressed files. There are a number of different compression schemes; the two most popular on non-Windows systems are gzip and bzip2. (You might have also encountered PKZIP archives and GNU Tar archives. Python has modules for them, too.)

The `gzip` module lets you create a stream object for reading or writing a gzip-compressed file. The stream object it gives you supports the `read()` method (if you opened it for reading) or the `write()` method (if you opened it for writing). That means you can use the methods you've already learned for regular files to *directly read or write a gzip-compressed file*, without creating a temporary file to store the decompressed data.

As an added bonus, it supports the `with` statement, too, so you can let Python automatically close your gzip-compressed file when you're done with it, as shown in Listing 11-17.

Listing 11-17. Reading Directly from a Compressed File

```
you@localhost:~$ python3
>>> import gzip
>>> with gzip.open('out.log.gz', mode='wb') as z_file:                          (1)
...     z_file.write('A nine mile walk is no joke, especially in the rain.'.encode('utf-8'))
...
>>> exit()
you@localhost:~$ ls -l out.log.gz                                               (2)
-rw-r--r--  1 mark mark     79 2009-07-19 14:29 out.log.gz
you@localhost:~$ gunzip out.log.gz                                              (3)
you@localhost:~$ cat out.log                                                    (4)
```

```
A nine mile walk is no joke, especially in the rain.
```

1. You should always open gzipped files in binary mode. (Note the `'b'` character in the mode argument.)

2. I constructed this example on Linux. If you're not familiar with the command line, this command is showing the *long listing* of the gzip-compressed file you just created in the Python shell. This Listing shows that the file exists and that it is 79 bytes long. That's actually larger than the string you started with! The gzip file format includes a fixed-length header that contains some metadata about the file, so it's inefficient for extremely small files.

3. The `gunzip` command (pronounced "gee-unzip") decompresses the file and stores the contents in a new file named the same as the compressed file but without the `.gz` file extension.

4. The `cat` command displays the contents of a file. This file contains the string you originally wrote directly to the compressed file `out.log.gz` from within the Python shell.

Standard Input, Output, and Error

Command-line gurus are already familiar with the concept of standard input, standard output, and standard error. This section is for the rest of us.

Standard output and standard error (commonly abbreviated `stdout` and `stderr`) are pipes that are built into every UNIX-like system, including Mac OS X and Linux. When you call the `print()` function, the thing you're printing is sent to the `stdout` pipe. When your program crashes and prints out a traceback, it goes to the `stderr` pipe. By default, both of these pipes are just connected to the terminal window where you are working; when your program prints something, you see the output in your terminal window (see Listing 11-18), and when a program crashes, you see the traceback in your terminal window too. In the graphical Python shell, the `stdout` and `stderr` pipes default to your "interactive window."

Listing 11-18. Understanding Standard Output

```
>>> for i in range(3):
...     print('PapayaWhip')          (1)
PapayaWhip
PapayaWhip
PapayaWhip
>>> import sys
>>> for i in range(3):
... sys.stdout.write('is the')       (2)
is theis theis the
>>> for i in range(3):
... sys.stderr.write('new black')    (3)
new blacknew blacknew black
```

1. The `print()` statement in a loop. Nothing surprising here.

2. `stdout` is defined in the `sys` module, and it is a stream object. Calling its `write` function will print out whatever string you give it. In fact, this is what the `print` function really does   it adds a carriage return to the end of the string you're printing and calls `sys.stdout.write`.

3. In the simplest case, `sys.stdout` and `sys.stderr` send their output to the same place: the Python IDE (if you're in one), or the terminal (if you're running Python from the command line). Like standard output, standard error does not add carriage returns for you. If you want carriage returns, you'll need to write carriage return characters.

`sys.stdout` and `sys.stderr` are stream objects, but they are write-only. Attempting to call their `read()` method will always raise an `IOError`, as shown in Listing 11-19.

Listing 11-19. Standard Output is Write-Only

```
>>> import sys
>>> sys.stdout.read()
Traceback (most recent call last):
  File "<stdin>", line 1, in <module>
IOError: not readable
```

Redirecting Standard Output

`sys.stdout` and `sys.stderr` are stream objects, albeit ones that support only writing. But they're not constants; they're variables. That means you can assign them a new value—any other stream object— to redirect their output, as shown in Listing 11-20.

Listing 11-20. Redirecting Standard Output

```
import sys
class RedirectStdoutTo:
    def __init__(self, out_new):
        self.out_new = out_new
    def __enter__(self):
        self.out_old = sys.stdout
        sys.stdout = self.out_new
    def __exit__(self, *args):
        sys.stdout = self.out_old
print('A')
with open('out.log', mode='w', encoding='utf-8') as a_file, RedirectStdoutTo(a_file):
    print('B')
print('C')
```

Listing 11-21 shows where each printed string went.

Listing 11-21. Redirected Output

```
you@localhost:~/diveintopython3/examples$ python3 stdout.py
A
C
you@localhost:~/diveintopython3/examples$ cat out.log
B
```

■ Did you get this error?

```
you@localhost:~/diveintopython3/examples$ python3 stdout.py
  File "stdout.py", line 15
    with open('out.log', mode='w', encoding='utf-8') as a_file, RedirectStdoutTo(a_file):
                                                                                       ^
SyntaxError: invalid syntax
```

If so, you're probably using Python 3.0. You should really upgrade to Python 3.1.

Python 3.0 supported the with statement, but each statement can use only one context manager. Python 3.1 allows you to chain multiple context managers in a single with statement.

Let's take the last part first (see Listing 11-22).

Listing 11-22. A Complicated "with" Statement

```
print('A')
with open('out.log', mode='w', encoding='utf-8') as a_file, RedirectStdoutTo(a_file):
    print('B')
print('C')
```

That's a complicated with statement. Let's rewrite it as something more recognizable (see Listing 11-23).

Listing 11-23. Nested "with" Statements

```
with open('out.log', mode='w', encoding='utf-8') as a_file:
    with RedirectStdoutTo(a_file):
        print('B')
```

As Listing 11-23 shows, you actually have *two* with statements, one nested within the scope of the other. The "outer" with statement should be familiar by now: it opens a UTF-8-encoded text file named out.log for writing and assigns the stream object to a variable named a_file. But that's not the only thing odd here (see Listing 11-24).

Listing 11-24. A "with" statement without an "as" clause

```
with RedirectStdoutTo(a_file):
```

Where's the as clause? The with statement doesn't actually require one. Just as you can call a function and ignore its return value, you can have a with statement that doesn't assign the with context to a variable. In this case, you're only interested in the side effects of the RedirectStdoutTo context.

What are those side effects? Take a look inside the RedirectStdoutTo class. This class is a custom context manager. Any class can be a context manager by defining two special methods: __enter__() and __exit__(), as shown in Listing 11-25.

Listing 11-25. A Custom Context Manager

```
class RedirectStdoutTo:
    def __init__(self, out_new):      (1)
        self.out_new = out_new
    def __enter__(self):              (2)
        self.out_old = sys.stdout
        sys.stdout = self.out_new
    def __exit__(self, *args):        (3)
        sys.stdout = self.out_old
```

1. The __init__() method is called immediately after an instance is created. It takesw one parameter: the stream object that you want to use as standard output for the life of the context. This method just saves the stream object in an instance variable so other methods can use it later.

2. The __enter__() method is a special class method; Python calls it when entering a context (that is, at the beginning of the with statement). This method saves the current value of sys.stdout in self.out_old; then redirects standard output by assigning self.out_new to sys.stdout.

3. The __exit__() method is another special class method; Python calls it when exiting the context (that is, at the end of the with statement). This method restores standard output to its original value by assigning the saved self.out_old value to sys.stdout.

Listing 11-26 puts it all together.

Listing 11-26. Putting it All Together

```
print('A')                                                              (1)
with open('out.log', mode='w', encoding='utf-8') as a_file, RedirectStdoutTo(a_file):  (2)
    print('B')                                                          (3)
print('C')                                                              (4)
```

1. This will print to the IDE "interactive window" (or the terminal, if running the script from the command line).

2. This `with` statement takes *a comma-separated list of contexts*. The comma-separated list acts like a series of nested `with` blocks. The first context listed is the "outer" block; the last one listed is the "inner" block. The first context opens a file; the second context redirects `sys.stdout` to the stream object that was created in the first context.

3. Because this `print()` statement is executed with the contexts created by the `with` statement, it will not print to the screen; it will write to the file `out.log`.

4. The `with` code block is over. Python has told each context manager to do whatever it is they do when exiting a context. The context managers form a last-in, first-out stack. Upon exiting, the second context changed `sys.stdout` back to its original value; then the first context closed the file named `out.log`. Because standard out has been restored to its original value, calling the `print()` function will once again print to the screen.

Redirecting standard error works exactly the same way, using `sys.stderr` instead of `sys.stdout`.

Further Reading Online

For more information on files, see the following online resources:

- *Reading and writing files*:
  http://docs.python.org/tutorial/inputoutput.html#reading-and-writing-files

- *io module*: http://docs.python.org/3.1/library/io.html

- *Stream objects*: http://docs.python.org/3.1/library/stdtypes.html#file-objects

- *Context manager types*: http://docs.python.org/3.1/library/stdtypes.html#context-manager-types

- *sys.stdout and sys.stderr*:
  http://docs.python.org/3.1/library/sys.html#sys.stdout

- *FUSE on Wikipedia*: http://en.wikipedia.org/wiki/Filesystem_in_Userspace

CHAPTER 12

■ ■ ■

XML

Most of the chapters in this book have centered around a piece of sample code. But XML isn't about code; it's about data. One common use of XML is "syndication feeds" that list the latest articles on a blog, forum, or other frequently-updated web site. Most popular blogging software can produce a feed and update it whenever new articles, discussion threads, or blog posts are published. You can follow a blog by "subscribing" to its feed, and you can follow multiple blogs with a dedicated "feed aggregator" like Google Reader.

Listing 12-1 shows the XML data we'll be working with in this chapter. It's a feed—specifically, an Atom syndication feed, as defined in RFC 4287.

Listing 12-1. An Atom Feed

```
<?xml version='1.0' encoding='utf-8'?>
<feed xmlns='http://www.w3.org/2005/Atom' xml:lang='en'>
  <title>dive into mark</title>
  <subtitle>currently between addictions</subtitle>
  <id>tag:diveintomark.org,2001-07-29:/</id>
  <updated>2009-03-27T21:56:07Z</updated>
  <link rel='alternate' type='text/html' href='http://diveintomark.org/'/>
  <link rel='self' type='application/atom+xml' href='http://diveintomark.org/feed/'/>
  <entry>
    <author>
      <name>Mark</name>
      <uri>http://diveintomark.org/</uri>
    </author>
    <title>Dive into history, 2009 edition</title>
    <link rel='alternate' type='text/html'
      href='http://diveintomark.org/archives/2009/03/27/dive-into-history-2009-edition'/>
    <id>tag:diveintomark.org,2009-03-27:/archives/20090327172042</id>
    <updated>2009-03-27T21:56:07Z</updated>
    <published>2009-03-27T17:20:42Z</published>
    <category scheme='http://diveintomark.org' term='diveintopython'/>
    <category scheme='http://diveintomark.org' term='docbook'/>
    <category scheme='http://diveintomark.org' term='html'/>
```

```
  <summary type='html'>Putting an entire chapter on one page sounds
    bloated, but consider this &amp;mdash; my longest chapter so far
    would be 75 printed pages, and it loads in under 5 seconds&amp;hellip;
    On dialup.</summary>
  </entry>
  <entry>
    <author>
      <name>Mark</name>
      <uri>http://diveintomark.org/</uri>
    </author>
    <title>Accessibility is a harsh mistress</title>
    <link rel='alternate' type='text/html'
      href='http://diveintomark.org/archives/2009/03/21/↵
accessibility-is-a-harsh-mistress'/>
    <id>tag:diveintomark.org,2009-03-21:/archives/20090321200928</id>
    <updated>2009-03-22T01:05:37Z</updated>
    <published>2009-03-21T20:09:28Z</published>
    <category scheme='http://diveintomark.org' term='accessibility'/>
    <summary type='html'>The accessibility orthodoxy does not permit people to
      question the value of features that are rarely useful and rarely used.</summary>
  </entry>
  <entry>
    <author>
      <name>Mark</name>
    </author>
    <title>A gentle introduction to video encoding, part 1: container formats</title>
    <link rel='alternate' type='text/html'
      href='http://diveintomark.org/archives/2008/12/18/give-part-1-container-formats'/>
    <id>tag:diveintomark.org,2008-12-18:/archives/20081218155422</id>
    <updated>2009-01-11T19:39:22Z</updated>
    <published>2008-12-18T15:54:22Z</published>
    <category scheme='http://diveintomark.org' term='asf'/>
    <category scheme='http://diveintomark.org' term='avi'/>
    <category scheme='http://diveintomark.org' term='encoding'/>
    <category scheme='http://diveintomark.org' term='flv'/>
    <category scheme='http://diveintomark.org' term='GIVE'/>
    <category scheme='http://diveintomark.org' term='mp4'/>
    <category scheme='http://diveintomark.org' term='ogg'/>
    <category scheme='http://diveintomark.org' term='video'/>
    <summary type='html'>These notes will eventually become part of a
      tech talk on video encoding.</summary>
  </entry>
</feed>
```

A 5-Minute Crash Course in XML

If you already know about XML, you can skip this section.

XML is a generalized way of describing hierarchical structured data. An XML *document* contains one or more *elements,* which are delimited by *start tags* and *end tags*. Listing 12-2 shows a complete (albeit boring) XML document.

Listing 12-2. A Complete XML Document

```
<foo>    (1)
</foo>   (2)
```

1. This is the *start tag* of the foo element.

2. This is the matching *end tag* of the foo element. Like balancing parentheses in writing or mathematics or code, every start tag much be *closed* (matched) by a corresponding end tag.

Elements can be *nested* to any depth, as shown in Listing 12-3. An element bar inside an element foo is said to be a *subelement* or *child* of foo.

Listing 12-3. Nested XML Elements

```
<foo>
  <bar></bar>
</foo>
```

The first element in every XML document is called the *root element*. An XML document can only have one root element. The document shown in Listing 12-4 is not an XML document, because it has two root elements.

Listing 12-4. Two Root Elements

```
<foo></foo>
<bar></bar>
```

Elements can have *attributes*, which are name-value pairs. Attributes are listed within the start tag of an element and separated by whitespace. *Attribute names* can not be repeated within an element. *Attribute values* must be quoted. You may use either single or double quotes, as shown in Listing 12-5.

Listing 12-5. Elements with Attributes

```
<foo lang='en'>                        (1)
  <bar id='papayawhip' lang="fr"></bar>   (2)
</foo>
```

1. The foo element has one attribute, named lang. The value of its lang attribute is en.

2. The bar element has two attributes, named id and lang. The value of its lang attribute is fr. This doesn't conflict with the foo element in any way. Each element has its own set of attributes.

If an element has more than one attribute, the ordering of the attributes is not significant. An element's attributes form an unordered set of keys and values, like a Python dictionary. There is no limit to the number of attributes you can define on each element.

Elements can have *text content*, as shown in Listing 12-6.

Listing 12-6. Elements with Text Content

```
<foo lang='en'>
  <bar lang='fr'>PapayaWhip</bar>
</foo>
```

Elements that contain no text and no children are *empty*, as shown in Listing 12-7.

Listing 12-7. An Empty Element

```
<foo></foo>
```

There is shorthand for writing empty elements. By putting a / character in the start tag, you can skip the end tag altogether. The XML document in Listing 12-7 could be written in shorthand instead, as in Listing 12-8.

Listing 12-8. Empty Element Shorthand

```
<foo/>
```

Just as Python functions can be declared in different *modules*, XML elements can be declared in different *namespaces*. Namespaces usually look like URLs. You use an xmlns declaration to define a *default namespace*, as shown in Listing 12-9. A namespace declaration looks similar to an attribute, but it has a different purpose.

Listing 12-9. A Default Namespace

```
<feed xmlns='http://www.w3.org/2005/Atom'>    (1)
  <title>dive into mark</title>               (2)
</feed>
```

1. The feed `element` is in the `http://www.w3.org/2005/Atom` namespace.

2. The `title` element is also in the `http://www.w3.org/2005/Atom` namespace. The namespace declaration affects the element where it's declared, plus all child elements.

You can also use an xmlns:prefix declaration to define a namespace and associate it with a *prefix*. Then each element in that namespace must be explicitly declared with the prefix, as shown in Listing 12-10.

Listing 12-10. A Prefixed Namespace

```
<atom:feed xmlns:atom='http://www.w3.org/2005/Atom'>    (1)
  <atom:title>dive into mark</atom:title>               (2)
</atom:feed>
```

1. The `feed` element is in the `http://www.w3.org/2005/Atom` namespace.

2. The `title` element is also in the `http://www.w3.org/2005/Atom` namespace.

As far as an XML parser is concerned, the previous two XML documents are *identical*. Namespace + element name = XML identity. Prefixes only exist to refer to namespaces, so the actual prefix name (`atom:`) is irrelevant. The namespaces match, the element names match, the attributes (or lack of attributes) match, and each element's text content matches, therefore the XML documents are the same.

Finally, XML documents can contain character encoding information on the first line, before the root element, as shown in Listing 12-11. (If you're curious how a document can contain information that needs to be known before the document can be parsed, Section F of the XML specification details how to resolve this Catch-22.)

Listing 12-11. Declaring Character Encoding

```
<?xml version='1.0' encoding='utf-8'?>
```

And now you know just enough XML to be dangerous!

The Structure of an Atom Feed

Think of a weblog, or in fact any web site with frequently updated content, like CNN.com. The site itself has a title (CNN.com), a subtitle (Breaking News, U.S., World, Weather, Entertainment & Video News), a last-updated date (updated 12:43 p.m. EDT, Sat May 16, 2009), and a list of articles posted at different times. Each article also has a title, a first-published date (and maybe also a last-updated date, if they published a correction or fixed a typo), and a unique URL.

The Atom syndication format is designed to capture all of this information in a standard format. My weblog and CNN.com are wildly different in design, scope, and audience, but they both have the same basic structure. CNN.com has a title; my blog has a title. CNN.com publishes articles; I publish articles.

At the top level is the *root element*, which every Atom feed shares: the `feed` element in the `http://www.w3.org/2005/Atom` namespace, as shown in Listing 12-12.

Listing 12-12. A Feed Element

```
<feed xmlns='http://www.w3.org/2005/Atom'   (1)
    xml:lang='en'>                          (2)
```

1. `http://www.w3.org/2005/Atom` is the Atom namespace.

2. Any element can contain an `xml:lang` attribute, which declares the language of the element and its children. In this case, the `xml:lang` attribute is declared once on the root element, which means the entire feed is in English.

An Atom feed contains several pieces of information about the feed itself. These are declared as children of the root-level `feed` element, as shown in Listing 12-13.

Listing 12-13. Feed-level Metadata

```
<feed xmlns='http://www.w3.org/2005/Atom' xml:lang='en'>
  <title>dive into mark</title>                                           (1)
  <subtitle>currently between addictions</subtitle>                       (2)
  <id>tag:diveintomark.org,2001-07-29:/</id>                              (3)
  <updated>2009-03-27T21:56:07Z</updated>                                 (4)
  <link rel='alternate' type='text/html' href='http://diveintomark.org/'/> (5)
```

1. The title of this feed is `dive into mark`.

2. The subtitle of this feed is `currently between addictions`.

3. Every feed needs a globally unique identifier. See RFC 4151 for how to create one.

4. This feed was last updated on March 27, 2009, at 21:56 GMT. This is usually equivalent to the last-modified date of the most recent article.

5. Now things start to get interesting. This `link` element has no text content, but it has three attributes: `rel`, `type`, and `href`. The `rel` value tells you what kind of link this is; `rel='alternate'` means that this is a link to an alternate representation of this feed. The `type='text/html'` attribute means that this is a link to an HTML page. And the link target is given in the `href` attribute.

Now we know that this is a feed for a site named "dive into mark" that is available at `http://diveintomark.org/` and was last updated on March 27, 2009.

■ Although the order of elements can be relevant in some XML documents, it is not relevant in an Atom feed.

After the feed-level metadata is the list of the most recent articles, as shown in Listing 12-14.

Listing 12-14. An Atom Entry

```
<entry>
  <author>                                                         (1)
    <name>Mark</name>
    <uri>http://diveintomark.org/</uri>
  </author>
  <title>Dive into history, 2009 edition</title>               (2)
  <link rel='alternate' type='text/html'                        (3)
    href='http://diveintomark.org/archives/2009/03/27/dive-into-history-2009-edition'/>
  <id>tag:diveintomark.org,2009-03-27:/archives/20090327172042</id>  (4)
  <updated>2009-03-27T21:56:07Z</updated>                       (5)
  <published>2009-03-27T17:20:42Z</published>
  <category scheme='http://diveintomark.org' term='diveintopython'/>  (6)
  <category scheme='http://diveintomark.org' term='docbook'/>
  <category scheme='http://diveintomark.org' term='html'/>
  <summary type='html'>Putting an entire chapter on one page sounds  (7)
    bloated, but consider this &amp;mdash; my longest chapter so far
    would be 75 printed pages, and it loads in under 5 seconds&amp;hellip;
    On dialup.</summary>
</entry>                                                         (8)
```

1. The author element tells who wrote this article: some guy named Mark, whom you can find loafing at http://diveintomark.org/. (This is the same as the alternate link in the feed metadata, but it doesn't have to be. Many weblogs have multiple authors, each with their own personal web site.)

2. The title element gives the title of the article, "Dive into history, 2009 edition."

3. As with the feed-level alternate link, this link element gives the address of the HTML version of this article.

4. Entries, like feeds, need a unique identifier.

5. Entries have two dates: a first-published date (published) and a last-modified date (updated).

6. Entries can have an arbitrary number of categories. This article is filed under diveintopython, docbook, and html.

7. The summary element gives a brief summary of the article. (There is also a content element, not shown here, if you want to include the complete article text in your feed.) This summary element has the Atom-specific type='html' attribute, which specifies that this summary is a snippet of HTML, not plain text. This is important, since it has HTML-specific entities in it (— and …) that should be rendered as "—" and "…" rather than displayed directly.

8. Finally, the end tag for the entry element signals the end of the metadata for this article.

Parsing XML

Python can parse XML documents in several ways. It has traditional DOM and SAX parsers like other programming languages, but I will focus on a different library called ElementTree. (See Listing 12-15.)

Listing 12-15. Introducing ElementTree

```
>>> import xml.etree.ElementTree as etree     (1)
>>> tree = etree.parse('examples/feed.xml')    (2)
>>> root = tree.getroot()                      (3)
>>> root                                        (4)
<Element {http://www.w3.org/2005/Atom}feed at cd1eb0>
```

1. The ElementTree library is part of the Python standard library, in xml.etree.ElementTree.

2. The primary entry point for the ElementTree library is the parse() function, which can take a filename or a file-like object. This function parses the entire document at once. If memory is tight, there are ways to parse an XML document incrementally instead.

3. The parse() function returns an object that represents the entire document. This is *not* the root element. To get a reference to the root element, call the getroot() method.

4. As expected, the root element is the feed element in the http://www.w3.org/ 2005/Atom namespace. The string representation of this object reinforces an important point: an XML element is a combination of its namespace and its tag name (also called the *local name*). Every element in this document is in the Atom namespace, so the root element is represented as {http://www.w3.org/2005/Atom}feed.

■ ElementTree represents XML elements as {namespace}localname. You'll see and use this format in multiple places in the ElementTree API.

Elements Are Lists

In the ElementTree, an element acts like a list. The items of the list are the element's children, as shown in Listing 12-16.

Listing 12-16. Getting the List of Child Elements

```
# continued from Listing 12-15
>>> root.tag                        (1)
'{http://www.w3.org/2005/Atom}feed'
>>> len(root)                       (2)
8
>>> for child in root:              (3)
...     print(child)                (4)
...
<Element {http://www.w3.org/2005/Atom}title at e2b5d0>
<Element {http://www.w3.org/2005/Atom}subtitle at e2b4e0>
<Element {http://www.w3.org/2005/Atom}id at e2b6c0>
<Element {http://www.w3.org/2005/Atom}updated at e2b6f0>
<Element {http://www.w3.org/2005/Atom}link at e2b4b0>
<Element {http://www.w3.org/2005/Atom}entry at e2b720>
<Element {http://www.w3.org/2005/Atom}entry at e2b510>
<Element {http://www.w3.org/2005/Atom}entry at e2b750>
```

1. The root element is {http://www.w3.org/2005/Atom}feed.

2. The "length" of the root element is the number of child elements.

3. You can use the element itself as an iterator to loop through all of its child elements.

4. As you can see from the output, there are indeed 8 child elements: all of the feed-level metadata (title, subtitle, id, updated, and link) followed by the three entry elements.

You may have guessed this already, but I want to point it out explicitly: the list of child elements only includes *direct children*. Each of the entry elements contains its own children, but those are not included in the list. They would be included in the list of each entry's children, but they are not included in the list of the feed's children. There are ways to find elements no matter how deeply nested they are; we'll look at two such ways later in this chapter.

Attributes Are Dictionaries

XML isn't just a collection of elements; each element can also have its own set of attributes. Once you have a reference to a specific element, you can easily get its attributes as a Python dictionary, as shown in Listing 12-17.

Listing 12-17. Getting a Dictionary of Attributes

```
# continued from Listing 12-16
# continuing from the previous example
>>> root.attrib                        (1)
{'{http://www.w3.org/XML/1998/namespace}lang': 'en'}
>>> root[4]                            (2)
<Element {http://www.w3.org/2005/Atom}link at e181b0>
>>> root[4].attrib                     (3)
{'href': 'http://diveintomark.org/',
 'type': 'text/html',
 'rel': 'alternate'}
>>> root[3]                            (4)
<Element {http://www.w3.org/2005/Atom}updated at e2b4e0>
>>> root[3].attrib                     (5)
{}
```

1. The attrib property is a dictionary of the element's attributes. The original markup here was <feed xmlns='http://www.w3.org/2005/Atom' xml:lang='en'>. The xml: prefix refers to a built-in namespace that every XML document can use without declaring it.

2. The fifth child—[4] in a 0-based list—is the link element.

3. The link element has three attributes: href, type, and rel.

4. The fourth child—[3] in a 0-based list—is the updated element.

5. The updated element has no attributes, so its .attrib is just an empty dictionary.

Searching for Nodes Within an XML Document

So far, we've worked with this XML document "from the top down," starting with the root element, getting its child elements, and so on throughout the document. But many uses of XML require you to find specific elements. The ElementTree API can do that, too. (See Listing 12-18.)

Listing 12-18. Searching for Specific Eelements

```
>>> import xml.etree.ElementTree as etree
>>> tree = etree.parse('examples/feed.xml')
>>> root = tree.getroot()
>>> root.findall('{http://www.w3.org/2005/Atom}entry')      (1)
[<Element {http://www.w3.org/2005/Atom}entry at e2b4e0>,
 <Element {http://www.w3.org/2005/Atom}entry at e2b510>,
 <Element {http://www.w3.org/2005/Atom}entry at e2b540>]
>>> root.tag
'{http://www.w3.org/2005/Atom}feed'
>>> root.findall('{http://www.w3.org/2005/Atom}feed')       (2)
[]
>>> root.findall('{http://www.w3.org/2005/Atom}author')     (3)
[]
```

1. The `findall()` method finds child elements that match a specific query. (More on the query format in a minute.)

2. Each element—including the root element, but also child elements—has a `findall()` method that finds all matching elements among the element's children. But why aren't there any results? Although it may not be obvious, this particular query searches only the element's children. Since the root **feed** element has no child named **feed**, this query returns an empty list.

3. This result may also surprise you. There is an **author** element in this document; in fact, there are three (one in each **entry**). But those **author** elements are not *direct children* of the root element; they are "grandchildren" (literally, a child element of a child element). If you want to look for **author** elements at any nesting level, you can do that, but the query format is slightly different.

The `findall()` method is also available on the **tree** object, as shown in Listing 12-19.

Listing 12-19. The tree.findall() Method

```
>>> tree.findall('{http://www.w3.org/2005/Atom}entry')      (1)
[<Element {http://www.w3.org/2005/Atom}entry at e2b4e0>,
 <Element {http://www.w3.org/2005/Atom}entry at e2b510>,
 <Element {http://www.w3.org/2005/Atom}entry at e2b540>]
>>> tree.findall('{http://www.w3.org/2005/Atom}author')     (2)
[]
```

1. For convenience, the **tree** object (returned from the `etree.parse()` function) has several methods that mirror the methods on the root element. The results are the same as if you had called the `tree.getroot().findall()` method.

2. Perhaps surprisingly, this query does not find the `author` elements in this document. Why not? Because this is just a shortcut for `tree.getroot().findall('{http://www.w3.org/2005/Atom}author')`, which means "find all the `author` elements that are children of the root element." The `author` elements are not children of the root element; they're children of the `entry` elements. Thus the query doesn't return any matches.

There is also a `find()` method that returns the first matching element (see Listing 12-20). This is useful for situations where you are expecting only one match, or if there are multiple matches, you care only about the first one.

Listing 12-20. The find() Method

```
>>> entries = tree.findall('{http://www.w3.org/2005/Atom}entry')          (1)
>>> len(entries)
3
>>> title_element = entries[0].find('{http://www.w3.org/2005/Atom}title')  (2)
>>> title_element.text
'Dive into history, 2009 edition'
>>> foo_element = entries[0].find('{http://www.w3.org/2005/Atom}foo')       (3)
>>> foo_element
>>> type(foo_element)
<class 'NoneType'>
```

1. You saw this in the previous example. It finds all the `atom:entry` elements.

2. The `find()` method takes an ElementTree query and returns the first matching element.

3. There are no elements in this entry named `foo`, so this returns `None`.

■ There is a "gotcha" with the `find()` method that will eventually bite you. In a Boolean context, ElementTree element objects will evaluate to `False` if they contain no children (that is, if `len(element)` is 0). This means that `if element.find('...')` is not testing whether the `find()` method found a matching element; it's testing whether that matching element has any child elements! To test whether the `find()` method returned an element, use `if element.find('...') is not None`.

There *is* a way to search for *descendant elements*—children, grandchildren, and any element at any nesting level. See Listing 12-21.

Listing 12-21. Searching for Grandchildren

```
>>> all_links = tree.findall('//{http://www.w3.org/2005/Atom}link')  (1)
>>> all_links
[<Element {http://www.w3.org/2005/Atom}link at e181b0>,
 <Element {http://www.w3.org/2005/Atom}link at e2b570>,
```

```
<Element {http://www.w3.org/2005/Atom}link at e2b480>,
<Element {http://www.w3.org/2005/Atom}link at e2b5a0>]
>>> all_links[0].attrib                                             (2)
{'href': 'http://diveintomark.org/',
 'type': 'text/html',
 'rel': 'alternate'}
>>> all_links[1].attrib                                             (3)
{'href': 'http://diveintomark.org/archives/2009/03/27/dive-into-history-2009-edition',
 'type': 'text/html',
 'rel': 'alternate'}
>>> all_links[2].attrib
{'href': 'http://diveintomark.org/archives/2009/03/21/accessibility-is-a-harsh-mistress',
 'type': 'text/html',
 'rel': 'alternate'}
>>> all_links[3].attrib
{'href': 'http://diveintomark.org/archives/2008/12/18/give-part-1-container-formats',
 'type': 'text/html',
 'rel': 'alternate'}
```

1. This query—`//{http://www.w3.org/2005/Atom}link`—is very similar to the previous examples, except for the two slashes at the beginning of the query. Those two slashes mean "don't just look for direct children; I want *any* elements, regardless of nesting level." So the result is a list of four `link` elements, not just one.

2. The first result *is* a direct child of the root element. As you can see from its attributes, this is the feed-level alternate link that points to the HTML version of the web site that the feed describes.

3. The other three results are each entry-level alternate links. Each `entry` has a single `link` child element, and because of the double slash at the beginning of the query, this query finds all of them.

What's that? You say you want the power of the `findall()` method, but you want to work with an iterator instead of building a complete list? ElementTree can do that, too (see Listing 12-22).

Listing 12-22. The getiterator() Method

```
>>> it = tree.getiterator('{http://www.w3.org/2005/Atom}link')   (1)
>>> next(it)                                                      (2)
<Element {http://www.w3.org/2005/Atom}link at 122f1b0>
>>> next(it)
<Element {http://www.w3.org/2005/Atom}link at 122f1e0>
>>> next(it)
<Element {http://www.w3.org/2005/Atom}link at 122f210>
>>> next(it)
<Element {http://www.w3.org/2005/Atom}link at 122f1b0>
>>> next(it)
Traceback (most recent call last):
  File "<stdin>", line 1, in <module>
StopIteration
```

1. The `getiterator()` method can take zero or one arguments. If called with no arguments, it returns an iterator that spits out every element and child element in the entire document. Or, as shown here, you can call it with an element name in standard ElementTree format. This returns an iterator that spits out only elements of that name.

2. Repeatedly calling the `next()` function with this iterator will eventually return every element of the document that matches the query you passed to the `getiterator()` method.

Overall, ElementTree's `findall()` method is a very powerful feature, but the query language can be a bit surprising. It is officially described as "limited support for XPath expressions." XPath is a W3C standard for querying XML documents. ElementTree's query language is similar enough to XPath to do basic searching, but dissimilar enough that it may annoy you if you already know XPath. Now let's look at a third-party XML library that extends the ElementTree API with full XPath support.

Going Further with lxml

lxml is an open-source third-party library that builds on the popular `libxml2` parser. It provides a 100% compatible ElementTree API (see Listing 12-23), then extends it with XPath 1.0 support and a few other niceties. There are installers available for Windows; Linux users should always try to use distribution-specific tools like `yum` or `apt-get` to install precompiled binaries from their repositories. Otherwise you'll need to install lxml manually.

■ Visit http://codespeak.net/lxml/ to download lxml and read installation instructions for your platform.

Listing 12-23. lxml Looks like ElementTree

```
>>> from lxml import etree                        (1)
>>> tree = etree.parse('examples/feed.xml')       (2)
>>> root = tree.getroot()                          (3)
>>> root.findall('{http://www.w3.org/2005/Atom}entry')  (4)
[<Element {http://www.w3.org/2005/Atom}entry at e2b4e0>,
 <Element {http://www.w3.org/2005/Atom}entry at e2b510>,
 <Element {http://www.w3.org/2005/Atom}entry at e2b540>]
```

1. Once imported, lxml provides the same API as the built-in ElementTree library.

2. `parse()` function: same as ElementTree.

3. `getroot()` method: also the same.

4. `findall()` method: exactly the same.

For large XML documents, lxml is significantly faster than the built-in ElementTree library. If you're only using the ElementTree API and want to use the fastest available implementation, you can try to import lxml and fall back to the built-in ElementTree. (See Listing 12-24.)

Listing 12-24. Use lxml if Available

```
try:
    from lxml import etree
except ImportError:
    import xml.etree.ElementTree as etree
```

But lxml is more than just a faster ElementTree. Its findall() method includes support for more complicated expressions, as shown in Listing 12-25.

Listing 12-25. Complex Queries with lxml

```
>>> import lxml.etree                                                          (1)
>>> tree = lxml.etree.parse('examples/feed.xml')
>>> tree.findall('//{http://www.w3.org/2005/Atom}*[@href]')                    (2)
[<Element {http://www.w3.org/2005/Atom}link at eeb8a0>,
 <Element {http://www.w3.org/2005/Atom}link at eeb990>,
 <Element {http://www.w3.org/2005/Atom}link at eeb960>,
 <Element {http://www.w3.org/2005/Atom}link at eeb9c0>]
>>> tree.findall("//{http://www.w3.org/2005/Atom}*[@href='http://diveintomark.org/']") (3)
[<Element {http://www.w3.org/2005/Atom}link at eeb930>]
>>> NS = '{http://www.w3.org/2005/Atom}'
>>> tree.findall('//{NS}author[{NS}uri]'.format(NS=NS))                        (4)
[<Element {http://www.w3.org/2005/Atom}author at eeba80>,
 <Element {http://www.w3.org/2005/Atom}author at eebba0>]
```

1. In this example, I'm going to import lxml.etree (instead of, say, from lxml import etree), to emphasize that these features are specific to lxml.

2. This query finds all elements in the Atom namespace, anywhere in the document, that have an href attribute. The // at the beginning of the query means "elements anywhere (not just as children of the root element)." {http://www.w3.org/2005/Atom} means "only elements in the Atom namespace." * means "elements with any local name." And [@href] means "has an href attribute."

3. The query finds all Atom elements with an href whose value is http://diveintomark.org/.

4. After doing some quick string formatting (because otherwise these compound queries get ridiculously long), this query searches for Atom author elements that have an Atom uri element as a child. This only returns two author elements, the ones in the first and second entry. The author in the last entry contains only a name, not a uri.

Not enough for you? lxml also integrates support for arbitrary XPath 1.0 expressions. I'm not going to go into depth about XPath syntax; that could be a whole book unto itself! But Listing 12-26 shows how it integrates into lxml.

Listing 12-26. XPath Queries in lxml

```
>>> import lxml.etree
```

```
>>> tree = lxml.etree.parse('examples/feed.xml')
>>> NSMAP = {'atom': 'http://www.w3.org/2005/Atom'}                    (1)
>>> entries = tree.xpath("//atom:category[@term='accessibility']/..",  (2)
...     namespaces=NSMAP)
>>> entries                                                           (3)
[<Element {http://www.w3.org/2005/Atom}entry at e2b630>]
>>> entry = entries[0]
>>> entry.xpath('./atom:title/text()', namespaces=NSMAP)              (4)
['Accessibility is a harsh mistress']
```

1. To perform XPath queries on namespaced elements, you need to define a
    namespace prefix mapping. This is just a Python dictionary.

2. Here is an XPath query. The XPath expression searches for **category** elements
    (in the Atom namespace) that contain a **term** attribute with the value
    accessibility. But that's not actually the query result. Look at the very end
    of the query string; did you notice the **/..** bit? It means "and then return the
    parent element of the **category** element you just found." So this single XPath
    query will find all entries with a child element of **<category
    term='accessibility'>**.

3. The **xpath()** function returns a list of ElementTree objects. In this document,
    there is only one entry with a **category** whose **term** is **accessibility**.

4. XPath expressions don't always return a list of elements. Technically, the
    DOM of a parsed XML document doesn't contain elements; it contains *nodes*.
    Depending on their type, nodes can be elements, attributes, or even text
    content. The result of an XPath query is a list of nodes. This query returns a list
    of text nodes: the text content (**text()**) of the **title** element (**atom:title**) that
    is a child of the current element (**./**).

Generating XML

Python's support for XML is not limited to parsing existing documents. You can also create XML
documents from scratch, as shown in Listing 12-27.

Listing 12-27. Creating an XML Document with the ElementTree API

```
>>> import xml.etree.ElementTree as etree
>>> new_feed = etree.Element('{http://www.w3.org/2005/Atom}feed',     (1)
...     attrib={'{http://www.w3.org/XML/1998/namespace}lang': 'en'})  (2)
>>> print(etree.tostring(new_feed))                                   (3)
<ns0:feed xmlns:ns0='http://www.w3.org/2005/Atom' xml:lang='en'/>
```

1. To create a new element, instantiate the **Element** class. You pass the element
    name (namespace + local name) as the first argument. This statement creates
    a **feed** element in the Atom namespace. This will be our new document's root
    element.

2. To add attributes to the newly created element, pass a dictionary of attribute names and values in the `attrib` argument. Note that the attribute name should be in the standard ElementTree format, `{namespace}localname`.

3. At any time, you can serialize any element (and its children) with the ElementTree `tostring()` function.

Was that serialization surprising to you? The way ElementTree serializes namespaced XML elements is technically accurate but not optimal. The sample XML document at the beginning of this chapter defined a *default namespace* (`xmlns='http://www.w3.org/2005/Atom'`). Defining a default namespace is useful for documents—like Atom feeds—where every element is in the same namespace, because you can declare the namespace once and declare each element with just its local name (`<feed>`, `<link>`, `<entry>`). There is no need to use any prefixes unless you want to declare elements from another namespace.

An XML parser won't "see" any difference between an XML document with a default namespace and an XML document with a prefixed namespace. The resulting DOMs of the serializations in Listings 12-28 and 12-29 are identical.

Listing 12-28. An XML document with a Prefixed Namespace

```
<ns0:feed xmlns:ns0='http://www.w3.org/2005/Atom' xml:lang='en'/>
```

Listing 12-29. An XML Document with a Default Namespace

```
<feed xmlns='http://www.w3.org/2005/Atom' xml:lang='en'/>
```

The only practical difference is that the second serialization is several characters shorter. If we were to recast our entire sample feed with an `ns0:` prefix in every start and end tag, it would add 4 characters per start tag times 79 tags, plus 4 characters for the namespace declaration itself, for a total of 320 characters. Assuming UTF-8 encoding, that's 320 extra bytes. (After gzipping, the difference drops to 21 bytes, but still, 21 bytes is 21 bytes.) Maybe that doesn't matter to you, but for something like an Atom feed, which may be downloaded several thousand times whenever it changes, saving a few bytes per request can quickly add up.

The built-in ElementTree library does not offer this fine-grained control over serializing namespaced elements, but `lxml` does, as shown in Listing 12-30.

Listing 12-30. Controlling Namespace Prefixes with lxml

```
>>> import lxml.etree
>>> NSMAP = {None: 'http://www.w3.org/2005/Atom'}                      (1)
>>> new_feed = lxml.etree.Element('feed', nsmap=NSMAP)                 (2)
>>> print(lxml.etree.tounicode(new_feed))                             (3)
<feed xmlns='http://www.w3.org/2005/Atom'/>
>>> new_feed.set('{http://www.w3.org/XML/1998/namespace}lang', 'en')  (4)
>>> print(lxml.etree.tounicode(new_feed))
<feed xmlns='http://www.w3.org/2005/Atom' xml:lang='en'/>
```

1. To start, define a namespace mapping as a dictionary. Dictionary values are namespaces; dictionary keys are the desired prefix. Using `None` as a prefix effectively declares a default namespace.

2. Now you can pass the lxml-specific nsmap argument when you create an element, and lxml will respect the namespace prefixes you've defined.

3. As expected, this serialization defines the Atom namespace as the default namespace and declares the feed element without a namespace prefix.

4. Oops, we forgot to add the xml:lang attribute. You can always add attributes to any element with the set() method. It takes two arguments: the attribute name in standard ElementTree format, then the attribute value. (This method is not lxml-specific. The only lxml-specific part of this example was the nsmap argument to control the namespace prefixes in the serialized output.)

Are XML documents limited to one element per document? No, of course not. You can easily create child elements, too, as shown in Listing 12-31.

Listing 12-31. Creating Child Elements with lxml

```
>>> title = lxml.etree.SubElement(new_feed, 'title',      (1)
...     attrib={'type':'html'})                           (2)
>>> print(lxml.etree.tounicode(new_feed))
<feed xmlns='http://www.w3.org/2005/Atom' xml:lang='en'><title type='html'/></feed>
>>> title.text = 'dive into &hellip;'                     (3)
>>> print(lxml.etree.tounicode(new_feed))                 (4)
<feed xmlns='http://www.w3.org/2005/Atom' xml:lang='en'><title type='html'>dive into ⤶
&amp;hellip;</title></feed>
>>> print(lxml.etree.tounicode(new_feed, pretty_print=True))  (5)
<feed xmlns='http://www.w3.org/2005/Atom' xml:lang='en'>
<title type='html'>dive into&amp;hellip;</title>
</feed>
```

1. To create a child element of an existing element, instantiate the SubElement class. The only required arguments are the parent element (new_feed in this case) and the new element's name. Since this child element will inherit the namespace mapping of its parent, there is no need to redeclare the namespace or prefix here.

2. You can also pass in an attribute dictionary. Keys are attribute names; values are attribute values.

3. As expected, the new title element was created in the Atom namespace, and it was inserted as a child of the feed element. Since the title element has no text content and no children of its own, lxml serializes it as an empty element (with the /> shortcut).

4. To set the text content of an element, simply set its .text property.

5. Now the title element is serialized with its text content. Any text content that contains less-than signs or ampersands needs to be escaped when serialized. lxml handles this escaping automatically.

6. You can also apply "pretty printing" to the serialization, which inserts line breaks after end tags, and after start tags of elements that contain child elements but no text content. In technical terms, lxml adds "insignificant whitespace" to make the output more readable.

You might also want to check out xmlwitch, another third-party library for generating XML. It makes extensive use of the `with` statement to make XML generation code more readable. `http://github.com/galvez/xmlwitch/tree/master`

Parsing Broken XML

The XML specification mandates that all conforming XML parsers employ "draconian error handling." That is, they must halt and catch fire as soon as they detect any sort of well-formedness error in the XML document. Well-formedness errors include mismatched start and end tags, undefined entities, illegal Unicode characters, and a number of other esoteric rules. This is in stark contrast to other common formats like HTML—your browser doesn't stop rendering a web page if you forget to close an HTML tag or escape an ampersand in an attribute value. (It is a common misconception that HTML has no defined error handling. Error handling is quite well-defined in the HTML 5 specification, but it's significantly more complicated than "halt and catch fire on first error.")

Some people (myself included) believe that it was a mistake for the inventors of XML to mandate draconian error handling. Don't get me wrong; I can certainly see the allure of simplifying the error-handling rules. But in practice, the concept of "well-formedness" is trickier than it sounds, especially for XML documents (like Atom feeds) that are published on the Web and served over HTTP. Despite the maturity of XML, which standardized on draconian error handling in 1997, surveys continually show a significant fraction of Atom feeds on the web are plagued with well-formedness errors.

So, I have both theoretical and practical reasons to parse XML documents "at any cost," that is, *not* to halt and catch fire at the first well-formedness error. If you find yourself wanting to do this too, `lxml` can help.

Listing 12-32 shows a fragment of a broken XML document. I've highlighted the well-formedness error.

Listing 12-32. A broken XML document

```
<?xml version='1.0' encoding='utf-8'?>
<feed xmlns='http://www.w3.org/2005/Atom' xml:lang='en'>
  <title>dive into &hellip;</title>
</feed>
```

That's an error, because the `&hellip;` entity is not defined in XML. (It is defined in HTML.) If you try to parse this broken feed with the default settings, `lxml` will choke on the undefined entity, as shown in Listing 12-33.

Listing 12-33. Parsing a Broken XML Document Fails by Default

```
>>> import lxml.etree
>>> tree = lxml.etree.parse('examples/feed-broken.xml')
Traceback (most recent call last):
  File "<stdin>", line 1, in <module>
  File "lxml.etree.pyx", line 2693, in lxml.etree.parse (src/lxml/lxml.etree.c:52591)
  File "parser.pxi", line 1478, in lxml.etree._parseDocument (src/lxml/lxml.etree.c:75665)
  File "parser.pxi", line 1507, in lxml.etree._parseDocumentFromURL ↵
```

```
(src/lxml/lxml.etree.c:75993)
  File "parser.pxi", line 1407, in lxml.etree._parseDocFromFile ↵
(src/lxml/lxml.etree.c:75002)
  File "parser.pxi", line 965, in lxml.etree._BaseParser._parseDocFromFile ↵
(src/lxml/lxml.etree.c:72023)
  File "parser.pxi", line 539, in lxml.etree._ParserContext._handleParseResultDoc ↵
(src/lxml/lxml.etree.c:67830)
  File "parser.pxi", line 625, in lxml.etree._handleParseResult ↵
(src/lxml/lxml.etree.c:68877)
  File "parser.pxi", line 565, in lxml.etree._raiseParseError (src/lxml/lxml.etree.c:68125)
lxml.etree.XMLSyntaxError: Entity 'hellip' not defined, line 3, column 28
```

To parse this broken XML document, despite its well-formedness error, you need to create a custom XML parser, as shown in Listing 12-34.

Listing 12-34. Parsing a Broken XML with a Custom Parser

```
>>> parser = lxml.etree.XMLParser(recover=True)            (1)
>>> tree = lxml.etree.parse('examples/feed-broken.xml', parser)  (2)
>>> parser.error_log                                       (3)
examples/feed-broken.xml:3:28:FATAL:PARSER:ERR_UNDECLARED_ENTITY: Entity 'hellip' ↵
not defined
>>> tree.findall('{http://www.w3.org/2005/Atom}title')
[<Element {http://www.w3.org/2005/Atom}title at ead510>]
>>> title = tree.findall('{http://www.w3.org/2005/Atom}title')[0]
>>> title.text                                             (4)
'dive into '
>>> print(lxml.etree.tounicode(tree.getroot()))            (5)
<feed xmlns='http://www.w3.org/2005/Atom' xml:lang='en'>
  <title>dive into </title>
</feed>
```

1. To create a custom parser, instantiate the lxml.etree.XMLParser class. It can take a number of different named arguments. The one we're interested in here is the recover argument. When set to True, the XML parser will try its best to "recover" from well-formedness errors.

2. To parse an XML document with your custom parser, pass the parser object as the second argument to the parse() function. Note that lxml does not raise an exception about the undefined … entity.

3. The parser keeps a log of the well-formedness errors that it has encountered. (This is actually true regardless of whether it is set to recover from those errors or not.)

4. Since it didn't know what to do with the undefined … entity, the parser just silently dropped it. The text content of the title element becomes 'dive into '.

5. As you can see from the serialization, the … entity didn't get moved; it was simply dropped.

It is important to reiterate that there is no guarantee of interoperability with "recovering" XML parsers. A different parser might decide that it recognized the … entity from HTML, and replace it with &hellip; instead. Is that "better"? Maybe. Is it "more correct"? No, they are both equally incorrect. The correct behavior (according to the XML specification) is to halt and catch fire. If you've decided not to do that, you're on your own.

Further Reading Online

- XML on Wikipedia.org: http://en.wikipedia.org/wiki/XML

- The ElementTree XML API:
  http://docs.python.org/3.1/library/xml.etree.elementtree.html

- Elements and Element Trees: http://effbot.org/zone/element.htm

- XPath Support in ElementTree: http://effbot.org/zone/element-xpath.htm

- The ElementTree iterparse Function:
  http://effbot.org/zone/element-iterparse.htm

- lxml project page: http://codespeak.net/lxml/

- Parsing XML and HTML with lxml: http://codespeak.net/lxml/1.3/parsing.html

- XPath and XSLT with lxml: http://codespeak.net/lxml/1.3/xpathxslt.html

- Xmlwitch: http://github.com/galvez/xmlwitch/tree/master

CHAPTER 13

■ ■ ■

Serializing Python Objects

The concept of *serialization* is simple. You have a data structure in memory that you want to save, reuse, or send to someone else. How can you do that? Well, that depends on how you want to save it, how you want to reuse it, and to whom you want to send it. Many games allow you to save your progress when you quit the game and pick up where you left off when you relaunch the game. (Actually, many non-gaming applications do this as well.) In this case, a data structure that captures "your progress so far" needs to be stored on disk when you quit and then loaded from disk when you relaunch. The data is meant to be used only by the same program that created it, never sent over a network, and never read by anything other than the program that created it. Therefore, the interoperability issues are limited to ensuring that later versions of the program can read data written by earlier versions.

For cases like this, the `pickle` module is ideal. It's part of the Python standard library, so it's always available. It's fast; the bulk of it is written in C, like the Python interpreter itself. And it can store arbitrarily complex Python data structures.

What can the `pickle` module store?

- All the native datatypes that Python supports: Booleans, integers, floating point numbers, complex numbers, strings, **bytes** objects, byte arrays, and **None**.

- Lists, tuples, dictionaries, and sets containing any combination of native datatypes; or any combination of other lists, tuples, dictionaries and sets up to the maximum nesting level that Python supports, which you can get by calling `sys.getrecursionlimit()`.

- Functions, classes, and instances of classes (with caveats).

If this isn't enough for you, the `pickle` module is also extensible. If you're interested in extensibility, check out the links in the "Further Reading Online" section at the end of the chapter.

A Quick Note About the Examples in this Chapter

This chapter tells a tale with two Python shells. All the examples in this chapter are part of a single story arc. You will be asked to switch back and forth between the two Python shells as I demonstrate the `pickle` and `json` modules.

To help keep things straight, open the Python shell and define a `shell` variable, as shown in Listing 13-1.

Listing 13-1. *Python Shell #1*

```
>>> shell = 1
```

Keep that window open. Now open another Python shell and define a shell variable, as shown in Listing 13-2.

Listing 13-2. *Python Shell #2*

```
>>> shell = 2
```

Throughout this chapter, I will use the shell variable to indicate which Python shell is being used in each example.

Saving Data to a Pickle File

The pickle module works with data structures. Let's build one (see Listing 13-3).

Listing 13-3. *Defining a Data Structure*

```
>>> shell                                                                    (1)
1
>>> entry = {}                                                               (2)
>>> entry['title'] = 'Dive into history, 2009 edition'
>>> entry['article_link'] = 'http://diveintomark.org/archives/2009/03/27/
dive-into-history-2009-edition'
>>> entry['comments_link'] = None
>>> entry['internal_id'] = b'\xDE\xD5\xB4\xF8'
>>> entry['tags'] = ('diveintopython', 'docbook', 'html')
>>> entry['published'] = True
>>> import time
>>> entry['published_date'] = time.strptime('Fri Mar 27 22:20:42 2009')      (3)
>>> entry['published_date']
time.struct_time(tm_year=2009, tm_mon=3, tm_mday=27, tm_hour=22, tm_min=20, ↵
tm_sec=42, tm_wday=4,
tm_yday=86, tm_isdst=-1)
```

1. Follow along in Python shell #1.

2. The idea here is to build a Python dictionary that could represent something useful such as an entry in an Atom feed (refer to Chapter 12). But I also want to ensure that it contains several different types of data to show off the pickle module. Don't read too much into these values.

3. The time module contains a data structure (time_struct) to represent a point in time (accurate to one millisecond) and functions to manipulate time structs. The strptime() function takes a formatted string and converts it to a time_struct. This string is in the default format, but you can control it with format codes. See the time module in the official Python documentation for more details.

That's a handsome-looking Python dictionary. Let's save it to a file (see Listing 13-4).

Listing 13-4. Saving a Data Structure to a File

```
>>> shell                                (1)
1
>>> import pickle
>>> with open('entry.pickle', 'wb') as f:   (2)
...     pickle.dump(entry, f)            (3)
...
```

1. This is still in Python shell #1.

2. Use the `open()` function to open a file. Set the file mode to `'wb'` to open the file for writing in binary mode. Wrap it in a `with` statement to ensure that the file is closed automatically when you're done with it. (Refer to Chapter 11 for more on files, binary mode, and the `with` statement.)

3. The `dump()` function in the `pickle` module takes a serializable Python data structure, serializes it into a binary, Python-specific format using the latest version of the pickle protocol, and saves it to an open file.

That last sentence was pretty important.

- The `pickle` module takes a Python data structure and saves it to a file.

- To do this, it *serializes* the data structure using a data format called the *pickle protocol.*

- The pickle protocol is Python-specific; there is no guarantee of cross-language compatibility. You probably couldn't take the `entry.pickle` file you just created and do anything useful with it in Perl, PHP, Java, or any other language.

- Not every Python data structure can be serialized by the `pickle` module. The pickle protocol has changed several times as new data types have been added to the Python language, but there are still limitations.

- As a result of these changes, there is no guarantee of compatibility between different versions of Python. Newer versions of Python support the older serialization formats, but older versions of Python do not support newer formats (because they don't support the newer data types).

- Unless you specify otherwise, the functions in the `pickle` module will use the latest version of the pickle protocol. This ensures that you have maximum flexibility in the types of data you can serialize, but it also means that the resulting file will not be readable by older versions of Python that do not support the latest version of the pickle protocol.

- The latest version of the pickle protocol is a binary format. Be sure to open your pickle files in binary mode, or else the data will get corrupted during writing.

Loading Data from a Pickle File

Now switch to your second Python shell—that is, not the one where you created the **entry** dictionary (see Listing 13-5).

Listing 13-5. Loading a Data Structure from a File

```
>>> shell                                  (1)
2
>>> entry                                  (2)
Traceback (most recent call last):
  File "<stdin>", line 1, in <module>
NameError: name 'entry' is not defined
>>> import pickle
>>> with open('entry.pickle', 'rb') as f:  (3)
...     entry = pickle.load(f)             (4)
...
>>> entry                                  (5)
{'comments_link': None,
 'internal_id': b'\xDE\xD5\xB4\xF8',
 'title': 'Dive into history, 2009 edition',
 'tags': ('diveintopython', 'docbook', 'html'),
 'article_link':
 'http://diveintomark.org/archives/2009/03/27/↵
dive-into-history-2009-edition',
 'published_date': time.struct_time(tm_year=2009, ↵
tm_mon=3, tm_mday=27,
 tm_hour=22, tm_min=20, tm_sec=42, tm_wday=4, ↵
tm_yday=86, tm_isdst=-1),
 'published': True}
```

1. This is Python shell #2.

2. There is no **entry** variable defined here. You defined an **entry** variable in Python shell #1, but that's a completely different environment with its own state.

3. Open the **entry.pickle** file you created in Python shell #1. The **pickle** module uses a binary data format, so you should always open pickle files in binary mode.

4. The **pickle.load()** function takes a stream object (refer to Chapter 11), reads the serialized data from the stream, creates a new Python object, re-creates the serialized data in the new Python object, and returns the new Python object.

5. Now the **entry** variable is a dictionary with familiar-looking keys and values.

The **pickle.dump()/pickle.load()** cycle results in a new data structure that is equal to the original data structure, as shown in Listing 13-6.

Listing 13-6. The pickle.dump/pickle.load Cycle

```
>>> shell                                    (1)
1
>>> with open('entry.pickle', 'rb') as f:    (2)
...     entry2 = pickle.load(f)              (3)
...
>>> entry2 == entry                          (4)
True
>>> entry2 is entry                          (4)
False
>>> entry2['tags']                           &#x2465;
('diveintopython', 'docbook', 'html')
>>> entry2['internal_id']
b'\xDE\xD5\xB4\xF8'
```

1. Switch back to Python shell #1.

2. Open the entry.pickle file.

3. Load the serialized data into a new variable: entry2.

4. Python confirms that the two dictionaries, entry and entry2, are equal. In this shell, you built entry from the ground up, starting with an empty dictionary and manually assigning values to specific keys. You serialized this dictionary and stored it in the entry.pickle file. Now you've read the serialized data from that file and created a perfect replica of the original data structure.

5. *Equality* is not the same as *identity*. I said you've created a *perfect replica* of the original data structure, which is true. But it's still a copy.

6. For reasons that will become clear later in this chapter, I want to point out that the value of the 'tags' key is a tuple, and the value of the 'internal_id' key is a bytes object.

Pickling Without a File

The examples in the previous section showed how to serialize a Python object directly to a file on disk. But what if you don't want or need a file? You can also serialize to a bytes object in memory, as shown in Listing 13-7.

Listing 13-7. Pickling Without a File

```
>>> shell
1
>>> b = pickle.dumps(entry)       (1)
>>> type(b)                       (2)
<class 'bytes'>
>>> entry3 = pickle.loads(b)      (3)
>>> entry3 == entry               (4)
True
```

1. The `pickle.dumps()` function (note the *s* at the end of the function name) performs the same serialization as the `pickle.dump()` function. Instead of taking a stream object and writing the serialized data to a file on disk, it simply returns the serialized data.

2. Because the pickle protocol uses a binary data format, the `pickle.dumps()` function returns a `bytes` object.

3. The `pickle.loads()` function (again, note the *s* at the end of the function name) performs the same deserialization as the `pickle.load()` function. Instead of taking a stream object and reading the serialized data from a file, it takes a `bytes` object containing serialized data, such as the one returned by the `pickle.dumps()` function.

4. The end result is the same: a perfect replica of the original dictionary.

Bytes and Strings Rear Their Ugly Heads Again

The pickle protocol has been around for many years, and it has matured as Python itself has matured. There are now four different versions of the pickle protocol:

- Python 1.x had two pickle protocols: a text-based format (version 0) and a binary format (version 1).

- Python 2.3 introduced a new pickle protocol (version 2) to handle new functionality in Python class objects. It is a binary format.

- Python 3.0 introduced another pickle protocol (version 3) with explicit support for `bytes` objects and byte arrays. It is a binary format.

Oh, look: the difference between bytes and strings rears its ugly head again (refer to Chapter 4). What this means in practice is that although Python 3 can read data pickled with protocol version 2, Python 2 cannot read data pickled with protocol version 3.

Debugging Pickle Files

What does the pickle protocol look like? Let's jump out of the Python shell for a moment and take a look at that `entry.pickle` file we created (see Listing 13-8).

Listing 13-8. Printing a Pickle File Is Not Useful

```
you@localhost:~/diveintopython3/examples$ ls -l entry.pickle
-rw-r--r-- 1 you  you  324 Aug  3 13:34 entry.pickle
you@localhost:~/diveintopython3/examples$ cat entry.pickle
comments_linkqNXtagsqXdiveintopythonqXdocbookqXhtmlq? ↵
qX publishedq?
XlinkXJhttp://diveintomark.org/archives/2009/03/27/↵
dive-into-history-2009-edition
q   Xpublished_dateq
ctime
struct_time
```

?qRqXtitleqXDive into history, 2009 editionqu.

That wasn't terribly helpful. You can see the strings, but other datatypes end up as unprintable (or at least unreadable) characters. Fields are not obviously delimited by tabs or spaces. This is not a format you would want to debug by yourself. But there *is* a way to disassemble a pickle file from within Python itself (see Listing 13-9).

Listing 13-9. Disassembling a Pickle File

```
>>> shell
1
>>> import pickletools
>>> with open('entry.pickle', 'rb') as f:
...     pickletools.dis(f)
    0: \x80 PROTO       3
    2: }    EMPTY_DICT
    3: q    BINPUT       0
    5: (    MARK
    6: X        BINUNICODE 'published_date'
   25: q        BINPUT       1
   27: c        GLOBAL       'time struct_time'
   45: q        BINPUT       2
   47: (        MARK
   48: M            BININT2     2009
   51: K            BININT1     3
   53: K            BININT1     27
   55: K            BININT1     22
   57: K            BININT1     20
   59: K            BININT1     42
   61: K            BININT1     4
   63: K            BININT1     86
   65: J            BININT      -1
   70: t            TUPLE       (MARK at 47)
   71: q        BINPUT       3
   73: }        EMPTY_DICT
   74: q        BINPUT       4
   76: \x86     TUPLE2
   77: q        BINPUT       5
   79: R        REDUCE
   80: q        BINPUT       6
   82: X        BINUNICODE 'comments_link'
  100: q        BINPUT       7
  102: N        NONE
  103: X        BINUNICODE 'internal_id'
  119: q        BINPUT       8
  121: C        SHORT_BINBYTES 'ÞÕ´ø'
  127: q        BINPUT       9
  129: X        BINUNICODE 'tags'
  138: q        BINPUT       10
  140: X        BINUNICODE 'diveintopython'
  159: q        BINPUT       11
```

```
161: X        BINUNICODE  'docbook'
173: q        BINPUT      12
175: X        BINUNICODE  'html'
184: q        BINPUT      13
186: \x87     TUPLE3
187: q        BINPUT      14
189: X        BINUNICODE  'title'
199: q        BINPUT      15
201: X        BINUNICODE  'Dive into history, 2009 edition'
237: q        BINPUT      16
239: X        BINUNICODE  'article_link'
256: q        BINPUT      17
258: X        BINUNICODE  'http://diveintomark.org/archives/
2009/03/27/dive-into-history-2009-edition'
337: q        BINPUT      18
339: X        BINUNICODE  'published'
353: q        BINPUT      19
355: \x88     NEWTRUE
356: u        SETITEMS    (MARK at 5)
357: .    STOP
highest protocol among opcodes = 3
```

The most interesting piece of information in that disassembly is on the last line because it includes the version of the pickle protocol with which this file was saved. There is no explicit version marker in the pickle protocol.

To determine which protocol version was used to store a pickle file, you need to look at the markers (*opcodes*) within the pickled data and use hard-coded knowledge of which opcodes were introduced with each version of the pickle protocol. The `pickle.dis()` function does exactly that, and it prints the result in the last line of the disassembly output. Listing 13-10 shows a function that returns just the version number without printing anything.

Listing 13-10. pickleversion.py

```python
import pickletools

def protocol_version(file_object):
    maxproto = -1
    for opcode, arg, pos in pickletools.genops(file_object):
        maxproto = max(maxproto, opcode.proto)
    return maxproto
```

Listing 13-11 shows the `pickleversion` module in action.

Listing 13-11. Getting the Version of a Pickle File

```python
>>> import pickleversion
>>> with open('entry.pickle', 'rb') as f:
...     v = pickleversion.protocol_version(f)
>>> v
3
```

Serializing Python Objects to be Read by Other Languages

The data format used by the `pickle` module is Python-specific. It makes no attempt to be compatible with other programming languages. If cross-language compatibility is one of your requirements, you need to look at other serialization formats. One such format is JSON. *JSON* stands for *JavaScript Object Notation*, but don't let the name fool you; JSON is explicitly designed to be usable across multiple programming languages.

Python 3 includes a `json` module in the standard library. Like the `pickle` module, the `json` module has functions for serializing data structures, storing the serialized data on disk, loading serialized data from disk, and unserializing the data back into a new Python object. But there are some important differences, too. First of all, the JSON data format is text-based, not binary. RFC 4627 defines the JSON format and how different types of data must be encoded as text. For example, a Boolean value is stored as either the five-character string `'false'` or the four-character string `'true'`. All JSON values are case-sensitive.

Second, as with any text-based format, there is the issue of whitespace. JSON allows arbitrary amounts of whitespace (spaces, tabs, carriage returns, and line feeds) between values. This whitespace is *insignificant*, which means that JSON encoders can add as much or as little whitespace as they like, and JSON decoders are required to ignore the whitespace between values. This allows you to *pretty-print* your JSON data, nicely nesting values within values at different indentation levels so you can read it in a standard browser or text editor. Python's `json` module has options for pretty-printing during encoding.

Third, there's the perennial problem of character encoding. JSON encodes values as plain text, but as you learned in Chapter 4, there ain't no such thing as "plain text." JSON must be stored in a Unicode encoding (UTF-32, UTF-16, or the default UTF-8), and section 3 of RFC 4627 defines how to tell which encoding is being used.

Saving Data to a JSON File

Serializing your data to a JSON file can be as easy as Listing 13-12.

Listing 13-12. Trying to Dump Our Data Structure to a JSON File

```
>>> shell
1
>>> basic_entry = {}                                        (1)
>>> basic_entry['id'] = 256
>>> basic_entry['title'] = 'Dive into history, 2009 edition'
>>> basic_entry['tags'] = ('diveintopython', 'docbook', 'html')
>>> basic_entry['published'] = True
>>> basic_entry['comments_link'] = None
>>> import json
>>> with open('basic.json', mode='w', encoding='utf-8') as f:   (2)
...     json.dump(basic_entry, f)                            (3)
```

1. We'll create a new data structure instead of reusing the existing `entry` data structure. Later in this chapter, you'll see what happens when we try to encode the more complex data structure in JSON.

2. JSON is a text-based format, which means you need to open this file in text mode and specify a character encoding. You can never go wrong with UTF-8.

213

3. Like the `pickle` module, the `json` module defines a `dump()` function, which takes a Python data structure and a writeable stream object. The `dump()` function serializes the Python data structure and writes it to the stream object. Doing this inside a `with` statement will ensure that the file is closed properly when we're done.

Listing 13-13 shows what the resulting JSON serialization looks like. JSON looks remarkably like a data structure you might define manually in JavaScript. This is no accident; you can actually use the JavaScript `eval()` function to "decode" JSON-serialized data. (The usual caveats about untrusted input apply, but the point is that JSON *is* valid JavaScript.) As such, JSON may already look familiar to you.

Listing 13-13. Printing a JSON File

```
you@localhost:~/diveintopython3/examples$ cat basic.json
{"published": true, "tags": ["diveintopython", "docbook", "html"],↵
 "comments_link": null,
"id": 256, "title": "Dive into history, 2009 edition"}
```

That's certainly more readable than a pickle file. But JSON can contain arbitrary whitespace between values, and the `json` module provides an easy way to take advantage of this to create even more readable JSON files, as shown in Listing 13-14.

Listing 13-14. Saving a JSON File with Added Whitespace

```
>>> shell
1
>>> with open('basic-pretty.json', mode='w', ↵
encoding='utf-8') as f:
...     json.dump(basic_entry, f, indent=2)                        (1)
```

1. If you pass an `indent` parameter to the `json.dump()` function, it will make the resulting JSON file more readable, at the expense of larger file size. The `indent` parameter is an integer. 0 means "put each value on its own line." A number greater than 0 means "put each value on its own line and use this number of spaces to indent nested data structures."

Listing 13-15 shows the resulting JSON file.

Listing 13-15. A Pretty-Printed JSON File

```
you@localhost:~/diveintopython3/examples$ ↵
cat basic-pretty.json
{
  "published": true,
  "tags": [
    "diveintopython",
    "docbook",
    "html"
  ],
```

```
   "comments_link": null,
   "id": 256,
   "title": "Dive into history, 2009 edition"
}
```

Mapping Python Datatypes to JSON

Because JSON is not Python-specific, there are some mismatches in its coverage of Python datatypes. Some of them are simply naming differences, but there are two important Python datatypes that are completely missing. See if you can spot them in Table 13-1.

Table 13-1. Mapping Python Datatypes to JSON

Notes	JSON	Python 3
	object	dictionary
	array	list
	string	string
	integer	integer
	Real number	float
*	True	True
*	False	False
*	Null	None

* All JSON values are case-sensitive.

Did you notice what was missing? Tuples and bytes! JSON has an array type, which the `json` module maps to a Python list, but it does not have a separate type for "frozen arrays" (tuples). And although JSON supports strings quite nicely, it has no support for **bytes** objects or byte arrays.

Serializing Datatypes Unsupported by JSON

Even if JSON has no built-in support for bytes, that doesn't mean you can't serialize **bytes** objects. The `json` module provides extensibility hooks for encoding and decoding unknown datatypes. (By "unknown," I mean "not defined in JSON." Obviously, the `json` module knows about byte arrays, but it's constrained by the limitations of the JSON specification.)

If you want to encode bytes or other datatypes that JSON doesn't support natively, you need to provide custom encoders and decoders for those types. Otherwise, you'll get an error message during serialization, as shown in Listing 13-16.

Listing 13-16. Trying to Serialize a Complex Python Data Structure to a JSON File

```
>>> shell
1
>>> entry                                                    (1)
{'comments_link': None,
 'internal_id': b'\xDE\xD5\xB4\xF8',
 'title': 'Dive into history, 2009 edition',
 'tags': ('diveintopython', 'docbook', 'html'),
 'article_link': 'http://diveintomark.org/archives/2009/03/27/↵
dive-into-history-2009-edition',
 'published_date': time.struct_time(tm_year=2009, tm_mon=3, ↵
tm_mday=27, tm_hour=22, tm_min=20, tm_sec=42, tm_wday=4, ↵
tm_yday=86, tm_isdst=-1),
 'published': True}
>>> import json
>>> with open('entry.json', 'w', encoding='utf-8') as f:   (2)
...     json.dump(entry, f)                                 (3)
...
Traceback (most recent call last):
  File "<stdin>", line 5, in <module>
  File "C:\Python31\lib\json\__init__.py", line 178, in dump
    for chunk in iterable:
  File "C:\Python31\lib\json\encoder.py", line 408, in _iterencode
    for chunk in _iterencode_dict(o, _current_indent_level):
  File "C:\Python31\lib\json\encoder.py", line 382, in _iterencode_dict
    for chunk in chunks:
  File "C:\Python31\lib\json\encoder.py", line 416, in _iterencode
    o = _default(o)
  File "C:\Python31\lib\json\encoder.py", line 170, in default
    raise TypeError(repr(o) + " is not JSON serializable")
TypeError: b'\xDE\xD5\xB4\xF8' is not JSON serializable
```

1. Okay, it's time to revisit the entry data structure. This has it all: a Boolean value, a None value, a string, a tuple of strings, a bytes object, and a time structure.

2. I know I've said it before, but it's worth repeating: JSON is a text-based format. Always open JSON files in text mode with a UTF-8 character encoding.

3. Well *that's* not good. What happened?

Here's what happened: the json.dump() function tried to serialize the bytes object b'\xDE\xD5\xB4\xF8', but it failed because JSON has no support for bytes objects. However, if storing bytes is important to you, you can define your own "mini-serialization format," as shown in Listing 13-17.

Listing 13-17. A Custom Serializer for Bytes

```
def to_json(python_object):                                    (1)
    if isinstance(python_object, bytes):                       (2)
        return {'__class__': 'bytes',
                '__value__': list(python_object)}              (3)
    raise TypeError(repr(python_object) + ' is not JSON serializable')  (4)
```

1. To define your own mini-serialization format for a datatype that JSON doesn't support natively, just define a function that takes a Python object as a parameter. This Python object will be the actual object that the `json.dump()` function is unable to serialize by itself—in this case, the `bytes` object `b'\xDE\xD5\xB4\xF8'`.

2. Your custom serialization function should check the type of the Python object that the `json.dump()` function passed to it. This is not strictly necessary if your function serializes only one datatype, but it makes it crystal clear what case your function is covering. It also makes it easier to extend if you need to add serializations for more datatypes later.

3. In this case, I chose to convert a `bytes` object into a dictionary. The `__class__` key will hold the original datatype (as a string, `'bytes'`), and the `__value__` key will hold the actual value. Of course, this can't be a `bytes` object; the entire point is to convert it into something that can be serialized in JSON! A `bytes` object is just a sequence of integers; each integer is somewhere in the range 0– 255. We can use the `list()` function to convert the `bytes` object into a list of integers. So `b'\xDE\xD5\xB4\xF8'` becomes [222, 213, 180, 248]. (Do the math! It works! The byte `\xDE` in hexadecimal is 222 in decimal, `\xD5` is 213, and so on.)

4. This line is important. The data structure you're serializing might contain types that neither the built-in JSON serializer nor your custom serializer can handle. In this case, your custom serializer must raise a `TypeError` so that the `json.dump()` function knows that your custom serializer did not recognize the type.

That's it; you don't need to do anything else. In particular, this custom serialization function *returns a Python dictionary*, not a string. You're not doing the entire serializing-to-JSON yourself; you're only doing the converting-to-a-supported-datatype part. The `json.dump()` function will do the rest.

Did the custom serializer do the trick? See Listing 13-18 to find out.

Listing 13-18. *Dumping to a JSON File with a Custom Serializer*

```
>>> shell
1
>>> import customserializer                                            (1)
>>> with open('entry.json', 'w', encoding='utf-8') as f:              (2)
...     json.dump(entry, f, default=customserializer.to_json)         (3)
...
Traceback (most recent call last):
  File "<stdin>", line 9, in <module>
    json.dump(entry, f, default=customserializer.to_json)
  File "C:\Python31\lib\json\__init__.py", line 178, in dump
    for chunk in iterable:
  File "C:\Python31\lib\json\encoder.py", line 408, in _iterencode
    for chunk in _iterencode_dict(o, _current_indent_level):
  File "C:\Python31\lib\json\encoder.py", line 382, in _iterencode_dict
    for chunk in chunks:
  File "C:\Python31\lib\json\encoder.py", line 416, in _iterencode
    o = _default(o)
  File "/Users/pilgrim/diveintopython3/examples/customserializer.py",↵
line 12, in to_json
    raise TypeError(repr(python_object) + ' is not JSON serializable')  (4)
TypeError: time.struct_time(tm_year=2009, tm_mon=3, tm_mday=27, ↵
tm_hour=22, tm_min=20, tm_sec=42, tm_wday=4, tm_yday=86, tm_isdst=-1) ↵
is not JSON serializable
```

1. The `customserializer` module is where you just defined the `to_json()` function in the previous example.

2. Text mode, UTF-8 encoding, yadda yadda. (You'll forget! I forget sometimes! And everything will work right up until the moment that it fails, and then it will fail most spectacularly.)

3. This is the important bit: to hook your custom conversion function into the `json.dump()` function, pass your function into the `json.dump()` function in the `default` parameter. (Hooray, everything in Python is an object!)

4. Okay, so it didn't actually work. But take a look at the exception. The `json.dump()` function is no longer complaining about being unable to serialize the `bytes` object. Now it's complaining about a completely different object: the `time.struct_time` object.

Although getting a different exception might not seem like progress, it really is! It'll just take one more tweak to get past this (see Listing 13-19).

Listing 13-19. A Custom Serializer for Multiple Data Types

```
import time

def to_json(python_object):
    if isinstance(python_object, time.struct_time):          (1)
        return {'__class__': 'time.asctime',
                '__value__': time.asctime(python_object)}     (2)
    if isinstance(python_object, bytes):
        return {'__class__': 'bytes',
                '__value__': list(python_object)}
    raise TypeError
```

1. Adding to our existing **customserializer.to_json()** function, we need to check whether the Python object (that the **json.dump()** function is having trouble with) is a **time.struct_time**.

2. If so, we'll do something similar to the conversion we did with the **bytes** object: convert the **time.struct_time** object to a dictionary that only contains JSON-serializable values. In this case, the easiest way to convert a datetime into a JSON-serializable value is to convert it to a string with the **time.asctime()** function. The **time.asctime()** function will convert that nasty-looking **time.struct_time** into the string **'Fri Mar 27 22:20:42 2009'**.

With these two custom conversions, the entire **entry** data structure should serialize to JSON without any further problems, as shown in Listing 13-20.

Listing 13-20. Successfully Dumping a Complex Data Structure to a JSON File

```
>>> shell
1
>>> with open('entry.json', 'w', encoding='utf-8') as f:
...     json.dump(entry, f, default=customserializer.to_json)
...
```

```
you@localhost:~/diveintopython3/examples$ ls -l example.json
-rw-r--r-- 1 you  you  391 Aug  3 13:34 entry.json
you@localhost:~/diveintopython3/examples$ cat example.json
{"published_date": {"__class__": "time.asctime", "__value__": ↵
"Fri Mar 27 22:20:42 2009"},
"comments_link": null, "internal_id": {"__class__": "bytes",↵
"__value__":
[222, 213, 180, 248]},
"tags": ["diveintopython", "docbook", "html"], "title": ↵
"Dive into history, 2009 edition",
"article_link": "http://diveintomark.org/archives/2009/03/27/
dive-into-history-2009-edition",
"published": true}
```

Loading Data from a JSON File

Like the `pickle` module, the `json` module has a `load()` function that takes a stream object, reads JSON-encoded data from it, and creates a new Python object that mirrors the JSON data structure, as shown in Listing 13-21.

Listing 13-21. Loading Data from a JSON File

```
>>> shell
2
>>> del entry                                          (1)
>>> entry
Traceback (most recent call last):
  File "<stdin>", line 1, in <module>
NameError: name 'entry' is not defined
>>> import json
>>> with open('entry.json', 'r', encoding='utf-8') as f:
...      entry = json.load(f)                          (2)
...
>>> entry                                              (3)
{'comments_link': None,
 'internal_id': {'__class__': 'bytes', '__value__':
[222, 213, 180, 248]},
 'title': 'Dive into history, 2009 edition',
 'tags': ['diveintopython', 'docbook', 'html'],
 'article_link': 'http://diveintomark.org/archives↵
/2009/03/27/
dive-into-history-2009-edition',
 'published_date': {'__class__': 'time.asctime', '__value__':
'Fri Mar 27 22:20:42 2009'},
 'published': True}
```

1. For demonstration purposes, switch to Python shell #2 and delete the `entry` data structure that you created earlier in this chapter with the `pickle` module.

2. In the simplest case, the `json.load()` function works the same as the `pickle.load()` function. You pass in a stream object and it returns a new Python object.

3. I have good news and bad news. Good news first: the `json.load()` function successfully read the `entry.json` file you created in Python shell #1 and created a new Python object that contained the data. Now the bad news: it didn't re-create the original `entry` data structure. The two values `'internal_id'` and `'published_date'` were re-created as dictionaries—specifically, the dictionaries with JSON-compatible values that you created in the `to_json()` conversion function.

`json.load()` doesn't know anything about any conversion function you might have passed to `json.dump()`. What you need is the opposite of the `to_json()` function—a function that will take a custom-converted JSON object and convert it back to the original Python datatype. Listing 13-22 shows such a function.

Listing 13-22. A Custom Unserializer for Bytes and Time Structs

```
# add this to customserializer.py
def from_json(json_object):                                    (1)
    if '__class__' in json_object:                             (2)
        if json_object['__class__'] == 'time.asctime':
            return time.strptime(json_object['__value__'])     (3)
        if json_object['__class__'] == 'bytes':
            return bytes(json_object['__value__'])             (4)
    return json_object
```

1. This conversion function also takes one parameter and returns one value. But the parameter it takes is not a string; it's a Python object—the result of deserializing a JSON-encoded string into Python.

2. All you need to do is check whether this object contains the '**__class__**' key that the **to_json()** function created. If so, the value of the '**__class__**' key will tell you how to decode the value back into the original Python datatype.

3. To decode the time string returned by the **time.asctime()** function, you use the **time.strptime()** function. This function takes a formatted datetime string (in a customizable format, but it defaults to the same format that **time.asctime()** defaults to) and returns a **time.struct_time**.

4. To convert a list of integers back into a **bytes** object, you can use the **bytes()** function.

That was it; there were only two datatypes handled in the **to_json()** function, and now those two datatypes are handled in the **from_json()** function. Now the **json.dump()**/**json.load()** cycle is complete, as shown in Listing 13-23.

Listing 13-23. The json.dump()/json.load() Cycle

```
>>> shell
2
>>> import customserializer
>>> with open('entry.json', 'r', encoding='utf-8') as f:
...       entry = json.load(f, object_hook=↵
customserializer.from_json)  (1)
...
>>> entry                                                      (2)
{'comments_link': None,
 'internal_id': b'\xDE\xD5\xB4\xF8',
 'title': 'Dive into history, 2009 edition',
 'tags': ['diveintopython', 'docbook', 'html'],
 'article_link': 'http://diveintomark.org/archives/2009/03/27/↵
dive-into-history-2009-edition',
 'published_date': time.struct_time(tm_year=2009, ↵
tm_mon=3, tm_mday=27,
 tm_hour=22, tm_min=20, tm_sec=42, tm_wday=4, tm_yday=86, ↵
 tm_isdst=-1),
 'published': True}
```

221

1. To hook the `from_json()` function into the deserialization process, pass it as the `object_hook` parameter to the `json.load()` function. Functions that take functions so handy!

2. The `entry` data structure now contains an `'internal_id'` key whose value is a `bytes` object. It also contains a `'published_date'` key whose value is a `time.struct_time` object.

There is one final glitch, though, as shown in Listing 13-24.

Listing 13-24. What About the Tuples?

```
>>> shell
1
>>> import customserializer
>>> with open('entry.json', 'r', encoding='utf-8') as f: ↵
...     entry2 = json.load(f, object_hook=
customserializer.from_json)
...
>>> entry2 == entry                                          (1)
False
>>> entry['tags']                                            (2)
('diveintopython', 'docbook', 'html')
>>> entry2['tags']                                           (3)
['diveintopython', 'docbook', 'html']
```

1. Even after hooking the `to_json()` function into the serialization and hooking the `from_json()` function into the deserialization, we still haven't re-created a perfect replica of the original data structure. Why not?

2. In the original `entry` data structure, the value of the `'tags'` key was a tuple of three strings.

3. But in the round-tripped `entry2` data structure, the value of the `'tags'` key is a *list* of three strings. JSON doesn't distinguish between tuples and lists; it has only a single list-like datatype, the array, and the `json` module silently converts both tuples and lists into JSON arrays during serialization. For most uses, you can ignore the difference between tuples and lists, but it's something to keep in mind as you work with the `json` module.

Further Reading Online

■ Many articles about the `pickle` module make references to `cPickle`. In Python 2, there were two implementations of the `pickle` module: one written in pure Python and another written in C (but still callable from Python). In Python 3, these two modules have been consolidated, so you should always just `import pickle`. You may find these articles useful, but you should ignore the now-obsolete information about `cPickle`.

On pickling with the `pickle` module:

- *pickle module*: http://docs.python.org/3.1/library/pickle.html

- *pickle and cPickle—Python object serialization*:
  http://www.doughellmann.com/PyMOTW/pickle/

- *Using* pickle: http://wiki.python.org/moin/UsingPickle

- *Python persistence management*:
  http://www.ibm.com/developerworks/library/l-pypers.html

On JSON and the `json` module:

- *json—JavaScript Object Notation Serializer*:
  http://www.doughellmann.com/PyMOTW/json/

- *JSON encoding and decoding with custom objects in Python*:
  http://blog.quaternio.net/2009/07/16/json-encoding-and-decoding-with-custom-objects-in-python/

On pickle extensibility:

- *Pickling class instances*:
  http://docs.python.org/3.1/library/pickle.html#pickling-class-instances

- *Persistence of external objects*: http://docs.python.org/3.1/library/pickle.html#persistence-of-external-objects

- *Handling stateful objects*: http://docs.python.org/3.1/library/pickle.html#handling-stateful-objects

CHAPTER 14

■ ■ ■

HTTP Web Services

HTTP web services are programmatic ways of sending and receiving data from remote servers using nothing but the operations of HTTP. If you want to get data from the server, use HTTP GET; if you want to send new data to the server, use HTTP POST. Some more advanced HTTP web service APIs also define ways of creating, modifying, and deleting data, using HTTP PUT and HTTP DELETE. In other words, the verbs built into the HTTP protocol (GET, POST, PUT, and DELETE) can map directly to application-level operations for retrieving, creating, modifying, and deleting data.

The main advantage of this approach is simplicity, and its simplicity has proven popular. Data— usually XML data—can be built and stored statically or generated dynamically by a server-side script, and all major programming languages (including Python, of course!) include an HTTP library for downloading it. Debugging is also easier; because each resource in an HTTP web service has a unique address (in the form of a URL), you can load it in your web browser and immediately see the raw data.

Here are some examples of HTTP web services:

- Google Data APIs (`http://code.google.com/apis/gdata/`) allow you to interact with a wide variety of Google services, including Blogger and YouTube.

- Flickr services (`http://www.flickr.com/services/api/`) allow you to upload and download photos from Flickr.

- The Twitter API (`http://apiwiki.twitter.com/`) allows you to publish status updates on Twitter.

Many more examples are available, and you'll find a more complete Listing at `http://www.programmableweb.com/apis/directory/1?sort=mashups`.

Python 3 comes with two different libraries for interacting with HTTP web services:

- `http.client` is a low-level library that implements RFC 2616, the HTTP protocol.

- `urllib.request` is an abstraction layer built on top of `http.client`. It provides a standard API for accessing both HTTP and file transfer protocol (FTP) servers, automatically follows HTTP redirects, and handles some common forms of HTTP authentication.

Which one should you use? Neither of them. Instead, you should use `httplib2`, an open source third-party library that implements HTTP more fully than `http.client` but provides a better abstraction than `urllib.request`.

To understand why `httplib2` is the right choice, you first need to understand HTTP.

Features of HTTP

There are five important features that all HTTP clients should support.

- Caching

- Last-modified checking

- ETags

- Compression

- Redirects

Caching

The most important thing to understand about any type of web service is that network access is incredibly expensive. I don't mean dollars-and-cents expensive (although bandwidth isn't free). I mean that an extraordinary amount of time is needed to open a connection, send a request, and retrieve a response from a remote server. Even on the fastest broadband connection, *latency* (the time it takes to send a request and start retrieving data in a response) can still be higher than you anticipated. A router misbehaves; a packet is dropped; an intermediate proxy is under attack — there's never a dull moment on the public Internet, and you probably can't do anything about it.

HTTP is designed with caching in mind. There is an entire class of devices (called caching proxies) whose only job is to sit between you and the rest of the world and minimize network access. Your company or Internet service provider (ISP) almost certainly maintains caching proxies, even if you're unaware of them. Caching proxies work because caching built into HTTP.

Listing 14-1 shows a concrete example of how caching works. You visit http://diveintomark.org in your browser. That page includes a background image, http://wearehugh.com/m.jpg. When your browser downloads that image, the server includes the HTTP headers shown in Listing 14-1.

Listing 14-1. Downloading an Image

```
HTTP/1.1 200 OK
Date: Sun, 31 May 2009 17:14:04 GMT
Server: Apache
Last-Modified: Fri, 22 Aug 2008 04:28:16 GMT
ETag: "3075-ddc8d800"
Accept-Ranges: bytes
Content-Length: 12405
Cache-Control: max-age=31536000, public
Expires: Mon, 31 May 2010 17:14:04 GMT
Connection: close
Content-Type: image/jpeg
```

The Cache-Control and Expires headers tell your browser (and any caching proxies between you and the server) that this image can be cached for up to a year. *A year!* And if, in the next year, you visit another page that also includes a link to this image, your browser will load the image from its cache *without generating any network activity whatsoever.*

But wait, it gets better. Let's say your browser purges the image from your local cache for some reason. Maybe it ran out of disk space or you manually cleared the cache. But the HTTP headers said that this data could be cached by public caching proxies (by virtue of that public keyword in the

Cache-Control header). Caching proxies are designed to have tons of storage space, probably far more than your local browser has allocated.

If your company or ISP maintains a caching proxy, the proxy may still have the image cached. When you visit http://diveintomark.org again, your browser will look in its local cache for the image, but it won't find it, so it will make a network request to try to download it from the remote server. However, if the caching proxy still has a copy of the image, the proxy will intercept that request and serve the image from *its* cache. That means that your request will never reach the remote server; in fact, it will never leave your company's network. That makes for a faster download (fewer network hops) and saves your company money (less data being downloaded from the outside world).

HTTP caching only works when everybody does their parts. On one side, servers need to send the correct headers in their response. On the other side, clients need to understand and respect those headers before they request the same data twice. The proxies in the middle are not a panacea; they can only be as smart as the servers and clients allow them to be.

Python's HTTP libraries do not support caching, but httplib2 does.

Last-Modified Checking

Some data never changes, while other data changes all the time. In between, there is a vast field of data that *might* have changed but hasn't. CNN.com's feed is updated every few minutes, but my weblog's feed may not change for days or weeks at a time. In the latter case, I don't want to tell clients to cache my feed for weeks at a time, because when I do actually post something, people may not read it for weeks (because they're respecting my cache headers which said not to bother checking this feed for weeks). On the other hand, I don't want clients downloading my entire feed once an hour if it hasn't changed!

HTTP has a solution to this dilemma, too. When you request data for the first time, the server can send back a Last-Modified header. This header contains exactly what it sounds like: the date that the data was changed. That background image referenced from http://diveintomark.org included a Last-Modified header, as shown in Listing 14-2.

Listing 14-2. Last-Modified Header

```
HTTP/1.1 200 OK
Date: Sun, 31 May 2009 17:14:04 GMT
Server: Apache
Last-Modified: Fri, 22 Aug 2008 04:28:16 GMT
ETag: "3075-ddc8d800"
Accept-Ranges: bytes
Content-Length: 12405
Cache-Control: max-age=31536000, public
Expires: Mon, 31 May 2010 17:14:04 GMT
Connection: close
Content-Type: image/jpeg
```

When you request the same data a second (or third or fourth) time, you can send an If-Modified-Since header with your request, with the date you got back from the server last time. If the data hasn't changed since then, the server sends back a special HTTP 304 status code, which indicates that this data hasn't changed since the last time the server asked for it. You can test this on the command line using curl, as shown in Listing 14-3.

Listing 14-3. Downloading with curl

```
you@localhost:~$ curl -I -H "If-Modified-Since: Fri, 22 Aug 2008 04:28:16 GMT" ↩
http://wearehugh.com/m.jpg
HTTP/1.1 304 Not Modified
Date: Sun, 31 May 2009 18:04:39 GMT
Server: Apache
Connection: close
ETag: "3075-ddc8d800"
Expires: Mon, 31 May 2010 18:04:39 GMT
Cache-Control: max-age=31536000, public
```

Why is this header an improvement? Because when the server sends a **304** response, *it doesn't resend the data*. All you get is the status code. Even after your cached copy has expired, last-modified checking ensures that you won't download the same data twice if it hasn't changed.

As an extra bonus, this **304** response also includes caching headers. Proxies will keep a copy of data even after it officially expires, in the hopes that the data hasn't *really* changed and the next request responds with a **304** status code and updated cache information.

Python's HTTP libraries do not support last-modified date checking, but **httplib2** does.

ETags

ETags are an alternate way to accomplish the same thing as the last-modified checking. With ETags, the server sends a hash code in an **ETag** header along with the data you requested (exactly how this hash is determined is entirely up to the server; the only requirement is that it changes when the data changes). That background image referenced from **http://diveintomark.org** had an **ETag** header, as shown in Listing 14-4.

Listing 14-4. ETag Header

```
HTTP/1.1 200 OK
Date: Sun, 31 May 2009 17:14:04 GMT
Server: Apache
Last-Modified: Fri, 22 Aug 2008 04:28:16 GMT
ETag: "3075-ddc8d800"
Accept-Ranges: bytes
Content-Length: 12405
Cache-Control: max-age=31536000, public
Expires: Mon, 31 May 2010 17:14:04 GMT
Connection: close
Content-Type: image/jpeg
```

The second time you request the same data, you include the ETag hash in an **If-None-Match** header of your request. If the data hasn't changed, the server will send back a **304** status code. As with the last-modified date checking, the server sends back *only* the **304** status code; it doesn't send you the same data a second time. By including the ETag hash in your second request, you're telling the server that there's no need to resend the same data if it still matches this hash, since you still have the data from the last time (see Listing 14-5).

Listing 14-5. curl Again with an If-None-Match Header

```
you@localhost:~$ curl -I -H "If-None-Match: \"3075-ddc8d800\"" http://wearehugh.com↵
/m.jpg (1)
HTTP/1.1 304 Not Modified
Date: Sun, 31 May 2009 18:04:39 GMT
Server: Apache
Connection: close
ETag: "3075-ddc8d800"
Expires: Mon, 31 May 2010 18:04:39 GMT
Cache-Control: max-age=31536000, public
```

1. ETags are commonly enclosed in quotation marks, but *the quotation marks are part of the value*. They are not delimiters; the only delimiter in the ETag header is the colon between ETag and "3075-ddc8d800". That means you need to send the quotation marks back to the server in the If-None-Match header.

Python's HTTP libraries do not support ETags, but httplib2 does.

Compression

When you talk about HTTP web services, you're almost always talking about moving text-based data back and forth over the wire. Maybe the data is XML; maybe it's JSON, or maybe it's just plain text. Regardless of the format, text compresses well. The example feed in Chapter 12 is 3070 bytes uncompressed but would be 941 bytes after gzip compression. That's just 30 percent of the original size!

HTTP supports several compression algorithms. The two most common types are gzip and deflate. When you request a resource over HTTP, you can ask the server to send it in compressed format. You include an Accept-encoding header in your request that lists which compression algorithms you support. If the server supports any of the same algorithms, it will send you back compressed data (with a Content-encoding header that tells you which algorithm it used). After that, it's up to you to decompress the data.

Python's HTTP libraries do not support compression, but httplib2 does.

Redirects

Cool URIs don't change, but many URIs are seriously uncool. Web sites get reorganized, and pages move to new addresses. Even web services can reorganize. A syndicated feed at http://example.com/index.xml might be moved to http://example.com/xml/atom.xml. Or an entire domain might move, as an organization expands and reorganizes, so http://www.example.com/index.xml becomes http://server-farm-1.example.com/index.xml.

Every time you request any kind of resource from an HTTP server, the server includes a status code in its response. Status code 200 means "everything's normal; here's the page you asked for." Status code 404 means "page not found" (you've probably seen 404 errors while browsing the Web).

Status codes in the 300s indicate some form of redirection. HTTP has several different ways of signifying that a resource has moved. The two most common techniques are status codes 301 and 302. Status code 301 is a *permanent redirect*; it means, "oops, that page was moved permanently" (and gives the new address in a Location header). If you get a 301 status code and a new address, you're supposed to use the new address from then on. Status code 302 is a temporary redirect; it means, "oops, that page got moved over here temporarily" (and gives the temporary address in a Location header). If you get a 302 status code and a new address, the HTTP specification says you should use the new address to get what you asked for, but the next time you want to access the same resource, you should retry the old address.

The urllib.request module automatically follows redirects when it receives the appropriate status code from the HTTP server, but it doesn't tell you that it did so. You'll end up getting data you asked for, but you'll never know that the underlying library "helpfully" followed a redirect for you. So you'll continue pounding away at the old address, and each time you'll get redirected to the new address, and each time the urllib.request module will "helpfully" follow the redirect. In other words, it treats permanent redirects the same as temporary redirects and results in two round trips instead of one, which is bad for the server and bad for you.

httplib2 handles permanent redirects for you. It will not only tell you that a permanent redirect occurred but will keep track of these redirects locally and automatically rewrite redirected URLs before requesting them.

How Not to Fetch Data Over HTTP

Let's say you want to download a resource over HTTP, such as an Atom feed. Since you're requesting a feed, you're not just going to download it once; you're going to download it over and over again (most feed readers will check for changes hourly). Let's fetch the data the quick-and-dirty way first (see Listing 14-6), and then I'll show you how you can do it better.

Listing 14-6. Quick-and-Dirty Data Fetching

```
>>> import urllib.request
>>> a_url = 'http://diveintopython3.org/examples/feed.xml'
>>> data = urllib.request.urlopen(a_url).read()    (1)
>>> type(data)                                      (2)
<class 'bytes'>
>>> print(data)
<?xml version='1.0' encoding='utf-8'?>
<feed xmlns='http://www.w3.org/2005/Atom' xml:lang='en'>
  <title>dive into mark</title>
  <subtitle>currently between addictions</subtitle>
  <id>tag:diveintomark.org,2001-07-29:/</id>
  <updated>2009-03-27T21:56:07Z</updated>
  <link rel='alternate' type='text/html' href='http://diveintomark.org/'/>
  ...
```

1. Downloading anything over HTTP is incredibly easy in Python; in fact, it's a one-liner. The urllib.request module has a handy urlopen() function that takes the address of the page you want and returns a file-like object that you can just read() from to get the full contents of the page. It just can't get any easier.

2. The urlopen().read() method always returns a bytes object, not a string. Remember, bytes are bytes; characters are an abstraction. HTTP servers don't deal in abstractions. If you request a resource, you get bytes. If you want that data as a string, you'll need to determine the character encoding and explicitly convert it to a string.

So what's wrong with the technique in Listing 14-6? During testing or development, there's nothing wrong with it. I use it all the time. I wanted the contents of the feed, and I got the contents of the feed. The same technique works for any web page. But once you start thinking in terms of a web service that you want to access on a regular basis (e.g., requesting this feed once an hour), you're being inefficient, and you're being rude.

What's On the Wire?

To see why Listing 14-6 is inefficient and rude, let's turn on the debugging features of Python's HTTP library and see what's being sent on the wire (i.e., over the network). Listing 14-7 shows what's going over the wire.

Listing 14-7. On the Wire When You Download the Quick-and-Dirty Way

```
>>> from http.client import HTTPConnection
>>> HTTPConnection.debuglevel = 1                                   (1)
>>> from urllib.request import urlopen
>>> response = urlopen('http://diveintopython3.org/examples/feed.xml')  (2)
send: b'GET /examples/feed.xml HTTP/1.1                              (3)
Host: diveintopython3.org                                           (4)
Accept-Encoding: identity                                           (5)
User-Agent: Python-urllib/3.1'                                      (6)
Connection: close
reply: 'HTTP/1.1 200 OK'
...further debugging information omitted...
```

1. As I mentioned at the beginning of this chapter, urllib.request relies on another standard Python library, http.client. Normally, you don't need to touch http.client directly (the urllib.request module imports it automatically). But we import it here so we can toggle the debugging flag on the HTTPConnection class that urllib.request uses to connect to the HTTP server.

2. Now that the debugging flag is set, information on the HTTP request and response is printed out in real time. As this Listing shows, when you request the Atom feed, the urllib.request module sends five lines to the server. The fifth line is just boilerplate, but the first four are interesting.

3. The first line specifies the HTTP verb you're using and the path of the resource (minus the domain name).

4. The second line specifies the domain name from which we're requesting this feed.

5. The third line specifies the compression algorithms that the client supports. As I mentioned earlier, urllib.request does not support compression by default.

6. The fourth line specifies the name of the library that is making the request. By default, this is Python-urllib plus a version number. Both urllib.request and httplib2 support changing the user agent, simply by adding a User-Agent header to the request (which will override the default value).

Listing 14-8 shows what the server sent back in its response.

Listing 14-8. Server Response to the Quick-and-Dirty Request

```
>>> print(response.headers.as_string())      (1)
Date: Sun, 31 May 2009 19:23:06 GMT          (2)
Server: Apache
Last-Modified: Sun, 31 May 2009 06:39:55 GMT (3)
ETag: "bfe-93d9c4c0"                          (4)
Accept-Ranges: bytes
Content-Length: 3070                          (5)
Cache-Control: max-age=86400                  (6)
Expires: Mon, 01 Jun 2009 19:23:06 GMT
Vary: Accept-Encoding
Connection: close
Content-Type: application/xml
>>> data = response.read()                    (7)
>>> len(data)
3070
```

1. The `response` returned from the `urllib.request.urlopen()` function contains all the HTTP headers the server sent back. It also contains methods to download the actual data; we'll get to that in a minute.

2. The server tells you when it handled your request.

3. This response includes a `Last-Modified` header.

4. This response includes an `ETag` header.

5. The data is 3070 bytes long. Notice what *isn't* here: a `Content-encoding` header. Your request stated that you only accept uncompressed data (`Accept-encoding: identity`), and sure enough, this response contains uncompressed data.

6. This response includes caching headers that state that this feed can be cached for up to 24 hours (86,400 seconds).

7. And finally, download the actual data by calling `response.read()`. As you can tell from the `len()` function, this downloads all 3070 bytes at once.

As you can see, this code is already inefficient: it asked for (and received) uncompressed data. I know for a fact that this server supports gzip compression, but you must opt in to HTTP compression. We didn't ask for it, so we didn't get it. That means we're downloading 3070 bytes when we could have just downloaded 941. Bad dog, no biscuit.

But wait, it gets worse! To see just how inefficient this code is, let's request the same feed a second time (see Listing 14-9).

Listing 14-9. The Quick-and-Dirty Feed Request, Again

```
# continued from the previous example
>>> response2 = urlopen('http://diveintopython3.org/examples/feed.xml')
send: b'GET /examples/feed.xml HTTP/1.1
Host: diveintopython3.org
Accept-Encoding: identity
User-Agent: Python-urllib/3.1'
Connection: close
reply: 'HTTP/1.1 200 OK'
…further debugging information omitted…
```

Notice anything peculiar about this request? It hasn't changed! It's exactly the same as the first request: no sign of If-Modified-Since or If-None-Match headers, no respect for the caching headers, and still no compression.

And what happens when you do the same thing twice? You get the same response—twice (see Listing 14-10).

Listing 14-10. Server Response to the Second Quick-and-Dirty Request

```
# continued from the previous example
>>> print(response2.headers.as_string())        (1)
Date: Mon, 01 Jun 2009 03:58:00 GMT
Server: Apache
Last-Modified: Sun, 31 May 2009 22:51:11 GMT
ETag: "bfe-255ef5c0"
Accept-Ranges: bytes
Content-Length: 3070
Cache-Control: max-age=86400
Expires: Tue, 02 Jun 2009 03:58:00 GMT
Vary: Accept-Encoding
Connection: close
Content-Type: application/xml
>>> data2 = response2.read()
>>> len(data2)                                  (2)
3070
>>> data2 == data                               (3)
True
```

1. The server is still sending the same array of smart headers: Cache-Control and Expires to allow caching, Last-Modified and ETag to enable not-modified tracking. Even the Vary: Accept-Encoding header hints that the server would support compression, if only you would ask for it. But you didn't.

2. Once again, fetching this data downloads the whole 3070 bytes.

3. These bytes are the exact same 3070 bytes you downloaded last time.

HTTP is designed to work better than this example allows. urllib speaks HTTP like I speak Spanish —enough to get by in a jam but not enough to hold a conversation. HTTP is a conversation. It's time to upgrade to a library that speaks HTTP fluently.

Introducing httplib2

Before you can use httplib2, you'll need to install it. Visit http://code.google.com/p/httplib2/, and download the latest version. httplib2 is available for Python 2.x and 3.x; make sure you get the Python 3 version, named something like httplib2-python3-0.5.0.zip.

Unzip the archive; open a terminal window, and go to the newly created httplib2 directory. On Windows, open the Start menu; select Run; type **cmd.exe**, and press Enter to open a command prompt. Listing 14-11 shows what to type once you've opened a command prompt.

Listing 14-11. Installing httplib2 on Windows

```
c:\Users\pilgrim\Downloads> dir
 Volume in drive C has no label.
 Volume Serial Number is DED5-B4F8
 Directory of c:\Users\pilgrim\Downloads
07/28/2009  12:36 PM    <DIR>          .
07/28/2009  12:36 PM    <DIR>          ..
07/28/2009  12:36 PM    <DIR>          httplib2-python3-0.5.0
07/28/2009  12:33 PM            18,997 httplib2-python3-0.5.0.zip
               1 File(s)         18,997 bytes
               3 Dir(s)  61,496,684,544 bytes free
c:\Users\pilgrim\Downloads> cd httplib2-python3-0.5.0
c:\Users\pilgrim\Downloads\httplib2-python3-0.5.0> c:\python31\python.exe setup.py install
running install
running build
running build_py
running install_lib
creating c:\python31\Lib\site-packages\httplib2
copying build\lib\httplib2\iri2uri.py -> c:\python31\Lib\site-packages\httplib2
copying build\lib\httplib2\__init__.py -> c:\python31\Lib\site-packages\httplib2
byte-compiling c:\python31\Lib\site-packages\httplib2\iri2uri.py to iri2uri.pyc
byte-compiling c:\python31\Lib\site-packages\httplib2\__init__.py to __init__.pyc
running install_egg_info
Writing c:\python31\Lib\site-packages\httplib2-python3_0.5.0-py3.1.egg-info
```

On Mac OS X, run the Terminal.app application in your /Applications/Utilities/ folder. On Linux, run the Terminal application, which is usually in your Applications menu under Accessories or System. Listing 14-12 shows what to type once you've opened a terminal window.

Listing 14-12. Installing httplib2 on Mac OS X or Linux

```
you@localhost:~/Desktop$ unzip httplib2-python3-0.5.0.zip
Archive:  httplib2-python3-0.5.0.zip
  inflating: httplib2-python3-0.5.0/README
  inflating: httplib2-python3-0.5.0/setup.py
  inflating: httplib2-python3-0.5.0/PKG-INFO
  inflating: httplib2-python3-0.5.0/httplib2/__init__.py
  inflating: httplib2-python3-0.5.0/httplib2/iri2uri.py
```

```
you@localhost:~/Desktop$ cd httplib2-python3-0.5.0/
you@localhost:~/Desktop/httplib2-python3-0.5.0$ sudo python3 setup.py install
running install
running build
running build_py
creating build
creating build/lib.linux-x86_64-3.0
creating build/lib.linux-x86_64-3.0/httplib2
copying httplib2/iri2uri.py -> build/lib.linux-x86_64-3.0/httplib2
copying httplib2/__init__.py -> build/lib.linux-x86_64-3.0/httplib2
running install_lib
creating /usr/local/lib/python3.0/dist-packages/httplib2
copying build/lib.linux-x86_64-3.0/httplib2/iri2uri.py -> /usr/local/lib/python3.0/↵
dist-packages/httplib2
copying build/lib.linux-x86_64-3.0/httplib2/__init__.py -> /usr/local/lib/python3.0/↵
dist-packages/httplib2
byte-compiling /usr/local/lib/python3.0/dist-packages/httplib2/iri2uri.py to iri2uri.pyc
byte-compiling /usr/local/lib/python3.0/dist-packages/httplib2/__init__.py to __init__.pyc
running install_egg_info
Writing /usr/local/lib/python3.0/dist-packages/httplib2-python3_0.5.0.egg-info
```

To use httplib2, create an instance of the httplib2.Http class, as shown in Listing 14-13.

Listing 14-13. The httplib2.Http Object

```
>>> import httplib2
>>> h = httplib2.Http('.cache')                                              (1)
>>> response, content = h.request('http://diveintopython3.org/examples/feed.xml')  (2)
>>> response.status                                                          (3)
200
>>> content[:52]                                                             (4)
b"<?xml version='1.0' encoding='utf-8'?>\r\n<feed xmlns="
>>> len(content)
3070
```

1. The primary interface to httplib2 is the Http object. For reasons you'll see in the next section, you should always pass a directory name when you create an Http object. The directory does not need to exist; httplib2 will create it if necessary.

2. Once you have an Http object, retrieving data is as simple as calling the request() method with the address of the data you want. This will issue an HTTP GET request for that URL (later in this chapter, you'll see how to issue other HTTP requests, like POST).

3. The request() method returns two values. The first is an httplib2.Response object, which contains all the HTTP headers the server returned. For example, a status code of 200 indicates that the request was successful.

4. The second value returned from the **request()** method is assigned to the **content** variable, and it contains the actual data that was returned by the HTTP server. The data is returned as a **bytes** object, not a string. If you want it as a string, you'll need to determine the character encoding and convert it yourself.

■ You probably need only one httplib2.Http object. There are valid reasons for creating more than one, but you should do so only if you know why you need them. Needing to request data from two different URLs is not a valid reason. For that, just reuse the Http object and call the request() method twice.

Why httplib2 Returns Bytes Instead of Strings

Bytes. Strings. What a pain. Why can't httplib2 just do the conversion for you? Well, the answer is complicated, because the rules for determining the character encoding are specific to the kind of resource you're requesting. How could httplib2 know what kind of resource you're requesting? It's usually listed in the Content-Type HTTP header, but that's an optional feature of HTTP, and not all HTTP servers include it. If that header is not included in the HTTP response, the client is left to guess (this guesswork is commonly called *content sniffing*, and it's never perfect.)

If you know what sort of resource you're expecting (an XML document in this case), perhaps you could just pass the returned bytes object to the xml.etree.ElementTree.parse() function. That'll work as long as the XML document includes information on its own character encoding (as this one does), but that's an optional feature, and not all XML documents do that. If an XML document doesn't include encoding information, the client is supposed to look at the enclosing transport (i.e., the Content-Type HTTP header, which can include a charset parameter).

But it gets worse. Now, character-encoding information can be in two places: within the XML document itself and within the Content-Type HTTP header. If the information is in *both* places, which one wins? According to RFC 3023 (I swear I am not making this up), if the media type given in the Content-Type HTTP header is application/xml, application/xml-dtd, application/xml-external-parsed-entity, or any one of the subtypes of application/xml such as application/atom+xml or application/rss+xml or even application/rdf+xml, then the precedence order is as follows:

1. The encoding given in the charset parameter of the Content-Type HTTP header

2. The encoding given in the encoding attribute of the XML declaration within the document

3. UTF-8

On the other hand, if the media type given in the Content-Type HTTP header is text/xml, text/xml-external-parsed-entity, or a subtype like text/AnythingAtAll+xml, then the encoding attribute of the XML declaration within the document is ignored completely, and the precedence order is as follows:

1. The encoding given in the charset parameter of the Content-Type HTTP header

2.   Plain ASCII (us-ascii encoding)

And that's just for XML documents. For HTML documents, web browsers have constructed such byzantine rules for content sniffing that we're still trying to figure them all out.

■ You can read the latest research on HTML content-sniffing rules at http://www.adambarth.com/papers/ 2009/barth-caballero-song.pdf.

Caching with httplib2

Remember in the previous section when I said you should always create an httplib2.Http object with a directory name? Caching is the reason (see Listing 14-14).

Listing 14-14. Caching with the httplib2.Http Object

```
>>> response2, content2 = h.request('http://diveintopython3.org/examples/feed.xml')   (1)
>>> response2.status                                                                   (2)
200
>>> content2[:52]                                                                      (3)
b"<?xml version='1.0' encoding='utf-8'?>\r\n<feed xmlns="
>>> len(content2)
3070
```

1.   This line shouldn't be terribly surprising. It's the same thing you did last time, except you're putting the result into two new variables.

2.   The HTTP status is once again 200, just like last time.

3.   The downloaded content is the same as last time, too.

So, who cares? Quit your Python interactive shell, and relaunch it with a new session, and I'll show you the reason in Listing 14-15.

Listing 14-15. Requesting a Cached Resource Again

```
# NOT continued from previous example!
# Please exit out of the interactive shell
# and launch a new one.
>>> import httplib2
>>> httplib2.debuglevel = 1                                                            (1)
>>> h = httplib2.Http('.cache')                                                        (2)
>>> response, content = h.request('http://diveintopython3.org/examples/feed.xml')      (3)
>>> len(content)                                                                       (4)
3070
>>> response.status                                                                    (5)
200
>>> response.fromcache                                                                 (6)
```

`True`

1. Let's turn on debugging and see what's on the wire. This is the `httplib2` equivalent of turning on debugging in `http.client`. `httplib2` will print all the data being sent to the server and some key information being sent back.

2. Create an `httplib2.Http` object with the same directory name as before.

3. Request the same URL as before. *Nothing appears to happen.* More precisely, nothing gets sent to the server, and nothing gets returned from the server. There is absolutely no network activity whatsoever.

4. Yet we did receive some data — in fact, we received all of it.

5. We also received an HTTP status code indicating that the request was successful.

6. Here's the rub: this response was generated from `httplib2`'s local cache. That directory name you passed in when you created the `httplib2.Http` object holds `httplib2`'s cache of all the operations it's ever performed.

■ If you want to turn on `httplib2` debugging, you need to set a module-level constant (`httplib2.debuglevel`) and create a new `httplib2.Http` object. If you want to turn off debugging, you need to change the same module-level constant and create a new `httplib2.Http` object.

You previously requested the data at this URL. That request was successful (`status: 200`). That response included not only the feed data, but also a set of caching headers that told anyone who was listening that they could cache this resource for up to 24 hours (`Cache-Control: max-age=86400`, which is 24 hours measured in seconds). `httplib2` understand and respects those caching headers, and it stored the previous response in the `.cache` directory (which you passed in when you create the `Http` object). That cache hasn't expired yet, so the second time you request the data at this URL, `httplib2` simply returns the cached result without ever hitting the network.

I say *simply*, but obviously, a lot of complexity is hidden behind that simplicity. `httplib2` handles HTTP caching *automatically* and *by default*. If for some reason you need to know whether a response came from the cache, you can check `response.fromcache`. Otherwise, it just works.

Now, suppose you have data cached, but you want to bypass the cache and rerequest it from the remote server. Browsers sometimes do this if the user specifically requests it. For example, pressing F5 refreshes the current page, but pressing Ctrl+F5 bypasses the cache and rerequests the current page from the remote server. You might think, "Oh, I'll just delete the data from my local cache and then request it again." You could do that, but remember that there may be more parties involved than just you and the remote server. What about those intermediate proxy servers? They're completely beyond your control, and they may still have that data cached and will happily return it to you, because (as far as they are concerned) their cache is still valid.

Instead of manipulating your local cache and hoping for the best, you should use the features of HTTP to ensure that your request actually reaches the remote server, as shown in Listing 14-16.

Listing 14-16. Bypassing the Cache

```
# continued from the previous example
>>> response2, content2 = h.request('http://diveintopython3.org/examples/feed.xml',
...      headers={'cache-control':'no-cache'})  (1)
connect: (diveintopython3.org, 80)           (2)
send: b'GET /examples/feed.xml HTTP/1.1
Host: diveintopython3.org
user-agent: Python-httplib2/$Rev: 259 $
accept-encoding: deflate, gzip
cache-control: no-cache'
reply: 'HTTP/1.1 200 OK'
...further debugging information omitted...
>>> response2.status
200
>>> response2.fromcache                       (3)
False
>>> print(dict(response2.items()))            (4)
{'status': '200',
 'content-length': '3070',
 'content-location': 'http://diveintopython3.org/examples/feed.xml',
 'accept-ranges': 'bytes',
 'expires': 'Wed, 03 Jun 2009 00:40:26 GMT',
 'vary': 'Accept-Encoding',
 'server': 'Apache',
 'last-modified': 'Sun, 31 May 2009 22:51:11 GMT',
 'connection': 'close',
 '-content-encoding': 'gzip',
 'etag': '"bfe-255ef5c0"',
 'cache-control': 'max-age=86400',
 'date': 'Tue, 02 Jun 2009 00:40:26 GMT',
 'content-type': 'application/xml'}
```

1. httplib2 allows you to add arbitrary HTTP headers to any outgoing request. In order to bypass *all* caches (not just your local disk cache but also any caching proxies between you and the remote server), add a no-cache header in the headers dictionary.

2. Now you see httplib2 initiating a network request. httplib2 understands and respects caching headers *in both directions* — as part of the incoming response *and* as part of the outgoing request. It noticed that you added the no-cache header, so it bypassed its local cache altogether and had no choice but to hit the network to request the data.

3. This response was *not* generated from your local cache. You knew that, of course, because you saw the debugging information on the outgoing request. But it's nice to have that programmatically verified.

4. The request succeeded; you downloaded the entire feed again from the remote server. Of course, the server also sent back a full complement of HTTP headers along with the feed data. That includes caching headers, which httplib2 uses to update its local cache, in the hopes of avoiding network access the *next* time you request this feed. Everything about HTTP caching is designed to maximize cache hits and minimize network access. Even though you bypassed the cache this time, the remote server would really appreciate it if you would cache the result for next time.

Handling Last-Modified and ETag Headers with httplib2

The Cache-Control and Expires caching headers are called *freshness indicators*. They tell caches in no uncertain terms that you can completely avoid all network access until the cache expires. And that's exactly the behavior you saw in the previous section: given a freshness indicator, httplib2 *does not generate a single byte of network activity* to serve up cached data (unless you explicitly bypass the cache, of course).

But what about the case where the data *might* have changed but hasn't? HTTP defines Last-Modified and ETag headers for this purpose. These headers are called *validators*. If the local cache is no longer fresh, a client can send the validators with the next request to see if the data has actually changed. If the data hasn't changed, the server sends back a 304 status code and no data. There's still a round-trip over the network, but you end up downloading fewer bytes, as shown in Listings 14-17 and 14-18.

Listing 14-17. A Resource That Hasn't Changed, Request 1

```
>>> import httplib2
>>> httplib2.debuglevel = 1
>>> h = httplib2.Http('.cache')
>>> response, content = h.request('http://diveintopython3.org/')   (1)
connect: (diveintopython3.org, 80)
send: b'GET / HTTP/1.1
Host: diveintopython3.org
accept-encoding: deflate, gzip
user-agent: Python-httplib2/$Rev: 259 $'
reply: 'HTTP/1.1 200 OK'
>>> print(dict(response.items()))                                  (2)
{'-content-encoding': 'gzip',
 'accept-ranges': 'bytes',
 'connection': 'close',
 'content-length': '6657',
 'content-location': 'http://diveintopython3.org/',
 'content-type': 'text/html',
 'date': 'Tue, 02 Jun 2009 03:26:54 GMT',
 'etag': '"7f806d-1a01-9fb97900"',
 'last-modified': 'Tue, 02 Jun 2009 02:51:48 GMT',
 'server': 'Apache',
 'status': '200',
 'vary': 'Accept-Encoding,User-Agent'}
>>> len(content)                                                   (3)
6657
```

1. Instead of the feed, this time we're going to download the site's home page, which is HTML. Since this is the first time you've ever requested this page, httplib2 has little to work with, and it sends out a minimum of headers with the request.

2. The response contains a multitude of HTTP headers but no caching information. However, it does include both an ETag and Last-Modified header.

3. At the time I constructed this example, this page was 6657 bytes. It's probably changed since then, but don't worry about it.

Listing 14-18. A Resource That Hasn't Changed, Request 2

```
>>> response, content = h.request('http://diveintopython3.org/')   (1)
connect: (diveintopython3.org, 80)
send: b'GET / HTTP/1.1
Host: diveintopython3.org
if-none-match: "7f806d-1a01-9fb97900"                              (2)
if-modified-since: Tue, 02 Jun 2009 02:51:48 GMT                   (3)
accept-encoding: deflate, gzip
user-agent: Python-httplib2/$Rev: 259 $'
reply: 'HTTP/1.1 304 Not Modified'                                 (4)
>>> response.fromcache                                             (5)
True
>>> response.status                                               (6)
200
>>> response.dict['status']                                       (7)
'304'
>>> len(content)                                                  (8)
6657
```

1. You request the same page again, with the same Http object (and the same local cache).

2. httplib2 sends the ETag validator back to the server in the If-None-Match header.

3. httplib2 also sends the Last-Modified validator back to the server in the If-Modified-Since header.

4. The server looks at these validators, looked at the page you requested, and determined that the page has not changed since you last requested it, so it sends back a 304 status code and no data.

5. Back on the client, httplib2 notices the 304 status code and loads the content of the page from its cache.

6. This line might be a bit confusing. There are really *two* status codes — 304 (returned from the server this time, which caused httplib2 to look in its cache) and 200 (returned from the server *last time*, and stored in httplib2's cache along with the page data). response.status returns the status from the cache.

7. If you want the raw status code returned from the server, you can get that by looking in **response.dict**, which is a dictionary of the actual headers returned from the server.

8. However, you still get the data in the **content** variable. Generally, you don't need to know why a response was served from the cache. You may not even care that it was served from the cache at all, and that's fine too. **httplib2** is smart enough to let you act dumb. By the time the **request()** method returns to the caller, **httplib2** has already updated its cache and returned the data to you.

Handling Compression with httplib2

HTTP supports two types of compression, and **httplib2** supports both of them (see Listing 14-19).

Listing 14-19. Downloading a Compressed Resource

```
>>> response, content = h.request('http://diveintopython3.org/')
connect: (diveintopython3.org, 80)
send: b'GET / HTTP/1.1
Host: diveintopython3.org
accept-encoding: deflate, gzip                          (1)
user-agent: Python-httplib2/$Rev: 259 $'
reply: 'HTTP/1.1 200 OK'
>>> print(dict(response.items()))
{'-content-encoding': 'gzip',                           (2)
 'accept-ranges': 'bytes',
 'connection': 'close',
 'content-length': '6657',
 'content-location': 'http://diveintopython3.org/',
 'content-type': 'text/html',
 'date': 'Tue, 02 Jun 2009 03:26:54 GMT',
 'etag': '"7f806d-1a01-9fb97900"',
 'last-modified': 'Tue, 02 Jun 2009 02:51:48 GMT',
 'server': 'Apache',
 'status': '304',
 'vary': 'Accept-Encoding,User-Agent'}
```

1. Every time **httplib2** sends a request, it includes an **Accept-Encoding** header to tell the server that it can handle either **deflate** or **gzip** compression.

2. In this case, the server has responded with a gzip-compressed payload. By the time the **request()** method returns, **httplib2** has already decompressed the body of the response and placed it in the **content** variable. If you're curious about whether or not the response was compressed, you can check **response['-content-encoding']**; otherwise, don't worry about it.

Handling Redirects with httplib2

HTTP defines two kinds of redirects: temporary and permanent. There's nothing special to do with temporary redirects except follow them, which httplib2 does automatically (see Listing 14-20).

Listing 14-20. Requesting a Temporarily Redirected Resource

```
>>> import httplib2
>>> httplib2.debuglevel = 1
>>> h = httplib2.Http('.cache')
>>> response, content = h.request('http://diveintopython3.org/examples/feed-302.xml')   (1)
connect: (diveintopython3.org, 80)
send: b'GET /examples/feed-302.xml HTTP/1.1                                              (2)
Host: diveintopython3.org
accept-encoding: deflate, gzip
user-agent: Python-httplib2/$Rev: 259 $'
reply: 'HTTP/1.1 302 Found'                                                              (3)
send: b'GET /examples/feed.xml HTTP/1.1                                                  (4)
Host: diveintopython3.org
accept-encoding: deflate, gzip
user-agent: Python-httplib2/$Rev: 259 $'
reply: 'HTTP/1.1 200 OK'
```

1. There is no feed at this URL. I've set up my server to issue a temporary redirect to the correct address.

2. This is the request.

3. And this is the response: 302 Found. Not shown here, this response also includes a Location header that points to the real URL.

4. httplib2 immediately turns around and follows the redirect by issuing another request for the URL given in the Location header: http://diveintopython3.org/examples/feed.xml.

Following a redirect is nothing more than this example shows. httplib2 sends a request for the URL you asked for. The server comes back with a response that says, "No, look over there instead." httplib2 sends another request for the new URL (see Listing 14-21).

Listing 14-21. Following a Temporary Redirect

```
# continued from the previous example
>>> response                                                                            (1)
{'status': '200',
 'content-length': '3070',
 'content-location': 'http://diveintopython3.org/examples/feed.xml',                    (2)
 'accept-ranges': 'bytes',
 'expires': 'Thu, 04 Jun 2009 02:21:41 GMT',
 'vary': 'Accept-Encoding',
 'server': 'Apache',
 'last-modified': 'Wed, 03 Jun 2009 02:20:15 GMT',
 'connection': 'close',
 '-content-encoding': 'gzip',                                                            (3)
```

```
'etag': '"bfe-4cbbf5c0"',
'cache-control': 'max-age=86400',                                          (4)
'date': 'Wed, 03 Jun 2009 02:21:41 GMT',
'content-type': 'application/xml'}
```

1. The **response** you get back from this single call to the **request()** method is the response from the final URL.

2. **httplib2** adds the final URL to the **response** dictionary, as **content-location**. This is not a header that came from the server; it's specific to **httplib2**.

3. Apropos of nothing, this feed is compressed.

4. And it's cacheable (this is important, as you'll see in a minute).

The **response** you get back gives you information about the *final* URL. What if you want more information about the intermediate URLs, the ones that eventually redirected to the final URL? **httplib2** lets you do that, too, as shown in Listing 14-22.

Listing 14-22. The Redirect Chain

```
# continued from the previous example
>>> response.previous                                                      (1)
{'status': '302',
 'content-length': '228',
 'content-location': 'http://diveintopython3.org/examples/feed-302.xml',
 'expires': 'Thu, 04 Jun 2009 02:21:41 GMT',
 'server': 'Apache',
 'connection': 'close',
 'location': 'http://diveintopython3.org/examples/feed.xml',
 'cache-control': 'max-age=86400',
 'date': 'Wed, 03 Jun 2009 02:21:41 GMT',
 'content-type': 'text/html; charset=iso-8859-1'}
>>> type(response)                                                         (2)
<class 'httplib2.Response'>
>>> type(response.previous)
<class 'httplib2.Response'>
>>> response.previous.previous                                            (3)
>>>
```

1. The **response.previous** attribute holds a reference to the previous response object that **httplib2** followed to get to the current response object.

2. Both **response** and **response.previous** are **httplib2.Response** objects.

3. 3. That means you can check **response.previous.previous** to follow the redirect chain backwards even further. (Consider a scenario in which one URL redirects to a second URL, which redirects to a third URL. It could happen!) In this case, we've already reached the beginning of the redirect chain, so the attribute is **None**.

What happens if you request the same URL again? See Listing 14-23.

Listing 14-23. Requesting the Resource in Listing 14-22 Again

```
# continued from the previous example
>>> response2, content2 = h.request('http://diveintopython3.org/examples/feed-302.xml')  (1)
connect: (diveintopython3.org, 80)
send: b'GET /examples/feed-302.xml HTTP/1.1                                               (2)
Host: diveintopython3.org
accept-encoding: deflate, gzip
user-agent: Python-httplib2/$Rev: 259 $'
reply: 'HTTP/1.1 302 Found'                                                               (3)
>>> content2 == content                                                                   (4)
True
```

1. This is the same URL and same `httplib2.Http` object (and therefore the same cache) as in Listing 14-22

2. The `302` response was not cached, so `httplib2` sends another request for the same URL.

3. Once again, the server responds with a `302`. But notice what *didn't* happen: there wasn't a second request for the final URL, `http://diveintopython3.org/examples/feed.xml`. That response was cached (recall the `Cache-Control` header that you saw in the previous example). Once `httplib2` received the `302 Found` code, it checked its cache *before* issuing another request. The cache contained a fresh copy of `http://diveintopython3.org/examples/feed.xml`, so there was no need to request it again.

4. By the time the `request()` method returns, it has read the feed data from the cache and returned it. Of course, it's the same as the data you received last time.

In other words, you don't have to do anything special for temporary redirects. `httplib2` will follow them automatically, and the fact that one URL redirects to another has no bearing on `httplib2`'s support for compression, caching, `ETags`, or any of the other features of HTTP.

Permanent redirects are just as simple (see Listing 14-24).

Listing 14-24. A Permanent Redirect

```
# continued from the previous example
>>> response, content = h.request('http://diveintopython3.org/examples/feed-301.xml')     (1)
connect: (diveintopython3.org, 80)
send: b'GET /examples/feed-301.xml HTTP/1.1
Host: diveintopython3.org
accept-encoding: deflate, gzip
user-agent: Python-httplib2/$Rev: 259 $'
reply: 'HTTP/1.1 301 Moved Permanently'                                                   (2)
>>> response.fromcache                                                                     (3)
True
```

1. Once again, this URL doesn't really exist. I've set up my server to issue a permanent redirect to `http://diveintopython3.org/examples/feed.xml`.

2. And here it is: status code **301**. But again, notice what *didn't* happen: there was no request to the redirect URL. Why not? Because it's already cached locally.

3. **httplib2** followed the redirect right into its cache.

But wait! There's more! Look at Listing 14-25.

Listing 14-25. Rerequesting a Permanently Redirected Resource

```
# continued from the previous example
>>> response2, content2 = h.request('http://diveintopython3.org/examples/feed-301.xml')    (1)
>>> response2.fromcache                                                                    (2)
True
>>> content2 == content                                                                    (3)
True
```

1. Here's the difference between temporary and permanent redirects: once **httplib2** follows a permanent redirect, all further requests for that URL will transparently be rewritten to the target URL *without hitting the network for the original URL*. Remember, debugging is still turned on, yet there is no output of network activity whatsoever.

2. Yes, this response was retrieved from the local cache.

3. Yes, you got the entire feed (from the cache).

HTTP. It works.

Beyond HTTP GET

HTTP web services are not limited to **GET** requests. What if you want to create something new? Whenever you post a comment on a discussion forum, update your weblog, publish your status on a microblogging service like Twitter or Identi.ca, you're probably already using HTTP **POST**.

Both Twitter and Identi.ca both offer a simple HTTP-based API for publishing and updating your status in 140 characters or less. Identi.ca's API documentation is available at **http://laconi.ca/trac/wiki/TwitterCompatibleAPI**.

Here's the information you'd use to update your status:

- *Identi.ca REST API method statuses and updates*: This updates the authenticating user's status and requires the **status** parameter specified later in this API. The request must be a **POST**.

- *URL*: **https://identi.ca/api/statuses/update.format**

- *Formats*: **xml**, **json**, **rss**, and **atom**

- *HTTP method*: **POST**

- *Requires authentication*: Yes

- *Parameter*: The **status** parameter is required, and it contains the text of your status update. You can URL encode it as necessary.

To publish a new message on Identi.ca, you need to issue an HTTP **POST** request to **http://identi.ca/api/statuses/update.**format.

The `format` bit is not part of the URL; you replace it with the data format you want the server to return in response to your request. If you want a response in XML, you would post the request to `https://identi.ca/api/statuses/update.xml`.

The request needs to include a parameter called `status`, which contains the text of your status update. And the request needs to be authenticated. Authenticated? Sure. To update your status on Identi.ca, you need to prove who you are. Identi.ca is not a wiki; only you can update your own status. Identi.ca uses HTTP Basic Authentication (also known as RFC 2617) over Secure Sockets Layer (SSL) to provide secure but easy-to-use authentication. `httplib2` supports both SSL and HTTP Basic Authentication, so this part is easy.

A `POST` request is different from a `GET` request, because it includes a payload. The *payload* is the data you want to send to the server. The once piece of data that this API method requires is `status`, and it should be URL encoded. URL encoding is a very simple serialization format that takes a set of key-value pairs (i.e., a dictionary) and transforms it into a string, as shown in Listing 14-26.

Listing 14-26. URL-Encoded Data

```
>>> from urllib.parse import urlencode             (1)
>>> data = {'status': 'Test update from Python 3'} (2)
>>> urlencode(data)                                (3)
'status=test+update+from+python+3'
```

1. Python comes with a utility function to URL encode a dictionary: `urllib.parse.urlencode()`.

2. This is the sort of dictionary that the Identi.ca API is looking for. It contains one key, `status`, whose value is the text of a single status update.

3. This is what the URL-encoded string looks like. This is the payload that will be sent on the wire to the Identi.ca API server in your HTTP `POST` request.

Let's see what it looks like on the wire (see Listing 14-27).

Listing 14-27. Posting a Message to Identi.ca

```
>>> from urllib.parse import urlencode
>>> import httplib2
>>> httplib2.debuglevel = 1
>>> h = httplib2.Http('.cache')
>>> data = {'status': 'Test update from Python 3'}
>>> h.add_credentials('diveintomark', 'MY_SECRET_PASSWORD', 'identi.ca')  (1)
>>> resp, content = h.request('https://identi.ca/api/statuses/update.xml',
...      'POST',                                                          (2)
...      urlencode(data),                                                 (3)
...      headers={'Content-Type': 'application/x-www-form-urlencoded'})   (4)
```

1. This is how `httplib2` handles authentication. Store your user name and password with the `add_credentials()` method. When `httplib2` tries to issue the request, the server will respond with a `401 Unauthorized` status code, and it will list that authentication methods it supports (in the `WWW-Authenticate` header). `httplib2` will automatically construct an `Authorization` header and request the URL again.

2. The second parameter is the type of HTTP request, in this case POST.

3. The third parameter is the payload to send to the server. We're sending the URL-encoded dictionary with a status message.

4. Finally, we need to tell the server that the payload is URL-encoded data.

■ The third parameter to the add_credentials() method is the domain in which the credentials are valid. You should always specify this! If you leave out the domain and later reuse the httplib2.Http object on a different authenticated site, httplib2 might end up leaking one site's user name and password to the other site.

Listing 14-28 shows what goes over the wire.

Listing 14-28. On the Wire When Posting a Message to Identi.ca

```
# continued from the previous example
send: b'POST /api/statuses/update.xml HTTP/1.1
Host: identi.ca
Accept-Encoding: identity
Content-Length: 32
content-type: application/x-www-form-urlencoded
user-agent: Python-httplib2/$Rev: 259 $
status=Test+update+from+Python+3'
reply: 'HTTP/1.1 401 Unauthorized'                      (1)
send: b'POST /api/statuses/update.xml HTTP/1.1          (2)
Host: identi.ca
Accept-Encoding: identity
Content-Length: 32
content-type: application/x-www-form-urlencoded
authorization: Basic SECRET_HASH_CONSTRUCTED_BY_HTTPLIB2  (3)
user-agent: Python-httplib2/$Rev: 259 $
status=Test+update+from+Python+3'
reply: 'HTTP/1.1 200 OK'                                (4)
```

1. After the first request, the server responds with a **401 Unauthorized** status code. httplib2 will never send authentication headers unless the server explicitly asks for them. This is how the server asks for them.

2. httplib2 immediately turns around and requests the same URL a second time.

3. This time, it includes the user name and password that you added with the add_credentials() method.

4. It worked!

What does the server send back after a successful request? That depends entirely on the web service API. In some protocols (like RFC 5023, the Atom Publishing Protocol), the server sends back a **201 Created** status code and the location of the newly created resource in the **Location** header. Identi.ca sends back a **200 OK** status code and an XML document containing information about the newly created resource (see Listing 14-29).

Listing 14-29. The Response from Identi.ca

```
# continued from the previous example
>>> print(content.decode('utf-8'))                              (1)
<?xml version="1.0" encoding="UTF-8"?>
<status>
 <text>Test update from Python 3</text>                         (2)
 <truncated>false</truncated>
 <created_at>Wed Jun 10 03:53:46 +0000 2009</created_at>
 <in_reply_to_status_id></in_reply_to_status_id>
 <source>api</source>
 <id>5131472</id>                                               (3)
 <in_reply_to_user_id></in_reply_to_user_id>
 <in_reply_to_screen_name></in_reply_to_screen_name>
 <favorited>false</favorited>
 <user>
  <id>3212</id>
  <name>Mark Pilgrim</name>
  <screen_name>diveintomark</screen_name>
  <location>27502, US</location>
  <description>tech writer, husband, father</description>
  <profile_image_url>http://avatar.identi.ca/3212-48-20081216000626.png</profile_image_url>
  <url>http://diveintomark.org/</url>
  <protected>false</protected>
  <followers_count>329</followers_count>
  <profile_background_color></profile_background_color>
  <profile_text_color></profile_text_color>
  <profile_link_color></profile_link_color>
  <profile_sidebar_fill_color></profile_sidebar_fill_color>
  <profile_sidebar_border_color></profile_sidebar_border_color>
  <friends_count>2</friends_count>
  <created_at>Wed Jul 02 22:03:58 +0000 2008</created_at>
  <favourites_count>30768</favourites_count>
  <utc_offset>0</utc_offset>
  <time_zone>UTC</time_zone>
  <profile_background_image_url></profile_background_image_url>
  <profile_background_tile>false</profile_background_tile>
  <statuses_count>122</statuses_count>
  <following>false</following>
  <notifications>false</notifications>
 </user>
</status>
```

1. Remember, the data returned by **httplib2** is always bytes, not a string. To convert it to a string, you need to decode it using the proper character encoding. Identi.ca's API always returns results in UTF-8, so that part is easy.

2. This is the text of the status message we just published.

3. This is the unique identifier for the new status message. Identi.ca uses this to construct a URL for viewing the message on the web. And here it is:

Beyond HTTP POST

HTTP isn't limited to GET and POST. Those are certainly the most common types of requests, especially in web browsers. But web service APIs can go beyond GET and POST, and httplib2 is ready, as shown in Listing 14-30.

Listing 14-30. Deleting a Post from Identi.ca

```
# continued from the previous example
>>> from xml.etree import ElementTree as etree
>>> tree = etree.fromstring(content)                                        (1)
>>> status_id = tree.findtext('id')                                         (2)
>>> status_id
'5131472'
>>> url = 'https://identi.ca/api/statuses/destroy/{0}.xml'.format(status_id) (3)
>>> resp, deleted_content = h.request(url, 'DELETE')                         (4)
```

1. The server returned XML, right? You know how to parse XML from reading Chapter 12.

2. The findtext() method finds the first instance of the given expression and extracts its text content. In this case, we're just looking for an <id> element.

3. Based on the text content of the <id> element, we can construct a URL to delete the status message we just published.

4. To delete a message, simply issue an HTTP DELETE request to that URL.

Listing 14-31 shows what goes over the wire.

Listing 14-31. On the Wire When Deleting a Post from Identi.ca

```
send: b'DELETE /api/statuses/destroy/5131472.xml HTTP/1.1       (1)
Host: identi.ca
Accept-Encoding: identity
user-agent: Python-httplib2/$Rev: 259 $
'
reply: 'HTTP/1.1 401 Unauthorized'                              (2)
send: b'DELETE /api/statuses/destroy/5131472.xml HTTP/1.1       (3)
Host: identi.ca
Accept-Encoding: identity
authorization: Basic SECRET_HASH_CONSTRUCTED_BY_HTTPLIB2        (4)
user-agent: Python-httplib2/$Rev: 259 $
'
reply: 'HTTP/1.1 200 OK'                                        (5)
>>> resp.status
200
```

1. This tells the API to delete this status message.

2. The server responds that you are not authorized to do that.

3. httplib2 requests the same URL again.

4. But this time, it adds the authorization header.

5. The server responds that the message has been deleted.

And just like that, poof, the previously published status message is gone:

251

Further Reading Online

For more information on `httplib2`, see the following:

- *The httplib2 project page*: http://code.google.com/p/httplib2/

- *More httplib2 code examples*: http://code.google.com/p/httplib2/wiki/ExamplesPython3

- *"Doing HTTP Caching Right*: Introducing httplib2" by Joe Gregorio: http://www.xml.com/pub/a/2006/02/01/doing-http-caching-right-introducing-httplib2.html

- *"httplib2 HTTP Persistence and Authentication" by Joe Gregorio*: http://www.xml.com/pub/a/2006/03/29/httplib2-http-persistence-and-authentication.html

For more information on HTTP caching, see the following:

- *"HTTP Caching Tutorial" by Mark Nottingham*: http://www.mnot.net/cache_docs

- *"How to control caching with HTTP headers" on Google Doctype*: http://code.google.com/p/doctype/wiki/ArticleHttpCaching

For more information on standards, see the following:

- *RFC 2616 (HTTP)*: http://www.ietf.org/rfc/rfc2616.txt

- *RFC 2617 (HTTP Basic Authentication)*: http://www.ietf.org/rfc/rfc2617.txt

- *RFC 1951 (DEFLATE Compressed Data Format Specification)*: http://www.ietf.org/rfc/rfc1951.txt

- RFC 1952 (GZIP File Format Specification): http://www.ietf.org/rfc/rfc1952.txt

■ ■ ■

## CHAPTER 15

Case Study: Porting chardet to Python 3

Unknown or incorrect character encoding is the number one cause of gibberish text on the web, in your inbox, and indeed across every computer system ever written. In Chapter 4, I talked about the history of character encoding and the creation of Unicode, the "one encoding to rule them all." I'd love it if I never had to see a gibberish character on a web page again because that would require that all authoring systems stored accurate encoding information, all transfer protocols were Unicode-aware, and every system that handled text maintained perfect fidelity when converting between encodings.

I'd also like a pony.

A Unicode pony.

A Unipony, as it were.

But I'll settle for character encoding auto-detection.

What Is Character Encoding Auto-Detection?

Character encoding auto-detection refers to the process of taking a sequence of bytes in an unknown character encoding, and then attempting to determine the encoding so you can read the text. It's like cracking a code when you don't have the decryption key.

Why Auto-Detection Is Difficult

Generally speaking, you can't auto-detect character encoding. However, some encodings are optimized for specific languages, and languages are not random. Some character sequences pop up all the time, while other sequences make no sense. A person fluent in English who opens a newspaper and finds "txzqJv 2!dasd0a QqdKjvz" will recognize instantly that this isn't an English word (even though it is composed entirely of letters you find in English words). By studying lots of "typical" words and sentences, a programmer could create a computer algorithm that simulates this kind of fluency and makes an educated guess about the language of a given piece of text.

In other words, encoding detection is really language detection, combined with knowledge of which languages tend to use which character encodings.

Auto-Encoding Algorithms

It turns out that that algorithms that detect character encoding exist; indeed, all major browsers have character encoding auto-detection because the web is full of pages that have no encoding information whatsoever. Mozilla Firefox contains an open source encoding auto-detection library. I ported the library to Python 2 and dubbed it the chardet module. This chapter takes you step-by-step through the process of porting the chardet module from Python 2 to Python 3.

Introducing the chardet Module

Before we set off porting the code, it would help if you understood how the original code worked! This is a brief guide to navigating the code itself. The chardet library is too large to include inline here, but you can download it at http://chardet.feedparser.org/download/.

The main entry point for the detection algorithm is universaldetector.py, which has one class, UniversalDetector. (You might think the main entry point is the detect function in chardet/__init__.py, but that's really just a convenience function that creates a UniversalDetector object, calls it, and returns its result.)

UniversalDetector handles five encoding categories:

- UTF-n with a Byte Order Mark (BOM). This includes UTF-8, both Big-Endian and Little-Endian variants of UTF-16, and all four byte-order variants of UTF-32.

- Escaped encodings, which are encoded in seven-bit ASCII, but non-ASCII characters start with an escape sequence. Examples include ISO-2022-JP (Japanese) and HZ-GB-2312 (Chinese).

- Multibyte encodings, where each character is represented by a variable number of bytes. Examples include Big5 (Chinese), SHIFT_JIS (Japanese), EUC-KR (Korean), and UTF-8 without a BOM.

- Single-byte encodings, where each character is represented by one byte. Examples include KOI8-R (Russian), windows-1255 (Hebrew), and TIS-620 (Thai).

- windows-1252, which is used primarily on Microsoft Windows by middle managers who wouldn't know a character encoding from a hole in the ground.

UTF-n with a BOM

If the text starts with a BOM, we can reasonably assume that the text is encoded in UTF-8, UTF-16, or UTF-32. (The BOM tells us exactly which one; that's what it's for.) This is handled inline in UniversalDetector, which returns the result immediately and without any further processing.

Escaped Encodings

If the text contains a recognizable escape sequence that might indicate an escaped encoding, UniversalDetector creates an EscCharSetProber (defined in escprober.py) and feeds it the text.

EscCharSetProber creates a series of state machines based on models of HZ-GB-2312, ISO-2022-CN, ISO-2022-JP, and ISO-2022-KR (defined in escsm.py). EscCharSetProber feeds the text to each of these state machines, one byte at a time. If any state machine ends up uniquely identifying the encoding, EscCharSetProber immediately returns the positive result to UniversalDetector, which returns it to the caller. If any state machine hits an illegal sequence, it is dropped and processing continues with the other state machines.

Multibyte Encodings

Assuming no BOM, `UniversalDetector` checks whether the text contains any high-bit characters. If so, it creates a series of "probers" for detecting multibyte encodings, single-byte encodings, and, as a last resort, `windows-1252`.

The multibyte encoding prober, `MBCSGroupProber` (defined in `mbcsgroupprober.py`), is really just a shell that manages a group of other probers, one for each multibyte encoding: `Big5`, `GB2312`, `EUC-TW`, `EUC-KR`, `EUC-JP`, `SHIFT_JIS`, and `UTF-8`. `MBCSGroupProber` feeds the text to each of these encoding-specific probers and checks the results. If a prober reports that it has found an illegal byte sequence, it is dropped from further processing (so that, for instance, any subsequent calls to `UniversalDetector.feed()` will skip that prober). If a prober reports that it is reasonably confident it has detected the encoding, `MBCSGroupProber` reports this positive result to `UniversalDetector`, which reports the result to the caller.

Most of the multibyte encoding probers are inherited from `MultiByteCharSetProber` (defined in `mbcharsetprober.py`). These probers hook up the appropriate state machine and distribution analyzer, letting `MultiByteCharSetProber` do the rest of the work. `MultiByteCharSetProber` runs the text through the encoding-specific state machine, one byte at a time, to look for byte sequences that would indicate a conclusive positive or negative result. At the same time, `MultiByteCharSetProber` feeds the text to an encoding-specific distribution analyzer.

The distribution analyzers (defined in `chardistribution.py`) use language-specific models of which characters are used most frequently. Once `MultiByteCharSetProber` has fed enough text to the distribution analyzer, it calculates a confidence rating based on the number of frequently-used characters, the total number of characters, and a language-specific distribution ratio. If the confidence is high enough, `MultiByteCharSetProber` returns the result to `MBCSGroupProber`. This prober returns the confidence rating to `UniversalDetector`, which returns it to the caller.

The case of Japanese is more difficult. Single-character distribution analysis is not always sufficient to distinguish between `EUC-JP` and `SHIFT_JIS`, so the `SJISProber` (defined in `sjisprober.py`) also uses two-character distribution analysis. `SJISContextAnalysis` and `EUCJPContextAnalysis` (both defined in `jpcntx.py` and both inheriting from a common `JapaneseContextAnalysis` class) check the frequency of Hiragana syllabary characters within the text. Once enough text has been processed, they return a confidence level to `SJISProber`, which checks both analyzers and returns the higher confidence level to `MBCSGroupProber`.

Single-Byte Encodings

The single-byte encoding prober, `SBCSGroupProber` (defined in `sbcsgroupprober.py`), is also just a shell that manages a group of other probers, one for each combination of single-byte encoding and language: `windows-1251`, `KOI8-R`, `ISO-8859-5`, `MacCyrillic`, `IBM855`, and `IBM866` (Russian); `ISO-8859-7` and `windows-1253` (Greek); `ISO-8859-5` and `windows-1251` (Bulgarian); `ISO-8859-2` and `windows-1250` (Hungarian); `TIS-620` (Thai); `windows-1255`, and `ISO-8859-8` (Hebrew).

`SBCSGroupProber` feeds the text to each of these encoding+language-specific probers and checks the results. These probers are all implemented as a single class, `SingleByteCharSetProber` (defined in `sbcharsetprober.py`), which takes a language model as an argument. The language model defines how frequently different two-character sequences appear in typical text. `SingleByteCharSetProber` processes the text and tallies the most frequently used two-character sequences. Once enough text has been processed, it calculates a confidence level based on the number of frequently-used sequences, the total number of characters, and a language-specific distribution ratio.

Hebrew is handled as a special case. If the text appears to be Hebrew based on two-character distribution analysis, HebrewProber (defined in hebrewprober.py) tries to distinguish between Visual Hebrew (where the source text is stored "backwards" line-by-line and then displayed verbatim, so it can be read from right to left) and Logical Hebrew (where the source text is stored in reading order and then rendered right-to-left by the client). Certain characters are encoded differently based on whether they appear in the middle of or at the end of a word, so we can make a reasonable guess about direction of the source text, and return the appropriate encoding (windows-1255 for Logical Hebrew or ISO-8859-8 for Visual Hebrew).

windows-1252

If UniversalDetector detects a high-bit character in the text, but none of the other multibyte or single-byte encoding probers return a confident result, it creates a Latin1Prober (defined in latin1prober.py) to try to detect English text in a windows-1252 encoding. This detection is inherently unreliable because English letters are encoded in the same way in many different encodings. The only way to distinguish windows-1252 is through commonly used symbols like smart quotes, curly apostrophes, copyright symbols, and the like. Latin1Prober automatically reduces its confidence rating to allow more accurate probers to win if at all possible.

Running 2to3

We're going to migrate the chardet module from Python 2 to Python 3. Python 3 comes with a utility script called 2to3, which takes Python 2 source code as input and auto-converts as much as it can to Python 3. In some cases, this is easy—a function was renamed or moved to a different module—but in other cases it can get quite complex. To get a sense of all that it *can* do, refer to Appendix A. In this chapter, we'll start by running 2to3 on the chardet package, but, as you'll see, a lot of work will remain after the automated tools have performed their magic.

The main chardet package is split across several different files, all in the same directory. The 2to3 script makes it easy to convert multiple files at once: just pass a directory as a command line argument, and 2to3 converts each of the files in turn, as shown in Listing 15-1.

Listing 15-1. Running the 2to3 Tool

```
C:\home\chardet> python c:\Python30\Tools\Scripts\2to3.py -w chardet\
RefactoringTool: Skipping implicit fixer: buffer
RefactoringTool: Skipping implicit fixer: idioms
RefactoringTool: Skipping implicit fixer: set_literal
RefactoringTool: Skipping implicit fixer: ws_comma
--- chardet\__init__.py (original)
+++ chardet\__init__.py (refactored)
@@ -18,7 +18,7 @@
   __version__ = "1.0.1"
```

```
 def detect(aBuf):
-    import universaldetector
+    from . import universaldetector
     u = universaldetector.UniversalDetector()
     u.reset()
     u.feed(aBuf)
--- chardet\big5prober.py (original)
+++ chardet\big5prober.py (refactored)
@@ -25,10 +25,10 @@
 # 02110-1301  USA
 ####################### END LICENSE BLOCK #######################

-from mbcharsetprober import MultiByteCharSetProber
-from codingstatemachine import CodingStateMachine
-from chardistribution import Big5DistributionAnalysis
-from mbcssm import Big5SMModel
+from .mbcharsetprober import MultiByteCharSetProber
+from .codingstatemachine import CodingStateMachine
+from .chardistribution import Big5DistributionAnalysis
+from .mbcssm import Big5SMModel

 class Big5Prober(MultiByteCharSetProber):
     def __init__(self):
--- chardet\chardistribution.py (original)
+++ chardet\chardistribution.py (refactored)
@@ -25,12 +25,12 @@
 # 02110-1301  USA
 ####################### END LICENSE BLOCK #######################

-import constants
-from euctwfreq import EUCTWCharToFreqOrder, EUCTW_TABLE_SIZE, ↵
EUCTW_TYPICAL_DISTRIBUTION_RATIO
-from euckrfreq import EUCKRCharToFreqOrder, EUCKR_TABLE_SIZE, ↵
EUCKR_TYPICAL_DISTRIBUTION_RATIO
-from gb2312freq import GB2312CharToFreqOrder, GB2312_TABLE_SIZE, ↵
GB2312_TYPICAL_DISTRIBUTION_RATIO
-from big5freq import Big5CharToFreqOrder, ↵
BIG5_TABLE_SIZE, BIG5_TYPICAL_DISTRIBUTION_RATIO
-from jisfreq import JISCharToFreqOrder, JIS_TABLE_SIZE, ↵
JIS_TYPICAL_DISTRIBUTION_RATIO
+from . import constants
+from .euctwfreq import EUCTWCharToFreqOrder, EUCTW_TABLE_SIZE, ↵
EUCTW_TYPICAL_DISTRIBUTION_RATIO
+from .euckrfreq import EUCKRCharToFreqOrder, EUCKR_TABLE_SIZE, ↵
EUCKR_TYPICAL_DISTRIBUTION_RATIO
+from .gb2312freq import GB2312CharToFreqOrder, GB2312_TABLE_SIZE, ↵
GB2312_TYPICAL_DISTRIBUTION_RATIO
+from .big5freq import Big5CharToFreqOrder, ↵
BIG5_TABLE_SIZE, BIG5_TYPICAL_DISTRIBUTION_RATIO
+from .jisfreq import JISCharToFreqOrder, ↵
JIS_TABLE_SIZE, JIS_TYPICAL_DISTRIBUTION_RATIO
```

```
ENOUGH_DATA_THRESHOLD = 1024
SURE_YES = 0.99
.
.
. (it goes on like this for a while)
.
.
RefactoringTool: Files that were modified:
RefactoringTool: chardet\__init__.py
RefactoringTool: chardet\big5prober.py
RefactoringTool: chardet\chardistribution.py
RefactoringTool: chardet\charsetgroupprober.py
RefactoringTool: chardet\codingstatemachine.py
RefactoringTool: chardet\constants.py
RefactoringTool: chardet\escprober.py
RefactoringTool: chardet\escsm.py
RefactoringTool: chardet\eucjpprober.py
RefactoringTool: chardet\euckrprober.py
RefactoringTool: chardet\euctwprober.py
RefactoringTool: chardet\gb2312prober.py
RefactoringTool: chardet\hebrewprober.py
RefactoringTool: chardet\jpcntx.py
RefactoringTool: chardet\langbulgarianmodel.py
RefactoringTool: chardet\langcyrillicmodel.py
RefactoringTool: chardet\langgreekmodel.py
RefactoringTool: chardet\langhebrewmodel.py
RefactoringTool: chardet\langhungarianmodel.py
RefactoringTool: chardet\langthaimodel.py
RefactoringTool: chardet\latin1prober.py
RefactoringTool: chardet\mbcharsetprober.py
RefactoringTool: chardet\mbcsgroupprober.py
RefactoringTool: chardet\mbcssm.py
RefactoringTool: chardet\sbcharsetprober.py
RefactoringTool: chardet\sbcsgroupprober.py
RefactoringTool: chardet\sjisprober.py
RefactoringTool: chardet\universaldetector.py
RefactoringTool: chardet\utf8prober.py
```

Now run the **2to3** script on the testing harness, **test.py** (see Listing 15-2).

Listing 15-2. Running the 2to3 Tool on test.py

```
C:\home\chardet> python c:\Python30\Tools\Scripts\2to3.py -w test.py
RefactoringTool: Skipping implicit fixer: buffer
RefactoringTool: Skipping implicit fixer: idioms
RefactoringTool: Skipping implicit fixer: set_literal
RefactoringTool: Skipping implicit fixer: ws_comma
```

```
--- test.py (original)
+++ test.py (refactored)
@@ -4,7 +4,7 @@
 count = 0
 u = UniversalDetector()
 for f in glob.glob(sys.argv[1]):
-        print f.ljust(60),
+        print(f.ljust(60), end=' ')
     u.reset()
     for line in file(f, 'rb'):
         u.feed(line)
@@ -12,8 +12,8 @@
     u.close()
     result = u.result
     if result['encoding']:
-        print result['encoding'], 'with confidence', result['confidence']
+        print(result['encoding'], 'with confidence', result['confidence'])
     else:
-        print '******** no result'
+        print('******** no result')
     count += 1
-print count, 'tests'
+print(count, 'tests')
RefactoringTool: Files that were modified:
RefactoringTool: test.py
```

Well, that wasn't so hard: all we had to do was convert a few imports and print statements. Speaking of which, what *was* the problem with all those import statements? To answer that, you need to understand how the chardet module is split into multiple files.

A Short Digression Into Multi-File Modules

chardet is a *multi-file module*. I could have chosen to put all the code in one file (named chardet.py), but I didn't. Instead, I made a directory (named chardet), and then I made an __init__.py file in that directory. If Python sees an __init__.py file in a directory, it assumes that all of the files in that directory are part of the same module. The module's name is the name of the directory. Files within the directory can reference other files within the same directory or even within subdirectories. But the entire collection of files is presented to other Python code as a single module, as if all the functions and classes were in a single .py file.

What goes in the __init__.py file? Nothing. Everything. Something in between. The __init__.py file doesn't need to define anything; it can be literally an empty file. Or you can use it to define your main entry point functions. Or you put all your functions in it. Or put all but one in it.

■ A directory with an __init__.py file is always treated as a multi-file module. Without an __init__.py file, a directory is just a directory of unrelated .py files.

Let's see how that works in practice (see Listing 15-3).

Listing 15-3. Importing the chardet Library

```
>>> import chardet
>>> dir(chardet)                    (1)
['__builtins__', '__doc__', '__file__', '__name__',
  '__package__', '__path__', '__version__', 'detect']
>>> chardet                         (2)
<module 'chardet' from 'C:\Python31\lib\site-packages\chardet\__init__.py'>
```

1. Other than the usual class attributes, the only thing in the chardet module is a detect() function.

2. Here's your first clue that the chardet module is more than just a file: the "module" is listed as the __init__.py file within the chardet/ directory.

Let's take a peek in that __init__.py file (see Listing 15-4).

Listing 15-4. chardet/__init__.py

```
def detect(aBuf):                               (1)
    from . import universaldetector            (2)
    u = universaldetector.UniversalDetector()
    u.reset()
    u.feed(aBuf)
    u.close()
    return u.result
```

1. The __init__.py file defines the detect() function, which is the main entry point into the chardet library.

2. But the detect() function has hardly any code! In fact, all it really does is import the universaldetector module and start using it. But where is universaldetector defined?

The answer lies in that odd-looking import statement, shown in Listing 15-5.

Listing 15-5. An Odd-Looking Import Statement

```
from . import universaldetector
```

Translated into English, this line means "import the universaldetector module that's in the same directory I am," where "I" is the chardet/__init__.py file. This is called a *relative import*. It's a way for the files within a multi-file module to reference each other, without worrying about naming conflicts with other modules you might have installed in your import search path. This import statement will look *only* for the universaldetector module within the chardet/ directory itself.

These two concepts—__init__.py and relative imports—mean that you can break up your module into as many pieces as you like. The chardet module comprises 36 .py files—36! Yet all you need to do to start using it is import chardet, after which you can call the main chardet.detect() function. Unbeknownst to your code, the detect() function is actually defined in the chardet/__init__.py file. And unbeknownst to you, the detect() function uses a relative import to reference a class defined in `chardet/universaldetector.py`, which in turn uses relative imports on five other files, all contained in the `chardet/` directory.

■ If you ever find yourself writing a large library in Python (or more likely, when you realize that your small library has grown into a large one), take the time to refactor it into a multi-file module. It's one of the many things Python is good at, so take advantage of it.

Fixing What 2to3 Can't

The 2to3 conversion script started the process of converting the chardet module from Python 2 to Python 3. However, it doesn't do everything for us. Let's walk through and resolve a handful of issues it doesn't handle automatically.

False Is Invalid Syntax

Now comes the real test: running the test harness against the test suite. The test suite is designed to cover all the possible code paths, so it's a good way to test our ported code to make sure there aren't any bugs lurking anywhere (see Listing 15-6).

Listing 15-6. Running the chardet Test Suite

```
C:\home\chardet> python test.py tests\*\*
Traceback (most recent call last):
  File "test.py", line 1, in <module>
    from chardet.universaldetector import UniversalDetector
  File "C:\home\chardet\chardet\universaldetector.py", line 51
    self.done = constants.False
                              ^
SyntaxError: invalid syntax
```

Hmm, we've hit a small snag. In Python 3, `False` is a reserved word, so you can't use it as a variable name. Let's look at `constants.py` to see where it's defined. Listing 15-7 shows the original version from `constants.py`, before the `2to3` script changed it.

Listing 15-7. constants.py, before conversion

```
import __builtin__
if not hasattr(__builtin__, 'False'):
    False = 0
    True = 1
else:
    False = __builtin__.False
    True = __builtin__.True
```

This piece of code is designed to enable this library to run under older versions of Python 2. Prior to Python 2.3, Python had no built-in `bool` type. This code detects the absence of the built-in constants `True` and `False`, and defines them if necessary.

However, Python 3 will always have a `bool` type, so this entire code snippet is unnecessary. The simplest solution is to replace all instances of `constants.True` and `constants.False` with `True` and `False`, respectively, then delete this dead code from `constants.py`.

This is why the line in `universaldetector.py` drops the reference to the `constants` module, as shown in Listings 15-8 and 15-9.

Listing 15-8. universaldetector.py, Before

```
self.done = constants.False
```

Listing 15-9. universaldetector.py, After

```
self.done = False
```

Ah, wasn't that satisfying? The code is shorter and more readable already.

No Module Named Constants

Now it's time to run `test.py` again and see how far it gets (see Listing 15-10).

Listing 15-10. Running the chardet Tests Again

```
C:\home\chardet> python test.py tests\*\*
Traceback (most recent call last):
  File "test.py", line 1, in <module>
    from chardet.universaldetector import UniversalDetector
  File "C:\home\chardet\chardet\universaldetector.py", line 29, in <module>
    import constants, sys
ImportError: No module named constants
```

What's that? No module named `constants`? Of course there's a module named `constants`! It's right there, in `chardet/constants.py`.

Remember when the `2to3` script fixed up all those import statements? This library has a lot of relative imports—that is, modules that import other modules within the same library—but *the logic behind relative imports has changed in Python 3*. In Python 2, you could just `import constants`, and it would look in the `chardet/` directory first. In Python 3, all import statements are absolute by default. If you want to do a relative import in Python 3, you need to be explicit about it, as shown in Listing 15-11.

Listing 15-11. A Relative Import

```
from . import constants
```

But wait: Wasn't the 2to3 script supposed to take care of import statements or you? Well, it did, but this particular import statement combines two different types of imports into one line: a relative import of the **constants** module within the library and an absolute import of the **sys** module that is pre-installed in the Python standard library. In Python 2, you could combine these into one import statement. In Python 3, you can't, and the 2to3 script isn't smart enough to split the import statement into two statements.

The solution is to split the import statement manually. So this two-in-one import needs to become two separate imports, as shown in Listings 15-12 and 15-13.

Listing 15-12. Importing Two Modules, Before

```
import constants, sys
```

Listing 15-13. Importing Two Modules, After

```
from . import constants
import sys
```

There are variations of this problem scattered throughout the **chardet** library. In some places, it's **import constants, sys**; in other places, it's **import constants, re**. The fix is the same: you need to split the import statement manually into two lines, one for the relative import and the other for the absolute import.

Onward!

Name 'file' Is Not Defined

And here we go again: we need to run **test.py** again to try to execute our test cases (see Listing 15-14).

Listing 15-14. Running the chardet Tests Again

```
C:\home\chardet> python test.py tests\*\*
tests\ascii\howto.diveintomark.org.xml
Traceback (most recent call last):
  File "test.py", line 9, in <module>
    for line in file(f, 'rb'):
NameError: name 'file' is not defined
```

This result surprised me because I've been using this idiom for as long as I can remember. In Python 2, the global **file()** function was an alias for the **open()** function, which was the standard way of opening text files for reading. In Python 3, the global **file()** function no longer exists, but the **open()** function still exists.

Thus, the simplest solution to the problem of the missing **file()** is to call the **open()** function instead, as shown in Listing 15-15.

Listing 15-15. Using open() Instead of file()

```
for line in open(f, 'rb'):
```

And that's all I have to say about that.

Can't Use a String Pattern on a Bytes-Like Object

Now things are starting to get interesting. And by "interesting," I mean "confusing as all hell" (see Listing 15-16).

Listing 15-16. A Confusing Error

```
C:\home\chardet> python test.py tests\*\*
tests\ascii\howto.diveintomark.org.xml
Traceback (most recent call last):
  File "test.py", line 10, in <module>
    u.feed(line)
  File "C:\home\chardet\chardet\universaldetector.py", line 98, in feed
    if self._highBitDetector.search(aBuf):
TypeError: can't use a string pattern on a bytes-like object
```

To debug this, let's see what `self._highBitDetector` is. It's defined in the `__init__` method of the `UniversalDetector` class, as shown in Listing 15-17.

Listing 15-17. UniversalDetector.__init__ Method

```
class UniversalDetector:
    def __init__(self):
        self._highBitDetector = re.compile(r'[\x80-\xFF]')
```

This pre-compiles a regular expression designed to find non-ASCII characters in the range, 128–255 (0x80–0xFF). Wait, that's not quite right; I need to be more precise with my terminology. This pattern is designed to find non-ASCII *bytes* in the range, 128-255.

And therein lies the problem.

In Python 2, a string was an array of bytes whose character encoding was tracked separately. If you wanted Python 2 to keep track of the character encoding, you had to use a Unicode string (u' ') instead. But in Python 3, a string is always what Python 2 called a Unicode string—that is, an array of Unicode characters (of possibly varying byte lengths). This regular expression is defined by a string pattern, but it can be used only to search a string—again, an array of characters. But what we're searching is not a string, it's a byte array. Looking at the traceback, we can see that this error occurred in `universaldetector.py`, as shown in Listing 15-18.

Listing 15-18. UniversalDetector.feed Method

```
def feed(self, aBuf):
    .
    .
    .
    if self._mInputState == ePureAscii:
        if self._highBitDetector.search(aBuf):
```

And what is aBuf? Let's backtrack further to a place that calls UniversalDetector.feed(). One place that calls it is the test harness, test.py (see Listing 15-19).

Listing 15-19. test.py Calling the UniversalDetector.feed Method

```
u = UniversalDetector()
.
.
.
for line in open(f, 'rb'):
    u.feed(line)
```

And here we find our answer: in the UniversalDetector.feed() method, aBuf is a line read from a file on disk. Look carefully at the parameters used to open the file: 'rb'. 'r' is for "read"; OK, big deal, we're reading the file. Ah, but 'b' is for "binary." Without the 'b' flag, this for loop would read the file, line by line, and convert each line into a string—an array of Unicode characters—according to the system default character encoding. But with the 'b' flag, this for loop reads the file, line by line, and stores each line exactly as it appears in the file, as an array of bytes. That byte array gets passed to UniversalDetector.feed(), and eventually, to the pre-compiled regular expression, self._highBitDetector, to search for high-bit... characters. But we don't have characters; we have bytes. Oops.

What we need this regular expression to search is not an array of characters, but an array of bytes.

Once you realize that, the solution is not difficult. Regular expressions defined with strings can search strings. Regular expressions defined with byte arrays can search byte arrays. To define a byte array pattern, we simply change the type of the argument we use to define the regular expression to a byte array, as shown in Listing 15-20. (There is one other case of this same problem, on the very next line.)

Listing 15-20. Changing a Regular Expression to Operate on Bytes

```
  class UniversalDetector:
      def __init__(self):
-         self._highBitDetector = re.compile(r'[\x80-\xFF]')
-         self._escDetector = re.compile(r'(\033|~{)')
+         self._highBitDetector = re.compile(b'[\x80-\xFF]')
+         self._escDetector = re.compile(b'(\033|~{)')
          self._mEscCharSetProber = None
          self._mCharSetProbers = []
          self.reset()
```

Searching the entire codebase for other uses of the re module turns up two more instances, in charsetprober.py. Again, the code is defining regular expressions as strings, but executing them on aBuf, which is a byte array. The solution is the same: define the regular expression patterns as byte arrays, as shown in Listing 15-21.

Listing 15-21. Fixing More Regular Expressions Changed from Bytes to Strings

```
class CharSetProber:
    .
    .
    .
    def filter_high_bit_only(self, aBuf):
-       aBuf = re.sub(r'([\x00-\x7F])+', ' ', aBuf)
+       aBuf = re.sub(b'([\x00-\x7F])+', b' ', aBuf)
        return aBuf

    def filter_without_english_letters(self, aBuf):
-       aBuf = re.sub(r'([A-Za-z])+', ' ', aBuf)
+       aBuf = re.sub(b'([A-Za-z])+', b' ', aBuf)
        return aBuf
```

Can't Convert 'bytes' Object to str Implicitly

Things get curiouser and curiouser... (see Listing 15-22).

Listing 15-22. Running the chardet Tests Again

```
C:\home\chardet> python test.py tests\*\*
tests\ascii\howto.diveintomark.org.xml
Traceback (most recent call last):
  File "test.py", line 10, in <module>
    u.feed(line)
  File "C:\home\chardet\chardet\universaldetector.py", line 100, in feed
    elif (self._mInputState == ePureAscii) and self._escDetector.search(self._mLastChar +
aBuf):
TypeError: Can't convert 'bytes' object to str implicitly
```

There's an unfortunate clash between our coding style and the Python interpreter here. The **TypeError** could be anywhere on that line, but the traceback doesn't tell us exactly where it is. It could be in the first or second conditional, and the traceback would look the same. To narrow it down, we can split the line in two by using a backslash (\\), as shown in Listing 15-23.

Listing 15-23. Splitting a Line of Code

```
elif (self._mInputState == ePureAscii) and \
    self._escDetector.search(self._mLastChar + aBuf):
```

Now re-run the test, as shown in Listing 15-24.

Listing 15-24. Running the chardet Tests Again

```
C:\home\chardet> python test.py tests\*\*
tests\ascii\howto.diveintomark.org.xml
Traceback (most recent call last):
  File "test.py", line 10, in <module>
    u.feed(line)
  File "C:\home\chardet\chardet\universaldetector.py", line 101, in feed
    self._escDetector.search(self._mLastChar + aBuf):
TypeError: Can't convert 'bytes' object to str implicitly
```

Aha! The problem was not in the first conditional (self._mInputState == ePureAscii), but in the second one. So what could cause a TypeError there? Perhaps you're thinking that the search() method is expecting a value of a different type, but that wouldn't generate this traceback. Python functions can take any value; if you pass the right number of arguments, the function will execute. It might *crash* if you pass it a value of a different type than it's expecting, but if that happened, the traceback would point to somewhere inside the function. But this traceback says it never got as far as calling the search() method, so the problem must be in that + operation that's trying to construct the value that it will eventually pass to the search() method.

We know from previous debugging that aBuf is a byte array. So what is self._mLastChar? It's an instance variable, defined in the reset() method, which is actually called from the __init__() method, as shown in Listing 15-25.

Listing 15-25. Defining self._mLastChar

```
class UniversalDetector:
    def __init__(self):
        self._highBitDetector = re.compile(b'[\x80-\xFF]')
        self._escDetector = re.compile(b'(\033|~{)')
        self._mEscCharSetProber = None
        self._mCharSetProbers = []
        self.reset()

    def reset(self):
        self.result = {'encoding': None, 'confidence': 0.0}
        self.done = False
        self._mStart = True
        self._mGotData = False
        self._mInputState = ePureAscii
        self._mLastChar = ''
```

And now we have our answer. Do you see it? self._mLastChar is a string, but aBuf is a byte array. You can't concatenate a string to a byte array, not even a zero-length string.

So what is self._mLastChar, anyway? Listing 15-26 shows the feed() method, just a few lines after the location where the trackback occurred.

Listing 15-26. Using self._mLastChar

```
if self._mInputState == ePureAscii:
    if self._highBitDetector.search(aBuf):
        self._mInputState = eHighbyte
    elif (self._mInputState == ePureAscii) and \
            self._escDetector.search(self._mLastChar + aBuf):
        self._mInputState = eEscAscii
self._mLastChar = aBuf[-1]
```

The calling function calls this `feed()` method repeatedly with a few bytes at a time. The method processes the bytes it was given (passed in as `aBuf`), then stores the last byte in `self._mLastChar` in case it's needed during the next call. (In a multibyte encoding, the `feed()` method might get called with half of a character, then called again with the other half.) Because `aBuf` is now a byte array instead of a string, `self._mLastChar` needs to be a byte array as well, as shown in Listing 15-27.

Listing 15-27. Making self._mLastChar a Byte Array

```
  def reset(self):
      .
      .
      .
-     self._mLastChar = ''
+     self._mLastChar = b''
```

Searching the entire codebase for "mLastChar" turns up a similar problem in `mbcharsetprober.py` (see Listing 15-28), but it tracks the last *two* characters instead of tracking the last character. The `MultiByteCharSetProber` class uses a list of one-character strings to track the last two characters. In Python 3, this class needs to use a list of integers because it's not really tracking characters; rather, it's tracking bytes (bytes are just integers from `0-255`).

Listing 15-28. Initializing self._mLastChar in MultiByteCharSetProber

```
  class MultiByteCharSetProber(CharSetProber):
      def __init__(self):
          CharSetProber.__init__(self)
          self._mDistributionAnalyzer = None
          self._mCodingSM = None
-         self._mLastChar = ['\x00', '\x00']
+         self._mLastChar = [0, 0]

      def reset(self):
          CharSetProber.reset(self)
          if self._mCodingSM:
              self._mCodingSM.reset()
          if self._mDistributionAnalyzer:
              self._mDistributionAnalyzer.reset()
-         self._mLastChar = ['\x00', '\x00']
+         self._mLastChar = [0, 0]
```

Unsupported Operand type(s) for +: 'int' and 'bytes'

I have good news, and I have bad news. The good news is that we're making progress (see Listing 15-29).

Listing 15-29. Running the chardet Tests Again

```
C:\home\chardet> python test.py tests\*\*
tests\ascii\howto.diveintomark.org.xml
Traceback (most recent call last):
  File "test.py", line 10, in <module>
    u.feed(line)
  File "C:\home\chardet\chardet\universaldetector.py", line 101, in feed
    self._escDetector.search(self._mLastChar + aBuf):
TypeError: unsupported operand type(s) for +: 'int' and 'bytes'
```

The bad news is that it doesn't always feel like progress.

But this is progress! Really! Even though the traceback calls out the same line of code, it's a different error than it used to be. Progress! So what's the problem now? The last time I checked, this line of code didn't try to concatenate an int with a byte array (bytes). In fact, you just spent a lot of time ensuring that self._mLastChar was a byte array. How did it turn into an int?

The answer lies not in the previous lines of code, but in the following lines, shown in Listing 15-30.

Listing 15-30. Setting self._mLastChar

```
if self._mInputState == ePureAscii:
    if self._highBitDetector.search(aBuf):
        self._mInputState = eHighbyte
    elif (self._mInputState == ePureAscii) and \
            self._escDetector.search(self._mLastChar + aBuf):
        self._mInputState = eEscAscii
self._mLastChar = aBuf[-1]
```

This error doesn't occur the first time the feed() method gets called; it occurs the *second time*, after self._mLastChar has been set to the last byte of aBuf. Well, what's the problem with that? Getting a single element from a byte array yields an integer, not a byte array. To see the difference, follow me to the interactive shell (see Listing 15-31).

Listing 15-31. Getting a Single Element from a Byte Array

```
>>> aBuf = b'\xEF\xBB\xBF'          (1)
>>> len(aBuf)
3
>>> mLastChar = aBuf[-1]
>>> mLastChar                       (2)
191
>>> type(mLastChar)                 (3)
<class 'int'>
>>> mLastChar + aBuf                (4)
Traceback (most recent call last):
  File "<stdin>", line 1, in <module>
```

```
TypeError: unsupported operand type(s) for +: 'int' and 'bytes'
>>> mLastChar = aBuf[-1:]              (5)
>>> mLastChar
b'\xbf'
>>> mLastChar + aBuf                   (6)
b'\xbf\xef\xbb\xbf'
```

1. Define a byte array with three bytes.

2. The last element of the byte array is 191.

3. That's an integer.

4. Concatenating an integer with a byte array doesn't work. You've now
   replicated the error you just found in universaldetector.py.

5. Ah, so here's the fix. Instead of taking the last element of the byte array, use list
   slicing to create a new byte array containing just the last element. That is, start
   with the last element and continue the slice until the end of the byte array.
   Now mLastChar is a one-byte array.

6. Concatenating a one-byte array with a three-byte array returns a new
   four-byte array.

So, to ensure that the feed() method in universaldetector.py continues to work no matter how
often it's called, you need to initialize self._mLastChar as a zero-length byte array, then *make sure it
stays a byte array* (see Listing 15-32).

Listing 15-32. Fixing self._mLastChar

```
        self._escDetector.search(self._mLastChar + aBuf):
    self._mInputState = eEscAscii
- self._mLastChar = aBuf[-1]
+ self._mLastChar = aBuf[-1:]
```

ord() Expected String of Length 1, but int Found

Tired yet? You're almost there (see Listing 15-33).

Listing 15-33. Running the chardet Tests Again

```
C:\home\chardet> python test.py tests\*\*
tests\ascii\howto.diveintomark.org.xml                          ascii with confidence 1.0
tests\Big5\0804.blogspot.com.xml
Traceback (most recent call last):
  File "test.py", line 10, in <module>
    u.feed(line)
  File "C:\home\chardet\chardet\universaldetector.py", line 116, in feed
    if prober.feed(aBuf) == constants.eFoundIt:
```

```
  File "C:\home\chardet\chardet\charsetgroupprober.py", line 60, in feed
    st = prober.feed(aBuf)
  File "C:\home\chardet\chardet\utf8prober.py", line 53, in feed
    codingState = self._mCodingSM.next_state(c)
  File "C:\home\chardet\chardet\codingstatemachine.py", line 43, in next_state
    byteCls = self._mModel['classTable'][ord(c)]
TypeError: ord() expected string of length 1, but int found
```

OK, so c is an int, but the ord() function was expecting a one-character string. Fair enough. But where is c defined? (See Listing 15-34.)

Listing 15-34. The next_state() function uses c, but doesn't define it

```
# codingstatemachine.py
def next_state(self, c):
    # for each byte we get its class
    # if it is first byte, we also get byte length
    byteCls = self._mModel['classTable'][ord(c)]
```

That's no help; it's just passed into the function. Let's pop the stack, as shown in Listing 15-35.

Listing 15-35. utf8prober Calls codingstatemachine

```
# utf8prober.py
def feed(self, aBuf):
    for c in aBuf:
        codingState = self._mCodingSM.next_state(c)
```

Do you see the issue now? In Python 2, aBuf was a string, so c was a one-character string. (That's what you get when you iterate over a string—all the characters, one by one.) But now, aBuf is a byte array, so c is an int, not a one-character string. In other words, there's no need to call the ord() function because c is already an int (see Listing 15-36).

Listing 15-36. c Is Already an int

```
  def next_state(self, c):
      # for each byte we get its class
      # if it is first byte, we also get byte length
-     byteCls = self._mModel['classTable'][ord(c)]
+     byteCls = self._mModel['classTable'][c]
```

Searching the entire codebase for instances of "ord(c)" uncovers similar problems in sbcharsetprober.py (see Listing 15-37).

Listing 15-37. More ord(c) Issues

```
# sbcharsetprober.py
def feed(self, aBuf):
    if not self._mModel['keepEnglishLetter']:
        aBuf = self.filter_without_english_letters(aBuf)
    aLen = len(aBuf)
    if not aLen:
        return self.get_state()
    for c in aBuf:
        order = self._mModel['charToOrderMap'][ord(c)]
```

It also uncovers problems in latin1prober.py (see Listing 15-38).

Listing 15-38. Still More ord(c) Issues

```
# latin1prober.py
def feed(self, aBuf):
    aBuf = self.filter_with_english_letters(aBuf)
    for c in aBuf:
        charClass = Latin1_CharToClass[ord(c)]
```

c is iterating over aBuf, which means it is an integer, not a one-character string. The solution is the same: change ord(c) to just plain c, as shown in Listing 15-39.

Listing 15-39. Even More ord(c) Issues

```
  # sbcharsetprober.py
  def feed(self, aBuf):
      if not self._mModel['keepEnglishLetter']:
          aBuf = self.filter_without_english_letters(aBuf)
      aLen = len(aBuf)
      if not aLen:
          return self.get_state()
      for c in aBuf:
-         order = self._mModel['charToOrderMap'][ord(c)]
+         order = self._mModel['charToOrderMap'][c]

  # latin1prober.py
  def feed(self, aBuf):
      aBuf = self.filter_with_english_letters(aBuf)
      for c in aBuf:
-         charClass = Latin1_CharToClass[ord(c)]
+         charClass = Latin1_CharToClass[c]
```

Unorderable Types: int() >= str()

Let's run the tests yet again, as shown in Listing 15-40.

Listing 15-40. Running the chardet Tests yet Again

```
C:\home\chardet> python test.py tests\*\*
tests\ascii\howto.diveintomark.org.xml                              ascii with confidence 1.0
tests\Big5\0804.blogspot.com.xml
Traceback (most recent call last):
  File "test.py", line 10, in <module>
    u.feed(line)
  File "C:\home\chardet\chardet\universaldetector.py", line 116, in feed
    if prober.feed(aBuf) == constants.eFoundIt:
  File "C:\home\chardet\chardet\charsetgroupprober.py", line 60, in feed
    st = prober.feed(aBuf)
  File "C:\home\chardet\chardet\sjisprober.py", line 68, in feed
    self._mContextAnalyzer.feed(self._mLastChar[2 - charLen :], charLen)
  File "C:\home\chardet\chardet\jpcntx.py", line 145, in feed
    order, charLen = self.get_order(aBuf[i:i+2])
  File "C:\home\chardet\chardet\jpcntx.py", line 176, in get_order
    if ((aStr[0] >= '\x81') and (aStr[0] <= '\x9F')) or \
TypeError: unorderable types: int() >= str()
```

So what's this all about? "Unorderable types"? Once again, the difference between byte arrays and strings is rearing its ugly head (see Listing 15-41).

Listing 15-41. Another Strings/Bytes Problem

```
class SJISContextAnalysis(JapaneseContextAnalysis):
    def get_order(self, aStr):
        if not aStr: return -1, 1
        # find out current char's byte length
        if ((aStr[0] >= '\x81') and (aStr[0] <= '\x9F')) or \
           ((aStr[0] >= '\xE0') and (aStr[0] <= '\xFC')):
            charLen = 2
        else:
            charLen = 1
```

And where does aStr come from? Let's pop the stack, as shown in Listing 15-42.

Listing 15-42. feed Method Calls get_order method

```
def feed(self, aBuf, aLen):
    .
    .
    .
    i = self._mNeedToSkipCharNum
    while i < aLen:
```

```
order, charLen = self.get_order(aBuf[i:i+2])
```

Oh look, it's our old friend, aBuf. As you might have guessed from every other issue we've encountered in this chapter, aBuf is a byte array. Here, the feed() method isn't just passing it on wholesale; it's slicing it. But as you saw earlier in this chapter, slicing a byte array returns a byte array, so the aStr parameter that gets passed to the get_order() method is still a byte array.

And what is this code trying to do with aStr? It's taking the first element of the byte array and comparing it to a string of length 1. That worked in Python 2 because aStr and aBuf were strings, aStr[0] would be a string, and you could compare strings for inequality. But in Python 3, aStr and aBuf are byte arrays, aStr[0] is an integer, and you can't compare integers and strings for inequality without coercing one of them explicitly.

In this case, there's no need to make the code more complicated. aStr[0] yields an integer; the values you're comparing aStr[0] to are all one-character string literals. If we change the values to integers, we don't need explicit type coercion. And while we're at it, let's change the variable name from aStr to aBuf, because it's not actually a string, as shown in Listing 15-43.

Listing 15-43. One-Character Strings Become Integers

```
  class SJISContextAnalysis(JapaneseContextAnalysis):
-     def get_order(self, aStr):
-       if not aStr: return -1, 1
+     def get_order(self, aBuf):
+       if not aBuf: return -1, 1
          # find out current char's byte length
-       if ((aStr[0] >= '\x81') and (aStr[0] <= '\x9F')) or \
-          ((aBuf[0] >= '\xE0') and (aBuf[0] <= '\xFC')):
+       if ((aStr[0] >= 0x81) and (aStr[0] <= 0x9F)) or \
+          ((aBuf[0] >= 0xE0) and (aBuf[0] <= 0xFC)):
            charLen = 2
        else:
            charLen = 1

          # return its order if it is hiragana
-       if len(aStr) > 1:
-           if (aStr[0] == '\202') and \
-              (aStr[1] >= '\x9F') and \
-              (aStr[1] <= '\xF1'):
-               return ord(aStr[1]) - 0x9F, charLen
+       if len(aBuf) > 1:
+           if (aBuf[0] == 0x202) and \
+              (aBuf[1] >= 0x9F) and \
+              (aBuf[1] <= 0xF1):
+               return aBuf[1] - 0x9F, charLen

        return -1, charLen

  class EUCJPContextAnalysis(JapaneseContextAnalysis):
-     def get_order(self, aStr):
-       if not aStr: return -1, 1
+     def get_order(self, aBuf):
```

```
+       if not aBuf: return -1, 1
            # find out current char's byte length
-       if (aStr[0] == '\x8E') or \
-           ((aStr[0] >= '\xA1') and (aStr[0] <= '\xFE')):
+       if (aBuf[0] == 0x8E) or \
+           ((aBuf[0] >= 0xA1) and (aStr[0] <= 0xFE)):
            charLen = 2
-       elif aStr[0] == '\x8F':
+       elif aBuf[0] == 0x8F:
            charLen = 3
        else:
            charLen = 1

        # return its order if it is hiragana
-   if len(aStr) > 1:
-           if (aStr[0] == '\xA4') and \
-               (aStr[1] >= '\xA1') and \
-               (aStr[1] <= '\xF3'):
-                   return ord(aStr[1]) - 0xA1, charLen
+   if len(aBuf) > 1:
+           if (aBuf[0] == 0xA4) and \
+               (aBuf[1] >= 0xA1) and \
+               (aBuf[1] <= 0xF3):
+                   return aBuf[1] - 0xA1, charLen

        return -1, charLen
```

Searching the entire codebase for occurrences of the ord() function uncovers the same problem in chardistribution.py (specifically, in the EUCTWDistributionAnalysis, EUCKRDistributionAnalysis, GB2312DistributionAnalysis, Big5DistributionAnalysis, SJISDistributionAnalysis, and EUCJPDistributionAnalysis classes. In each case, the fix is similar to the change we made to the EUCJPContextAnalysis and SJISContextAnalysis classes in jpcntx.py.

Global Name 'reduce' Is not Defined

Let's head once more into the breach (see Listing 15-44).

Listing 15-44. Running the chardet Tests (Again!)

```
C:\home\chardet> python test.py tests\*\*
tests\ascii\howto.diveintomark.org.xml                          ascii with confidence 1.0
tests\Big5\0804.blogspot.com.xml
Traceback (most recent call last):
  File "test.py", line 12, in <module>
    u.close()
  File "C:\home\chardet\chardet\universaldetector.py", line 141, in close
    proberConfidence = prober.get_confidence()
  File "C:\home\chardet\chardet\latin1prober.py", line 126, in get_confidence
    total = reduce(operator.add, self._mFreqCounter)
NameError: global name 'reduce' is not defined
```

According to the official *What's New In Python 3.0* guide, the `reduce()` function has been moved out of the global namespace and into the `functools` module. Quoting the guide: "Use `functools.reduce()` if you really need it; however, 99 percent of the time an explicit `for` loop is more readable" (see Listing 15-45).

Listing 15-45. reduce() Is No Longer a Global Function

```
def get_confidence(self):
    if self.get_state() == constants.eNotMe:
        return 0.01

    total = reduce(operator.add, self._mFreqCounter)
```

The `reduce()` function takes two arguments—a function and a list (strictly speaking, any iterable object will do)—and applies the function cumulatively to each item of the list. In other words, this is a fancy and roundabout way of adding up all the items in a list and returning the result.

This monstrosity was so common that Python added a global `sum()` function, as shown in Listing 15-46.

Listing 15-46. Use sum() Instead of reduce()

```
  def get_confidence(self):
      if self.get_state() == constants.eNotMe:
          return 0.01

-     total = reduce(operator.add, self._mFreqCounter)
+     total = sum(self._mFreqCounter)
```

You're no longer using the `operator` module, so you can remove that `import` from the top of the file as well, as shown in Listing 15-47.

Listing 15-47. Deleting an Import

```
  from .charsetprober import CharSetProber
  from . import constants
- import operator
```

Please work. Please work. Please work (see Listing 15-48)?

Listing 15-48. Running the chardet Tests for the Last Time (No, Really!)

```
C:\home\chardet> python test.py tests\*\*
tests\ascii\howto.diveintomark.org.xml          ascii with confidence 1.0
tests\Big5\0804.blogspot.com.xml                Big5 with confidence 0.99
tests\Big5\blog.worren.net.xml                  Big5 with confidence 0.99
tests\Big5\carbonxiv.blogspot.com.xml           Big5 with confidence 0.99
tests\Big5\catshadow.blogspot.com.xml           Big5 with confidence 0.99
tests\Big5\coolloud.org.tw.xml                  Big5 with confidence 0.99
tests\Big5\digitalwall.com.xml                  Big5 with confidence 0.99
```

```
tests\Big5\ebao.us.xml                      Big5 with confidence 0.99
tests\Big5\fudesign.blogspot.com.xml        Big5 with confidence 0.99
tests\Big5\kafkatseng.blogspot.com.xml      Big5 with confidence 0.99
tests\Big5\ke207.blogspot.com.xml           Big5 with confidence 0.99
tests\Big5\leavesth.blogspot.com.xml        Big5 with confidence 0.99
tests\Big5\letterlego.blogspot.com.xml      Big5 with confidence 0.99
tests\Big5\linyijen.blogspot.com.xml        Big5 with confidence 0.99
tests\Big5\marilynwu.blogspot.com.xml       Big5 with confidence 0.99
tests\Big5\myblog.pchome.com.tw.xml         Big5 with confidence 0.99
tests\Big5\oui-design.com.xml               Big5 with confidence 0.99
tests\Big5\sanwenji.blogspot.com.xml        Big5 with confidence 0.99
tests\Big5\sinica.edu.tw.xml                Big5 with confidence 0.99
tests\Big5\sylvia1976.blogspot.com.xml      Big5 with confidence 0.99
tests\Big5\tlkkuo.blogspot.com.xml          Big5 with confidence 0.99
tests\Big5\tw.blog.xubg.com.xml             Big5 with confidence 0.99
tests\Big5\unoriginalblog.com.xml           Big5 with confidence 0.99
tests\Big5\upsaid.com.xml                   Big5 with confidence 0.99
tests\Big5\willythecop.blogspot.com.xml     Big5 with confidence 0.99
tests\Big5\ytc.blogspot.com.xml             Big5 with confidence 0.99
tests\EUC-JP\aivy.co.jp.xml                 EUC-JP with confidence 0.99
tests\EUC-JP\akaname.main.jp.xml            EUC-JP with confidence 0.99
tests\EUC-JP\arclamp.jp.xml                 EUC-JP with confidence 0.99
.
.
.
316 tests
```

Holy crap, it actually works! /me *does a little dance.*

Lessons Learned

Converting the chardet project from Python 2 to Python 3 has required some significant effort. However, porting any non-trivial amount of code from Python 2 to Python 3 is going to be a pain. There's no way around it. It's hard.

The automated 2to3 tool is helpful as far as it goes, but it will only do the easy parts: function renames, module renames, syntax changes. It's an impressive piece of engineering, but in the end it's just an intelligent search-and-replace bot.

The number one porting problem in this library was the difference between strings and bytes. In this case that seems obvious, because the whole point of the chardet library is to convert a stream of bytes into a string. But "a stream of bytes" comes up more often than you might think. Reading a file in "binary" mode (as seen in Chapter 11)? You'll get a stream of bytes. Fetching a web page or calling a web API (as seen in Chapter 14)? These return a stream of bytes, too.

You need to understand your program. Thoroughly. Preferably because you wrote it. At the very least, you need to be comfortable with all its quirks and musty corners. The bugs are everywhere.

Test cases are essential; don't port anything without them. The *only* reason I have any confidence that chardet works in Python 3 is that I started with a test suite that exercised all major code paths. If you don't have any tests, write some tests before you start porting to Python 3. If you have a few tests, write more. If you have a lot of tests, then the real fun can begin.

CHAPTER 16

■ ■ ■

Packaging Python Libraries

So you want to release a Python script, library, framework, or application. Excellent. The world needs more Python code.

Python 3 comes with a packaging framework called *Distutils*. Distutils is many things: a build tool (for you), an installation tool (for your users), a package metadata format (for search engines), and more. It integrates with the Python Package Index (PyPI), a central repository for open source Python libraries (see http://pypi.python.org/).

All these facets of Distutils center around the *setup script*, traditionally called setup.py. In fact, you've already seen several Distutils setup scripts in this book. You used Distutils to install httplib2 in Chapter 14 and again to install chardet in Chapter 15.

In this chapter, you'll learn how the setup scripts for chardet and httplib2 work, and you'll step through the process of releasing your own Python software. The setup script for chardet is shown in Listing 16-1.

Listing 16-1. setup.py

```python
# chardet's setup.py
from distutils.core import setup
setup(
    name = "chardet",
    packages = ["chardet"],
    version = "1.0.2",
    description = "Universal encoding detector",
    author = "Mark Pilgrim",
    author_email = "mark@diveintomark.org",
    url = "http://chardet.feedparser.org/",
    download_url = "http://chardet.feedparser.org/download/python3-chardet-1.0.1.tgz",
    keywords = ["encoding", "i18n", "xml"],
    classifiers = [
        "Programming Language :: Python",
        "Programming Language :: Python :: 3",
        "Development Status :: 4 - Beta",
        "Environment :: Other Environment",
        "Intended Audience :: Developers",
        "License :: OSI Approved :: GNU Library or Lesser General Public License (LGPL)",
```

```
        "Operating System :: OS Independent",
        "Topic :: Software Development :: Libraries :: Python Modules",
        "Topic :: Text Processing :: Linguistic",
        ],
    long_description = """\
Universal character encoding detector
-------------------------------------

Detects
 - ASCII, UTF-8, UTF-16 (2 variants), UTF-32 (4 variants)
 - Big5, GB2312, EUC-TW, HZ-GB-2312, ISO-2022-CN (Traditional and Simplified Chinese)
 - EUC-JP, SHIFT_JIS, ISO-2022-JP (Japanese)
 - EUC-KR, ISO-2022-KR (Korean)
 - KOI8-R, MacCyrillic, IBM855, IBM866, ISO-8859-5, windows-1251 (Cyrillic)
 - ISO-8859-2, windows-1250 (Hungarian)
 - ISO-8859-5, windows-1251 (Bulgarian)
 - windows-1252 (English)
 - ISO-8859-7, windows-1253 (Greek)
 - ISO-8859-8, windows-1255 (Visual and Logical Hebrew)
 - TIS-620 (Thai)

This version requires Python 3 or later; a Python 2 version is available separately.
"""

)
```

■ chardet and httplib2 are open source, but there's no requirement that you release your own Python libraries under any particular license. The process described in this chapter will work for any Python software, regardless of license.

Things Distutils Can't Do for You

Releasing your first Python package is a daunting process. (Releasing your second one is a little easier.) Distutils tries to automate as much of it as possible, but there are some things you simply must do yourself:

Choose a license. This is a complicated topic, fraught with politics and peril. If you want to release your software as open source, I humbly offer five pieces of advice:

- Don't write your own license.

- Don't write your own license.

- Don't write your own license.

- It doesn't need to be GPL, but it needs to be GPL-compatible: http://www.dwheeler.com/essays/gpl-compatible.html.

- Don't write your own license.

Classify your software using the PyPI classification system. I'll explain more later in this chapter.

Write a "read me" file. Don't skimp on this. At a minimum, it should give your users an overview of what your software does and how to install it.

Directory Structure

To start packaging your Python software, you need to get your files and directories in order. The `httplib2` directory is shown in Listing 16-2.

Listing 16-2. Project Directory Structure

```
httplib2/                (1)
|
+--README.txt            (2)
|
+--setup.py              (3)
|
+--httplib2/             (4)
   |
   +--__init__.py
   |
   +--iri2uri.py
```

1. Make a root directory to hold everything. Give it the same name as your Python module.

2. To accomodate Windows users, your "read me" file should include a `.txt` extension, and it should use Windows-style carriage returns. Just because *you* use a fancy text editor that runs from the command line and includes its own macro language, you don't need to make life difficult for your users. (Your users use Notepad. Sad but true.) Even if you're on Linux or Mac OS X, your fancy text editor undoubtedly has an option to save files with Windows-style carriage returns.

3. Your Distutils setup script should be named `setup.py` unless you have a good reason not to do so. *You do not have a good reason not to do so.*

4. If your Python software is a single `.py` file, you should put it in the root directory along with your "read me" file and your setup script. But `httplib2` is not a single `.py` file; it's a multifile module (see Chapter 15). But that's okay! Just put the `httplib2` directory in the root directory, so you have an `__init__.py` file within an `httplib2/` directory within the `httplib2/` root directory. That's not a problem; in fact, it will simplify your packaging process.

The `chardet` directory looks slightly different. Like `httplib2`, it's a multifile module, so there's a `chardet/` directory within the `chardet/` root directory. In addition to the `README.txt` file, `chardet` has HTML-formatted documentation in the `docs/` directory. The `docs/` directory contains several `.html` and `.css` files and an `images/` subdirectory, which contains several `.png` and `.gif` files. (This will be important later.) Also, in keeping with the convention for (L)GPL-licensed software, it has a separate file called

COPYING.txt, which contains the complete text of the LGPL. Listing 16-3 shows the complete directory structure.

Listing 16-3. chardet Project Directory Structure

```
chardet/
|
+--COPYING.txt
|
+--setup.py
|
+--README.txt
|
+--docs/
|   |
|   +--index.html
|   |
|   +--usage.html
|   |
|   +--images/ ...
|
+--chardet/
    |
    +--__init__.py
    |
    +--big5freq.py
    |
    +--...
```

Writing Your Setup Script

The Distutils setup script is a Python script. In theory, it can do anything Python can do. In practice, it should do as little as possible, in as standard a way as possible. Setup scripts should be boring. The more exotic your installation process is, the more exotic your bug reports will be.

The first line of every Distutils setup script is always the same (see Listing 16-4).

Listing 16-4. First Line of Every setup.py Script

```
from distutils.core import setup
```

This line imports the **setup()** function, which is the main entry point into Distutils. Ninety-five percent of all Distutils setup scripts consist of a single call to **setup()** and nothing else. (I totally just made up that statistic, but if your Distutils setup script is doing more than calling the Distutils **setup()** function, you should have a good reason. Do you have a good reason? I didn't think so.)

The **setup()** function can take dozens of parameters. For the sanity of everyone involved, you must use named arguments for every parameter (see Chapter 1). This is not merely a convention; it's a hard requirement. Your setup script will crash if you try to call the **setup()** function with non-named arguments.

The following named arguments are required:

- *name*: the name of the package.

- *version*: the version number of the package.

- *author*: your full name.

- *author_email*: your e-mail address.

- *url*: the home page of your project. This can be your PyPI package page if you don't have a separate project web site.

Although not required, I recommend that you also include the following in your setup script:

- *description*: a one-line summary of the project.

- *long_description*: a multiline string in reStructuredText format (see http://docutils.sourceforge.net/rst.html). PyPI converts this to HTML and displays it on your package page.

- *classifiers*: a list of specially formatted strings described in the next section.

■ Setup script metadata is defined in PEP 314 (http://www.python.org/dev/peps/pep-0314/).

Now let's look at the **chardet** setup script. It has all these required and recommended parameters, plus one I haven't mentioned yet: **packages**. (See Listing 16-5.)

Listing 16-5. setup.py Script for chardet

```
from distutils.core import setup
setup(
    name = 'chardet',
    packages = ['chardet']
    version = '1.0.2',
    description = 'Universal encoding detector',
    author='Mark Pilgrim',
    ...
)
```

The **packages** parameter highlights an unfortunate vocabulary overlap in the distribution process. We've been talking about the *package* as the thing you're building (and potentially Listing in the Python "Package" Index). But that's not what this **packages** parameter refers to. It refers to the fact that the **chardet** module is a multifile module, sometimes known as a *package*. The **packages** parameter tells Distutils to include the **chardet/** directory, its **__init__.py** file, and all the other **.py** files that constitute the **chardet** module. That's kind of important; all this happy talk about documentation and metadata is irrelevant if you forget to include the actual code!

Classifying Your Package

PyPI contains thousands of Python libraries. Proper classification metadata will allow people to find yours more easily. PyPI lets you browse packages by classifier (see http://pypi.python.org/pypi?:action=browse). You can even select multiple classifiers to narrow your search. Classifiers are not invisible metadata that you can just ignore!

To classify your software, pass a `classifiers` parameter to the Distutils `setup()` function. The `classifers` parameter is a list of strings. These strings are *not* freeform. All classifier strings should come from the master list on PyPI (see http://pypi.python.org/pypi?:action=list_classifiers).

Classifiers are optional. You can write a Distutils setup script without any classifiers at all. Don't do that! You should *always* include at least these classifiers:

- *Programming Language*: In particular, you should include both `"Programming Language :: Python"` and `"Programming Language :: Python :: 3"`. If you do not include them, your package will not show up in the PyPI list of Python three-compatible libraries (see http://pypi.python.org/pypi?:action=browse&c=533&show=all), which linked from the sidebar of every single page of `pypi.python.org`.

- *License*: This is *the absolute first thing I look for* when I'm evaluating third-party libraries. Don't make me hunt for this vital information. Don't include more than one license classifier unless your software is explicitly available under multiple licenses. (Don't release software under multiple licenses unless you're forced to do so. And don't force other people to do so. Licensing is enough of a headache; don't make it worse.)

- *Operating System*: If your software runs only on Windows (or Mac OS X or Linux), I want to know sooner rather than later. If your software runs anywhere without any platform-specific code, use the classifier `"Operating System :: OS Independent"`. Multiple `Operating System` classifiers are necessary only if your software requires specific support for each platform. (This is not common.)

I also recommend that you include the following classifiers:

- *Development Status*: Is your software beta quality? Alpha quality? Pre-alpha? Pick one. Be honest.

- *Intended Audience*: Who would download your software? The most common choices are `Developers`, `End Users/Desktop`, `Science/Research`, and `System Administrators`.

- *Framework*: If your software is a plugin for a larger Python framework like Django or Zope, include the appropriate `Framework` classifier. If not, omit it.

- *Topic*: There are many topics to choose from (see http://pypi.python.org/pypi?:action=list_classifiers); choose all that apply.

Examples of Good Package Classifiers

By way of example, Listing 16-6 shows the classifiers for Django, a production-ready, cross-platform, BSD-licensed web application framework that runs on your web server. (Django is not yet compatible with Python 3, so the `Programming Language :: Python :: 3` classifier is not listed.)

Listing 16-6. Django Package Classifiers

```
Programming Language :: Python
License :: OSI Approved :: BSD License
Operating System :: OS Independent
Development Status :: 5 - Production/Stable
Environment :: Web Environment
Framework :: Django
Intended Audience :: Developers
Topic :: Internet :: WWW/HTTP
Topic :: Internet :: WWW/HTTP :: Dynamic Content
Topic :: Internet :: WWW/HTTP :: WSGI
Topic :: Software Development :: Libraries :: Python Modules
```

Listing 16-7 shows the classifiers for **chardet**, the character encoding detection library covered in Chapter 15. **chardet** is beta quality, cross-platform, Python 3-compatible, LGPL-licensed, and intended for developers to integrate into their own products.

Listing 16-7. chardet Package Classifiers

```
Programming Language :: Python
Programming Language :: Python :: 3
License :: OSI Approved :: GNU Library or Lesser General Public License (LGPL)
Operating System :: OS Independent
Development Status :: 4 - Beta
Environment :: Other Environment
Intended Audience :: Developers
Topic :: Text Processing :: Linguistic
Topic :: Software Development :: Libraries :: Python Modules
```

Listing 16-8 shows the classifiers for **httplib2**, the HTTP client library covered in Chapter 14. **httplib2** is beta quality, cross-platform, MIT-licensed, and intended for Python developers.

Listing 16-8. httplib2 Package Classifiers

```
Programming Language :: Python
Programming Language :: Python :: 3
License :: OSI Approved :: MIT License
Operating System :: OS Independent
Development Status :: 4 - Beta
Environment :: Web Environment
Intended Audience :: Developers
Topic :: Internet :: WWW/HTTP
Topic :: Software Development :: Libraries :: Python Modules
Specifying Additional Files with a Manifest
```

By default, Distutils will include the following files in your release package:

- `README.txt`

- `setup.py`

- The `.py` files needed by the multifile modules listed in the `packages` parameter

- The individual `.py` files listed in the `py_modules` parameter

That will cover all the files in the `httplib2` project. But for the `chardet` project, we also want to include the `COPYING.txt` license file and the entire `docs/` directory that contains images and HTML files. To tell Distutils to include these additional files and directories when it builds the `chardet` release package, you need a *manifest file*.

A manifest file is a text file called `MANIFEST.in`. Place it in the project's root directory, next to `README.txt` and `setup.py`. Manifest files are *not* Python scripts; they are text files that contain a series of "commands" in a Distutils-defined format. Manifest commands allow you to include or exclude specific files and directories.

Listing 16-9 shows the manifest file for the `chardet` project.

Listing 16-9. A Manifest File

```
include COPYING.txt                               (1)
recursive-include docs *.html *.css *.png *.gif   (2)
```

1. The first line is self-explanatory: include the `COPYING.txt` file from the project's root directory.

2. The second line is a bit more complicated. The `recursive-include` command takes a directory name and one or more file names. The file names aren't limited to specific files; they can include wildcards. This line means "See that `docs/` directory in the project's root directory? Look in there (recursively) for `.html`, `.css`, `.png`, and `.gif` files. I want all of them in my release package."

All manifest commands preserve the directory structure that you set up in your project directory. That `recursive-include` command will not put a bunch of `.html` and `.png` files in the root directory of the release package. It will maintain the existing `docs/` directory structure, but include only those files inside that directory that match the given wildcards. (I didn't mention it earlier, but the `chardet` documentation is actually written in XML and converted to HTML by a separate script. I don't want to include the XML files in the release package, just the HTML and the images.)

■ Manifest files have their own unique format. See "Specifying the files to distribute" (`http://docs.python.org/3.1/distutils/sourcedist.html#manifest`) and "the manifest template commands" (`http://docs.python.org/3.1/distutils/commandref.html#sdist-cmd`) for details.

To reiterate: you need to create a manifest file only if you want to include files that Distutils doesn't include by default. If you do need a manifest file, it should include only the files and directories that Distutils wouldn't otherwise find on its own.

Checking Your Setup Script for Errors

There's a lot to keep track of. Distutils comes with a built-in validation command that checks that all the required metadata is present in your setup script. For example, if you forget to include the **version** parameter, Distutils will remind you, as shown in Listing 16-10.

Listing 16-10. Checking Your Setup Script for Errors

```
c:\Users\pilgrim\chardet> c:\python31\python.exe setup.py check
running check
warning: check: missing required meta-data: version
```

Once you include a **version** parameter (and all the other required bits of metadata), the **check** command will not output any other warnings, as shown in Listing 16-11.

Listing 16-11. Checking Your Setup Script: No Errors

```
c:\Users\pilgrim\chardet> c:\python31\python.exe setup.py check
running check
```

Creating a Source Distribution

Distutils supports building multiple types of release packages. At a minimum, you should build a "source distribution" that contains your source code, your Distutils setup script, your "read me" file, and whatever additional files you want to include. To build a source distribution, pass the **sdist** command to your Distutils setup script, as shown in Listing 16-12.

Listing 16-12. Creating a Source Distribution

```
c:\Users\pilgrim\chardet> c:\python31\python.exe setup.py sdist
running sdist
running check
reading manifest template 'MANIFEST.in'
writing manifest file 'MANIFEST'
creating chardet-1.0.2
creating chardet-1.0.2\chardet
creating chardet-1.0.2\docs
creating chardet-1.0.2\docs\images
copying files to chardet-1.0.2...
copying COPYING -> chardet-1.0.2
copying README.txt -> chardet-1.0.2
copying setup.py -> chardet-1.0.2
copying chardet\__init__.py -> chardet-1.0.2\chardet
copying chardet\big5freq.py -> chardet-1.0.2\chardet
...
copying chardet\universaldetector.py -> chardet-1.0.2\chardet
copying chardet\utf8prober.py -> chardet-1.0.2\chardet
copying docs\faq.html -> chardet-1.0.2\docs
copying docs\history.html -> chardet-1.0.2\docs
```

```
copying docs\how-it-works.html -> chardet-1.0.2\docs
copying docs\index.html -> chardet-1.0.2\docs
copying docs\license.html -> chardet-1.0.2\docs
copying docs\supported-encodings.html -> chardet-1.0.2\docs
copying docs\usage.html -> chardet-1.0.2\docs
copying docs\images\caution.png -> chardet-1.0.2\docs\images
copying docs\images\important.png -> chardet-1.0.2\docs\images
copying docs\images\note.png -> chardet-1.0.2\docs\images
copying docs\images\permalink.gif -> chardet-1.0.2\docs\images
copying docs\images\tip.png -> chardet-1.0.2\docs\images
copying docs\images\warning.png -> chardet-1.0.2\docs\images
creating dist
creating 'dist\chardet-1.0.2.zip' and adding 'chardet-1.0.2' to it
adding 'chardet-1.0.2\COPYING'
adding 'chardet-1.0.2\PKG-INFO'
adding 'chardet-1.0.2\README.txt'
adding 'chardet-1.0.2\setup.py'
adding 'chardet-1.0.2\chardet\big5freq.py'
adding 'chardet-1.0.2\chardet\big5prober.py'
...
adding 'chardet-1.0.2\chardet\universaldetector.py'
adding 'chardet-1.0.2\chardet\utf8prober.py'
adding 'chardet-1.0.2\chardet\__init__.py'
adding 'chardet-1.0.2\docs\faq.html'
adding 'chardet-1.0.2\docs\history.html'
adding 'chardet-1.0.2\docs\how-it-works.html'
adding 'chardet-1.0.2\docs\index.html'
adding 'chardet-1.0.2\docs\license.html'
adding 'chardet-1.0.2\docs\supported-encodings.html'
adding 'chardet-1.0.2\docs\usage.html'
adding 'chardet-1.0.2\docs\images\caution.png'
adding 'chardet-1.0.2\docs\images\important.png'
adding 'chardet-1.0.2\docs\images\note.png'
adding 'chardet-1.0.2\docs\images\permalink.gif'
adding 'chardet-1.0.2\docs\images\tip.png'
adding 'chardet-1.0.2\docs\images\warning.png'
removing 'chardet-1.0.2' (and everything under it)
```

Several things to note here include the following:

- Distutils noticed the manifest file (MANIFEST.in).

- Distutils successfully parsed the manifest file and added the additional files we wanted: COPYING.txt and the HTML and image files in the docs/ directory.

- If you look in your project directory, you'll see that Distutils created a dist/ directory. Within the dist/ directory is the .zip file that you can distribute.

Listing 16-13 shows the resulting .zip file.

Listing 16-13. The Source Distribution

```
c:\Users\pilgrim\chardet> dir dist
 Volume in drive C has no label.
 Volume Serial Number is DED5-B4F8

 Directory of c:\Users\pilgrim\chardet\dist

07/30/2009  06:29 PM    <DIR>          .
07/30/2009  06:29 PM    <DIR>          ..
07/30/2009  06:29 PM           206,440 chardet-1.0.2.zip
               1 File(s)        206,440 bytes
               2 Dir(s)  61,424,635,904 bytes free
```

Creating a Graphical Installer

In my opinion, every Python library deserves a graphical installer for Windows users. It's easy to make (even if you don't run Windows yourself), and Windows users appreciate it.

Distutils can create a graphical Windows installer for you, by passing the bdist_wininst command to your Distutils setup script, as shown in Listing 16-14.

Listing 16-14. Creating a Windows Installer

```
c:\Users\pilgrim\chardet> c:\python31\python.exe setup.py bdist_wininst
running bdist_wininst
running build
running build_py
creating build
creating build\lib
creating build\lib\chardet
copying chardet\big5freq.py -> build\lib\chardet
copying chardet\big5prober.py -> build\lib\chardet
...
copying chardet\universaldetector.py -> build\lib\chardet
copying chardet\utf8prober.py -> build\lib\chardet
copying chardet\__init__.py -> build\lib\chardet
installing to build\bdist.win32\wininst
running install_lib
creating build\bdist.win32
creating build\bdist.win32\wininst
creating build\bdist.win32\wininst\PURELIB
creating build\bdist.win32\wininst\PURELIB\chardet
copying build\lib\chardet\big5freq.py -> build\bdist.win32\wininst\PURELIB\chardet
copying build\lib\chardet\big5prober.py -> build\bdist.win32\wininst\PURELIB\chardet
...
```

```
copying build\lib\chardet\universaldetector.py -> build\bdist.win32\wininst\PURELIB\chardet
copying build\lib\chardet\utf8prober.py -> build\bdist.win32\wininst\PURELIB\chardet
copying build\lib\chardet\__init__.py -> build\bdist.win32\wininst\PURELIB\chardet
running install_egg_info
Writing build\bdist.win32\wininst\PURELIB\chardet-1.0.2-py3.1.egg-info
creating 'c:\users\pilgrim\appdata\local\temp\tmp2f4h7e.zip' and adding '.' to it
adding 'PURELIB\chardet-1.0.2-py3.1.egg-info'
adding 'PURELIB\chardet\big5freq.py'
adding 'PURELIB\chardet\big5prober.py'
...
adding 'PURELIB\chardet\universaldetector.py'
adding 'PURELIB\chardet\utf8prober.py'
adding 'PURELIB\chardet\__init__.py'
removing 'build\bdist.win32\wininst' (and everything under it)
c:\Users\pilgrim\chardet> dir dist
Volume in drive C has no label.
 Volume Serial Number is AADE-E29F

 Directory of c:\Users\pilgrim\chardet\dist

07/30/2009  10:14 PM    <DIR>          .
07/30/2009  10:14 PM    <DIR>          ..
07/30/2009  10:14 PM           371,236 chardet-1.0.2.win32.exe
07/30/2009  06:29 PM           206,440 chardet-1.0.2.zip
               2 File(s)        577,676 bytes
               2 Dir(s)  61,424,070,656 bytes free</samp>
```

Building Installable Packages for Other Operating Systems

Distutils can help you build installable packages for Linux users. In my opinion, this probably isn't worth your time. If you want your software distributed for Linux, your time would be better spent working with community members who specialize in packaging software for major Linux distributions.

For example, my chardet library is in the Debian GNU/Linux repositories (http://packages.debian.org/python-chardet) and therefore in the Ubuntu repositories as well (http://packages.ubuntu.com/python-chardet). I had nothing to do with it; the packages just showed up there one day. The Debian community has its own policies for packaging Python libraries, and the Debian python-chardet package is designed to follow these conventions. And because the package lives in Debian's repositories, Debian users will receive security updates and/or new versions, depending on the system-wide settings they've chosen to manage their own computers.

The Linux packages that Distutils builds offer none of these advantages. Your time is better spent elsewhere.

Adding Your Software to the Python Package Index

Uploading software to the Python Package Index is a three-step process:

1. Register yourself.

2. Register your software.

3. Upload the packages you created with setup.py sdist and setup.py bdist_*.

To register yourself, go to the PyPI user registration page (http://pypi.python.org/pypi?:action=register_form). Enter your desired username and password, provide a valid e-mail address, and click the Register button. (If you have a PGP or GPG key, you can also provide it. If you don't have one or don't know what that means, don't worry about it.) Check your e-mail; within a few minutes, you should receive a message from PyPI with a validation link. Click the link to complete the registration process.

Now you need to register your software with PyPI and upload it. You can do this all in one step, as shown in Listing 16-15.

Listing 16-15. Uploading to the Python Package Index

```
c:\Users\pilgrim\chardet> c:\python31\python.exe setup.py register sdist ↵
 bdist_wininst upload                                                      (1)
running register
We need to know who you are, so please choose either:
 1. use your existing login,
 2. register as a new user,
 3. have the server generate a new password for you (and email it to you), or
 4. quit
Your selection [default 1]: 1                                              (2)
<samp>Username: MarkPilgrim                                                (3)
<samp>Password:
Registering chardet to http://pypi.python.org/pypi                        (4)
Server response (200): OK
running sdist                                                             (5)
... output trimmed for brevity ...
running bdist_wininst                                                     (6)
... output trimmed for brevity ...
running upload                                                           (7)
Submitting dist\chardet-1.0.2.zip to http://pypi.python.org/pypi
Server response (200): OK
Submitting dist\chardet-1.0.2.win32.exe to http://pypi.python.org/pypi
Server response (200): OK
I can store your PyPI login so future submissions will be faster.
(the login will be stored in c:\home\.pypirc)
Save your login (y/N)?n                                                   (8)
```

1. When you release your project for the first time, Distutils will add your software to the Python Package Index and give it its own URL. Every time after that, it will simply update the project metadata with any changes you may have made in your `setup.py` parameters. Next, it builds a source distribution (`sdist`) and a Windows installer (`bdist_wininst`) and then uploads them to PyPI (`upload`).

2. Type **1** or just press Enter to select "use your existing login".

3. Enter the username and password you selected on the the PyPI user registration page. Distuils will not echo your password; it will not even echo asterisks in place of characters. Just type your password and press Enter.

4. Distutils registers your package with the Python Package Index…

5. …builds your source distribution…

6. …builds your Windows installer…

7. …and uploads them both to the Python Package Index.

8. If you want to automate the process of releasing new versions, you need to save your PyPI credentials in a local file. This is completely insecure and completely optional.

Congratulations! You now have your own page on the Python Package Index! The address is `http://pypi.python.org/pypi/NAME`, where *NAME* is the string you passed in the `name` parameter in your `setup.py` file.

If you want to release a new version, just update your `setup.py` with the new version number and then run the same upload command again (see Listing 16-16).

Listing 16-16. Uploading New Versions to the Python Package Index

```
c:\Users\pilgrim\chardet> c:\python31\python.exe setup.py register ↵
 sdist bdist_wininst upload
```

The Many Possible Futures of Python Packaging

Distutils is not the be-all and end-all of Python packaging, but as of this writing (August 2009), it's the only packaging framework that works in Python 3. There are a number of other frameworks for Python 2; some focus on installation, and others focus on testing and deployment. Some or all of them may end up being ported to Python 3 in the future.

These frameworks focus on installation:

- *Setuptools*: http://pypi.python.org/pypi/setuptools

- *Pip*: http://pypi.python.org/pypi/pip

- *Distribute*: http://bitbucket.org/tarek/distribute/

These focus on testing and deployment:

- *virtualenv*: http://pypi.python.org/pypi/virtualenv

- *zc.buildout*: http://pypi.python.org/pypi/zc.buildout

- *Paver*: http://www.blueskyonmars.com/projects/paver/

- *Fabric*: http://fabfile.org/

- *py2exe*: http://www.py2exe.org/

Further Reading Online

For more information, refer to the following sources:

On Distutils:

- *Distributing Python Modules with Distutils*:
  http://docs.python.org/3.1/distutils/

- *Core Distutils functionality lists all the possible arguments to the setup() function*:
  http://docs.python.org/3.1/distutils/apiref.html#module-distutils.core

- *Distutils Cookbook*: http://wiki.python.org/moin/Distutils/Cookbook

- *PEP 370: Per user site-packages directory*:
  http://www.python.org/dev/peps/pep-0370/

- *PEP 370 and "environment stew"*: http://jessenoller.com/2009/07/19/
  pep-370-per-user-site-packages-and-environment-stew/

On other packaging frameworks:

- *The Python packaging ecosystem*: http://groups.google.com/group/
  django-developers/msg/5407cdb400157259

- *On packaging*: http://www.b-list.org/weblog/2008/dec/14/packaging/

- *A few corrections to "On packaging"*:
  http://blog.ianbicking.org/2008/12/14/a-few-corrections-to-on-packaging/

- *Why I like Pip*: http://www.b-list.org/weblog/2008/dec/15/pip/

- *Python packaging: a few observations:* http://cournape.wordpress.com/2009/
  04/01/python-packaging-a-few-observations-cabal-for-a-solution/

- *Nobody expects Python packaging!*:
  http://jacobian.org/writing/nobody-expects-python-packaging/

APPENDIX A

■ ■ ■

Porting Code to Python 3 with 2to3

Virtually all Python 2 programs need at least some tweaking to run properly under Python 3. To help with this transition, Python 3 comes with a utility script called **2to3**, which takes your actual Python 2 source code as input and auto-converts as much as it can to Python 3. Chapter 15 described how to run the **2to3** script and showed some things it can't fix automatically. This appendix documents what it *can* fix automatically.

print Statement

In Python 2, **print** was a statement. Whatever you wanted to print simply followed the **print** keyword. In Python 3, **print()** is a function. Whatever you want to print, pass it to **print()** like any other function, as shown in Table A-1.

Table A-1. The print() Statement

Notes	Python 2	Python 3
(1)	`print`	`print()`
(2)	`print 1`	`print(1)`
(3)	`print 1, 2`	`print(1, 2)`
(4)	`print 1, 2,`	`print(1, 2, end=' ')`
(5)	`print >>sys.stderr, 1, 2, 3`	`print(1, 2, 3, file=sys.stderr)`

1. To print a blank line, call **print()** without any arguments.
2. To print a single value, call **print()** with one argument.
3. To print two values separated by a space, call **print()** with two arguments.

4. This one is a little tricky. In Python 2, if you ended a `print` statement with a comma, it would print the values separated by spaces, print a trailing space, and then stop without printing a carriage return. In Python 3, the way to do this is to pass `end=' '` as a keyword argument to the `print()` function. The `end` argument defaults to `'\n'` (a carriage return), so overriding it will suppress the carriage return after printing the other arguments.

5. In Python 2, you could redirect the output to a pipe (such as `sys.stderr`) by using the `>>pipe_name` syntax. In Python 3, the way to do this is to pass the pipe in the `file` keyword argument. The `file` argument defaults to `sys.stdout` (standard out), so overriding it will output to a different pipe instead.

Unicode String Literals

Python 2 had two string types: Unicode strings and non-Unicode strings. Python 3 has one string type: Unicode strings, as shown in Table A-2.

Table A-2. *Unicode String Literals*

Notes	Python 2	Python 3
(1)	`u'PapayaWhip'`	`'PapayaWhip'`
(2)	`ur'PapayaWhip\foo'`	`r'PapayaWhip\foo'`

1. Unicode string literals are simply converted into string literals, which are always Unicode in Python 3.

2. Unicode raw strings (in which Python does not auto-escape backslashes) are converted to raw strings. In Python 3, raw strings are always Unicode.

unicode() Global Function

Python 2 had two global functions to coerce objects into strings: `unicode()` to coerce them into Unicode strings and `str()` to coerce them into non-Unicode strings. Python 3 has only one string type, Unicode strings, so the `str()` function is all you need. (The `unicode()` function no longer exists.) See Table A-3.

Table A-3. *The unicode() Global Function*

Python 2	Python 3
unicode(anything)	str(anything)

long Datatype

Python 2 had separate `int` and `long` types for non-floating-point numbers. An `int` could not be any larger than `sys.maxint`, which varied by platform. Longs were defined by appending an L to the end of the number, and they could be, well, longer than ints. In Python 3, there is only one integer type, called `int`, which mostly behaves like the `long` type in Python 2. Because there are no longer two types, there is no need for special syntax to distinguish them (see Table A-4).

Table A-4. *long Datatypes*

Notes	Python 2	Python 3
(1)	x = 1000000000000L	X = 1000000000000
(2)	x = 0xFFFFFFFFFFFFFL	x = 0xFFFFFFFFFFFFF
(3)	long(x)	int(x)
(4)	type(x) is long	type(x) is int
(5)	isinstance(x, long)	isinstance(x, int)

1. Base 10 long integer literals become base 10 integer literals.

2. Base 16 long integer literals become base 16 integer literals.

3. In Python 3, the old `long()` function no longer exists because longs don't exist. To coerce a variable to an integer, use the `int()` function.

4. To check whether a variable is an integer, get its type and compare it with `int`, not `long`.

5. You can also use the `isinstance()` function to check datatypes; again, use `int`, not `long`, to check for integers.

<> Comparison

Python 2 supported `<>` as a synonym for `!=`, the not-equals comparison operator. Python 3 supports the `!=` operator, but not `<>`, as shown in Table A-5.

Table A-5. <> Comparison

Notes	Python 2	Python 3
(1)	if x <> y:	if x != y:
(2)	if x <> y <> z:	if x != y != z:

   1.   This is a simple comparison between two values.

   2.   This is a more complex comparison between three values.

has_key() Dictionary Method

In Python 2, dictionaries had a **has_key()** method to test whether the dictionary had a certain key. In Python 3, this method no longer exists. Instead, you need to use the **in** operator. (See Table A-6.)

Table A-6. has_key() Dictionary Method

Notes	Python 2	Python 3
(1)	a_dictionary.has_key('PapayaWhip')	'PapayaWhip' in a_dictionary
(2)	a_dictionary.has_key(x) or a_dictionary.has_key(y)	x in a_dictionary or y in a_dictionary
(3)	a_dictionary.has_key(x or y)	(x or y) in a_dictionary
(4)	a_dictionary.has_key(x + y)	(x + y) in a_dictionary
(5)	x + a_dictionary.has_key(y)	x + (y in a_dictionary)

   1.   The simplest form.

   2.   The **in** operator takes precedence over the **or** operator, so there is no need for parentheses here.

   3.   On the other hand, you *do* need parentheses here, for the same reason: **in** takes precedence over **or**. Note that this code is completely different from the previous line. Python interprets **x or y** first, which results in either **x** (if **x** is **true** in a Boolean context) or **y**. Then it takes that singular value and checks whether it is a key in **a_dictionary**.

   4.   The **in** operator takes precedence over the + operator, so this form technically doesn't need parentheses, but **2to3** includes them anyway.

   5.   This form definitely needs parentheses because the **in** operator takes precedence over the + operator.

Dictionary Methods that Return Lists

In Python 2, many dictionary methods returned lists. The most frequently used methods were `keys()`, `items()`, and `values()`. In Python 3, all these methods return dynamic views. In some contexts, this is not a problem. If the method's return value is immediately passed to another function that iterates through the entire sequence, it makes no difference whether the actual type is a list or a view. In other contexts, it matters a great deal. If you were expecting a complete list with individually addressable elements, your code will choke because views do not support indexing. (See Table A-7.)

Table A-7. Dictionary Methods that Return Lists

Notes	Python 2	Python 3
(1)	`a_dictionary.keys()`	`list(a_dictionary.keys())`
(2)	`a_dictionary.items()`	`list(a_dictionary.items())`
(3)	`a_dictionary.iterkeys()`	`iter(a_dictionary.keys())`
(4)	`[i for i in a_dictionary.iterkeys()]`	`[i for i in a_dictionary.keys()]`
(5)	`min(a_dictionary.keys())`	No Change

1. `2to3` errs on the side of safety, converting the return value from `keys()` to a static list with the `list()` function. This will always work, but it will be less efficient than using a view. You should examine the converted code to see whether a list is absolutely necessary (or whether a view would do).

2. Another view-to-list conversion with the `items()` method. `2to3` will do the same thing with the `values()` method.

3. Python 3 does not support the `iterkeys()` method anymore. Use `keys()` and convert the view to an iterator with the `iter()` function, if necessary.

4. `2to3` recognizes when the `iterkeys()` method is used inside a list comprehension and converts it to the `keys()` method without wrapping it in an extra call to `iter()`. It works because views are iterable.

5. `2to3` recognizes that the `keys()` method is immediately passed to a function that iterates through an entire sequence, so there is no need to convert the return value to a list first. The `min()` function will happily iterate through the view instead. This applies to `min()`, `max()`, `sum()`, `list()`, `tuple()`, `set()`, `sorted()`, `any()`, and `all()`.

Renamed or Reorganized Modules

Several modules in the Python Standard Library have been renamed. Several other modules that are related to each other have been combined or reorganized to make their association more logical.

http

In Python 3, several related HTTP modules have been combined into a single package, http, as shown in Table A-8.

Table A-8. http Module Reorganization

Notes	Python 2	Python 3
(1)	import httplib	import http.client
(2)	import Cookie	import http.cookies
(3)	import cookielib	import http.cookiejar
(4)	import BaseHTTPServer	import http.server
	import SimpleHTTPServer	
	import CGIHttpServer	

1. The http.client module implements a low-level library that can request HTTP resources and interpret HTTP responses.

2. The http.cookies module provides a Pythonic interface to browser cookies that are sent in a Set-Cookie: HTTP header.

3. The http.cookiejar module manipulates the actual files on disk that popular web browsers use to store cookies.

4. The http.server module provides a basic HTTP server.

urllib

Python 2 had a rat's nest of overlapping modules to parse, encode, and fetch URLs. In Python 3, they have all been refactored and combined in a single package, urllib, as shown in Table A-9.

Table A-9. urllib Module Reorganization

Notes	Python 2	Python 3
(1)	import urllib	import urllib.request, urllib.parse, urllib.error
(2)	import urllib2	import urllib.request, urllib.error
(3)	import urlparse	import urllib.parse
(4)	import robotparser	import urllib.robotparser

Notes	Python 2	Python 3
(5)	`from urllib import FancyURLopener`	`from urllib.request import FancyURLopener`
	`from urllib import urlencode`	`from urllib.parse import urlencode`
(6)	`from urllib2 import Request`	`from urllib.request import Request`
	`from urllib2 import HTTPError`	`from urllib.error import HTTPError`

1. The old `urllib` module in Python 2 had a variety of functions, including `urlopen()` for fetching data; and `splittype()`, `splithost()`, and `splituser()` for splitting a URL into its constituent parts. These functions have been reorganized more logically within the new `urllib` package. 2to3 will also change all calls to these functions so they use the new naming scheme.

2. The old `urllib2` module in Python 2 has been folded into the `urllib` package in Python 3. All your `urllib2` favorites—the `build_opener()` method, Request objects, and `HTTPBasicAuthHandler` and friends—are still available.

3. The `urllib.parse` module in Python 3 contains all the parsing functions from the old `urlparse` module in Python 2.

4. The `urllib.robotparser` module parses `robots.txt` files.

5. The `FancyURLopener` class, which handles HTTP redirects and other status codes, is still available in the new `urllib.request` module. The `urlencode()` function has moved to `urllib.parse`.

6. The Request object is still available in `urllib.request`, but constants such as `HTTPError` have been moved to `urllib.error`.

Did I mention that 2to3 will rewrite your function calls, too? For example, if your Python 2 code imports the `urllib` module and calls `urllib.urlopen()` to fetch data, 2to3 will fix both the import statement and the function call, as shown in Table A-10.

Table A-10. Fixing urllib.urlopen()

Python 2	Python 3
`import urllib`	`import urllib.request`
`print urllib.urlopen(A_URL).read()`	`import urllib.parse`
	`import urllib.error`
	`print(urllib.request.urlopen(A_URL).read())`

dbm

All the various DBM clones are now in a single package: `dbm`. If you need a specific variant such as GNU DBM, you can import the appropriate module within the `dbm` package, as shown in Table A-11.

Table A-11. *dbm Module Reorganization*

Python 2	Python 3
import dbm	import dbm.ndbm
import gdbm	import dbm.gnu
import dbhash	import dbm.bsd
import dumbdbm	import dbm.dumb
import anydbm import whichdb	import dbm

xmlrpc

XML-RPC is a lightweight method of performing remote RPC calls over HTTP. The XML-RPC client library and several XML-RPC server implementations are now combined in a single package, `xmlrpc`, as shown in Table A-12.

Table A-12. *The xmlrpc Module Reorganization*

Python 2	Python 3
import xmlrpclib	import xmlrpc.client
import DocXMLRPCServer import SimpleXMLRPCServer	import xmlrpc.server

Other Modules

Python 3 also renames a potpourri of other modules, as shown in Table A-13.

Table A-13. *Miscellaneous Module Reorganization*

Notes	Python 2	Python 3

(1)	try:
	    import cStringIO as StringIO
	except ImportError:
	    import StringIO
		import io

Notes	Python 2	Python 3

(2)	`try:`
	    `import cPickle as pickle`
	`except ImportError:`
	    `import pickle`
		`import pickle`

(3)	`import __builtin__`	`import builtins`
(4)	`import copy_reg`	`import copyreg`
(5)	`import Queue`	`import queue`
(6)	`import SocketServer`	`import socketserver`
(7)	`import ConfigParser`	`import configparser`
(8)	`import repr`	`import reprlib`
(9)	`import commands`	`import subprocess`

1. A common idiom in Python 2 was to try to `import cStringIO as StringIO`. If that failed, it tried to import `import StringIO` instead. Do not do this in Python 3; the `io` module does it for you. It will find the fastest implementation available and use it automatically.

2. A similar idiom was used to import the fastest pickle implementation. Do not do this in Python 3; the `pickle` module does it for you.

3. The `builtins` module contains the global functions, classes, and constants used throughout the Python language. Redefining a function in the `builtins` module will redefine the global function everywhere. That is exactly as powerful and scary as it sounds.

4. The `copyreg` module adds pickle support for custom types defined in C.

5. The `queue` module implements a multiproducer, multiconsumer queue.

6. The `socketserver` module provides generic base classes for implementing different kinds of socket servers.

7. The `configparser` module parses INI-style configuration files.

8. The `reprlib` module reimplements the built-in `repr()` function, with additional controls on how long the representations can be before they are truncated.

9. The `subprocess` module allows you to spawn processes, connect to their pipes, and obtain their return codes.

Relative Imports Within a Package

In Python 2, when modules within a package need to reference each other, you use `import foo` or `from foo import Bar`. The Python 2 interpreter first searches within the current package to find `foo.py` and then moves on to the other directories in the Python search path (`sys.path`).

Python 3 works a bit differently. Instead of searching the current package, it goes directly to the Python search path. If you want one module within a package to import another module in the same package, you need to explicitly provide the relative path between the two modules. Suppose that you had a package with multiple files in the same directory (see Listing A-1).

Listing A-1. chardet Directory Structure

```
chardet/
|
+--__init__.py
|
+--constants.py
|
+--mbcharsetprober.py
|
+--universaldetector.py
```

Now suppose that `universaldetector.py` needs to import the entire `constants.py` file and one class from `mbcharsetprober.py`. How do you do it? Table A-14 shows the new syntax.

Table A-14. Relative Imports Within a Multifile Module

Notes	Python 2	Python 3
(1)	`import constants`	`from . import constants`
(2)	`from mbcharsetprober import MultiByteCharSetProber`	`from .mbcharsetprober import MultiByteCharsetProber`

1. When you need to import an entire module from elsewhere in your package, use the new `from . import` syntax. The period is actually a relative path from this file (`universaldetector.py`) to the file you want to import (`constants.py`). In this case, they are in the same directory (thus the single period). You can also import from the parent directory (`from .. import anothermodule`) or a subdirectory.

2. To import a specific class or function from another module directly into your module's namespace, prefix the target module with a relative path, minus the trailing slash. In this case, `mbcharsetprober.py` is in the same directory as `universaldetector.py`, so the path is a single period. You can also import from the parent directory (from ..anothermodule import AnotherClass) or a subdirectory.

next() Iterator Method

In Python 2, iterators had a next() method that returned the next item in the sequence. That's still true in Python 3, but there is now also a global next() function that takes an iterator as an argument, as shown in Table A-15.

Table A-15. The next() Iterator Method

Notes	Python 2	Python 3
(1)	`anIterator.next()`	`next(anIterator)`
(2)	`a_function_that_returns_an_iterator().next()`	`next(a_function_that_returns_an_iterator())`

(3)	`class A:`
	`    def next(self):`
	`        pass`
		`class A:`
		`    def __next__(self):`
		`        pass`

(4)	`A:`
	`ef next(self, x, y):`
	`    pass`
		No Change

(5)	`next = 42`
	`for an_iterator in`↵
	`  a_sequence_of_iterators:`
	`    an_iterator.next()`
		`next = 42`
		`for an_iterator in a_sequence_of_iterators:`
		`    an_iterator.__next__()`

1. In the simplest case, instead of calling an iterator's next() method, you now pass the iterator itself to the global next() function.

2. If you have a function that returns an iterator, call the function and pass the result to the next() function. (The 2to3 script is smart enough to convert it properly.)

3. If you define your own class and mean to use it as an iterator, define the __next__() special method.

4. If you define your own class and just happen to have a method named next() that takes one or more arguments, 2to3 will not touch it. This class cannot be used as an iterator because its next() method takes arguments.

5. This one is a bit tricky. If you have a local variable named next, it takes precedence over the new global next() function. In this case, you need to call the iterator's special __next__() method to get the next item in the sequence. (Alternatively, you could also refactor the code so the local variable wasn't named next, but 2to3 will not do that for you automatically.)

filter() Global Function

In Python 2, the `filter()` function returned a list, the result of filtering a sequence through a function that returned `True` or `False` for each item in the sequence. In Python 3, the `filter()` function returns an iterator, not a list, as shown in Table A-16.

Table A-16. *filter() Returns an Iterator*

Notes	Python 2	Python 3
(1)	`filter(a_function, a_sequence)`	`list(filter(a_function, a_sequence))`
(2)	`list(filter(a_function, a_sequence))`	No Change
(3)	`filter(None, a_sequence)`	`[i for i in a_sequence if i]`
(4)	`. in filter(None, a_sequence):`	No Change
(5)	`[i for i in filter(a_function, ↵` `a_sequence)]`	No Change

1. In the most basic case, **2to3** will wrap a call to `filter()` with a call to `list()`, which simply iterates through its argument and returns a real list.

2. However, if the call to `filter()` is *already* wrapped in `list()`, **2to3** will do nothing because the fact that `filter()` is returning an iterator is irrelevant.

3. For the special syntax of `filter(None, ...)`, **2to3** will transform the call into a semantically equivalent list comprehension.

4. In contexts like **for** loops, which iterate through the entire sequence anyway, no changes are necessary.

5. Again, no changes are necessary because the list comprehension will iterate through the entire sequence, and it can do that just as well if `filter()` returns an iterator as if it returns a list.

map() Global Function

In much the same way as `filter()`, the `map()` function now returns an iterator, as shown in Table A-17. (In Python 2, it returned a list.)

Table A-17. map() Returns an Iterator

Notes	Python 2	Python 3
(1)	`map(a_function, 'PapayaWhip')`	`list(map(a_function, 'PapayaWhip'))`
(2)	`map(None, 'PapayaWhip')`	`list('PapayaWhip')`
(3)	`map(lambda x: x+1, range(42))`	`[x+1 for x in range(42)]`
(4)	`. in map(a_function, a_sequence):`	No Change
(5)	`[i for i in map(a_function, ↵ a_sequence)]`	No Change

1. As with `filter()`, in the most basic case, `2to3` will wrap a call to `map()` with a call to `list()`.

2. For the special syntax of `map(None, ...)`, the identity function, `2to3` will convert it to an equivalent call to `list()`.

3. If the first argument to `map()` is a lambda function, `2to3` will convert it to an equivalent list comprehension.

4. In contexts such as `for` loops, which iterate through the entire sequence anyway, no changes are necessary.

5. Again, no changes are necessary because the list comprehension will iterate through the entire sequence, and it can do that just as well if `map()` returns an iterator as if it returns a list.

reduce() Global Function

In Python 3, the `reduce()` function has been removed from the global namespace and placed in the `functools` module, as shown in Table A-18.

Table A-18. The reduce() Global Function

Python 2	Python 3
`reduce(a, b, c)`	`from functools import reduce` `reduce(a, b, c)`

apply() Global Function

Python 2 had a global function called **apply()**, which took a function **f** and a list **[a, b, c]** and returned **f(a, b, c)**. You can accomplish the same thing by calling the function directly and passing it the list of arguments preceded by an asterisk. In Python 3, the **apply()** function no longer exists; you must use the asterisk notation, as shown in Table A-19.

Table A-19. The apply() Global Function

Notes	Python 2	Python 3
(1)	`apply(a_function, a_list_of_args)`	`a_function(*a_list_of_args)`
(2)	`apply(a_function, a_list_of_args,` `a_dictionary_of_named_args)`	`a_function(*a_list_of_args,` `**a_dictionary_of_named_args)`
(3)	`apply(a_function, a_list_of_args + z)`	`a_function(*a_list_of_args + z)`
(4)	`apply(aModule.a_function,` `a_list_of_args)`	`aModule.a_function(*a_list_of_args)`

1. In the simplest form, you can call a function with a list of arguments (an actual list such as **[a, b, c]**) by prepending the list with an asterisk (*). This is exactly equivalent to the old **apply()** function in Python 2.

2. In Python 2, the **apply()** function could actually take three parameters: a function, a list of arguments, and a dictionary of named arguments. In Python 3, you can accomplish the same thing by prepending the list of arguments with an asterisk (*) and the dictionary of named arguments with two asterisks (**).

3. The + operator, used here for list concatenation, takes precedence over the * operator, so there is no need for extra parentheses around **a_list_of_args + z**.

4. The **2to3** script is smart enough to convert complex **apply()** calls, including calling functions within imported modules.

intern() Global Function

In Python 2, you could call the **intern()** function on a string to intern it as a performance optimization. In Python 3, the **intern()** function has been moved to the **sys** module, as shown in Table A-20.

Table A-20. The intern() Global Function

Python 2	Python 3
intern(aString)	sys.intern(aString)

exec Statement

Just as the print statement became a function in Python 3, so too has the exec statement. The exec() function takes a string that contains arbitrary Python code and executes it as if it were just another statement or expression. exec() is like eval(), but even more powerful and evil. The eval() function can evaluate only a single expression, but exec() can execute multiple statements, imports, or function declarations—essentially an entire Python program in a string. See Table A-21.

Table A-21. The exec Statement

Notes	Python 2	Python 3
(1)	exec codeString	exec(codeString)
(2)	exec codeString in a_global_namespace	exec(codeString, a_global_namespace)
(3)	exec codeString in a_global_namespace, a_local_namespace	exec(codeString, a_global_namespace, a_local_namespace)

1. In the simplest form, the 2to3 script simply encloses the code-as-a-string in parentheses because exec() is now a function instead of a statement.

2. The old exec statement could take a namespace, a private environment of globals in which the code-as-a-string would be executed. Python 3 can also do this; just pass the namespace as the second argument to the exec() function.

3. Even fancier, the old exec statement could also take a local namespace (like the variables defined within a function). In Python 3, the exec() function can do that, too.

execfile Statement

Like the old exec statement, the old execfile statement will execute strings as if they were Python code. Where exec took a string, execfile took a file name. In Python 3, the execfile statement has been eliminated. If you really need to take a file of Python code and execute it (but you're not willing to simply import it), you can accomplish the same thing by opening the file, reading its contents, calling the global compile() function to force the Python interpreter to compile the code, and then calling the new exec() function. See Table A-22.

Table A-22. *The execfile Statement*

Python 2	Python 3
execfile('a_filename')	exec(compile(open('a_filename').read(), 'a_filename', 'exec'))

repr Literals (Backticks)

In Python 2, there was a special syntax of wrapping any object in backticks (such as `` `x` ``) to get a representation of the object. In Python 3, this capability still exists, but you can no longer use backticks to get it. Instead, use the global `repr()` function. See Table A-23.

Table A-23. *repr literals*

Notes	Python 2	Python 3
(1)	`` `x` ``	repr(x)
(2)	`` `'PapayaWhip' + `2`` ``	repr('PapayaWhip' + repr(2))

1. Remember that x can be anything: a class, a function, a module, a primitive datatype, and so on. The `repr()` function works on everything.

2. In Python 2, backticks could be nested, leading to this sort of confusing (but valid) expression. The 2to3 tool is smart enough to convert this into nested calls to `repr()`.

try...except Statement

The syntax for catching exceptions has changed slightly between Python 2 and Python 3, as shown in Table A-24.

Table A-24. *The try...except Statement*

Notes	Python 2	Python 3

(1)	```python
	try:
	    import mymodule
	except ImportError, e
	    pass
	``
		``python
		try:
		    import mymodule
		except ImportError as e:
		    pass
		``

(2)	```python
	try:
	    import mymodule
	except (RuntimeError, ImportError), e
	    pass
	``
		``python
		try:
		    import mymodule
		except (RuntimeError, ImportError) ⏎
		    as e:
		    pass
		``

(3)	```python
	try:
	    import mymodule
	except ImportError:
	    pass
	``
		No Change

(4)	```python
	try:
	    import mymodule
	except:
	    pass
	``
		No Change

1. Instead of a comma after the exception type, Python 3 uses a new keyword: **as.**

2. The **as** keyword also works for catching multiple types of exceptions at once.

3. If you catch an exception but don't actually care about accessing the exception object itself, the syntax is identical between Python 2 and Python 3.

4. Similarly, if you use a fallback to catch *all* exceptions, the syntax is identical.

■You should never use a fallback to catch *all* exceptions when importing modules (or most other times). Doing so will catch things such as `KeyboardInterrupt` (if the user pressed `Ctrl+C` to interrupt the program) and can make it more difficult to debug errors.

raise Statement

The syntax for raising your own exceptions has changed slightly between Python 2 and Python 3, as shown in Table A-25.

Table A-25. The raise Statement

Notes	Python 2	Python 3
(1)	`raise MyException`	No Change
(2)	`raise MyException, 'error message'`	`raise MyException('error message')`
(3)	`raise MyException, 'error message', a_traceback`	`raise MyException('error message').with_traceback(a_traceback)`
(4)	`raise 'error message'`	Unsupported

1. In the simplest form, raising an exception without a custom error message, the syntax is unchanged.

2. The change becomes noticeable when you want to raise an exception with a custom error message. Python 2 separated the exception class and the message with a comma; Python 3 passes the error message as a parameter.

3. Python 2 supported a more complex syntax to raise an exception with a custom traceback (stack trace). You can do this in Python 3 as well, but the syntax is quite different.

4. In Python 2, you could raise an exception with no exception class, just an error message. In Python 3, this is no longer possible. **2to3** will warn you that it was unable to fix this automatically.

throw Method on Generators

In Python 2, generators have a `throw()` method. Calling `a_generator.throw()` raises an exception at the point where the generator was paused and then returns the next value yielded by the generator function. In Python 3, this functionality is still available, but the syntax is slightly different, as shown in Table A-26.

Table A-26. *The throw Method on Generators*

Notes	Python 2	Python 3
(1)	a_generator.throw(MyException)	No Change
(2)	a_generator.throw(MyException, 'error message')	A_generator.throw(MyException('error message'))
(3)	a_generator.throw('error message')	Unsupported

1. In the simplest form, a generator throws an exception without a custom error message. In this case, the syntax has not changed between Python 2 and Python 3.

2. If the generator throws an exception *with* a custom error message, you need to pass the error string to the exception when you create it.

3. Python 2 also supported throwing an exception with *only* a custom error message. Python 3 does not support this, and the **2to3** script will display a warning telling you that you will need to fix this code manually.

xrange() Global Function

In Python 2, there were two ways to get a range of numbers: **range()**, which returned a list, and **xrange()**, which returned an iterator. In Python 3, **range()** returns an iterator, and **xrange()** doesn't exist. (See Table A-27.)

Table A-27. *The xrange() Global Function*

Notes	Python 2	Python 3
(1)	xrange(10)	Range(10)
(2)	a_list = range(10)	a_list = list(range(10))
(3)	[i for i in xrange(10)]	[i for i in range(10)]
(4)	for i in range(10):	No Change
(5)	sum(range(10))	No Change

1. In the simplest case, the **2to3** script will simply convert **xrange()** to **range()**.

2. If your Python 2 code used **range()**, the **2to3** script does not know whether you needed a list or whether an iterator would do. It errs on the side of caution and coerces the return value into a list by calling the **list()** function.

3. If the **xrange()** function was inside a list comprehension, there is no need to coerce the result to a list because the list comprehension will work just fine with an iterator.

4. Similarly, a **for** loop will work just fine with an iterator, so there is no need to change anything here.

5. The **sum()** function will also work with an iterator, so **2to3** makes no changes here, either. Similar to dictionary methods that return views instead of lists, this applies to **min()**, **max()**, **sum()**, **list()**, **tuple()**, **set()**, **sorted()**, **any()**, and **all()**.

raw_input() and input() Global Functions

Python 2 had two global functions for asking the user for input on the command line. The first, called **input()**, expected the user to enter a Python expression (and returned the result). The second, called **raw_input()**, just returned whatever the user typed. This was wildly confusing for beginners and widely regarded as a "wart" in the language. Python 3 excises this wart by renaming **raw_input()** to **input()**, so it works the way everyone naively expects it to work. (See Table A-28.)

Table A-28. The raw_input() and input() Global Functions

Notes	Python 2	Python 3
(1)	raw_input()	input()
(2)	raw_input('prompt')	input('prompt')
(3)	input()	eval(input())

1. In the simplest form, **raw_input()** becomes **input()**.

2. In Python 2, the **raw_input()** function could take a prompt as a parameter. This has been retained in Python 3.

3. If you actually need to ask the user for a Python expression to evaluate, use the **input()** function and pass the result to **eval()**.

func_* Function Attributes

In Python 2, code within functions can access special attributes about the function itself. In Python 3, these special function attributes have been renamed for consistency with other attributes, as shown in Table A-29.

Table A-29. The func_* Function Attributes

Notes	Python 2	Python 3
(1)	a_function.func_name	a_function.__name__
(2)	a_function.func_doc	a_function.__doc__
(3)	a_function.func_defaults	a_function.__defaults__
(4)	a_function.func_dict	a_function.__dict__
(5)	a_function.func_closure	a_function.__closure__
(6)	a_function.func_globals	a_function.__globals__
(7)	a_function.func_code	a_function.__code__

1. The __name__ attribute (previously func_name) contains the function's name.

2. The __doc__ attribute (previously func_doc) contains the docstring defined in the function's source code.

3. The __defaults__ attribute (previously func_defaults) is a tuple containing default argument values for those arguments that have default values.

4. The __dict__ attribute (previously func_dict) is the namespace supporting arbitrary function attributes.

5. The __closure__ attribute (previously func_closure) is a tuple of cells that contain bindings for the function's free variables.

6. The __globals__ attribute (previously func_globals) is a reference to the global namespace of the module in which the function was defined.

7. The __code__ attribute (previously func_code) is a code object representing the compiled function body.

xreadlines() I/O Method

In Python 2, file objects had an xreadlines() method that returned an iterator that would read the file one line at a time. This was useful in for loops, among other places. In fact, it was so useful, later versions of Python 2 added the capability to file objects themselves.

In Python 3, the xreadlines() method no longer exists. 2to3 can fix the simple cases, but some edge cases will require manual intervention. (See Table A-30.)

Table A-30. The xreadlines() I/O Method

Notes	Python 2	Python 3
(1)	`for line in a_file.xreadlines():`	`for line in a_file:`
(2)	`for line in a_file.xreadlines(5):`	`No Change (broken)`

1. If you used to call `xreadlines()` with no arguments, `2to3` will convert it to just the file object. In Python 3, this will accomplish the same thing: read the file one line at a time and execute the body of the `for` loop.

2. If you used to call `xreadlines()` with an argument (the number of lines to read at a time), `2to3` will not fix it, and your code will fail with an `AttributeError: '_io.TextIOWrapper' object has no attribute 'xreadlines'`. You can manually change `xreadlines()` to `readlines()` to get it to work in Python 3. (The `readlines()` method now returns an iterator, so it is just as efficient as `xreadlines()` was in Python 2.)

lambda Functions that Take a Tuple Instead of Multiple Parameters

In Python 2, you could define anonymous `lambda` functions that took multiple parameters by defining the function as taking a tuple with a specific number of items. In effect, Python 2 would "unpack" the tuple into named arguments, which you could then reference (by name) within the `lambda` function. In Python 3, you can still pass a tuple to a `lambda` function, but the Python interpreter will not unpack the tuple into named arguments. Instead, you will need to reference each argument by its positional index. (See Table A-31.)

Table A-31. The lambda Functions

Notes	Python 2	Python 3
(1)	`lambda (x,): x + f(x)`	`lambda x1: x1[0] + f(x1[0])`
(2)	`lambda (x, y): x + f(y)`	`lambda x_y: x_y[0] + f(x_y[1])`
(3)	`lambda (x, (y, z)): x + y + z`	`lambda x_y_z: x_y_z[0] + x_y_z[1][0] + x_y_x_y_z[1][1]`
(4)	`lambda x, y, z: x + y + z`	`Unchanged`

1. If you had defined a lambda function that took a tuple of one item, in Python 3 that would become a lambda with references to x1[0]. The name x1 is autogenerated by the 2to3 script, based on the named arguments in the original tuple.

2. A lambda function with a two-item tuple (x, y) gets converted to x_y with positional arguments x_y[0] and x_y[1].

3. The 2to3 script can even handle lambda functions with nested tuples of named arguments. The resulting Python 3 code is a bit unreadable, but it works the same as the old code did in Python 2.

4. You can define lambda functions that take multiple arguments. Without parentheses around the arguments, Python 2 just treats it as a lambda function with multiple arguments; within the lambda function, you simply reference the arguments by name, just like any other function. This syntax still works in Python 3.

Special Method Attributes

In Python 2, class methods can reference the class object in which they are defined, as well as the method object itself. im_self is the class instance object; im_func is the function object; im_class is the class of im_self. In Python 3, these special method attributes have been renamed to follow the naming conventions of other attributes. See Table A-32 for a complete list.

Table A-32. Special Method Attributes

Python 2	Python 3
aClassInstance.aClassMethod.im_func	aClassInstance.aClassMethod._func_
aClassInstance.aClassMethod.im_self	aClassInstance.aClassMethod._self_
aClassInstance.aClassMethod.im_class	aClassInstance.aClassMethod._self_._class_

__nonzero__ Special Method

In Python 2, you could build your own classes that could be used in a Boolean context. For example, you could instantiate the class and then use the instance in an if statement. To do this, you defined a special __nonzero__() method that returned True or False, and it was called whenever the instance was used in a Boolean context. In Python 3, you can still do this, but the name of the method has changed to __bool__(). (See Table A-33.)

Table A-33. Special Method Attributes

Notes	Python 2	Python 3

(1)	class A:
	    def __nonzero__(self):
	        pass
		class A:
		    def __bool__(self):
		        pass

(2)	class A:
	    def __nonzero__(self, x, y):
	        pass
		No Change

1. Instead of __nonzero__(), Python 3 calls the __bool__() method when evaluating an instance in a Boolean context.

2. However, if you have a __nonzero__() method that takes arguments, the 2to3 tool will assume that you were using it for some other purpose, and it will not make any changes.

Octal Literals

The syntax for defining base 8 (octal) numbers has changed slightly between Python 2 and Python 3, as shown in Table A-34.

Table A-34. Octal Literals

Python 2	Python 3
x = x = 0755	x = x = 0o755

sys.maxint

Because of the integration of the long and int types, the sys.maxint constant is no longer accurate. Because the value might still be useful in determining platform-specific capabilities, it has been retained but renamed as sys.maxsize. See Table A-35.

Table A-35. sys.maxint

Notes	Python 2	Python 3
(1)	from sys import maxint	from sys import maxsize
(2)	a_function(sys.maxint)	a_function(sys.maxsize)

1. `maxint` becomes `maxsize`.

2. Any usage of `sys.maxint` becomes `sys.maxsize`.

callable() Global Function

In Python 2, you could check whether an object was callable (like a function) with the global `callable()` function. In Python 3, this global function has been eliminated. To check whether an object is callable, check for the existence of the `__call__()` special method. (See Table A-36.)

Table A-36. The callable() Global Function

Python 2	Python 3
`callable(anything)`	`hasattr(anything, '__call__')`

zip() Global Function

In Python 2, the global `zip()` function took any number of sequences and returned a list of tuples. The first tuple contained the first item from each sequence, the second tuple contained the second item from each sequence, and so on. In Python 3, `zip()` returns an iterator instead of a list. (See Table A-37.)

Table A-37. The zip() Global Function

Notes	Python 2	Python 3
(1)	`zip(a, b, c)`	`list(zip(a, b, c))`
(2)	`d.join(zip(a, b, c))`	No Change

1. In the simplest form, you can get the old behavior of the `zip()` function by wrapping the return value in a call to `list()`, which will run through the iterator that `zip()` returns and return a real list of the results.

2. In contexts that already iterate through all the items of a sequence (such as this call to the `join()` method), the iterator that `zip()` returns will work just fine. The 2to3 script is smart enough to detect these cases and make no change to your code.

StandardError Exception

In Python 2, `StandardError` was the base class for all built-in exceptions other than `StopIteration`, `GeneratorExit`, `KeyboardInterrupt`, and `SystemExit`. In Python 3, `StandardError` has been eliminated; use `Exception` instead. See Table A-38.

Table A-38. *The StandardError Exception*

Python 2	Python 3
x = StandardError()	x = Exception()
x = StandardError(a, b, c)	x = Exception(a, b, c)

types Module Constants

The **types** module contains a variety of constants to help you determine the type of an object. In Python 2, it contained constants for all primitive types like **dict** and **int**. In Python 3, these constants have been eliminated; just use the primitive type name instead. (See Table A-39 for a complete list.)

Table A-39. *The types Module Constants*

Python 2	Python 3
types.UnicodeType	str
types.StringType	bytes
types.DictType	dict
types.IntType	int
types.LongType	int
types.ListType	list
types.NoneType	type(None)
types.BooleanType	bool
types.BufferType	memoryview
types.ClassType	type
types.ComplexType	complex
types.EllipsisType	type(Ellipsis)
types.FloatType	float
types.ObjectType	object

Python 2	Python 3
types.NotImplementedType	type(NotImplemented)
types.SliceType	slice
types.TupleType	tuple
types.TypeType	type
types.XRangeType	range

types.StringType gets mapped to bytes instead of str because a Python 2 "string" (not a Unicode string, just a regular string) is really just a sequence of bytes in a particular character encoding.

isinstance() Global Function

The isinstance() function checks whether an object is an instance of a particular class or type. In Python 2, you could pass a tuple of types, and isinstance() would return True if the object was any of those types. In Python 3, you can still do this, but passing the same type twice is deprecated. See Table A-40.

Table A-40. The isinstance() Global Function

Python 2	Python 3
isinstance(x, (int, float, int))	isinstance(x, (int, float))

basestring Datatype

Python 2 had two string types: Unicode and non-Unicode. But there was also another type: basestring. It was an abstract type, a superclass for both the str and unicode types. It couldn't be called or instantiated directly, but you could pass it to the global isinstance() function to check whether an object was a Unicode or non-Unicode string. In Python 3, there is only one string type, so basestring has no reason to exist. (See Table A-41.)

Table A-41. The basestring Datatype

Python 2	Python 3
isinstance(x, basestring)	isinstance(x, str)

itertools Module

Python 2.3 introduced the `itertools` module, which defined variants of the global `zip()`, `map()`, and `filter()` functions that returned iterators instead of lists. In Python 3, those global functions return iterators, so those functions in the `itertools` module have been eliminated, as shown in Table A-42. (There are still lots of useful functions in the `itertools` module—just not these.)

Table A-42. *The itertools Module*

Notes	Python 2	Python 3
(1)	`itertools.izip(a, b)`	`zip(a, b)`
(2)	`itertools.imap(a, b)`	`map(a, b)`
(3)	`itertools.ifilter(a, b)`	`filter(a, b)`
(4)	`from itertools import imap, izip, foo`	`from itertools import foo`

1. Instead of `itertools.izip()`, just use the global `zip()` function.

2. Instead of `itertools.imap()`, just use `map()`.

3. `itertools.ifilter()` becomes `filter()`.

4. The `itertools` module still exists in Python 3; it just doesn't have the functions that have migrated to the global namespace. The `2to3` script is smart enough to remove the specific imports that no longer exist, while leaving other imports intact.

sys.exc_type, sys.exc_value, sys.exc_traceback

Python 2 had three variables in the **sys** module that you could access while an exception was being handled: **sys.exc_type**, **sys.exc_value**, and **sys.exc_traceback**. (Actually, these variables date all the way back to Python 1.) Ever since Python 1.5, these variables have been deprecated in favor of **sys.exc_info**, which is a tuple that contains all three values. In Python 3, these individual variables have finally gone away; you must use **sys.exc_info**. See Table A-43.

Table A-43. *The sys.exc_type and Friends*

Python 2	Python 3
`sys.exc_type`	`sys.exc_info()[0]`
`sys.exc_value`	`sys.exc_info()[1]`
`sys.exc_traceback`	`sys.exc_info()[2]`

List Comprehensions Over Tuples

In Python 2, if you wanted to code a list comprehension that iterated over a tuple, you did not need to put parentheses around the tuple values. In Python 3, explicit parentheses are required. See Table A-44.

Table A-44. List Comprehensions Over Tuples

Python 2	Python 3
`[i for i in 1, 2]`	`[i for i in (1, 2)]`

os.getcwdu() Function

Python 2 had a function named `os.getcwd()`, which returned the current working directory as a (non-Unicode) string. Because modern file systems can handle directory names in any character encoding, Python 2.3 introduced `os.getcwdu()`. The `os.getcwdu()` function returned the current working directory as a Unicode string. In Python 3, there is only one string type (Unicode), so `os.getcwd()` is all you need. See Table A-45.

Table A-45. The os.getcwdu() Function

Python 2	Python 3
`os.getcwdu()`	`os.getcwd()`

Metaclasses

In Python 2, you could create metaclasses either by defining the `metaclass` argument in the class declaration, or by defining a special class-level `__metaclass__` attribute. In Python 3, the class-level attribute has been eliminated, as shown in Table A-46.

Table A-46. Metaclasses

Notes	Python 2	Python 3
(1)	`Class C(metaclass=PapayaMeta):` `    pass`	Unchanged
(2)	`class Whip:` `    __metaclass__ = PapayaMeta`	`class Whip(metaclass=PapayaMeta):` `    pass`
(3)	`class C(Whipper, Beater):` `    __metaclass__ = PapayaMeta`	`class C(Whipper, Beater, metaclass=PapayaMeta):` `    pass`

1. Declaring the metaclass in the class declaration worked in Python 2 and it still works the same in Python 3.

2. Declaring the metaclass in a class attribute worked in Python 2, but it doesn't work in Python 3.

3. The 2to3 script is smart enough to construct a valid class declaration, even if the class is inherited from one or more base classes.

Matters of Style

The rest of the "fixes" listed here aren't really fixes per se. That is, the things they change are matters of style, not substance. They work just as well in Python 3 as they do in Python 2, but the developers of Python have a vested interest in making Python code as uniform as possible. To that end, there is an official Python style guide (*PEP 8*) that outlines (in excruciating detail) all sorts of nitpicky details that you almost certainly don't care about. And given that 2to3 provides such a great infrastructure for converting Python code from one thing to another, the authors took it upon themselves to add a few optional features to improve the readability of your Python programs.

set() Literals (Explicit)

In Python 2, the only way to define a literal set in your code was to call set(a_sequence). This still works in Python 3, but a clearer way of doing it is to use the new set literal notation: curly braces. This works for everything except empty sets because dictionaries also use curly braces, so {} is an empty dictionary, not an empty set. See Table A-47.

■The 2to3 script will not fix set() literals by default. To enable this fix, specify -f set_literal on the command line when you call 2to3.

Table A-47. The set() Literals

Before	After
set([1, 2, 3])	{1, 2, 3}
set((1, 2, 3))	{1, 2, 3}
set([i for i in a_sequence])	{i for i in a_sequence}

buffer() Global Function (Explicit)

Python objects implemented in C can export a *buffer interface*, which allows other Python code to directly read and write a block of memory. (It is exactly as powerful and scary as it sounds.) In Python 3, `buffer()` has been renamed to `memoryview()`, as shown in Table A-48. (It's a little more complicated than that, but you can almost certainly ignore the differences.)

■The `2to3` script will not fix the `buffer()` function by default. To enable this fix, specify `-f buffer` on the command line when you call `2to3`.

Table A-48. *The buffer() Global Function*

Before	After
`x = buffer(y)`	`x = memoryview(y)`

Whitespace Around Commas (Explicit)

Despite being draconian about whitespace for indenting and outdenting, Python is actually quite liberal about whitespace in other areas. Within lists, tuples, sets, and dictionaries, whitespace can appear before and after commas with no ill effects. However, the Python style guide states that commas should be preceded by zero spaces and followed by one. Although this is purely an aesthetic issue (the code works either way in both Python 2 and Python 3), the `2to3` script can optionally fix this for you, as shown in Table A-49.

■By default, the `2to3` script will not fix whitespace around commas. To enable this fix, specify `-f wscomma` on the command line when you call `2to3`.

Table A-49. *Whitespace Around Commas*

Before	After
`a ,b`	`a, b`
`{a :b}`	`{a: b}`

Common Idioms (Explicit)

There were a number of common idioms built up in the Python community. Some, such as the `while 1:` loop, date back to Python 1. (Python didn't have a true Boolean type until version 2.3, so developers used `1` and `0` instead.) Modern Python programmers should train their brains to use modern versions of these idioms instead. (See Table A-50.)

■The 2to3 script will not fix common idioms by default. To enable this fix, specify -f idioms on the command line when you call 2to3.

Table A-50. Common Idioms

Before	After

While 1:
    do_stuff()
	while True:
	    do_stuff()

type(x) == T	isinstance(x, T)
type(x) is T	isinstance(x, T)
a_list = list(a_sequence) a_list.sort() do_stuff(a_list)	a_list = sorted(a_sequence) do_stuff(a_list)

APPENDIX B

■ ■ ■

Special Method Names

A few special method names are covered elsewhere in this book: "magic" methods that Python invokes when you use certain syntax. Using special methods, your classes can act like sequences, like dictionaries, like functions, like iterators, or even like numbers! This appendix serves both as a reference for the special methods you've seen already and a brief introduction to some of the more esoteric ones.

Basics

If you read Chapter 7, you've already seen the most common special method: the `__init__()` method. The majority of classes I write end up needing some initialization. There are also a few other basic special methods that are especially useful for debugging your custom classes, as shown in Table B-1.

Table B-1. Basic Special Methods

Notes	You Want...	So You Write...	And Python Calls...
(1)	to initialize an instance	`x = MyClass()`	`x.__init__()`
(2)	the "official" representation as a string	`repr(x)`	`x.__repr__()`
(3)	the "informal" value as a string	`str(x)`	`x.__str__()`
(4)	the "informal" value as a byte array	`bytes(x)`	`x.__bytes__()`
(5)	the value as a formatted string	`format(x, format_spec)`	`x.__format__(format_spec)`

1. The `__init__()` method is called *after* the instance is created. If you want to control the actual creation process, use the `__new__()` method.

2. By convention, the `__repr__()` method should return a string that is a valid Python expression.

3. The `__str__()` method is also called when you `print(x)`.

327

4. New in Python 3 since the **bytes** type was introduced.

5. By convention, **format_spec** should conform to the format specification mini-language (see http://www.python.org/doc/3.1/library/string.html#formatspec). **decimal.py** in the Python standard library provides its own **__format__()** method.

Classes that Act Like Iterators

In Chapter 7, you saw how to build an iterator from the ground up using the **__iter__()** and **__next__()** methods. Table B-2 shows all the special methods for iterators.

Table B-2. Special Methods for Iterators

Notes	You Want...	So You Write...	And Python Calls...
(1)	to iterate through a sequence	iter(seq)	seq.__iter__()
(2)	to get the next value from an iterator	next(seq)	seq.__next__()
(3)	to create an iterator in reverse order	reversed(seq)	seq.__reversed__()

1. The **__iter__()** method is called whenever you create a new iterator. It's a good place to initialize the iterator with initial values.

2. The **__next__()** method is called whenever you retrieve the next value from an iterator.

3. The **__reversed__()** method is uncommon. It takes an existing sequence and returns an iterator that yields the items in the sequence in reverse order, from last to first.

As you saw in Chapter 7, a **for** loop can act on an iterator (see Listing B-1).

Listing B-1. A "for" Loop

```
for x in seq:
    print(x)
```

Python 3 will call **seq.__iter__()** to create an iterator and then call the **__next__()** method on that iterator to get each value of x. When the **__next__()** method raises a **StopIteration** exception, the **for** loop ends gracefully.

Computed Attributes

As you saw in Chapter 7, individual instances of a class can define attributes. Python 3 gives you fine-grained control over how these attributes are accessed (see Table B-3).

Table B-3. Special Methods for Computed Attributes

Notes	You Want...	So You Write...	And Python Calls...
(1)	to get a computed attribute (unconditionally)	`x.my_property`	`x.__getattribute__('my_property')`
(2)	to get a computed attribute (fallback)	`x.my_property`	`x.__getattr__('my_property')`
(3)	to set an attribute	`x.my_property = ` ↵ `value`	`x.__setattr__('my_property', value)`
(4)	to delete an attribute	`del x.my_property`	`x.__delattr__('my_property')`
(5)	to list all attributes and methods	`dir(x)`	`x.__dir__()`

1. If your class defines a __getattribute__() method, Python will call it on *every reference to any attribute or method name* (except special method names because that would cause an unpleasant infinite loop).

2. If your class defines a __getattr__() method, Python will call it only after looking for the attribute in all the normal places. If an instance x defines an attribute color, x.color will *not* call x.__getattr__('color'); it will simply return the already-defined value of x.color.

3. The __setattr__() method is called whenever you assign a value to an attribute.

4. The __delattr__() method is called whenever you delete an attribute.

5. The __dir__() method is useful if you define a __getattr__() or __getattribute__() method. Normally, calling dir(x) would list only the regular attributes and methods. If your __getattr()__ method handles a color attribute dynamically, dir(x) would not list color as one of the available attributes. Overriding the __dir__() method allows you to list color as an available attribute, which is helpful for other people who want to use your class without digging into the internals of it.

The distinction between the __getattr__() and __getattribute__() methods is subtle but important. I can explain it with two examples. The first is shown in Listing B-2.

Listing B-2. Computed Attributes

```
class Dynamo:
    def __getattr__(self, key):
        if key == 'color':          (1)
            return 'PapayaWhip'
        else:
            raise AttributeError     (2)
```

```
>>> dyn = Dynamo()
>>> dyn.color                        (3)
'PapayaWhip'
>>> dyn.color = 'LemonChiffon'
>>> dyn.color                        (4)
'LemonChiffon'
```

1. The attribute name is passed into the __getattr()__ method as a string. If the name is 'color', the method returns a value. (In this case, it's just a hard-coded string, but you would normally do some sort of computation and return the result.)

2. If the attribute name is unknown, the __getattr()__ method needs to raise an AttributeError exception; otherwise, your code will silently fail when accessing undefined attributes. (Technically, if the method doesn't raise an exception or explicitly return a value, it returns None, the Python null value. This means that *all* attributes not explicitly defined will be None, which is almost certainly not what you want.)

3. The dyn instance does not have an attribute named color, so the __getattr__() method is called to provide a computed value.

4. After explicitly setting dyn.color, the __getattr__() method will no longer be called to provide a value for dyn.color because dyn.color is already defined on the instance.

On the other hand, the __getattribute__() method is absolute and unconditional (see Listing B-3).

Listing B-3. An Unconditional Computed Attribute

```
class SuperDynamo:
    def __getattribute__(self, key):
        if key == 'color':
            return 'PapayaWhip'
        else:
            raise AttributeError

>>> dyn = SuperDynamo()
>>> dyn.color                        (1)
'PapayaWhip'
>>> dyn.color = 'LemonChiffon'
>>> dyn.color                        (2)
'PapayaWhip'
```

1. The __getattribute__() method is called to provide a value for dyn.color.

2. Even after explicitly setting dyn.color, the __getattribute__() method *is still called* to provide a value for dyn.color. If present, the __getattribute__() method *is called unconditionally* for every attribute and method lookup, even for attributes that you explicitly set after creating an instance.

■ If your class defines a __getattribute__() method, you probably also want to define a __setattr__() method and coordinate between them to keep track of attribute values. Otherwise, any attributes you set after creating an instance will disappear into a black hole.

You need to be extra careful with the __getattribute__() method because it is also called when Python looks up a method name on your class. See Listing B-4.

Listing B-4. Trying to Set an Unconditional Computed Attribute

```
class Rastan:
    def __getattribute__(self, key):
        raise AttributeError          (1)
    def swim(self):
        pass

>>> hero = Rastan()
>>> hero.swim()                       (2)
Traceback (most recent call last):
  File "<stdin>", line 1, in <module>
  File "<stdin>", line 3, in __getattribute__
AttributeError
```

1. This class defines a __getattribute__() method that always raises an AttributeError exception. No attribute or method lookups will succeed.

2. When you call hero.swim(), Python looks for a swim() method in the Rastan class. This lookup goes through the __getattribute__() method because all attribute and method lookups go through the __getattribute__() method. In this case, the __getattribute__() method raises an AttributeError exception, so the method lookup fails and the method call fails.

Classes that Act Like Functions

You can make an instance of a class callable—exactly like a function is callable—by defining the __call__() method, as shown in Table B-4.

Table B-4. Special Method for Functions

You Want...	So You Write...	And Python Calls...
to "call" an instance like a function	my_instance()	my_instance.__call__()

The zipfile module uses this to define a class that can decrypt an encrypted zip file with a given password. The zip decryption algorithm requires you to store state during decryption. Defining the decryptor as a class allows you to maintain this state within a single instance of the decryptor class. The state is initialized in the __init__() method and updated as the file is decrypted. But because the class is also callable like a function, you can pass the instance as the first argument of the map() function, as shown in Listing B-5.

Listing B-5. An Excerpt from zipfile.py

```
class _ZipDecrypter:
    .
    .
    .

    def __init__(self, pwd):
        self.key0 = 305419896              (1)
        self.key1 = 591751049
        self.key2 = 878082192
        for p in pwd:
            self._UpdateKeys(p)

    def __call__(self, c):                 (2)
        assert isinstance(c, int)
        k = self.key2 | 2
        c = c ^ (((k * (k^1)) >> 8) & 255)
        self._UpdateKeys(c)
        return c
    .
    .
    .

zd = _ZipDecrypter(pwd)                     (3)
bytes = zef_file.read(12)
h = list(map(zd, bytes[0:12]))             (4)
```

1. The _ZipDecryptor class maintains state in the form of three rotating keys, which are later updated in the _UpdateKeys() method (not shown here).

2. The class defines a __call__() method, which makes class instances callable like functions. In this case, the __call__() method decrypts a single byte of the zip file; then updates the rotating keys based on the byte that was decrypted.

3. zd is an instance of the _ZipDecryptor class. The pwd variable is passed to the __init__() method, where it is stored and used to update the rotating keys for the first time.

4. Given the first 12 bytes of a zip file, decrypt them by mapping the bytes to zd, in effect calling zd 12 times, which invokes the __call__() method 12 times and then updates its internal state and returns a resulting byte 12 times.

Classes that Act Like Sequences

If your class acts as a container for a set of values (that is, if it makes sense to ask whether your class "contains" a value), it should probably define the special methods (shown in Table B-5) that make it act like a sequence.

Table B-5. Special Methods for Sequences

You Want...	So You Write...	And Python Calls...
the length of a sequence	len(seq)	seq.__len__()
to know whether a sequence contains a specific value	x in seq	seq.__contains__(x)

The `cgi` module uses these methods in its `FieldStorage` class, which represents all the form fields or query parameters submitted to a dynamic web page (see Listing B-6).

Listing B-6. A Script that Responds to http://example.com/search?q=cgi

```
import cgi
fs = cgi.FieldStorage()
if 'q' in fs:                                          (1)
  do_search()

# An excerpt from cgi.py that explains how that works
class FieldStorage:
    .
    .
    .
    def __contains__(self, key):                       (2)
        if self.list is None:
            raise TypeError('not indexable')
        return any(item.name == key for item in self.list)  (3)

    def __len__(self):                                 (4)
        return len(self.keys())                        (5)
```

1. Once you create an instance of the `cgi.FieldStorage` class, you can use the `in` operator to check whether a particular parameter was included in the query string.

2. The `__contains__()` method is the magic that makes this work.

3. When you say `if 'q' in fs`, Python looks for the `__contains__()` method on the `fs` object, which is defined in `cgi.py`. The value `'q'` is passed into the `__contains__()` method as the `key` argument.

4. The same `FieldStorage` class also supports returning its length, so you can say `len(fs)` and it will call the `__len__()` method on the `FieldStorage` class to return the number of query parameters that it identified.

5. The `self.keys()` method checks whether `self.list is None`, so the `__len__` method doesn't need to duplicate this error checking.

Classes that Act Like Dictionaries

Extending the previous section a bit, you can define classes that not only respond to the in operator and the len() function but also act like full-blown dictionaries by returning values based on keys (see Table B-6).

Table B-6. Special Methods for Dictionaries

You Want...	So You Write...	And Python Calls...
to get a value by its key	x[key]	x.__getitem__('key')
to set a value by its key	x[key] = value	x.__setitem__('key', value)
to delete a key-value pair	del x[key]	x.__delitem__('key')
to provide a default value for missing keys	x[nonexistent_key]	x.__missing__('nonexistent_key')

The FieldStorage class from the cgi module also defines these special methods, which means you can do things like Listing B-7.

Listing B-7. A Script that Responds to http://example.com/search?q=cgi

```
import cgi
fs = cgi.FieldStorage()
if 'q' in fs:
  do_search(fs['q'])                        (1)

# An excerpt from cgi.py that shows how it works
class FieldStorage:
.
.
.
    def __getitem__(self, key):             (2)
        if self.list is None:
            raise TypeError('not indexable')
        found = []
        for item in self.list:
            if item.name == key: found.append(item)
        if not found:
            raise KeyError(key)
        if len(found) == 1:
            return found[0]
        else:
            return found
```

1. The fs object is an instance of cgi.FieldStorage, but you can still evaluate expressions such as fs['q'].

2. fs['q'] invokes the __getitem__() method with the key parameter set to 'q'. It then looks up in its internally maintained list of query parameters (self.list) for an item whose .name matches the given key.

Classes that Act Like Numbers

Using the appropriate special methods, you can define your own classes that act like numbers. That is, you can add them, subtract them, and perform other mathematical operations on them. This is how fractions are implemented—the Fraction class implements these special methods; then you can use mathematical operators on them, as shown in Listing B-8.

Listing B-8. Fractions Are Like Numbers

```
>>> from fractions import Fraction
>>> x = Fraction(1, 3)
>>> x / 3
Fraction(1, 9)
```

Table B-7 shows the special methods required to implement a number-like class.

Table B-7. Special Methods for Numbers

You Want...	So You Write...	And Python Calls...
addition	x + y	x.__add__(y)
subtraction	x - y	x.__sub__(y)
multiplication	x * y	x.__mul__(y)
division	x / y	x.__truediv__(y)
floor division	x // y	x.__floordiv__(y)
modulo (remainder)	x % y	x.__mod__(y)
floor division and modulo	divmod(x, y)	x.__divmod__(y)
raise to power	x ** y	x.__pow__(y)
left bit-shift	x << y	x.__lshift__(y)
right bit-shift	x >> y	x.__rshift__(y)
bitwise and	x & y	x.__and__(y)

You Want...	So You Write...	And Python Calls...
bitwise xor	x ^ y	x.__xor__(y)
bitwise or	x | y	x.__or__(y)

That's all well and good if x is an instance of a class that implements those methods. But what if it doesn't implement one of them? Or worse, what if it implements it, but it can't handle certain kinds of arguments? For example, look at Listing B-9.

Listing B-9. A "for" Loop

```
>>> from fractions import Fraction
>>> x = Fraction(1, 3)
>>> 1 / x
Fraction(3, 1)
```

This is *not* a case of taking a **Fraction** and dividing it by an integer (as in the previous example). That case was straightforward: x / 3 calls x.__truediv__(3), and the __truediv__() method of the **Fraction** class handles all the math. But integers don't "know" how to do arithmetic operations with fractions. So why does this example work?

There is a second set of arithmetic special methods with *reflected operands*. Given an arithmetic operation that takes two operands (for example, x / y), there are two ways to go about it:

- Tell x to divide itself by y.

- Tell y to divide itself into x.

The special methods in Table B-7 take the first approach: given x / y, they provide a way for x to say "I know how to divide myself by y." The set of special methods in Table B-8 tackle the second approach: they provide a way for y to say "I know how to be the denominator and divide myself into x."

Table B-8. More Special Methods for Numbers

You Want...	So You Write...	And Python Calls...
addition	x + y	y.__radd__(x)
subtraction	x - y	y.__rsub__(x)
multiplication	x * y	y.__rmul__(x)
division	x / y	y.__rtruediv__(x)
floor division	x // y	y.__rfloordiv__(x)
modulo (remainder)	x % y	y.__rmod__(x)

You Want...	So You Write...	And Python Calls...
floor division and modulo	divmod(x, y)	y.__rdivmod__(x)
raise to power	x ** y	y.__rpow__(x)
left bit-shift	x << y	y.__rlshift__(x)
right bit-shift	x >> y	y.__rrshift__(x)
bitwise and	x & y	y.__rand__(x)
bitwise xor	x ^ y	y.__rxor__(x)
bitwise or	x | y	y.__ror__(x)

But wait! There's more! If you're doing in-place operations such as x /= 3, there are even more special methods you can define, as shown in Table B-9.

Table B-9. Even More Special Methods for Numbers

You Want...	So You Write...	And Python Calls...
in-place addition	x += y	x.__iadd__(y)
in-place subtraction	x -= y	x.__isub__(y)
in-place multiplication	x *= y	x.__imul__(y)
in-place division	x /= y	x.__itruediv__(y)
in-place floor division	x //= y	x.__ifloordiv__(y)
in-place modulo	x %= y	x.__imod__(y)
in-place raise to power	x **= y	x.__ipow__(y)
in-place left bit-shift	x <<= y	x.__ilshift__(y)
in-place right bit-shift	x >>= y	x.__irshift__(y)

You Want...	So You Write...	And Python Calls...
in-place bitwise and	x &= y	x.__iand__(y)
in-place bitwise xor	x ^= y	x.__ixor__(y)
in-place bitwise or	x |= y	x.__ior__(y)

For the most part, the in-place operation methods are not required. If you don't define an in-place method for a particular operation, Python will try the methods. For example, to execute the expression x /= y, Python will do the following:

- Try calling x.__itruediv__(y). If this method is defined and returns a value other than NotImplemented, you're done.

- Try calling x.__truediv__(y). If this method is defined and returns a value other than NotImplemented, the old value of x is discarded and replaced with the return value, just as if you had done x = x / y instead.

- Try calling y.__rtruediv__(x). If this method is defined and returns a value other than NotImplemented, the old value of x is discarded and replaced with the return value.

So you need to define only in-place methods such as the __itruediv__() method if you want to do some special optimization for in-place operands. Otherwise, Python will essentially reformulate the in-place operand to use a regular operand plus a variable assignment.

There are also a few *unary* mathematical operations you can perform on number-like objects by themselves, as shown in Table B-10.

Table B-10. *Special Methods for Unary Operations*

You Want...	So You Write...	And Python Calls...
negative number	-x	x.__neg__()
positive number	+x	x.__pos__()
absolute value	abs(x)	x.__abs__()
inverse	~x	x.__invert__()
complex number	complex(x)	x.__complex__()
integer	int(x)	x.__int__()
floating point number	float(x)	x.__float__()

You Want...	So You Write...	And Python Calls...
number rounded to nearest integer	`round(x)`	`x.__round__()`
number rounded to nearest n digits	`round(x, n)`	`x.__round__(n)`
smallest integer >= x	`math.ceil(x)`	`x.__ceil__()`
largest integer <= x	`math.floor(x)`	`x.__floor__()`
truncate x to nearest integer toward 0	`math.trunc(x)`	`x.__trunc__()`
number as a list index	`a_list[x]`	`a_list[x.__index__()]`

Classes that Can Be Compared

I broke this section out from the previous one because comparisons are not strictly the purview of numbers. Many datatypes can be compared: strings, lists, or even dictionaries. If you're creating your own class and it makes sense to compare your objects to other objects, you can use the special methods listed in Table B-11 to implement comparisons.

Table B-11. *Special Methods for Comparisons*

You Want...	So You Write...	And Python Calls...
equality	`x == y`	`x.__eq__(y)`
inequality	`x != y`	`x.__ne__(y)`
less than	`x < y`	`x.__lt__(y)`
less than or equal to	`x <= y`	`x.__le__(y)`
greater than	`x > y`	`x.__gt__(y)`
greater than or equal to	`x >= y`	`x.__ge__(y)`
truth value in a Boolean context	`if x:`	`x.__bool__()`

■ If you define an __lt__() method but no __gt__() method, Python will use the __lt__() method with operands swapped. However, Python will not combine methods. For example, if you define an __lt__() method and an __eq()__ method and try to test whether x <= y, Python will not call __lt__() and __eq()__ in sequence; it will call only the __le__() method.

Classes that Can Be Serialized

Python supports serializing and unserializing arbitrary objects. (Most Python references call this process *pickling* and *unpickling*.) It can be useful for saving state to a file and restoring it later. All the native datatypes support pickling. If you create a custom class that needs special handling during serializing and unserializing, you can use the special methods shown in Table B-12.

Table B-12. Special Methods for Serialization

You Want...	So You Write...	And Python Calls...
a custom object copy	copy.copy(x)	x.__copy__()
a custom object deepcopy	copy.deepcopy(x)	x.__deepcopy__()
to get an object's state before pickling	pickle.dump(x, file)	x.__getstate__()
to serialize an object	pickle.dump(x, file)	x.__reduce__()
to serialize an object (new pickling protocol)	pickle.dump(x, file, protocol_version)	x.__reduce_ex__(protocol_version)
control over how an object is created during unpickling	x = pickle.load(file)	x.__getnewargs__()
to restore an object's state after unpickling	x = pickle.load(file)	x.__setstate__()

To re-create a serialized object, Python needs to create a new object that looks like the serialized object, set the values of all the attributes on the new object. The __getnewargs__() method controls how the object is created; then the __setstate__() method controls how the attribute values are restored.

Classes that Can Be Used in a "with" Block

Python 3 supports the with statement, which allows you to access an object's properties and methods without explicitly referencing the object every time. A with block defines a runtime context; you "enter" the context when you execute the `with` statement, and you "exit" the context after you execute the last statement in the block.

Any class can be used in a `with` block; no special methods are required. The Python interpreter will automatically set up the runtime context and dispatch all the property and method lookups to your class. However, if you want your class to do something special upon entering or exiting a runtime context, you can define the special methods shown in Table B-13.

Table B-13. *Special Methods for Context Managers*

You Want...	So You Write...	And Python Calls...
do something special when entering a `with` block	`with x:`	`x.__enter__()`
do something special when leaving a `with` block	`with x:`	`x.__exit__()`

This is how the `with` *file* idiom works, as shown in Listing B-10.

Listing B-10. An Excerpt from io.py

```
def _checkClosed(self, msg=None):
    '''Internal: raise an ValueError if file is closed
    '''
    if self.closed:
        raise ValueError('I/O operation on closed file.'
                         if msg is None else msg)

def __enter__(self):
    '''Context management protocol.  Returns self.'''
    self._checkClosed()                              (1)
    return self                                      (2)

def __exit__(self, *args):
    '''Context management protocol.  Calls close()'''
    self.close()                                     (3)
```

1. The file object defines both an __enter__() and an __exit__() method. The __enter__() method checks that the file is open; if it's not, the _checkClosed() method raises an exception.

2. The __enter__() method should almost always return `self`, which is the object that the `with` block will use to dispatch properties and methods.

3. After the `with` block, the file object automatically closes. How? In the __exit__() method, it calls `self.close()`.

■ The __exit__() method will always be called, even if an exception is raised inside the with block. In fact, if an exception is raised, the exception information will be passed to the __exit__() method. See "With Statement Context Managers" (http://www.python.org/doc/3.1/reference/datamodel.html#with-statement-context-managers) for more details.

For more on context managers, see Chapter 11.

Really Esoteric Stuff

If you know what you're doing, you can gain almost complete control over how classes are compared, how attributes are defined, and what kinds of classes are considered subclasses of your class.

Table B-14. Esoteric Special Methods

You Want...	So You Write...	And Python Calls...
a class constructor	x = MyClass()	x.__new__()
a class destructor	del x	x.__del__()
only a specific set of attributes to be defined		x.__slots__()
a custom hash value	hash(x)	x.__hash__()
to get a property's value	x.color	type(x).__dict__['color'].__get__ˊ (x, type(x))
to set a property's value	x.color = 'PapayaWhip'	type(x).__dict__['color'].__set__ˊ (x, 'PapayaWhip')
to delete a property	del x.color	type(x).__dict__['color'].__del__ˊ (x)
to control whether an object is an instance of your class	isinstance(x, MyClass)	MyClass.__instancecheck__(x)
to control whether a class is a subclass of your class	issubclass(C, MyClass)	MyClass.__subclasscheck__(C)
to control whether a class is a subclass of your abstract base class	issubclass(C, MyABC)	MyABC.__subclasshook__(C)

Further Reading Online

For more information on modules mentioned in this appendix, see the following resources:

- *zipfile module*: http://docs.python.org/3.1/library/zipfile.html

- *cgi module*: http://docs.python.org/3.1/library/cgi.html

- *collections module*: http://www.python.org/doc/3.1/library/collections.html

- *math module*: http://docs.python.org/3.1/library/math.html

- *pickle module*: http://docs.python.org/3.1/library/pickle.html

- *copy module*: http://docs.python.org/3.1/library/copy.html

- *abc (abstract base classes) module*: http://docs.python.org/3.1/library/abc.html

For other light reading, see the following resources:

- *Format specification mini-language*:
  http://www.python.org/doc/3.1/library/string.html#formatspec

- *Python data model*: http://www.python.org/doc/3.1/reference/datamodel.html

- *Built-in types*: http://www.python.org/doc/3.1/library/stdtypes.html

- *PEP 357: Allowing Any Object to be Used for Slicing*:
  http://www.python.org/dev/pcps/pep-0357/

- PEP 3119: Introducing Abstract Base Classes:
  http://www.python.org/dev/peps/pep-3119/

APPENDIX C

■ ■ ■

Where to Go From Here

Free tutorials exist for a number of topics that I decided not to cover in this book. If you want to explore advanced Python 3 topics or peruse working Python 3 code, I recommend these starting points.

For more information on decorators, please see the following:

- *"Function Decorators" by Ariel Ortiz:*
  `http://programmingbits.pythonblogs.com/27_programmingbits/archive/↵50_function_decorators.html`

- *"More on Function Decorators" by Ariel Ortiz:*
  `http://programmingbits.pythonblogs.com/27_programmingbits/archive/↵51_more_on_function_decorators.html`

- *"Charming Python: Decorators Make Magic Easy" by David Mertz:*
  `http://www.ibm.com/developerworks/linux/library/l-cpdecor.html`

- *Function definitions in the official Python documentation:*
  `http://docs.python.org/reference/compound_stmts.html#function`

For more information on descriptors, please see the following:

- *"How-To Guide for Descriptors" by Raymond Hettinger:*
  `http://users.rcn.com/python/download/Descriptor.htm`

- *"Charming Python: Python Elegance and Warts, Part 2" by David Mertz:*
  `http://www.ibm.com/developerworks/linux/library/l-python-elegance-2.html`

- *"Python Descriptors" by Mark Summerfield:*
  `http://www.informit.com/articles/printerfriendly.aspx?p=1309289`

- *Descriptor invocation in the official Python documentation:*
  `http://docs.python.org/3.1/reference/datamodel.html#invoking-descriptors`

For more information on metaclasses, please see the following:

- *"Metaclass Programming in Python" by David Mertz and Michele Simionato:*
  `http://www.ibm.com/developerworks/linux/library/l-pymeta.html`

- *"Metaclass Programming in Python, Part 2" by David Mertz and Michele Simionato*: `http://www.ibm.com/developerworks/linux/library/l-pymeta2/`

- *"Metaclass Programming in Python, Part 3" by David Mertz and Michele Simionato*: `http://www.ibm.com/developerworks/linux/library/l-pymeta3.html`

As Python 3 is relatively new, there is a dearth of compatible libraries. Here are some of the places to look for code that works with Python 3:

- *Python Package Index's list of Python 3 packages*: `http://pypi.python.org/pypi?:action=browse&c=533&show=all`

- *Python Cookbook's list of Python 3 recipes*: `http://code.activestate.com/recipes/langs/python/tags/python3/`

- *Google Project Hosting's list of Python 3 projects*: `http://code.google.com/hosting/search?q=label:python3`

- *SourceForge's list of Python 3 projects:* `http://sourceforge.net/search/?words=%22python+3%22`

- *GitHub's list of Python 3 projects*: `http://github.com/search?type=Repositories&language=python&q=python3`

- *BitBucket's list of Python 3 projects*: `http://bitbucket.org/repo/all/?name=python3`

Finally, Doug Hellman's Python Module of the Week series is a fantastic guide to many of the modules in the Python standard library:

- `http://www.doughellmann.com/PyMOTW/`

Index

■Symbols & Numbers

■A

Y

Z

You Need the Companion eBook

Your purchase of this book entitles you to buy the companion PDF-version eBook for only $10. Take the weightless companion with you anywhere.

We believe this Apress title will prove so indispensable that you'll want to carry it with you everywhere, which is why we are offering the companion eBook (in PDF format) for $10 to customers who purchase this book now. Convenient and fully searchable, the PDF version of any content-rich, page-heavy Apress book makes a valuable addition to your programming library. You can easily find and copy code—or perform examples by quickly toggling between instructions and the application. Even simultaneously tackling a donut, diet soda, and complex code becomes simplified with hands-free eBooks!

Once you purchase your book, getting the $10 companion eBook is simple:

❶ Visit **www.apress.com/promo/tendollars/**.

❷ Complete a basic registration form to receive a randomly generated question about this title.

❸ Answer the question correctly in 60 seconds, and you will receive a promotional code to redeem for the $10.00 eBook.

Apress®
THE EXPERT'S VOICE™

233 Spring Street, New York, NY 10013

Offer valid through 4/10.